Towards Cultural Psychology of Religion

Jacob A. Belzen

Towards Cultural Psychology of Religion

Principles, Approaches, Applications

Jacob A. Belzen
Faculty of Humanities
University of Amsterdam
Oude Turfmarkt 147
1012 GC Amsterdam
The Netherlands
belzen@hum.uva.nl

ISBN 978-90-481-3490-8   e-ISBN 978-90-481-3491-5
DOI 10.1007/978-90-481-3491-5
Springer Dordrecht Heidelberg London New York

Library of Congress Control Number: 2010922791

© Springer Science+Business Media B.V. 2010
No part of this work may be reproduced, stored in a retrieval system, or transmitted in any form or by any means, electronic, mechanical, photocopying, microfilming, recording or otherwise, without written permission from the Publisher, with the exception of any material supplied specifically for the purpose of being entered and executed on a computer system, for exclusive use by the purchaser of the work.

Printed on acid-free paper

Springer is part of Springer Science+Business Media (www.springer.com)

Acknowledgements

Although none of the chapters in this book have ever been published in their present form, parts of them draw significantly on papers that were previously published. I am grateful to the publishers for granting permission to re-use material from the following publications:

Chapter 2

The historicocultural approach in the psychology of religion: Perspectives for inter-disciplinary research. *Journal for the Scientific Study of Religion*, 1997, *36*, 358–371. (Oxford: Wiley-Blackwell.)

Chapter 3

Cultural psychology of religion: Profile of an interdisciplinary approach. *Research in the Social Scientific Study of Religion*, 2009, *20*, 103–129. (Leiden: Brill.)

Chapter 4

The cultural-psychological approach to religion: Contemporary debates on the object of the discipline. *Theory and Psychology*, 1999, *9*, 229–256. (London: Sage.)

Chapter 5

Methodological issues in the psychology of religion: Towards another paradigm? *Journal of Psychology*, 2006, *140*, 5–28. (Washington: Heldref.)

Chapter 6

Studying the specificity of spirituality: Lessons from the psychology of religion. *Mental Health, Religion and Culture*, 2009, *12*, 205–222. (London: Routledge.)

Chapter 7

Methodological concerns in the psychology of religion: Continuities, losses and transforming perspectives. *Religion*, 2005, *35*, 137–165. (Oxford: Elsevier.)

Chapter 8

Culture and the 'dialogical self': Toward a secular cultural psychology of religion. In: Straub, J., Weidemann, D., Kölbl, C., & Zielke, B. (Eds.) (2006), *Pursuit of Meaning: Advances in Cultural and Cross-Cultural Psychology* (pp. 129–152). (Bielefeld: Transcript.)

Chapter 9

Religion as embodiment: Cultural-psychological concepts and methods in the study of conversion among "Bevindelijken". *Journal for the Scientific Study of Religion*, 1999, *38*, 236–253. (Oxford: Wiley-Blackwell.)

Chapter 10

Religion, culture and psychopathology. Cultural-psychological reflections on religion in a case of manslaughter in The Netherlands. *Pastoral Psychology*, 2000, *48*, 415–435. (New York: Springer.)

Chapter 11

Psychic functioning and mental health: The role of religion in personal life. In: Belzen, J.A., & Geels, A. (Eds.) (2008), *Autobiography and the Psychological Study of Religious lives* (pp. 117–157). Amsterdam-New York: Rodopi (International Series in the Psychology of Religion, Volume 15.)

Chapter 12

Religion and social order – psychological factors in Dutch pillarization, especially among the Calvinists. In: Belzen, J.A. (Ed.) (2001), *Psychohistory in Psychology of Religion: Interdisciplinary Studies* (pp. 205–238). Amsterdam-New York: Rodopi. (International Series in the Psychology of Religion, Volume 12.)

Preface

The aims pursued in this book are quite modest. The text is not an introduction in the traditional sense to any psychological subdiscipline or field of application, nor does it present anything essentially new. Rather, it shows 'work in progress', as it attempts to contribute to an integration of two differently structured, but already existing fields within psychology. In order to explain this, it is probably best to say a few words about how the book came into being and about what it hopes to achieve.

As a project, the volume owes very much to others. While lecturing in places ranging from South Africa to Canada and from California through European countries to Korea, colleagues have often urged me to come up with a volume on 'cultural psychology of religion'. For reasons that should become clear in the text, I feel uncomfortable with such a demand. To my understanding, there exists no single cultural psychology of religion. Rather, there are ever expanding numbers of divergent types of psychologies, some of which are applied to understanding religious aspects of human lives or to researching specific religious phenomena, while others are not. Within this heterogeneous field that is, correctly or not, still designated as 'psychology', there are also many approaches that are sometimes referred to as 'cultural psychology' or as 'culturally sensitive psychologies'. It would be worthwhile applying many of these to research on religious phenomena, but at present not too many are in fact so applied.

As I resisted the idea of writing an 'introduction', a 'handbook' or a 'companion' to cultural psychologies of religion, Joao Edenio Reis Valle and Marcio Fabri, both from Sao Paulo, suggested I should at least bring together a number of previously published papers in which I advocate cultural psychological approaches to the study of religion and that offer a specimen of the kind of interdisciplinary work I envision. Indeed, this is what this collection attempts: it tries, through a number of essays that may each be read separately, to serve as an 'appetizer' to possible ways of doing cultural psychology of religion. It hopes to make the reader aware of the possibility of applying cultural psychological approaches within the psychology of religion, and it hopes to stimulate others to indulge in this type of research. The volume owes much to the anonymous reviewers of the manuscript and to the editors of journals and other media in which the various chapters were initially published, as well as to comments made at the final stage by Ray Paloutzian, Ulrike Popp-Baier,

vii

Hessel Zondag and others. Supporters of the project from the field of cultural psychology include Carl Ratner, Jürgen Straub and Jaan Valsiner, all of whom I gratefully acknowledge.

A volume like this has limitations of several kinds. Many such limitations are due to the person of the author. Colleagues from especially the USA have often remarked how different the kind of work represented here is from what is being done in so-called mainstream psychology in the USA. The work is seen as European, and if it is true I am grateful for it and proud of it. Yet, whether I like it or not, it also has to be admitted that throughout the work it will remain visible that the author is Dutch, educated and trained primarily in the Netherlands, doing research mainly in that country. None of this, however, is a problem within the type of psychological knowledge and research represented here: as all knowledge is limited and situated, so is everything that is offered and proposed here. Cultural psychologists do not strive for universally valid knowledge: such is left to other branches of scholarship, working on such foundations of human psychic functioning as may be analyzed using natural science approaches. Cultural psychology does not deny or trivialize such foundations. But it does remind us of the limits that inevitably go with such approaches as well: for next to being impossible without genetic, neurological, chemical and many other foundations approachable by natural sciences, psychic phenomena are instigated and regulated by cultural conditions, determinations and limitations to human conduct, such as conventions, norms, beliefs, practices and many others more. Cultural psychologists urge their colleagues in other fields not to forget about these, but to come up with types of knowledge additional to those discovered by psychologists collaborating with neurologists or geneticists. By consequence, the type of knowledge cultural psychologists provided is valid first and foremost (and sometimes even only) at the place and at the moment it was developed. Therefore, what this book has to offer is not a paradigm of how to do cultural psychological research on whatever religion wherever on the planet. It does not offer a recipe at all, but rather an *appetizer*: it provides an invitation to take notice of and to get involved in this kind of research, by offering examples of how cultural psychological approaches can be applied to the study of specific forms of religion. That these examples deal largely with the so-called *gereformeerden* (Reformed, a subclass of Calvinism) in the Netherlands has mainly to do with my situatedness as a researcher and an author: the Reformed have been and continue to constitute an important, in itself not homogeneous, religious subculture in the Netherlands, to which I myself have never belonged (nor did my family), but which I happened to come across in some of my earliest research projects and that I have some in-depth knowledge about. (And lest anyone thinks I would be particularly fond of *gereformeerden*, I have included in chapter 10 also an analysis of an incident they have always been embarrassed about.)

Next to gratitude for moral support provided by colleagues from many countries, this volume owes a debt also to others who helped out with many practical things, esp. to Fraser Watts, the director of the Psychology and Religion Research Group at the University of Cambridge (UK), who invited me to be a visiting Fellow during the Fall of 2008 and to shelter at Queens' College away from the many distractions

Preface ix

from intellectual work that prevail at the University of Amsterdam. I am grateful for the opportunity to share ideas from this book with members of his Research Group and for the opportunity to see what a truly academic setting can look like.

Hopefully, this collection conveys some of the enthusiasm with which the studies have been pursued: contrary to the tendency to tailor empirical phenomena according to theoretical categories and to press them into the moulds provided by research methods, cultural psychology allows the researcher to remain close to the lived reality of subjects' lives, seeking by necessity collaboration with other approaches that try to interpret these lives and their vicissitudes. Although they are just like every other scientific and reflective approach apt to reducing complexity, cultural psychologies try to resist the tendency to reductionism found so often in research on religion and to help to deconstruct scientific prejudices and all too easy answers to all too simple questions. Paradoxically, the aims pursued by this volume will be achieved if readers put it aside as insufficient and not good enough, asking for more and for better, and are consequently inspired to try to come up with such themselves. *Bon appétit!*

Amsterdam, Cambridge

Jacob A. Belzen
New Year's Eve 2008

Contents

Introduction

1 Building Bridges 3

What Is Psychology of Religion? 3
Psychological Research: on Religion? 8
The Relationship Between Cultural Psychology and Psychology
of Religion 12
Once More: The Modest Aims of This Book 16

Part I Principles

**2 A Hermeneutical, Interdisciplinary Approach to the Study
of Religion** 23

Towards a Human Scientific Psychology of Religion? 23
Psychology in the Plural 24
The Object of Psychology of Religion: A Product of Culture 25
A Cultural-Psychological Approach 26
The Historicity of Human Subjectivity 28
The Double Perspective: Historical and Cultural 29
Variants of a Diachronic Cultural Psychology 30
　Historical Psychology 30
　Psychological Historiography 31
　Psychohistory 32
Psychohistory: An Example of the Interdisciplinary
Character of Cultural Psychology of Religion 33

3 Cultural Psychology of Religion 37

Introducing Cultural Psychology: Initial Distinctions 37
Contemporary Research in Cultural Psychology 40
　On the Difference Between Cross-cultural Psychology
　and Cultural Psychology 40

xi

Examples of Current Fields of Research	41
Cultural Psychology of Religion	43
The Interdisciplinary Character of Cultural Psychology of Religion	43
Theories in Contemporary Cultural Psychology and Their Application to Religion	44
Examples	48
Closing Words	50

4 The Way Out of Contemporary Debates on the Object of the Discipline 53

Introduction	53
Debates on the Object of the Psychology of Religion: Tema Con Variazoni?	54
Defensive Motives?	58
The Cultural Psychological Approach: A New Vista?	60
Religion and the Perspective of Cultural Psychology: Closing Remarks	63

Part II Approaches

5 Methodological Issues 69

The Relationship Between Psychology of Religion and General Psychology	69
The Role of Philosophical Presuppositions	72
Two Methodological Mainstreams in General Psychology	73
Hermeneutical Research as Empirical Psychology	77
How to Assess Qualitative Research	79
On the Psychology of Religion	80

6 When Psychology Turns to Spirituality 83

Research on Research: A Metapsychological Perspective	83
Psychology Does Not Define Spirituality	85
What Type of Psychology Do We Need in Order to Approach Spiritual Acts and Activities?	88
Hidden Agendas in the Psychology of Religion and Spirituality	90
The Specificity of Religious and Spiritual Conduct	93
Recommendations for Empirical Research	96

7 The Question of the Specificity of Religion 101

Introduction: Psychology and Its Methodology	101
Wundt Contra James	105
The Varieties in Germany	106

Contents

xiii

Questionnaires and Statistics Versus Case-Studies............................ 108
Methodological Preferences in the Psychology of Religion.................... 109
Experiments Versus Questionnaires... 112
The Genetic Approach Versus Experiments 115
Wundtian Psychology of Religion 118
Problems with Wundt's *Völkerpsychologie* 119
Ongoing Debates, Regained Perspectives................................... 124

**8 A Cultural Psychological Promise to the Study of Religiosity:
Background and Context of the "Dialogical Self"** 129
The Dialogical Self.. 129
The Origin of the Idea of Cultural Psychology............................. 131
Professional Training 131
Personal Background 133
Vision of Psychology 133
The Combination of Cultural Psychology
and the Psychology of Religion 134
Cultural Psychology: Program and Preliminary Achievements 137
Conclusions... 140
Deconfessionalizing of the Psychology of Religion..................... 140
Toward a Cultural Psychology of Religion............................. 142

Part III   Applications

9   Religion as Embodiment.. 147
Psychology of Religion and Cultural Analysis............................. 147
The *Bevindelijke* Tradition... 149
Bevindelijke Spirituality: Am I Converted…? 151
Obstacles to Empirical Research 155
Variants of Cultural Psychology 157
Body, Culture and Religion.. 159
Concluding Comments.. 162

10   Religion, Culture and Psychopathology............................... 165
Introduction: The Necessity of a Multiple Perspective..................... 165
Narrative Psychology and Analysis of Religion 168
Kill the Devil: A Case of Religious Pathology? 170
The Spiritual Background.. 171
The Events in Betuwe 173
The Role of Religion.. 176

11   Psychopathology and Religion 181
The Role of Autobiography in Psychology 181
The Spiritual Autobiography as Source for the Psychology
of Religion 185

The Narrative Construction of the Self 191
Doetje's Psychic Energy: Self-psychological Reflections 195
Psychological Hypotheses and Empirical Historical Research 203
The Function of the Autobiography for Mrs. Reinsberg 206
Religiosity in Relation to Mental Health 207
Religion and the Transformation of the Self 211

12 Religion and the Social Order 215
Introduction: "Pillarization" 215
The Motives Behind Pillarization 220
The Beginnings of Pillarization: Case Study – Calvinist
Mental Health Care 222
Brief History of the Calvinist Mind 227
Religion and Identity 232

Bibliography 239

Index 275

Introduction

Chapter 1
Building Bridges

Invitations to Cultural Psychologies of Religion

Very generally formulated, the aim of this book is to plea for an approach to "religion" from a cultural psychological perspective. However, even though refraining from any jargon, this formulation may easily evoke all kinds of problems in understanding. For what is meant by "religion" (the word is not without reason written between quotation marks! Such usually indicates a problem of some kind …)? What is to be understood by an approach to "religion"? And what is a cultural psychological perspective? The easiest answer to such questions would be: Just read this book! Having done so, you should know what was meant. Admittedly, this doesn't sound too satisfactory, and it may even suggest the author is too lazy to answer appropriate questions. It seems more adequate, therefore, to explain at least some general terms and to preclude misunderstandings, even before the book really commences. Let us then circumscribe the aim of this volume once more, but a little differently, in a way that will hopefully help to situate it. As this is going to be a book in the field of cultural psychology as much as in that of psychology of religion, it aims to contribute to an integration of cultural psychology into the psychology of religion. This perhaps sounds more familiar to some people than others, who may not know what to think of when hearing the additional term "psychology of religion." Let us start then by saying something about this discipline, its possibilities and its problems, and work our way up to its relationship with cultural psychology, in order to explain what kind of book this is going to be (and not going to be!) and what can be expected from its main corpus.

What Is Psychology of Religion?

Should one desire to do so, one could easily sing the praises of the present status of the psychology of religion: never before have there been so many psychological publications on religion, so many meetings and conferences, such an interest – within as well as outside academia – in what psychology may have to say about religiosity and spirituality. Networks are being established, journals founded, people

J.A. Belzen, *Towards Cultural Psychology of Religion: Principles, Approaches, Applications*,
DOI 10.1007/978-90-481-3491-5_1, © Springer Science+Business Media B.V. 2010

appointed – the field truly seems to be doing well. From someone who makes his living from the psychology of religion, one might perhaps expect praise such as this. Yet, an academic may also be expected to be earnest and serious; and, given that, I immediately want to express more concern than praise. Not that anything I said is wrong or untrue: it is just not the whole truth. At the very least I should point out the similarity of the current situation to that of a century ago: in those days too the psychology of religion was rapidly gaining an audience and both within and outside psychology there were journals founded and organizations established. But we should especially not forget what happened between these two peaks in activity: the enormous decline of the discipline. As this book is not going to be about history, I am not going to ruminate about the reasons for the earlier decline and the present growth of the field. In the background, there are some concerns I want to comment on briefly, however, and I hope to suggest some remedies. Before doing so, I should first add a little nuance to what I've said about the present blossoming of the discipline.

There certainly is great interest in what psychology might have to say about "religion," religiosity and spirituality. Any book store offers dozens of books on these themes, sometimes entire sections devoted to the subject; and there are workshops and seminars offered on psychology and spirituality, and so on. It is important to realize, however, that not everything psychological about "religion" is psychology of religion. Stated even more strongly: it is most likely that the majority of those books and activities do not belong to the psychology of religion. This position grants that the expression "psychology of religion" may itself give rise to problems of understanding. Briefly, what is not meant by the expression is a psychology that belongs to, is part of, or articulates or serves the perspective of any single "religion." Psychology of religion is therefore no "religious psychology" (as the discipline was, misleadingly, called for many decades).[1] In the psychology of religion the aim and purpose is to use psychological instruments (like theories, concepts, insights, methods and techniques) to analyze and understand "religion." This needs to be done from a scholarly, distant perspective, remaining as personally detached as possible, as is required in all of the *Religionswissenschaften*, those scholarly disciplines dealing with "religion" such as the history, sociology, anthropology, archaeology and

---

[1]The term "religious psychology" is misleading though not necessarily wrong, if understood as analogous to terms like "social psychology," "clinical psychology" and so on. Evidently, social psychology is not social in itself: it is the psychology about the social dimension of human life and its impact on psychic functioning; clinical psychology is not clinical itself: it is about mental dysfunctions, that may be in need of clinical treatment, and so on. Likewise, religious psychology can be understood to refer to branches of psychology dealing with religion or religious life. As the term may nevertheless raise misunderstandings, however, I shall, in accordance with what has become customary today, speak of "psychology of religion" and restrict the use of "religious psychology" to refer to types of psychology that are, in one way or another, religious in themselves. Trying to introduce a neologism like "psychology on religion", though a correct one perhaps, would not contribute much clarity.

What Is Psychology of Religion?

economics of religion, and several others.[2] I immediately grant that each religious tradition contains a great deal of psychological insight – that counselors, spiritual directors and other psychologically gifted religious professionals have considerable insight into human psychic functioning (cf. Marcus 2003; see also the accounts by Aronson (2004), Dockett et al. (2003) and Levine (2000), for examples from the Buddhist traditions). This cannot, however, be considered scientific psychological knowledge – just as knowledge generated by novelists, philosophers and poets is also not called scientific knowledge.[3] Further, there is considerable knowledge and insight of a psychological kind that is directly related to or founded in religious ideas. Well-known examples include C.G. Jung's psychology and the many publications of esoteric and transpersonal perspectives: interesting as they may be, these are not usually considered part of the psychology of religion, not even by the authors themselves (cf., e.g., Faiver et al. 2001; Corbett 1996; Young-Eisendraht and Muramoto 2002; Young-Eisendrath and Miller 2000).

Psychology of religion is neither to be identified with what is sometimes indicated as "psychology and religion" or as "the dialogue between psychology and theology." This field, with quite a number of practitioners, is a subfield of theology or of religious studies, and at universities or colleges is usually found within those departments. (For powerful critiques of "religious studies" as an academic branch as such, see Fitzgerald (2000, 2007) and McCutcheon (2003).) Ever since modern psychology came into being, numerous theologians and other religious thinkers have had a lively interest in this discipline – focusing on a subject that has always been of prime concern to theologians too: the human soul. I am not going to dwell on how the understanding of the "soul" rapidly changed and diverged between the two academic fields, and how especially psychology hastened to get rid of the concept of the "soul." The only point now is that many theologians, either because of their practical work as pastors or due to more systematic academic interests, closely

---

[2] I strongly prefer the term "sciences of religion" (*Religionswissenschaften*) to the term "religious studies." The former I understand to be the conglomerate of all scientific approaches to "religion" (however understood), practiced from the perspective of the different disciplines that might be relevant to investigating any "religious" phenomenon or state of affairs (but ideally pursued from an interdisciplinary perspective); and they are usually situated at a department for the advancement of that specific discipline. "Religious studies" is usually an indication of a department or a style that derivates from a (formerly) theological department or discourse, even though it sometimes claims to be rooted in a scholarly discipline like the history of religion. History of religion, however, is very often a kind of interpretative enterprise, not engaging in any empirical historical work, but mainly commenting on research done previously by others. Needless to say, such interpretive work can be brilliant, whereas most empirical work can be very boring.... For a related view, see Segal (2006). Needless to say too, that psychology of religion is, by definition, one of the "sciences of religion."

[3] This is not to say that these kinds of knowledge would be of less value than scientific knowledge! On the contrary, as should become clear, I am well aware of the very limited value of scientific knowledge, especially in the human sciences like psychology; for the moment, I want merely to distinguish the different types of knowledge.

followed developments in modern psychology and tried to relate to these in their own work. Some even integrated parts of psychology into their thinking or became at least deeply influenced by what psychology, or what branches of scholarship focusing on human experiences, had to say (see, e.g. Tillich, Pannenberg or Schillebeeckx). None of this, however, constitutes psychology of religion, understood in the very modest and general sense just mentioned. Only a very limited number of theologians turned to the psychology of religion in the proper sense; some of them even turned into psychologists of religion themselves, taking up theories, methods and techniques from a relevant psychological school and setting out to conduct empirical research or to at least produce psychological analyses of religious phenomena (see e.g. Batson et al. 1993; Girgensohn 1921/1930; Malony and Lovekin 1985; Vergote 1983/1997). In general, however, scholars from "psychology and religion" or from the "psychology and theology dialogue" remained interested primarily in broad theoretical issues – more in psychological theories in general than in practicing empirical psychological work, whether on "religion" or otherwise (Angel 2006; Crocket 2007; Browning 1987; Gundry 2006; Homans 1968, 1970, 1979, 1989, Jonte-Pace 2001, 2003; Parsons et al. 2008; Santner 2001). To someone primarily interested in theoretical issues, "psychology and religion" will be far more attractive than the inevitably very limited scope and results of any psychology of religion (which at best relates to "psychology and religion" only as a small element of a much larger whole, see Jonte-Pace and Parsons 2001). For by virtue of their training and their need to participate in discussions and in the media of their professional peers, psychologists of religion – who follow trends within psychology in general – have often narrowed down their research and reflections to small scale questions that are not so interesting to people from the "psychology and theology dialogue." Typically, the latter acquaint themselves mostly with what is probably the most theoretical of all psychological schools, psychoanalysis. As a consequence, students in religious studies usually hear only the grand, but by now a bit hoary, theories of Freud and Jung (Palmer 1997; Vandermeersch 1974/1991), only seldom about more recent developments in psychoanalysis (Jacobs and Capps 1997; Jones 1991, 1996; Leupin 2004), and hardly ever about other branches of psychology, whether related to research on "religion" or not (Gundry 2006; Jonte-Pace and Parsons 2001; notable exceptions in this regard being Bulkeley (2005), Turner (2008), and Watts (2002)).

As I do not wish this chapter to become merely an enumeration of all kinds of psychology related to "religion" that are not psychology of religion, I shall mention only one more category: so-called pastoral psychology (for recent introductions, cf. Klessmann 2004; Watts et al. 2002). Work done in this field is often of good scholarly quality, but it is the intention behind the work that makes the difference to the psychology of religion in the proper sense: pastoral psychology serves religious purposes; it is the psychology that helps the pastor, a psychology developed and practiced to facilitate the aims of (usually Christian) churches. There is hardly anything wrong with this, of course, and within pastoral psychology people are very often well acquainted with and employ the psychology of religion; the point is that the latter is, in principal, neutral towards its object: it does not want to foster nor to

What Is Psychology of Religion?

combat "religion," only to analyze and understand it (Belzen 1995–1996).[4] Similarly, psychology of religion in not to be identified with any integration of psychology and theology, or of psychology and Christianity. (For information on that "movement", see Stevenson et al. 2007.) Here too, the psychological study of religion is not an end in itself, but a kind of handmaiden to a religiously inspired goal.

A critical reply to all of this might be that, regarded in this way, there seems not to be very much psychology of religion at all! That is essentially correct. If we take by way of example the largest organization for psychology in the world, the American Psychological Association, and its psychology of religion division, which is mid-sized among APA divisions, we should realize that the large majority of its 2,500-plus membership is not very interested in the psychology of religion in its proper sense.[5] Most of the members are psychologists with a private interest in "religion," of whom quite a number are interested in integrating "religion" into their professional work as, especially, clinical professionals (Cashwell and Young 2005; Frame 2003; Fukuyama and Sevig 1999; Miller 2002; Richards and Bergin 1997; Sperry 2001; West 2000). Also recall that prior to 1992, Division 36 was for years called "psychologists interested in religious issues", and that there are strong forces at work that would either like to return to that name or change it into "psychology of religion and spirituality," cf. the discussions in the Division's *Newsletter* from the beginning of this century. The psychology of religion is therefore a field of very moderate size with a limited number of practitioners worldwide.[6] This field is doing relatively well and there are indeed praises to be sung, albeit that one should know what one is singing praises about and also what kind of praises can be sung at all.

---

[4] I admit that the picture painted here is too simple, perhaps too optimistic: most psychologists of religion do have some private reasons for being involved in this work, reasons that may be partly religious too; yet, as in all sciences of religion, psychology of religion should observe an epistemological *episteme* in the Husserlian sense: it should refrain from passing judgment on axiological pronunciations and on claims to ontological truth of the religions it studies. This position is difficult to master and requires considerable training to even begin to understand it. However, the attempt to do justice to religions other than one's own and to be critical toward one's own religion as well, are essential elements for any scientific study of religion. In Chapter 6 I will deal with this issue in some detail.

[5] To complicate things, but more importantly, to make this account more truthful to the actual situation: although psychology of religion is usually practiced by psychologists, this is not necessarily so. Classic studies have been published by psychiatrists like Meissner (1992) and Rizzuto (1979), both working from a psychoanalytic perspective. Also people coming from and employed at a theological or religious studies department sometimes contribute genuine psychological studies of a religious phenomenon. (Though usually restricting themselves to working with psychoanalytic theories, they often choose very interesting topics, like the person of Jesus of Nazareth (Capps 2000; Watts 2007), the Bible (Ellens and Rollins 2004; Rollins 1999), religious violence (Ellens 2004; Jones 2008) and many others more). And on the other hand, psychologists also sometimes add to the "psychology and religion" literature, as, e.g. Johnson and Jones 2000; Olson 2002; Roberts and Talbot 1997. The distinctions made in this chapter do not aim to present categories with strict boundaries, they have heuristic value only.

[6] One finds excellent reviews of theories in the field, especially of the older ones, in Wulff (1997) and an up-to-date overview of contemporary empirical research in Hood et al. (2009).

I would like to mention only a few indicators of the vitality of the field, which include the many empirical investigations reviewed by, e.g., Beit-Hallahmi and Argyle. In 1997 they published an updated version of their 1975 *Social Psychology of Religion*; and when the two volumes are compared it is impressive to see how much more recent empirical work is included. (The same conclusion can be reached when comparing the subsequent editions of the best available review of empirical research in general – that by Hood et. al. 2009.) Another example: about 20 years ago not a single introduction to the field existed, but now we have several (e.g., Argyle 2000; Hemminger 2003; Loewenthal 2000). To a great extent this certainly is the result of the ever-increasing number of psychological investigations and publications in general, and also of the fact that "religion" is a much less taboo theme within psychology than it was just a few years ago (even the American Psychological Association recently published a number of best-selling books on the subject, cf. volumes like Richards and Bergin 1997, 2000; Shafranske 1996a; Sperry and Shafranske 2005). If, however, we ask whether there has been much progress in the psychology of religion (next to quantitative growth), the answer needs to be more modest: it very much remains to be determined whether we have actually learned more about "religion" over the last 20 years, or whether we deal more adequately with "religion" in psychological research and other branches of professional psychological work. I would especially like to draw attention to one very problematic point.

Psychological Research: on Religion?

Many are the problems with the object of our discipline. As we have seen above, the object of the psychology of religion can be determined as "religion" – it sounds very easy, almost tautological. It is by no means clear what "religion" is, however. To roughly summarize the entire literature on the definition of "religion" (cf., e.g., Platvoet and Molendijk 1999; Greil and Bromley 2003), let me point out that "religion" is much too broad a term; it fails altogether to subsume the worldwide multitude of phenomena called "religion" into a single, comprehensive, universally valid definition or concept (cf. Feil 1986, 1997; Fitzgerald 2007; Haußig 1999; Kippenberg 2001). For the psychology of religion this is a problem, but not a special or a specific one: the definition and conceptualization of "religion" is a problem to all sciences of religion and can probably be better solved by philosophers and phenomenologists of religion than by psychologists of religion (who may however contribute to reflection on the problem to some extent, see Chapter 7). For psychologists, especially after having taken notice of cultural psychological reflections, the solution may pragmatically consist in doing research on phenomena that can with some authority – be it even only common sense, in a certain society – be referred to as "religious," *provided* – and this is essential – the psychologist understands that her results cannot, or at least cannot easily, be generalized to other phenomena also called "religious." (I shall return to this instantly. But I shall first try to explain why I come up with whatproposal.) For psychologists, as for other scientists studying religion, it would be far more adequate to state they have been doing research on this or that phenomenon from this or that tradition on this or that location, than to claim to have been doing research on "religion." As there is no need for empirical researchers on religion to try to settle what should or should not be understood by the designation "religion," they may turn to the investigation of phenomena generally accepted as being religious. (And following William James, I would even recommend selecting intensive as opposed to liminal cases of what is considered religion or religiosity.) As this sounds terribly clumsy, it may perhaps be best to continue, even in this book, to use the word "religion," understood in the problematic but modest sense just pointed out.

The definition and conceptualization of religion being primarily an issue for philosophers of religion (and probably for practitioners of "religious studies," cf. McCutcheon 1999, 2003), there is another question to which I wish to draw attention: does the psychology of religion have much to say at all about that diffuse object, religion? This question is both central and vital to the psychology of religion. For if this question is answered in the negative, we should immediately ask, What has the psychology of religion been doing for more than a century now? What does the recent growth of this field really constitute other than and more than just an increase of activities under the label "psychology of religion"? In all likelihood we will probably have to admit that most of the work in the psychology of religion is not about religion, not about the phenomena usually regarded as religious (not about rituals, prayer or martyrdom, not about miracles, visions and appearances, not about worship, priests and saints – to mention just a few phenomena that are commonly considered to be religious, although this is probably not always correct). At best, most of the psychology of religion is about religiosity, about the individual-personal counterpart of some type of religion (Belzen 2005a). To a large extent this is understandable: psychology is the science of the "psyche": it is about psychic functioning, and as this is most easily investigated via individual subjects, Western psychology at large certainly has had an inclination toward the individual and the personal.[7] I can only touch upon it briefly here, but an oft-observed tragedy is that psychology nowadays hardly deals with individuals and persons anymore, but just with presumed isolated psychic processes or even with some variables only (Fox and Prilleltensky 1997). Across academic psychology the experiment is considered the ideal research method: it is able to detect and distinguish variables that can then be manipulated under experimental conditions and thereby generating solid knowledge. One of the problems with this approach, however, is its limited external validity: even if it were possible to dissect psychic processes into units that can be measured and manipulated, results from studies in laboratory settings would hardly apply to the much more complex, far less predictable and almost uncontrollable real-life situations outside the laboratory.

---

[7] Although it may seem niggling to some, I like to continue to distinguish between a theory and what the theory is about. Psychology consists of theories, and what is part of such theories is correctly called "psychological", belonging to the science (logos) of the psyche; what psychological theories are about, however, should correctly be referred to as "psychic". So, with "psychic" I do not mean clairvoyant or telepathic but the aspects of empirical reality dealt with in psychologies.

Moreover, as concerns religion, one wonders whether it is at all subject to experimentation. The psychology of religion naturally orients itself to psychology in general, however, and consequently quite a number of psychologists of religion have attempted to distinguish just such variables; although it should be noted that the majority of empirical studies are not experimental, but correlational (Hood and Belzen 2005).

Following such trends in psychology in general, research in the psychology of religion has focused on individual religiosity (Hill and Hood 1999), often assessed only by a rating scale and correlated with one other issue (e.g., general satisfaction and subjective well-being, stress, adjustment, affective disorders, trauma and intervention, addiction, care-giving for disabled elders, abuse, blood pressure, burnout, etc.). Yet one must ask whether psychology in general did not make a major theoretical and methodological mistake in focusing almost exclusively on the individual. Psychology has done so in an ill-understood effort to mirror the natural sciences: it naturalizes its object of study. Its *modus operandi* is marked by de-subjectivization and de-contextualization as it tries to produce universally valid results. It is precisely this last assumption which needs to be challenged, however, as has been the case in the history of psychology time and time again. Even the founding father of experimental psychology, Wilhelm Wundt, contested the view that in order to understand higher psychic processes it is sufficient to restrict oneself to investigating individuals. As other researchers have made clear, numerous psychic processes (e.g., thinking, learning, memory, etc.) are dependent upon and conditioned by language and other aspects of our acculturation (Cole 1996). The relationship between culture and psychic functioning cannot be studied experimentally, but needs to be investigated by methods developed in other human and social sciences, such as history, sociology, anthropology, and others. Wundt already concluded that psychology must consist of two branches: an experimental, physiological individual psychology and what he called *Völkerpsychologie*, what we would today perhaps call a social scientific psychology or even better a cultural psychology. In Wundt's opinion psychology should not only take individual psychic processes as its objects, but also topics such as language, justice, ethics, customs, society and religion. All of these are clearly elements of culture: none of them is produced by a single individual but they are products of the coordinated action of a plurality of individuals. Language, for example, is not dependent upon the individual – it is the other way round: in order to be able to speak, an individual must adapt to a pre-existing language. It is the same with other domains of culture: in order to survive and become fully human, every infant must be acculturated, must become a participant in culture. This is equally applicable to religion, according to Wundt, and he therefore declared the psychological study of religion to be possible only by means of cultural psychology.

In my opinion Wundt's insights remain largely valid. As I shall argue in Chapter 7, it is tragic that they have been so quickly forgotten unlike his experimental and individual psychology. There are many reasons for this – that I cannot recount here in detail, as this is not going to be a study in history. But a very important one is certainly the rise of behaviorism in the USA, which focused expressly on individuals, largely disregarding how they interacted with culture. Moreover, in the early days promises were far more common than convincing results. Wundt developed his ideas at the same time that philosophers such as Dilthey and Rickert differentiated between the natural sciences and the humanities or cultural sciences. Those working in the latter sciences had come to realize that human functioning can be and in effect is very different at other times and in other places. They did not yet have the proper instruments (theories, concepts or research methods) to explore and conceptualize these insights, however. Wundt also lacked such essential tools and employed notions like "folkspirit and folksoul," "prehistory and history," "individual and society," none of which are psychological concepts. Even then, and increasingly ever since, psychologists have oriented themselves overwhelmingly toward the more prestigious natural sciences and have thereby largely lost sight of the social scientific component of their discipline. Since then, many theories compatible with Wundt's plea for a cultural psychology have been developed (although they have not usually been applied within the psychology of religion); but very often either those theories were neglected (as happened to William James' *Principles,* Belzen 2005b, 2006), or they were formulated by persons who have come to be regarded as non-psychologists within the historiography of the history of psychology (for example George Herbert Mead or Norbert Elias).

This having been said, I am not simply and naively going to propose a "return to Wundt," or to anyone, in this book. History proceeds whimsically, dialectically at best; there is no way to return to a past position nor is there much use in attempting to do so (for the past isn't around anymore, things have changed). What we can and should do, however, is to take notice of what our predecessors said and did in order to take advantage in the present situation. Moreover, I think Wundt was exaggerating: although I agree with him that religion is clearly a phenomenon on the level of culture (not of the individual), I disagree with his position that investigation of individual religiosity is useless. I do see religiosity as one of the subjects for the psychology of religion, but two important points need to be taken into consideration: first, religiosity should be studied as the result of the subject's being embedded in religion at a cultural level; and second, psychology should not forget to try to say something about religion as a cultural phenomenon too. Much of this also pertains to spirituality, which quite a number of psychologists of religion have recently come to regard as the main object of the psychology of religion. (In Chapter 6 I shall deal in more detail with this issue and with the possibilities and problems that relate to it.) What I shall propose in the following chapters of this book is to try to pursue the psychology of "religion" including "religiosity" and "spirituality" from the perspective of cultural psychology. As it must be tedious to readers to see such words constantly between quotation marks, and even more to be confronted with a circumscription time and again of what is and what is not meant by such a word, I shall just write: religiosity and spirituality, as with the word religion, mainly for reasons of elegance and simplicity. This does not imply that there is any single and clear understanding of what these terms stand for; nor does it mean I would assume a "common core" to exist to all that is called religion or religious or spirituality or spiritual (Hill 2000; Hill and Pargament 2003; Hood 2003a; Zinnbauer and Pargament 2005). As indicated, these are not issues to be settled by psychologists. For a psychologist, the remedy exists in doing research on persons, phenomena, events and in general on states of affairs that others than psychologists have designated as religion or as religious. As I shall defend later at greater length in this book from a cultural psychological perspective, my plea will be to do research on such phenomena that are plainly recognizable as religious in a given culture, not to draw conclusions true and valid for all religions (for there exists no religion-in-general, there is no religion-as-such, separable from other cultural entities and manifestations). The desire for such conclusions is inappropriate when it comes to research into any of the phenomena that are high on the cultural psychological agenda: research for what might be true of all human functioning, regardless of cultural context, is *not* an aim for cultural psychology. (But it may well be for other branches of psychology, like evolutionary psychology, neuropsychology or physiological psychology. Acknowledging the importance of these approaches, in themselves just as partial as any cultural psychological approach, a cultural psychologist will probably still be tempted to look for cultural impact, even at the levels on which these psychologies are operating, and not without reason. It is even questionable whether any specifically human functioning exists without relation to culture.) Not pretending to achieve results that are valid always and everywhere, cultural psychological research into specific forms of religion does give rise to heuristic hypotheses about the possible intertwining of religion and psychic functioning at other places and at different times and about ways to investigate this.

The Relationship Between Cultural Psychology and Psychology of Religion

Naturally, at this point the argumentation could switch to an exposition of what cultural psychology is, or of what is usually meant by it. Such, however, will be attempted in almost all of the following chapters. Therefore, at this point, a few words should suffice, especially to make clear the relationship to other psychological approaches to the study of religion. First of all, just as with religion, I shall usually speak of cultural psychology in the singular, although this is not entirely correct: there exists no single cultural psychology, there only exist cultural psychological theories, and an even larger number of culturally inclusive psychological approaches and concepts. It is just for convenience sake that we speak of cultural psychology as if it were a homogeneous enterprise. But the cultural psychological perspectives referred to or drawn on in this book should not be identified with cross-cultural psychology: these are separate approaches working with different conceptions of culture. Cross-cultural psychology operates with a rather traditional understanding of culture, conceiving it as a variable that possibly influences behavior, and comparatively investigating how experience and behavior, attitudes, social relationships etc. present themselves within different cultural conditions. Cultural psychology, on the contrary, stresses that all of these are essentially cultural: they are the effect of culture, as opposed to only being influenced by culture. All cultural patterns of acting, thinking and experiencing are created, adopted and promulgated by a number of individuals jointly. Such patterns are supra-individual (social) rather than individual;

and they are artifactual rather than natural. Therefore, psychological phenomena are cultural insofar as they are social artifacts, i.e., insofar as their content, mode of operation and dynamic relationships are (a) socially created and shared by a number of individuals, and (b) integrated with other social artifacts (Ratner 2002, p. 9). Being an interdisciplinary approach, cultural psychology has a number of natural allies: as human conduct and functioning changes over time and as any state of affairs needs a genetic explanation, cultural psychology lines up with historical scholarship to interpret the present. When studying contemporary subjects, it also and in addition relates to disciplines like sociology, ethnomethodology and anthropology. Especially when dealing with non-Western subjects or when making comparisons between subjects from various countries, the confusion with "cross-cultural psychology" (Berry 1992; Bouvy 1994; Grad et al. 1996; Moghaddam et al. 1993) occurs. But, again, the latter approach usually takes existing Western psychological constructs, and tests for their presence in other cultures, while cultural psychology is inclined to ground theoretical categories in terms of the specific cultures from which they are derived (Much 1995).

Let us now turn to the relationship between cultural psychologies and the psychologies of religion as they are usually pursued today. Let us take a look again on a kind of "meta"-level, not to give an account of the goals and results of either cultural psychology or psychology of religion, but rather to compare them one to another. Some brief comments should help to bring the two fields more clearly into focus. As just noted, from a historical perspective, the fields of cultural psychology and of psychology of religion have a number of things in common. They were both prominent in the days that psychology developed into an independent branch of scholarship; they both suffered from the narrowing down of perspectives in psychology; and they both enjoy a recent come-back (cf. the almost simultaneous publication of handbooks for cultural psychology by Kitayama and Cohen 2007, and Valsiner and Rosa 2007, and of handbooks for psychology of religion and spirituality by Bucher 2007, and Paloutzian and Park 2005). The similar history led, however, to a major change in their relationship: whereas initially they were related (as with Wundt), nowadays there is not much of an overlap between the two fields anymore, and a new rapprochement needs to be brought about, to the benefit especially of the psychology of religion. (The handbooks on cultural psychology each devote one chapter to religion; the handbooks on psychology of religion and spirituality contain nothing about cultural psychology.) All meaningful human conduct is cultural, but some domains of human psychic functioning are more cultural than others. It will be self-evident that phenomena typically investigated on a psychophysiological level are less prone to cultural influence than perceptual phenomena, and that these again are less cultural in nature than what personality psychologists are doing research on. Phenomena like nationalism, honor, gratitude and many more that precisely make the world a human world are almost entirely cultural, however. This does not imply – a point that for didactical reasons should be iterated time and again – that on this level of human functioning psychophysiology doesn't play a role: to all human functioning all levels that can be distinguished in psychological analyses are relevant! In psychic phenomena like cognitive development, meaning giving, mourning, memory, sense of self, however conceptualized, processes central to genetics, physiology, neurology and many other sciences play a more evident role. The issue is that for an embracing understanding of certain phenomena under scrutiny, sometimes an approach from one corner of psychology may be more relevant than from another corner of psychology. To explore the different forms of identity formation found in various cultures or the psychic aspects of diverging practices in different religions, one is probably better off with an approach that takes historical and socio-cultural factors into account than with an approach rooted in biopsychology only. (Not that the latter is impossible: recently a number of studies have been published that fruitfully integrate cognitive psychological perspectives into anthropological and even into archeological research, see Cohen 2007; Whitehouse and Laidlaw 2004; Whitehouse and Martin 2004. The only comment a cultural psychologist would make here, is that cognitive functioning as such is not universally identical:, we find the impact of culture also on a cognitive level, cf. Kotre 1995; Miller 1999; Wang and Ross 2007.)

If we have understood this correctly, we can avoid two all too common misunderstandings. First, cultural psychologists do not always or do not exclusively do research on phenomena that are mostly cultural in nature. Cultural psychologists do not only engage in research into cultural phenomena like citizenship, traffic, marriage, circumcision, etc. Cultural psychologists could investigate all other subjects about which psychologists in general are doing research, only they are especially keen on how culture instigates and regulates them. Second, in so doing, cultural psychologists do not primarily try to understand complex functioning in terms of theories designed to explain less complex functioning (which is to a large extent just reductionism). Without denying that factors appropriate to a lesser complex level of psychic functioning are significant, cultural psychologists turn to culturally sensitive approaches to discuss the phenomena under scrutiny. They do this even to such an extent that quite a number of psychologists, oriented other than towards culture, reproach the cultural psychologists of having left psychology altogether and of becoming engaged in history or sociology or anthropology or another "culturological" approach. As I shall try to show, this is a reproach that may have been understandable some decades ago, but which is no longer valid: by now, cultural psychologists have developed and are drawing on a great number of theories and concepts that try to conceptualize precisely the nexus between "culture," however understood, and "human psychic functioning," however conceptualized. But, indeed, in research their modus operandi is characterized by an interdisciplinary approach: they will try to conduct their investigations by examining real life situations; they will work together with anthropologists, sociologists, historians, folklorists, linguists, and with representatives of whatever discipline may help to answer their questions (Boesch and Straub 2006; Straub and Werbik 1999).

What should be clear from this brief exposition is that there are some major differences between cultural psychology and psychology of religion. One may rightly say of both that they are characterized by multiplicity: as with cultural psychology, one can do psychology of religion in many different ways. But whereas a valid psychology could ignore religion, no valid psychology can afford to be culturally insensitive.

Any psychology that aspires to be more embracing than just an idea or a concept, must take into account the cultural nature of human psychic functioning. But while every psychology can be employed in research on religion, it need not necessarily do so. If research and theory in the psychology of religion have brought to light anything, it is this: religion is not a property of human psychic functioning; it is the opposite: in all religions the entire range of psychic functioning manifests itself. Therefore, research into the psychophysiological underpinnings of a type of behavior such as prayer is well possible, just as it is possible to do research into the psychophysiological underpinnings of swimming, reading, planning a holiday. But in order to understand why this child prays to Allah and another to the Virgin Mary, or even to understand why such prayer can have become so important for an adult that she or he would rather die than discontinue practicing it, psychophysiological knowledge is not of prime relevance. To explore the particularities of any religious behavior – it should be emphasized again: there is nothing that is true of all behavior called religious; not even prayer is considered the same in all religions or as centrally important as in the example just given – and the attitudes, meanings, emotions and practices that go with it, one is better advised to turn to cultural approaches. But this is only the case, of course, if one is interested in doing research on any type of religious conduct; such research is not a requirement that must be fulfilled by any psychology to be sound. To the different types of psychology, religion is first and foremost a field of application. Religion can be approached from any psychology (though some psychological perspectives are more appropriate than others). Such research into religion is not an urgent issue for psychology, however; it is urgent for persons interested, for whatever reasons, in religions; and it is pressing for society, as religions are of great importance to numerous participants of almost all societies. To the extent that psychology of religion has any importance, it derives its importance entirely from the relevance religion has to societies as well as to individuals.

Formulated somewhat more in slogans: cultural psychology is not only about culture, about cultural artifacts, etc.; cultural psychological viewpoints should be included in and should be driving any psychology. Psychology of religion is a heterogeneous field, consisting of all the efforts that have been undertaken to understand religious phenomena from the perspectives of, in principle, all psychologies that could have been applied to religion. Cultural psychology, understood as culturally sensitive forms of psychology, is a must; psychologies can only neglect the cultural nature of human psychic functioning to their detriment. Religion, however, can be neglected for a long time before any psychology will have to be criticized as invalid.

A number of further comparisons can now be made between cultural psychology and psychology of religion; and these will need less explanation. Cultural psychology is a very broad, in principle infinite field; psychology of religion is a rather limited field (for it is "only" about religions, however broadly one may define these). Both fields are rapidly expanding, but whereas contributions are made from literally all continents to cultural psychology, psychology of religion is a field practiced almost exclusively in the United States of America. (It seems the American Psychological Association is the only national organization for psychology having a division for psychology of religion.) Although the number of research areas in cultural psychology is infinite (viz. all psychic phenomena, screened for their cultural nature, plus all cultural phenomena, screened for their psychic aspect), the number of areas of psychology of religion is in principle only a subset of that larger cultural number (viz. all religious phenomena). And whereas the number of possible objects for research in the psychology of religion is countless, in fact, this subdiscipline has dealt almost exclusively with (Protestant and Roman Catholic) subjects from the Western part of Christianity (with the notably exception of the research on "cults" or "new religious movements"). At best, one could say, psychology of religion has dealt with monotheistic traditions, as illustrated by a recent handbook (Hood et al. 1996; Spilka et al. 2003), which uses the Cross, the Crescent and Star of David as illustrations on its cover. (But in fact, that cover even misrepresents the actual situation, as there are hardly any psychological studies on Islamic forms of religion.) The heterogeneity within cultural psychology is much larger than in psychology of religion: cultural psychologists draw on an ever increasing number of new psychological approaches; the majority of psychologists of religion draw on theories that count as mainstream in social and personality psychology, in psychoanalysis and developmental psychology. In contrast to the enormous number of topics that could have been researched, psychologists of religion mainly restricted themselves to topics like religious experiences (under which almost everything could be counted, but which usually means phenomena referred to as conversion or mysticism), and a few other topics like socialization and development of religiosity during the life span, and issues related to mental health, as can readily be seen from any introduction. (Next to these, numerous publications have touched upon the so-called intrinsic versus extrinsic religious orientation.) Being a field of application, research on religion has never led to innovations within psychology (numerous psychological theories have been applied to religion, but no theory has ever been developed because of research on religion). Cultural psychology on the contrary is in danger of losing itself in an ever expanding number of so-called "new ideas" (many of which still need to be assessed as to how "new" they are indeed, if valid at all).

Once More: The Modest Aims of This Book

The situation being as described, the conclusion from the previous section can only be that there seems to be not much of a relationship between cultural psychology and psychology of religion. That conclusion is essentially correct. Although some cultural psychologists now and then refer to some religious phenomenon, as it were in passing (Boesch 2000; Gergen 1993, 1999; Gone et al. 1999; Much and Mahapatra 1995; Sampson 1996), or if they want to give an example, there is hardly any theory in the field of cultural psychology that has elaborated at length on any religious phenomenon or that has given a specific type of religious functioning its proper place. Moreover the number of studies on religion conducted from an explicitly cultural psychological point of view is very limited. Certainly, from psychoanalytic perspectives there have always been studies on religion (Belzen 2009a;

Once More: The Modest Aims of This Book

Black 2006; Faber 2004; Meissner 1984; Vergote 1978/1988; Winer and Anderson 2007). But they are limited in number, and very often not very culturally sensitive in character. The situation calls for a change, as rapid and as radical as possible. As no single form of religious functioning is universal, and as no single form of religious psychic functioning can be properly understood without taking cultural factors into account, psychology of religion should have been within the paramount fields of psychology striving for cultural inclusiveness in its theories and methods. As it is not, the psychology of religion is in urgent need of a rapprochement with cultural psychology. In what way could this book contribute to that noble goal?

There are a number of possibilities, most of which I have not chosen, which I should shortly explain. One possibility would be to review the psychology of religion as we know it today (which would then lead to the conclusion that "the" psychology of religion does not exist, but that there are a great number of psychological publications, from various perspectives, on religious phenomena); and to point out time and time again where, why and how a cultural psychological addition or even improvement is needed. Not only would such an approach be quite boring to read, it would also be unacceptably arrogant: as if someone from a cultural psychological perspective could tell all the rest of the psychologists of religion where they failed and could tell them what to do next! Such an approach would be entirely at odds with the pluralistic approach I favor. I don't think that many of the existing psychological approaches should ever be canceled or forbidden: the only thing I plead for is the extension of the number of approaches in the psychological research into religion to include cultural psychological ones. I hope to put forward good enough reasons for doing so.

Another possibility – though it is a rather unrealistic one – would have been to try to develop a cultural psychological theory that would explicitly focus on, or at least include, religions, or a specific cultural entity designated religious. This would certainly be interesting, and let's hope someone pretentious will do that in some future. It is rather unrealistic, however, as hardly anyone ever sat down with the intention to come up with a new psychological theory, and then indeed stood up with something valuable. This is not the way science, or any scholarship, proceeds. This possibility, moreover, would be at odds with another firmly held convention of mine: there are so many interesting and worthwhile psychological approaches and theories already, some of them abandoned or forgotten without any good reason, that it is quite unnecessary to try to develop a new one. Rather: let existing psychological approaches show what they are able to come up with if and when they turn to religion as a possible subject to do research on.

A third possibility, then, would have been to try to do a review of existing cultural psychological theories and their possible relations to research on religion. Yet, this would have been, as we say in Dutch, a kind of "swimming on the dry," as there would be only very little actual research to report and it would result in mainly articulating hopes and wishes, without much chance of factual implementation.

Still another possibility would have been to present an in-depth investigation into some religious phenomenon or person or event from a cultural psychological perspective. This again is certainly interesting and proper to do. This is the possibility

I have always chosen for my own work (e.g. Belzen 2004a), but it too has serious limits. First of all, despite all the energy, time and other resources it takes to come up with one such piece of completed research, it will be just that: one piece of research, whatever its qualities may be. It will be one example only. And a second limitation, as concerns my work, is that the research has primarily taken place in a Dutch context, and – quite apart from the troublesome necessity of translation – why would there be much interest in results from research about a Dutch religious phenomenon? (As I briefly pointed out already and as should become plain from the following chapters: the results from cultural psychological research are primarily valid in the context in which the research was done; they are not easily generalized to other contexts. A good piece of research in this vein can hardly be replicated or even repeated: it draws its value from other criteria successfully met, see Chapter 5.)

At best, a piece of cultural psychological research is inspiring to others, raising hypotheses (or perhaps also objections), animating others to engage in something similar, inviting others to try to do something akin. Most cultural psychological investigations cannot aspire to possess paradigmatic value in the sense classically discussed by Kuhn (1962); hardly any other psychological investigation can either. What can be done, however, is to offer an example: to describe briefly, especially if in translation to foreigners, what has been done in the type of research reported on and what kind of results have been achieved. With this fifth possibility, one probably better presents one's reasoning and one's reasons for doing what one has done, than fatigue the reader with details from an alien context. The risk one takes with such an enterprise will be evident. To readers from the same context or country, such a brief report will fail inexcusable precisely on the point of displaying culturological knowledge and competence: the description will be insufficiently thick (in the sense of Geertz 1973); the analysis insufficiently profound. With a non-expert, precisely the opposite reaction may be expected: why all those details, why all those reflections, about something such a reader will probably never encounter? Such risks must be taken, however: the limits to and situatedness of results are endemic to all psychological research (and probably not only to this type of research, Geertz 1983). Precisely for this reason, I also provide a little historical information on some cultural psychological theories in Chapters 7 and 8; this is not done for the sake of writing history – these chapters are not pieces of history – but rather to show the situatedness of all psychological theory and theorizing. Ideas never come out of the blue; but especially in the social and human sciences, theorizing is intrinsically tied up with its diverse contexts, also with the context of discovery; different cultures lead to different theories, and so do different periods of time within the same culture.

Despite the risks – and there are more than the ones I mentioned! – I have opted for this last possibility. Therefore, the present book is not a textbook on "cultural psychology of religion" (by now, it should be clear that such a thing does not yet exist); it is not an overview of cultural psychology in general; nor is it even a systematic introduction to research on religion from a cultural psychological perspective. The aim is much more modest: the book strives to present a number of *invitations to* cultural psychology of religion; at best it will function as an appetizer, as *a step towards* cultural psychological approaches of religion. Part I outlines and situates cultural psychology, as I understand it, and articulates what I value about it. Conceived as an interdisciplinary approach, necessarily practiced in combination with other culturological sciences, it provides the opportunity to approach the specific religious phenomenon one wants to investigate in the context of a more "real life" situation than many other approaches from psychology. Often theory-driven and through interest in fundamental theoretical questions, a cultural psychological approach promises to resolve some of the old debates that have haunted the psychology of religion for over a century now. The hope for Part II is that it will become clear to the reader that an array of cultural psychological theories and concepts exist, many of which could well be employed in research on religion, religiosity and spirituality. And finally, Part III attempts to convince the reader that despite all the limitations that go with it, it is indeed possible and worthwhile to apply cultural psychological perspectives to research on religious phenomena. I present some pieces of interdisciplinary empirical research into phenomena related to or from one of the religious subcultures of the Netherlands that happened to have been one of my objects of research. That is, the examples are taken from areas where psychological perspectives could be combined with methods and viewpoints from other social sciences such as anthropology (Chapter 9), psychopathology (Chapter 10), history (Chapters 10–12) and sociology (Chapter 12). I leave it to reader to judge whether psychology has indeed contributed anything to the exploration of the phenomena under scrutiny. None of these studies can serve as a model; but the least we can say, probably, is that without the employment and integration of psychology, anthropologists, psychiatrists, historians and sociologists would have given different accounts, would probably have asked different questions and have searched for other materials to base their answers on.

Summarizing then, the aims of this book are threefold: (1) to point out to psychologists of religion that cultural psychology is a viable approach within psychology at large, that in all its heterogeneity may be fruitfully applied in research on religious phenomena; (2) to draw the attention of cultural psychologists to religious phenomena as possible and even interesting objects for psychological research and introduce them to a number of central issues in contemporary psychology of religion; (3) to bring some examples, from just one corner of the enormous field that is open to an interdisciplinary approach like cultural psychology, of the kind of research that could be done when one tries to engage in cultural psychology of religion.

Part I
Principles

Chapter 2
A Hermeneutical, Interdisciplinary Approach to the Study of Religion

Towards a Human Scientific Psychology of Religion?

To many, psychology of religion – especially as an academic discipline – is still a rarity. Either it is considered – usually because of theological a priori's – to be an impossibility; or it is regarded as superfluous – often because of personal lack of interest and sometimes even animosity towards religion. On the other hand, there exists outside academic psychology a broad stream of psychology-like approaches to religion and spirituality, contaminating psychology with, or using it on behalf of, religious "salvation." In a way, even an undertaking like pastoral psychology might come under this label. Although all these psychological and psychology-like approaches are dealing with religion, they are not usually regarded as psychology of religion in the proper sense. The aim and intention of the latter is not salutary: it is more modest and only tries to figure out some psychological aspects of religion (cf. Vergote 1983/1997). (Although this may sound tautological, it has to be hammered away at time and time again.) Psychology of religion as it has developed laboriously but steadily over the last few decades, therefore defines itself as a branch of psychology and orients itself towards the different branches of academic psychology in general (and not, for example, towards theology). Psychology of religion, by consequence, shares much of the fate of psychology in general. Next to benefiting from the strength of academic psychology in general, however, psychology of religion is threatened by the same dangers. The "crisis in psychology," which seems to have been spoken of ever since Karl Bühler's publication by the same name (1927), seems to exist in this subdiscipline of psychology as well. This crisis has been delineated by Amedeo Giorgi (1976) in terms of lack of unity, lack of relevance, and problematic self-understanding as a science. Even if, in a post-modern era, one might be inclined to hail pluriformity in psychology, Giorgi's second and third reproaches still seem to hold. The many lamentations, from various sides, about psychology's restricted value for a fundamental understanding of human beings, its having lost sight of the peculiarities of the individual, its non-generalizability of the results obtained on middle class white students, and many more well known drawbacks seem likewise to pertain to psychology of religion and need not be repeated at length here. In spite of (or perhaps because of) dealing with small-scale questions, concepts and manipulated variables, and in spite

J.A. Belzen, *Towards Cultural Psychology of Religion: Principles, Approaches, Applications*,
DOI 10.1007/978-90-481-3491-5_2, © Springer Science+Business Media B.V. 2010

23

of its ever increasing refinement of scales and sophisticated statistical techniques, psychology is criticized for not observing sufficiently, not going deeply enough into, the phenomena it wants to explore, especially not when constructing its "measuring instruments." One of the main reasons for this lack of relevance is, according to Giorgi, psychology's problematic self-understanding. Because it chose to emulate the natural sciences it could not solve this fundamental dilemma: being faithful to the demands of the life-world and not doing justice to science, or remaining faithful to the requirements of science and precisely because of that, not doing justice to the life-world. To Giorgi, phenomena have to be approached as they present themselves in the world and therefore "the kind of science psychology should be must be constructed from within the viewpoint of the 'world.' For the world of man, psychology must be a human science" (Giorgi 1976, p. 293).

Very eloquently brought forward, pleas like Giorgi's, however, in turn have often been criticized as being too abstract, too philosophical, not practical enough. Pleading for a different psychology, namely for psychology as a human science, these (usually phenomenological) spokesmen would offer no real alternative. They would complain, but not show how to do it better. Is this reproach justified? In the years in which Giorgi was writing it may have been true that human scientific psychology was still in the process of understanding and defining itself, but since then much has happened. Innovating approaches such as social constructionism (Gergen 1985; Shotter 1993b), narrative psychology (Bruner 1990, 1992; Josselson and Lieblich 1993), rhetorical psychology (Billig 1987, 1991), discursive psychology (Edwards and Potter 1992; Harré and Gillett 1994; Harré and Stearns 1995) – to name just a few – present themselves as viable alternatives that are promising for psychology of religion as well. And besides that, one should not exaggerate: in earlier decades there have always been psychological efforts to approach subjects and phenomena in the plenitude of daily human life. Rather than criticize or review existing psychology of religion, in this chapter I want to draw attention to the renewed awareness of the historico-cultural dimension of the object of psychology and to plead for bringing cultural psychology to the study of religion. In spite of recent suggestions to present it as something "new" (perhaps because journals like *Culture & Psychology* and *Psychocultural* are relatively recently founded: both since 1995), it will try to show that historico-cultural psychology has a long tradition and offers fruitful ways for drawing psychology of religion out of its isolation. Sociohistorical psychology (as it is sometimes also referred to, Ratner 1991, 1993) presents perspectives for collaboration with scholars from various different but nevertheless related fields and, most importantly, offers attractive opportunities for studying religiosity in vivo. Let us take a look at some of its basic considerations, in order to take advantage of what it has to offer to psychology of religion.

Psychology in the Plural

The fact that religiosity is highly diverse in terms of time, culture and the individual can facilitate an initial screening of the many divergent psychologies and mini-psychologies. In theoretical psychology, or in the philosophy of psychology, the diverse domains of theory formation in psychology is usually subdivided into two or three groups. People refer to mechanistic, organistic and hermeneutic theories which exhibit successive levels of mounting complexity as a result of the increasing historico-cultural determinacy of the object and the results of the research (Sanders and Rappard 1982; Strien 1993). While in mechanistic and organistic theories the tendency is to disregard the historico-cultural determinacy of human reality as much as possible, in hermeneutic psychologies this is deemed both impossible and undesirable. Therefore, hermeneutical psychology seems the obvious ally in studying religiosity.

These and other philosophy-of-science divisions of the different psychologies stem from an older but not entirely dated bipartite division, about which we shall have more to say in Chapter 7; here just some remarks should suffice. The distinction between the natural and the human sciences, a distinction put forward around 1900, is admittedly no longer adhered to today in its rigorous form: the related distinctions between explaining and understanding, between nomothetic and idiographic research, could no longer be very strictly maintained. Still, in these terms there was and is a reference to a problem which played a large role in psychology, in the past as much as in the present. The question is: Must psychology be conceived and practiced in the manner of the natural sciences or should it study its object in the manner of the human sciences?

Wilhelm Wundt, who is regarded as the founder of the natural–scientific approach in psychology, stated in his day that psychology would have to be plural. Psychology can only turn to the experiment as an auxiliary method if it seeks to examine the "elementary psychicprocesses"; but if it seeks to study the higher psychicprocesses it has to consult other sciences for orientation (Wundt 1900–1909; for more information on Wundt and his work in cultural psychology, see Chapter 7). Wundt's own suggestion was that psychologists should consult history. Since his day, psychology has been fractured by a fault line which no one wants and which any number of theoreticians have repeatedly tried to bridge. Perhaps it must even be acknowledged that much theory formation in psychology occurs today in Western universities outside of the so-called psychological institutes. In striving for scientific objectivity and prestige, mainstream psychology has mostly concentrated on one pole of Wundt's research program: it naturalizes its object of study; its *modus operandi* is marked by de-subjectivization and de-contextualization. When orienting themselves according to this mainstream approach (cf., e.g. Brown 1987; Paloutzian 1996; Paloutzian and Park 2005), large parts of psychology of religion run the same risks.

The Object of Psychology of Religion: A Product of Culture

Religiosity, as so many aspects characteristic of human beings, is a culturally constituted phenomenon in which psychic life expresses itself. Decades ago psychologists like Vygotsky (1978) had already pointed out that the higher psychic functions have a double origin: first a cultural and, after appropriation, an individual one.

All concrete phenomena belonging to the reality of the psychic are determined by cultural encadration. All knowing, experiencing, action, wanting and fantasizing can only be grasped in light of the individual's historico-cultural situatedness and mediation. Emotions, for example, are not irrational eruptions of purely natural and unavoidable reactions. In contrast to what is currently thought, they turn out rather to be characterized by convictions, evaluations, and wishes, whose content is not given by nature but determined by systems of convictions, values and mores of particular cultural communities. Emotions are socio-culturally determined patterns of experience and expression, which are acquired and then expressed in specific social situations (Armon-Jones 1986). The various behavioral, physiological and cognitive reactions which belong to the syndrome which is a specific emotion are not necessarily emotional in and of themselves. Ultimately emotions are based on the same physiological processes, which underlie all other behavior. What makes a syndrome specifically emotional, however, is the way in which the different responses are organized and interpreted within a certain context. To put it succinctly, emotions conform to pre-existing cultural paradigms: they are socially-construed syndromes, temporary social roles, which encompass an assessment of the situation by the person in question and are interpreted as passions instead of actions (Averill 1985). Further, in the course of the so-called civilization process (Elias 1939/1978–82) which can be described for Western society, certain emotions, it turns out, are not only regulated but even created (see also Foucault 1975/1977). Human subjectivity in its totality is always subject to specific historico-cultural conditions: there is no meaningful conduct that is not culturally constituted. It has to be understood in light of cultural contexts; and this does not mean to find out how the postulated constant articulates itself again and again in different contexts (this only results in knowledge about "cultural variation") but to trace how a specific cultural context made the specific action, knowledge and experience possible. Accordingly, psychology of religion, like history, anthropology and linguistics, is an interpretive science: it focuses its attention on meanings and searches out the rules according to which meaning originates in a cultural situation.

A Cultural-Psychological Approach

A psychology which seeks to study something as specifically human and entirely culturally determined as religiosity will therefore be well-advised to orient itself towards various hermeneutical psychologies (cf., e.g. Messer et al. 1988; Terwee 1989; Widdershoven and Boer 1990; Mooij and Widdershoven 1992) and to consult recent developments like narrative theory, which are used today to help explore the relation between culture and the human subject. Narrative psychology, for example, directs one's attention to the role which available leading stories play in the construction and articulation of identity. It tells us that humans think and act, feel and fantasize in accordance with narrative structures and shape their lives in conformity with stories (cf. Sarbin 1986a). In this connection some psychologists, inspired or not inspired by Ricoeur (1977/1992), go so far as to view the "self" – the object of

A Cultural-Psychological Approach

much discussion in anthropology and psychology – as a "story" (Schafer 1983). In Chapters 10 and 11 I shall provide some examples of the employment of narrative psychology in research of some religious phenomena.

It goes without saying that there is no denial here, out of reaction, of the role that physical or psychophysical factors play in human subjectivity. On the contrary, in the historical-hermeneutic school of psychology now evolving there is plenty of room for the body which a human being is. In line with such divergent seminal thinkers as Portmann (1951), Gehlen (1961), but also Lacan (1966), the physical is here conceived of as a complex of potentialities which need a complement of cultural care and regulation in order to become the basic material from which the psyche can originate (Stam 1998; Voestermans and Verheggen 2007).

Further, it is pointed out in this psychology – along the lines of Merleau-Ponty (1945/1962) – that the body, belonging as it does to a certain life form and shaped by its practices, possesses an intentionality of its own (Merwe and Voestermans 1995). One must not underestimate the cultural-psychological perspective referred to here; it is still tricky enough to think through its implications. It cuts across numerous ideas which in the last few centuries have come to be common to Western thought.

Its point is not only that human action, cognition and experience have consistently assumed variable forms in different cultures. Its viewpoint is more radical than that. It stresses that human subjectivity *as a whole* is culturally constituted. Somewhat aphoristically this perspective can be found articulated in the work of Clifford Geertz, an anthropologist who has had considerable influence in cultural psychology of religion: "There is no such thing as human nature independent of culture" (1973, p. 49). One of the implications of this position is that psychology must attempt, much more forcefully than it has up until now, to recover and understand how by their culture human beings have become who they are. A psychology which does not study the human being using the analogy of a mechanism but seeks to understand the almost infinite plasticity of human subjectivity, inquires into the effects of culture. It seeks to find out how a given culture incarnates itself, how it takes possession of the subject and shapes his ("second"; Boer 1980/1983) nature.

In other words, whenever a person wishes to undertake a psychological study of a specific religiosity, he will have to re-situate it in a specific (sub-)cultural segment which, by a certain mode of treatment, i.e. by the way it speaks to and treats people, passes down the frameworks for individual experience and expression. In contrast to what is usually done in the natural sciences, the investigators, if they want to make a psychological study of any form of meaningful life, should as much as possible approach the subjects in their ordinary everyday reality (Voestermans 1992). In contemporary research, common techniques like experiments, tests and questionnaires are ill-adapted to this demand and are abandoned in cultural psychology in favor of so-called "experience-friendly" methods like the interview, participatory observation and self-confrontation. As every sound intellectual endeavor, cultural psychology argues for modesty: "the search for stable patterns and long-range predictions in human psychological phenomena would probably not be the proper goal of the science. The role of the psychologist as a knowledgeable person would be to help in understanding, reading and interpreting behavioral episodes within the culture, and informing people about the potentialities of action within the range of possibilities in the culture. Thus the research would be a co-participant in the joint construction of reality, rather than an authority to control and predict the future of a person" (Misra and Gergen 1993, p. 237).

The Historicity of Human Subjectivity

Cultural psychology consists in a synchronic and a diachronic. The synchronic variant works with living subjects from contemporary cultures, its obvious ally are disciplines like anthropology and sociology; we shall say more about it in the chapters on methodology and on research on spirituality (Chapters 5 and 6). The diachronic or historic variant of cultural psychology has historians as natural allies. Leaving the synchronic variant aside for now, I want to try to elaborate a little more on the preceding thoughts with the aid of the much less well known diachronic variant of cultural psychology. But first we should realize that this historical variant is a logical necessity because of the *historical nature* of psychology's object.

In striving to understand religiosity, a hermeneutical psychology always meets the subject at an intersection of corporeality and a complex of cultural meaning. Usually it encounters a human being at a time when the latter has already completed a certain stage in his or her life's journey. When it asks the traveler about his identity, the person she or he is, it inquires into her or his history, into the maturation process the individual has undergone to become the person she is. The relation between a human being and (her or his) culture, after all, is not a natural but a historical one. A hermeneutical psychology is continually confronted by history, since, on the one hand, a human being is shaped by a culture which has reached a certain (historical) stage of its development and, on the other hand, every individual is the outcome of a process of becoming, of an idiosyncratic history within a particular historico-cultural context. To function as a human being and not to become a Kaspar Hauser, the individual must after all more or less harmoniously fit herself into a specific culture. In the case of the study of contemporary subjects it is also of lasting importance to conceptualize this historical character of the relation between culture and the body which every individual is.

In so doing one can take either the culture or the individual body as the starting point. Thus structuralist-inspired psychologists of culture have tried to grasp the way in which the culture takes possession of the individual subject. In the history which every human being undergoes, socialization is set in motion by social definitions which existed prior to the birth of the individual and which assign her place in the human cultural order into which the subject, saying "I," will later insert herself. These definitions are continued, strengthened and confirmed by the corresponding (social) treatment of the individual and are transformed into a quasi-naturalness. The "habitus" (Bourdieu 1980/1990), which thus originates as a product of history, starts then to produce its own history in conformity with the schemes engendered by history. In that way a habitus, about which we will have more to say in later chapters, ensures the active presence of past experiences which have crystallized in the form of schemes of perception, thought and action. The past, thus present, guarantees that a person becomes the bearer of the culture which produced her.

Psychoanalysis is, of course, another and perhaps more familiar example of conceptualizing the relation between culture and the individual which takes its starting point in the body. Its reflection on the vicissitudes of the "drive," this boundary concept between soul and body, offers important contributions by fixing its attention on the very earliest experiences of the human child and by reminding us that subjectivity, in all of its manifestations, also inevitably bears the marks of vulnerable moments in the individual's life history, of a relation to dynamic tension implying the possibility of failures which may later, in an extreme way, come to expression in the various forms of pathology known to psychology. With respect to every act and experience, therefore, one can and must raise the question concerning the place it occupies in the individual life story, in the life history of the person in question (Jüttemann and Thomae 1987). Accordingly, in psychotherapy and other practical psychologies which, in contrast to academic psychology, were never devoid of hermeneutic bias (Strien 1986), people usually understand by "meaning" the particular significance that can only be grasped from within the history of the individual. Thus Freud defines the meaning of a psychic process as "the intention it serves and its position in a psychical continuity. For most of our researches we can replace 'sense' by 'intention' or 'purpose'" (1917/1971, p. 40), that is to say, by terms which convey an intentional connection.

The Double Perspective: Historical and Cultural

In such a historicizing approach, whether one proceeds from the culture or the body is a difference of emphasis. Ultimately psychology's aim is to understand something that has taken shape at the point of intersection between the two. For a psychological understanding of meaningful action and experience it is therefore necessary to apply a double perspective: the perspective of the meaning shared by a cultural community in general as well as that of the personal meaning which can only be understood in terms of the individual life history. Even a deviation, understood as a symbol (in the sense of Lorenzer 1977), can thus be interrogated as to its meaning, since in deviating from the surrounding order it can be a manifestation of the underlying psychic conflict. I deliberately say "can be" since not every deviation points to psychopathology; and, on the other hand, the (apparent) absence of conflict need not indicate psychic health. Psychology cannot say anything in advance about a person's health and sickness and will only make statements about them after it has examined a concrete individual against the background of her culture and life history.

To a very large extent, therefore, psychology of religion is a historicizing science (see also Belzen 2000b). Hermeneutical psychologists and historians also frequently resemble each other in the concrete ways in which they operate: they favor

30 A Hermeneutical, Interdisciplinary Approach to the Study of Religion

attending to the concrete and specific, the individual and qualitative aspects of the person (see also Chapters 5 and 11). In his exposition of the so-called "indication paradigm" Ginzburg (1986/1989) puts both groups of practitioners of the individualizing approach in the same category as Sherlock Holmes. Psychology and history, however, not only follow a frequently similar way of working but may also go hand-in-hand materially. I want to comment on some of the ways in which this may happen shortly.

Variants of a Diachronic Cultural Psychology

I will set aside possible combinations like "a psychology of history" and "the history of psychology." As can be surmised by now, I consider a psychology of history problematic: psychology can no more make history as such the object of investigation than it can explain religion or culture. Psychology does not explain history; the reverse, rather, is true: history may account for (the rise and the decline of varieties of) psychology. Secondly, the historiography of psychology is an obvious place for an encounter between psychology and historical science. It has, however, grown into a special discipline all by itself, with its own organizations and publications, and will not be dealt with in this volume.

Let us turn instead briefly now to (a) historical psychology, (b) psychological historiography, and (c) so-called psychohistory, and consider their relation to psychology of religion. All three can be regarded as belonging to a continuum between psychology and history or to an area where psychology and historiography overlap. Historical psychology is still mainly the business of psychologists; psychological historiography is the business of historians; while psychohistory is a kind of natural intersection between the two.

Historical Psychology

Historical psychology is not "dated" psychology: that kind of psychology would belong to the history of psychology. Historical psychology is a modern psychology: it comes into being when the cultural-psychological perspective is expanded diachronically, not synchronically or cross-culturally; it is a natural part of cultural psychology. Just as subjects differ to the extent that they live in different contemporary cultures, so they also differ in their subjectivity in each successive historic era of the same culture. In psychology, however, people in general still consistently proceed on the assumption that "in essence" human beings were always and everywhere the same. In the meantime a sufficient number of studies have been made which invalidate this assumption. In historical psychology it has been adequately demonstrated that even if one remains within a single culture, the phenomena which psychologists so eagerly study – phenomena like cognition, emotion, memory,

Variants of a Diachronic Cultural Psychology

personality, identity, mental illness – are historically determined (Danziger 2008; Hutschemaekers 1990; Peeters 1974, 1993). And this is true not only in the trivial sense that in earlier times people thought, desired or felt something different than they do today, but in the more radical sense that in earlier times people thought, desired or felt in a different way. The course of life, cognitive development, memory – each of them was different and used to function differently in earlier times (Olbrich 1986; Ingleby and Nossent 1986; Huls 1986; Sonntag 1990; Carruthers 1990). For a psychology which considers itself scientific to the degree that it attempts to uncover unchanging laws, this is hard to swallow. For this psychology, culturally and historically determined variability in human conduct and experience is actually only disturbing, an error in measurement for which compensation must be made in statistical analysis. It is fearful of the conclusion which Gergen (1973) drew from these considerations for his own discipline: social psychology, according to him, is the historiography of the present, the recording of how a thing is at the moment of investigation. The facts with which it operates are historical and do not permit generalization. Historical psychology for that reason calls for relativization and modesty: it raises the question whether present-day psychological concepts can be applied at all in a context different from that in which they were developed.

It may be considered characteristic for historical psychology that it has its starting point in present-day psychology. It has a mild as well as a critical variant: the mild variant believes it is able, by means of historical research, to arrive at an additional validation of (present-day) psychological knowledge (Runyan 1982, 1988). The critical variant, in contrast, continually points to the limited validity of such knowledge. Like a bug in the fur of established psychology, it keeps alive the critical awareness that as an academic enterprise psychology is just as much a historical product as the object for which it wants to be the science (Danziger 1990, 1997). Its point of entry reminds the historiography of psychology that it describes the construction of psychological objects, not the history of discoveries. *Mutatis mutandis* all of these considerations apply to psychology of religion as well (see, e.g. Hermsen 2006).

Psychological Historiography

Clearly related, of course, but still different, is the somewhat older psychological historiography or the history of mentalities (Vovelle 1982/1990). Being as a rule but little concerned with the systematics and nomenclature of any twentieth-century psychology whatsoever, great historians such as Huizinga, Ariès, Fèbvre, Le Roy Ladurie and Le Goff focus their attention on psychologically relevant phenomena such as anxiety, hate, smell, hearing and visual perception (Anders 1956; Ariès and Béjin 1984/1986; Corbin 1982/1986; Delumeau 1982/1990; Kamper 1977; Lowe 1982; Schivelbusch 1977/1979). They describe and analyze how in earlier times these phenomena were different both in form and in content, and how they have changed over the course of centuries. If these authors were read more by psychologists, they would be constant reminders of the "actuality-centered" character of present-day psychological investigation. Psychological historiography has been the primary source of inspiration of historical psychology. Since the psychology of religion is a part of (more) general psychology, it is understandable that there exists no historical psychology of religion: the theoretical and methodological tools of the psychology of religion, after all, are those of psychology in general. In contrast to what has often been implied by older psychologists of religion (e.g. Rümke 1939/1952), who conceptualized religiosity by analogy with a natural or biological drive, there are no specifically religious psychic functions, functions either religious in themselves or only found in religious people; consequently, no specifically psychology-of-religion concepts or methods exist. (By calling his volume a *dictionary*, Dunde (1993) therefore ran the risk of creating an anachronistic misunderstanding.) On the other hand, a historiography dealing with the same themes as psychology of religion does in fact exist, though it hardly refers to this subdiscipline: fine studies have been published on the psycho(patho)logical aspects of spiritual and religious themes. Just think of such works as those of Fèbvre (1942/1982), Keith Thomas (1971), King (1983), Cohen (1986), Demos (1988), Rubin (1994) and Pultz (2007).

Psychohistory

Concerning psychohistory, the third and most interdisciplinary form of a possible relation between psychology and history to which I wish to draw attention, there are a number of prejudices and misunderstandings, not least, of course, due to the existence of bad examples. To focus on these examples in forming a judgment seems unfair. Let me try to correct a couple of these misunderstandings. In general, psychohistory can be defined as the systematic use of scientific psychology in historical investigation. In all its unpretentiousness this definition nevertheless does call attention to a potential advantage of the psychohistorical *modus operandi*: one who turns to the past, after all, always uses one or another psychology, and certainly when reviewing themes relevant to this field. Now, instead of doing this altogether uncritically, or mindlessly applying the homegrown common sense one happens to have inherited, psychohistory attempts to follow a carefully thought-out procedure. Though not a guarantee of infallibility, such a considered attempt is nevertheless more preferable than unreasoned psychological dilettantism. In the same way that disciplines such as sociology or economics can be integrated with historiography (cf., e.g., Burke 1980; Bairoch 1993) and yield an additional perspective, so this can be done with psychology too. Here it is also the case that psychohistory and the psychology of religion share a similar fate: they are accused of reductionism, of explaining history or religion in terms of psychology. This representation of the state of affairs is obviously incorrect; it has already been sufficiently refuted above. Contrary to what was still even relatively recently being maintained in a professional journal of psychology, psychohistory is *not* "the most extreme representative of the assumption that much of culture is shaped by the psychodynamics of the individual psyche" (Gadlin 1992, p. 888). Far from being reductionistic, psychohistory, as presented for example by Erikson, may be considered exemplary in its attempt to recognize the individual intertwinement of an instinct-driven body and the symbolic order. A good psychobiography requires triple-entry bookkeeping. The individual under study needs to be understood on three complementary levels: (a) the body and all that constitutionally comes with it; (b) the ego as idiosyncratic synthesis of experience; and c) the social structures within which the individual life history is realized and whose ethos and mythos shape the subject and, in the case of exceptional individuals, is shaped by the subject.

Psychohistory, for that matter, in no way needs to limit itself to the genre of biography and to the utilization of psychoanalysis. These are additional misunderstandings which need to be cleared up. Although the lion's share of psychohistorical production is still made up of biographical and psychoanalytical studies, there is no logical necessity for this. It does have to be recognized, however, that psychoanalysis in its reflection on the interpretive process in therapy offers a valuable tool for helping in the analysis of the interpretive work of the historian (Röckelein 1993). The number of studies in which an attempt is made to conduct other than exclusively biographical investigations with diverse forms of psychology is growing (Belzen 2004a; Schultz 2005). In two ways, heuristically as well as hermeneutically, one can also employ, say, personality theory, social or developmental psychology, in historical investigation. The views developed in these branches of psychology can draw the attention of historians to certain themes which would probably otherwise remain un- or underexposed. In the second place, psychological theories or viewpoints may furnish additional possibilities for the interpretation of sources. I would be the last to sing the praises of the attainments of academic psychology, but it seems hard to deny that it has produced some knowledge of motivation and emotion, social interaction, decision behavior, human development and personal life stories which, for all their limitations, exceeds the level of common sense. These and many other psychologically namable processes have played a role in the lives of past individuals, groups, organizations, institutions, also *in religiosis* (Belzen and Geels 2008).

Psychohistory: An Example of the Interdisciplinary Character of Cultural Psychology of Religion

The aims of this chapter remain modest: there is no pretension here of opening entirely new avenues to psychology of religion. This discipline usually has had some awareness of the historico-cultural embeddedness of the phenomena and, consequently, there always have been efforts to combine psychology with other areas of scholarship in studying religion. Let us, as an example, consider briefly the last mentioned example again: psychohistory.

There is a striking historical relationship between the psychology of religion and psychohistory. Stanley Hall, one of the founders of the present-day psychology of religion and founder and publisher of the first professional journal in this field, attempted to make a psychohistorical study of Jesus Christ, an attempt which did not gain a following (Hall 1917). Usually, however, psychohistory is viewed as having started with Freud's study of Leonardo da Vinci (1910/1964). And it is well-known that Freud is also considered the patriarch of the psychoanalytic psychology of religion. The era of steady growth in contemporary professional psychohistory begins with a study which at the same time became one of the most popular classics in the psychology of religion, viz. *Young Man Luther* by Erik Erikson (1958). It would seem that there is some sort of kinship between the psychology of religion and psychohistory: both great and small in the psychology of religion have made psychohistorical contributions, especially from psychoanalytic perspectives, of course. Just consider Pfister's studies on Zinzendorf (1910) and Sadhu Sundar Singh (1926); Vergote's (1978/1988) study of Teresa of Avila and other mystics; the work of Sundén (1959/1966, 1987); his pupils (Källstad 1974, 1978, 1987; Wikström 1980; Holm 1987) and many other Scandinavian colleagues (Geels 1980; Åkerberg 1975, 1978, 1985; Hoffman 1982); Meissner (1992) on Loyola; Rizzuto (1998) on Freud; Capps (1997) on founding fathers of our own discipline; also the numerous studies on Augustine should be mentioned (Capps and Dittes 1990; Dixon 1999). As examples of psychohistorical psychology of religion which do not confine themselves to the study of a single individual we can mention Freud (1913/1964), Pfister (1944/1948), Carroll (1986 and 2002), Haartman (2004) and Meissner (1995), while Festinger et al. (1956), Belzen (2001a, 2004a) and Bucher (2004) offer examples that also employed something other than psychoanalytic tools.

I do not suggest that any of these examples can claim paradigmatic status in a Kuhnian sense (Kuhn 1962). Nor do I want to suggest that contemporary cultural psychology, in either its synchronic and diachronic variants, is a modern legitimation of this kind of previous work. I do want to suggest, however, that theories and methodology as they are developed in contemporary cultural psychology will be an impetus to any psychology that strives for studying an evasive and variable phenomenon like religiosity. Acknowledging that psychological phenomena are developing products of historico-cultural constitution, is something else and something more than combining psychology with an interest in religious phenomena from other times and places (as, e.g., with Jung (1938/1969) who – quite the opposite of cultural psychology – searched for the same psychological archetypes in various places). It is also different from carrying a psychological interest into the study of the history of religions, as with admittedly great authors such as VanderLeeuw (1926), Söderblom (1908) or Andrae (1932). Some kind of progress could be achieved if psychologists of religion would no longer just confine themselves to commenting (from their "armchairs," as it were) on research previously conducted by others – as in most of the studies mentioned in the last paragraph. Psychologists of religion should preferably turn into interdisciplinary empirical workers. Collaborating with ethnomethodologists and anthropologists, cross-cultural psychologists of religion might, for example, modify their research instruments in order to apply them to or develop alternative ones for other than western populations (cf. Herdt and Stephen 1989). Evidently, such a procedure is impossible for the historicizing branch of cultural psychology of religion. However, as pointed out, psychological questioning and hermeneutics can be combined with thorough empirical historical research of primary sources (e.g. Geels 1989; Meissner 1992; Belzen 2004a), as I shall try to show in Part III of this book. Both these suggestions to integrate viewpoints and methodology from anthropology or history are but examples, yet they would present a step forward in comparison with the "mere" (and all too easily forgotten) awareness that all data and interpretation in psychology of religion are limited by culture and time. Both would be expressions of seriously trying to take into account that the objects of psychology of religion are cultural and historical phenomena that require appropriate approaches in psychological research.

Thus taking up Wundt's seminal suggestion in a new and reflective way, psychology of religion will enlarge its foundations, competence and applicability, and will make a contribution to a truly human scientific psychology. Moreover, after so many complaints that much of academic psychology of religion, especially in its analytical–statistical branch, is disappointing (Nørager 1996), this strategy will make its results relevant and interesting to an even broader audience of scholars and general public. A number of psychologists of religion have been on this track already: they usually are to some extent aware of the cultural and historical make-up of the phenomena they investigate – probably more than psychologists in general, and perhaps precisely because of their often being located in other than psychological departments, with historians, anthropologists and philosophers. To them, contemporary historico-cultural psychology is an encouragement. To other psychologists of religion, it should – for the sake of their own object! – be a challenge to start collaborating with scholars from neighboring disciplines. Only this time preferably not only with neuroscientists and mathematicians, but also with anthropologists and historians.

Chapter 3
Cultural Psychology of Religion

Perspectives, Challenges and Possibilities

Introducing Cultural Psychology: Initial Distinctions

After having situated a cultural psychological approach to religion and religiosity in the larger hermeneutical camp within the social and human sciences, it should by now be appropriate to introduce cultural psychology in some more detail. As one can imagine, like psychology in general, cultural psychology is a rather broad, heterogeneous enterprise to which many well-known psychologists have made significant contributions. It is important to realize from the onset that cultural psychology is not a psychology entirely different from other kinds of psychology as developed during the discipline's past; neither is it one of its separate subdisciplines or simply a field of application. Broadly stated, cultural psychology is an approach within psychology that attempts to describe, investigate and interpret the interrelatedness of culture and human psychic functioning. It is the branch of psychology that tries to take seriously the superficially trivial observation that these would not exist without each other, that culture is therefore a major factor in all meaningful human conduct, and that traces of human involvement can be detected in all expressions of culture. By "culture" this kind of psychology usually means a system of signs, rules, symbols and practices that on the one hand structure the human realm of action, structures that are on the other hand constantly being (re)constructed and transformed by human action and praxis. It may be instructive to divide cultural psychology into several variants, subsections which are obviously not entirely independent from one another and cannot all be justly dealt with in this chapter.

(a) First of all, and vital to the development of psychology as a body of knowledge, attitudes and skills, cultural psychology investigates how culture constitutes, facilitates and regulates human subjectivity and its expression in diverse psychic functions and processes as postulated and conceptualized by different psychological schools and theories (e.g. perception, memory, mental health, the self, the unconscious, etc.). It is important to note, that the concept of culture employed here is a dynamic one, it does not just mean "context" or "situation." In the words of Ernst Boesch, a major German representative of contemporary cultural psychology (Lonner and Hayes 2007; Simao 2008):

J.A. Belzen, *Towards Cultural Psychology of Religion: Principles, Approaches, Applications*, DOI 10.1007/978-90-481-3491-5_3, © Springer Science+Business Media B.V. 2010

Culture is a field of action, whose contents range from objects made and used by human beings to institutions, ideas and myths. Being an action field, culture offers possibilities of, but by the same token stipulates conditions for, action; it circumscribes goals which can be reached by certain means, but establishes limits, too, for correct, possible and also deviant action. The relationship between the different material as well as ideational contents of the cultural field of action is a systemic one; i.e. transformations in one part of the system can have an impact in any other part. As an action field, culture not only includes and controls action, but is also continuously transformed by it; therefore, culture is as much a process as a structure. (Boesch 1991, p. 29)

With such a conception of culture, cultural psychology goes beyond the common understanding of culture in psychology at large. Whereas contemporary psychology generally recognizes that not only human interactions are influenced by culture, but that also individuals' feelings, thinking, experiences and behavior are shaped by it: cultural psychology conceives of these as being inherently cultural – as being the result of human embeddedness in culture, which is therefore to be considered as a genuine element of all human functioning relevant for psychology.[1] This form of cultural psychology will be dealt with at greater length in this chapter. It is the form of cultural psychology usually developed by psychologists. (This latter remark should not be surprising, for, as we shall see in a moment, there are also other academic disciplines that use or even make contributions to psychology as a scientific enterprise.)

All conditions and determinants of psychic functioning, whether they are limitative (like psychophysical makeup or social and geographical conditions), operative (like acquired, learned activities), or normative (like rules and norms), are always cultural-historically variable (cf. Peeters 1994). Therefore, this first variant of cultural psychology consists, roughly, in two forms: a synchronic and a diachronic one. In both forms there is a realization of the historical nature of culture (in its various manifestations) and therefore of human psychic functioning. Yet, in the first form, the emphasis is on psychic functions and processes in contemporary subjects; there is an abstraction of historical variation. In the second form, however, the historical changes in human psychic functioning are being investigated and explained on the basis of modifications in cultural conditions and determinations. Cultural psychology as a whole is an interdisciplinary approach, as will be readily understood with this first of its variants: in both forms of the first variant distinguished here, cultural psychology is in need of collaboration with other disciplines from the social and human sciences. In the synchronic form, psychology relies on information, and sometimes theories, concepts and skills from disciplines like anthropology, sociology, politicology. In the second one, historiography, and sometimes even evolutionary biology (Atran 2002, 2007), are among the obvious partners in theorizing and research.

---

[1] Cultural psychologists usually define meaningful action or conduct as the object of psychology. Obviously, there are also forms of human behavior that are not intentional or not regulated by meaning (like drawing back one's hand from a hot object; although even in the way this is done, there exists cultural variation).

Introducing Cultural Psychology: Initial Distinctions

(b) Secondly, numerous publications have traditionally been devoted to efforts to detect and determine the human involvement in all kinds of cultural products. Whereas in the first variant of cultural psychology, the understanding of culture is more or less anthropological, on a macro-level, in this second variant usually a much more elitist and restricted concept of culture is employed. Attention is given to products of so-called "high culture," like novels, movies, operas and other arts, but also to entire areas like peace and war, sports, advertising, organizations, international affairs, and to important domains like socialization, sexuality and courting, labor, death and dying. Each of these subjects can and is also being studied by other scholarly disciplines to which psychology in such cases often relates as an auxiliary discipline. In fields (to be distinguished from disciplines!) like cultural studies, education or arts, the discipline of psychology is often called upon to explore the human involvement in the phenomena studied. In these cases typically some kind or another of psychology (very often: psychoanalysis) is applied. Although this may be and has been done by psychologists (again: especially psychoanalysts) themselves, it is often done by researchers and authors without formal psychological training. Or, if psychologists are hired in these contexts, they obviously are serving another goal than the development of (new) psychological theory.

In this second variant of cultural psychology, considerable attention has been given to a variety of religious phenomena, contributing substantially to the psychology of religion-literature. Not only numerous "great" psychologists, especially from the psychoanalytic tradition, have been writing explicitly on religion from the perspective of the psychological approach or theory developed by themselves (e.g., Freud, Jung, Erikson, Allport, Maslow, Fromm), but psychological approaches or theories have often been utilized by scholars other than psychologists to analyze some religious phenomenon. The latter has been done by authors with a psycho(patho)logical training (e.g. Pruyser 1983; Rizzuto 1979; Meissner 1992, 1996; Kakar 1982, 1991; Stählin 1914b), but frequently also by scholars with a (primary) background in theology, sciences of religion, or religious studies in general (e.g. Beth 1927, 1931a, b; Pfister 1910, 1926, 1944/1948; Sundén 1959/1966; Girgensohn 1921/1930; Holm 1990; Kripall 1995; Parsons 1999; Vergote 1978/1988, 1983/1997). As such work is covered at some length in other excellent reviews (as in Wulff 1997), this variant of cultural psychology will be left out of consideration in the remainder of this chapter.

(c) A third variant of cultural psychology will be mentioned here even more briefly. It is common to find an understanding among cultural psychologists that different cultural contexts, different times as well as different places, produce different psychologies, partly as a result of their being developed with or on subjects who are psychically differently constituted (cf. Gomperts 1992; Zeegers 1988), and that the history of psychology is not about natural facts, but about socially generated constructions (cf. Danziger 1990, 1997). Therefore, within cultural psychology there is, on the one hand, attention to so-called indigenous psychologies: the psychologies as developed and employed by local people (as distinguished from Euro-American psychologists, who produced almost all of the present "academic" psychological knowledge), also in other parts of the world than on both sides of the Atlantic (e.g., Much 1995; Ratner 2008). On the other hand, there is also a fair amount of attention devoted to the history of psychology as a Western enterprise. As will be clear, in this third variant there is again collaboration with experts on local cultures (whether academically trained in the Western tradition, like anthropologists, or not) and with historians, especially intellectual historians (or with historicizing philosophers), cf. Belzen (1991a, 2007), Laucken (1998), Paranjpe (1998).

Let us now turn to a closer exploration of the first variant just distinguished, to the form of cultural psychology concentrating on the cultural basis of human psychic functioning, developed as an integral part of psychology.

Contemporary Research in Cultural Psychology

On the Difference Between Cross-cultural Psychology and Cultural Psychology

As many cultural psychologists point out, it is important to distinguish between cross-cultural psychology and cultural psychology in the proper sense.[2] The two disciplines work with different conceptions of culture, cross-cultural psychology operating with a rather traditional understanding of culture: it conceives of culture as a variable that may possibly have influence on behavior, and it investigates comparatively how experiences and behavior, attitudes, social relationships etc. present themselves within different cultural conditions. In its most straightforward form, individuals who match for age, sex, education and other relevant variables, but belong to different ethnic groups or live in different geographical regions, are compared with regard to the psychic phenomenon the particular investigation focuses on. This type of research has contributed greatly to the present sensitivity to the cultural variations in human ways of experiencing and of being in general (Vijver et al. 2008). Such comparative cultural studies often aim to determine culturally invariant forms of human expression, and considers these – in covariance with sociobiological perspectives – as anthropological constants, e.g. in research on emotions. From this approach, culture tends to be viewed merely as a qualification on the generality of psychological effects or as a moderator variable, but not as a constituent process that is implicated in explaining psychological phenomena (Billmann-Mahecha 2001).

On the contrary, cultural psychology in a proper sense stresses that cultural patterns of acting, thinking and experiencing are created, adopted and promulgated by a number of individuals jointly. Such patterns are supra-individual (social) rather than individual, and they are artefactual rather than natural. Therefore, psychological

---

[2] Recently, authors from both traditions are trying to open up a dialogue and to look for commonalities instead of stressing differences (cf. e.g. Kitayama and Cohen 2007; Matsumoto 1994a, b, 1996; Ratner 2008; Valsiner and Rosa 2007).

phenomena are cultural insofar as they are social artifacts, i.e., insofar as their content, mode of operation and dynamic relationships are a) socially created and shared by a number of individuals, and b) integrated with other social artifacts (Ratner 2002, p. 9). For example, conversion is a phenomenon found within certain religions, having a different meaning within different subgroups of such religions, being the result of certain patterns of religious practice, in their turn related to certain religious doctrines and rituals. In cultural psychology usually the meaning of some form of action (or thought or experience) is central, not the action as such (which could be, and in fact often is, studied by other social and human sciences too). Culture, also cultural practices, is conceived of as symbolic: it is considered to do more than merely represent preexisting realities and regulate behavior. Rather, culture is seen as creating (social) reality, whose existence rests partly on such cultural definitions. With this, cultural psychology recognizes the open and indeterminate relationship between cultural meanings, practices and material forces. It is recognized that not only social institutions (e.g. marriage, school), roles (e.g. bride, student) and artifacts (e.g. wedding ring, lecture notes), but also psychological concepts (e.g. the self, emotion, mind) and epistemological categories (e.g. time) depend, in part, on cultural distinctions embodied in language categories, discourse, and everyday social practices.

The main contrast between the two forms of psychology investigating the role of culture in psychological phenomena is therefore conceptual, not methodological. Cultural psychology views culture and psychology as mutually constitutive and treats basic psychological processes as culturally dependent, if not also, in certain cases, as culturally variable. Cross-cultural psychology, on the other hand, treats psychological processes as formed independently from culture, with cultural impacting on their display, but not on their basic way of functioning (Miller 2001, p. 38). In order to not remain too abstract, let us consider some pieces of research in contemporary cultural psychology.

Examples of Current Fields of Research

According to contemporary cultural psychologists, working with a more nuanced and process-oriented understanding of culture, realizing and determining its impact on psychic functioning will broaden psychological theory. And indeed, with regard to a number of basic issues in psychology like cognition, emotion, the self, well-being, self-esteem, motivation, cultural psychological research has contributed to the elaboration of new theoretical frameworks (Kitayama and Cohen 2007). A core insight from the cognitive revolution has been that individuals in making sense of experience go beyond information given, rather than merely passively "processing" it (Bruner 1990). An act of interpretation mediates between stimulus and response. Such interpretation necessarily draws on culturally available systems of meaning. Culturally different settings require different activities, leading to different (cognitive) abilities. Thus, to refer to just one example, it was found that arithmetical problem-solving goes on differently, leading to different results, in different situations. Lave et al. (1984) found, for example, that whereas 98% of problems were correctly solved by subjects when engaged in grocery shopping, only 59% of an equal kind of questions were answered correctly by the same subjects when tested in a classroom. These researchers argue further that problem-solving is not a disembodied mental activity, but belongs to, and is specific to, the kind of situation the subject is involved in. In general, cognition is viewed as constituted, in part, by the concrete practical activities in which it is situated and the cultural tools on which it depends (Miller 1999, p. 87). Likewise, emotions are not just the same ones, differing only in degree across cultures, but are different in different cultures, i.e. some emotions exist in some cultures and not in other ones. Emotions are characterized by beliefs, judgments, and desires – the content of which is not natural but is determined by the systems of cultural belief, value and mores of particular communities. They are not natural responses elicited by natural features which a situation may possess, but socio-culturally determined patterns of experience and expression which are acquired, and subsequently feature in, specific social situations (Armon-Jones 1986).

Also in the conceptions of the self – understood as an individual's understanding and experience of the own psychic functioning – and in related modes of psychic functioning, qualitative differences exist between individuals from cultural communities characterized by contrasting self-related cultural meanings and practices (Kitayama et al. 2007). Thus, the researchers Shweder and Bourne (1984) showed that, in descriptions of persons, Oriyan Indians – as compared to Euro-Americans – place greater emphasis on actions than on abstract traits, while more frequently making reference to the context. (Instead of describing a friend as, e.g., "friendly," Oriyan Indians would say that she or he "brings cakes to my family on festival days.") Recent extensions of this type of research indicate that theory of mind understanding does not spontaneously develop toward an endpoint of trait psychology, but that it proceeds in directions that reflect the contrasting epistemological assumptions of local cultural communities (Lillard 1998; Miller 2002). Another example: the fundamental attribution error (i.e. a bias to overemphasize dispositional relative to situational explanations of behavior) was formerly assumed to be universal, but research now suggests that Asians may be less vulnerable to it than North Americans (Lee et al. 1996; Morris et al. 1995).

With regard to self-esteem and well-being, cultural research implies that strategies of self-enhancement and defensive self-promotion to maintain positive feelings about the self are culturally variable, with Japanese populations emphasizing a culturally supported self-critical stance and Chinese populations emphasizing maintaining harmony within groups. The tendencies for reported self-esteem and life satisfaction to be higher among North-American than among Asian cultural populations (Diener and Diener 1995) probably does not indicate more successful patterns of adaptation to be linked with individualism. Moreover, the research in this area suggests that psychological measures of self-esteem are biased by conceptions of norms, practices and self-conceptions as individualistic, and may therefore not be able to capture central goals for the self in cultures that emphasize fulfillment of interpersonal responsibilities and interdependence (Miller 2001, p. 33).

Cultural Psychology of Religion

With regard to motivation, recent cultural work challenges some common assumptions that link agency with individualism; its shows that agency is experienced qualitatively in different ways in contrasting cultural communities. In cultural groups where the self tends to be conceptualized as inherently social rather than as inherently autonomous, individuals are more prone to experience their true selves as expressed in the realization of social expectations rather than in acting autonomously. Also, Miller and Bersoff (1994) showed that whereas Americans interpret helping as more endogenously motivated and satisfying when individuals are acting autonomously rather than in response to social expectations, Indians regard helping in both cases as just as endogenously motivated and satisfying. Likewise, Iyengar and Lepper (1999) found that Euro-American children show less intrinsic motivation when choices on anagram and game tasks were made for them by their mothers or by their peer groups, but that Asian-American children display highest levels when acting to fulfill the expectations of these trusted others. Extending this type of cultural research to issues of socialization, it has been shown that not only the meaning but also the adaptive consequences of particular modes of socialization are culturally dependent. Whereas in Euro-American cultural communities authoritarian modes of parenting tend to be associated with more maladaptive outcomes than are less controlling authoritative modes of parenting, Korean adolescents associate greater perceived parental warmth with greater perceived parental control, concordant with the Korean view of parents as having a responsibility to exercise authority over their children, failure to exercise it being experienced as parental neglect (Berndt et al. 1993; Miller 2001).

Cultural Psychology of Religion

The Interdisciplinary Character of Cultural Psychology of Religion

In psychology at large, the sensitivity for the cultural character of the phenomena being researched has largely been lost. All too often, researchers take their results to be cross-culturally valid: there is usually no realization that results obtained (frequently only on Western middle class white students) may only be valid for the sample chosen, and even that only for the time being. Therefore, in spite of (or perhaps because of) dealing with small-scale questions, concepts and manipulated variables, and in spite of it ever increasing refinement of scales and sophisticated statistical techniques, psychology is often criticized for not observing sufficiently, not going deeply enough into the phenomena it wants to explore, especially not when constructing its "measuring instruments" (cf. also Belzen 1997b).

Among the interdisciplinary authors from the founding days of psychology and other social sciences there were also scholars who are now frequently remembered as the founding fathers of sociology such as Max Weber (1904/1984) and Émile Durkheim (1912). Yet, although one finds interesting (cultural) psychological approaches with them, especially in their work on religion, they are hardly ever read by psychologists anymore. Awareness of the cultural character of the religious phenomena under scrutiny was since the beginning of the twentieth century also found with a number of theologians, who had developed into historians of religion or into comparative scholars of religion (Andrae 1926, 1932; VanderLeeuw 1926, 1928, 1932; Sierksma 1950, 1956/1980; Söderblom 1908, 1916, 1939). Very frequently, such scholars turned to psychology for interpretation of their findings (cf. Sharpe 1986). But as psychology in general narrowed down its perspectives, it lost its attractiveness to comparative scholars of religion and to others who would otherwise have been interested in psychology. If at all, they oriented themselves to psychoanalytical psychology. The work of this group of scholars – not developing new psychological theory themselves, but using psychological viewpoints within another discipline or enterprise – largely belongs to the second form of cultural psychology distinguished in the first paragraph of this chapter, and will be left out of consideration here.

In current cultural psychology, there is a return to the interdisciplinary approach from the former days (Jahoda 1993, 2007). As one of the social sciences, psychology is in need of close collaboration with, e.g., historians, sociologists and anthropologists. Accepting that culture is a major constituting and regulating force in people's self-definition, conduct and experience also require a different kind of research than is usual in mainstream psychology of religion. The particular religious "form of life" (Wittgenstein) the human being is embedded in, can then no longer be neglected in favor of searching for some presumably inherent and invariable psychic structures. On the contrary, it is necessary to study people *engaging* in their particular "form of life," not to take them out of it by submitting them to experiments, tests or questionnaires in the "laboratory." Accordingly, researchers have to turn to participant observation, analysis of personal documents, interviews, group discussions and other ecologically valid techniques. Further, it becomes necessary to study not the isolated individual, but also the beliefs, values and rules that are prevalent in a particular cultural situation, together with the patterns of social relatedness and interaction that characterize that situation. In any case, it appears erroneous to try to study the "individual mind" as such. Psychology cannot fulfill this task without the aid of other cultural sciences.

Theories in Contemporary Cultural Psychology and Their Application to Religion

In contemporary cultural psychology a variety of concepts and theories is employed, drawing from different strains of thoughts (Triandis 2007). As there is no space here to cover the range even approximately, let us take a brief look at just some of them, and see what a concept like *habitus* means, what the theory of the dialogical self and other narrative approaches stand for, and what theories of "action" (or "activity") have put forward.

Cultural Psychology of Religion

The notion that psychological phenomena depend on practical activities has a long tradition, ranging from Marx and Engels, to Dewey and contemporary thinkers like Bourdieu. Religious people very often cannot explain on a cognitive level why they perform as they do, for example, in rituals. (Even the question as posed by a researcher, say, would be odd, as we will see in a case of empirical research reported in Chapter 9.) Most often they have no knowledge of the "official" rationales for certain conduct. Accordingly Roman Catholics cannot account for their behavior during Mass, nor can Buddhists for the reasons for experiencing grief as they do (Obeyesekere 1985). Yet people perform perfectly in accordance with the expectations of their religious (sub)culture, often with a competence and to an extent that a foreigner will never learn to manage. Religion regulates conduct, although this conduct cannot be conceived of as the conscious following of rules. People's conduct – in the broadest sense, also including their perception, thinking, emotion, needs, etc. – is regulated according to a scheme or structure that is not consciously known. This scheme is not even of a primarily cognitive nature at all, but is something belonging to the body. People act not because they know consciously what to do: it is as if their body knows for them. Affect, for example, is not the result of properly knowing how to feel – it is ruled by an immediate corporeal structure. Bourdieu (1980/1990) calls this structure *habitus* – it is this structure that generates and structures people's actions. Although these structures are personally embodied, they are not individual: they characterize the (sub)culture and are derived from the patterns in the participant's conduct. They belong to both the individual and a (sub)culture; in fact, they are precisely the nexus between an individual and a cultural institution. Unlike western secularized societies, religion in most cultures is not just a specific practice performed on specific occasions. In such cultures, religion is transmitted through practice, "without raising to the level of discourse. The child mimics other people's actions rather than 'models.' Body praxis speaks directly to motor function, in the form of a pattern of postures that is both individual and systematic, being bound up with a whole system of objects, and charged with a host of special meanings and values" (Bourdieu 1980/1990, pp. 73–74). The same applies to those western subcultures where religion is still predominantly a shaping and integrating force. For example: it is because he carries, in his body, the *habitus* of a Hindu from India, that a believer thinks, reacts, feels and behaves as an Indian Hindu, in fact *is* an Indian Hindu, and not because he would know the specifics of the doctrine, the ethical rules or the rituals. The believer usually is *not* aware of these specifics. Not being individual, the *habitus* is itself structured by social practices: its dispositions are durably inculcated by the possibilities and impossibilities, freedoms and necessities, opportunities and prohibitions inscribed in the objective conditions. It is in social practices that the *habitus* can be observed at work: being (re)produced and producing conduct itself.

To what extent ever the *habitus* may be non-cognitive or operating in a way nonconscious to the actor, the conduct that results does mean something, both to the actor and to other cultural participants. This meaning is rooted in both personal life history and culturally available meanings. Analysis of activity must take into account the "forms of life" that are the context of meaning. This culturally available meaning can only be traced and analyzed at the level of text: words, proverbs, stories, myths, articulated symbols. However true it may be that without the analysis of activity, cultural psychology is only telling half of the story (Ratner 1996), it remains true that cultural knowledge, symbols, concepts and words, laid down in and maintained by linguistic conventions, stimulate and organize psychological phenomena. Here narrative psychology can be seen as an obvious ally in any analysis of religiosity. It points out that in the course of their life, people hear and assimilate stories, which enable them to develop "schemes" which give direction to their experience and conduct – schemes with whose help they can then make sense out of a potential stimulation overload (Howard 1991). To each developing story, and in every situation with which they are confronted, people bring an acquired catalogue of "plots" which is used to make sense out of the story or situation (Mancuso and Sarbin 1983). Here lies a possibility of applying narrative psychology to religious phenomena. For, whatever religion may be besides this, it is in any case also a reservoir of verbal elements, stories, interpretations, prescriptions and commandments, which in their power to determine experience and conduct and in their legitimization possess narrative character. Clifford Geertz's definition of religion, which is most widely disseminated in cultural psychology, points to the central importance of "stories," of linguistically transmitted and given reality: "a religion is a system of symbols which act to establish powerful, pervasive and long-lasting moods and motivations in men by formulating conceptions of a general order of existence and clothing those conceptions with such an aura of factuality that the moods and motivations seem uniquely realistic" (1973, p. 90). In order to effect a connection with narrative psychology, one need only take the word "symbols" in this definition and give it more precise content with the aid of "stories and practices." (In this connection one must realize that both practices and "conceptions" again employ stories to explain and legitimate themselves.) In other words: people who, among the various culturally available life forms, have also been introduced to, or have appropriated, a religious life form, have at their disposal a system of interpretation and conduct which (narratively) prefigures reality for them. Thus in every situation, expectations, interpretations and actions can be brought to bear which have been derived from a religious horizon of understanding and which, under certain circumstances, confirm and reinforce this understanding. Indeed, precisely those persons and groups are considered deeply devout who succeed, with the greatest frequency, spontaneously and perseveringly, to activate this religious horizon of understanding and who are in a position – despite the paradoxes they are confronted with – to overcome their own problems of religious interpretation and to act in harmony with the system of interpretation and conduct they have appropriated as well as with the "stories" that have been handed down to them.

Activity theory was seminally lined out by Vygotsky (Veresov 1999) and elaborated in the cultural- historical Russian tradition initiated by him (Leontiev 1978, 1981; Luria 1971, 1976; Vygotsky 1978, 1998). Vygotsky enumerated three cultural factors that influence psychic functioning:

1. Activities such as producing goods, raising children, educating the populace, devising and implementing laws, treating disease, playing, and producing art

Cultural Psychology of Religion

2. Artifacts including tools, books, paper, pottery, weapons, eating utensils, clocks, clothing, buildings, furniture, toys, and technology
3. Concepts about things and people, e.g. the succession of forms that the content of person has taken in the life of human beings in different societies with their system of law, religion, customs, social structures, and mentality (Mauss 1938/1985, p. 3, in Ratner 2002, p. 10)

Vygotsky emphasized the dependence of psychic functioning on these three cultural factors, and the dominance of activities over the other two. (Ratner 2002 correctly pointed out that the real situation is more complex and dynamic: it contains reciprocal influence among the factors, and it is animated by intentionality, teleology, or agency.) Vygotsky stated: "The structures of higher mental functions represent a cast of collective social relations between people. These structures are nothing other than a transfer into the personality of an inward relation of a social order that constitutes the basis of the social structure of the human personality" (1998, pp. 169–170). Another member of the "cultural-historical" school in psychology initiated by Vygotsky wrote similarly that "changes take place in the course of historical development in the general character of men's consciousness that are engendered by changes in their mode of life" (Leontiev 1981, p. 22).

According to activity theorists, activity, artifacts and cultural concepts need to be explored by psychologists to understand psychic functioning of individuals in a particular culture. This is not a task to be left to scholars other than psychologists, as one has to look outside the individual to comprehend the content, mode of operation, and dynamics of psychological phenomena, constituted as they are by cultural factors and processes. Gerth and Mills (1953) pointed out that activities are internally divided into roles, and that each role entails distinctive rights, responsibilities, norms, opportunities, limitations, rewards and qualifications. (The activity of religion, e.g., includes the roles of believer and usually of some kind of priest, both more often than not divided into a host of religious categories as penitent, possessed, enlightened, etc., or such as pastor, baptizer, minister, exorcist, etc.) The distinctive characteristics of a role shape the occupant's psychic functioning, for it is by her or his experience in enacting various roles, that the person incorporates certain objectives and values which steer and direct her or his conduct, as well as the elements of her or his psychic structure. Fulfilling a role requires psychic training: it involves learning what to do, as well as the meaning of what to do. "His [sic] memory, his sense of time and space, his perception, his motives, his conception of his self, his psychological functions are shaped and steered by the specific configuration of roles which he incorporates from his society" (Gerth and Mills 1953, p. 11; cf. also Ratner (2002), for an actualized outline of activity theory, integrating numerous contemporary research findings and extensive discussions of its relation to other cultural psychological approaches).

The concept of the (social) role is an excellent device for a cultural psychological approach to religion, as it designates a historically specific set of norms, rights, responsibilities and qualifications that pertain not only to persons and/or situations actually present, but also to those from the realm of religious stories, symbols and discourse in general. Roles are specific, distinctive ways of acting and interacting, and the concept can be used to designate the functioning (action, but also corresponding attitudes, emotions and expectations) on the part of the actual believer as well as to the (anticipated) conduct of the beings from an immaterial realm as stipulated by the divers religions, as the Swedish psychologist of religion Hjalmar Sundén (1959/1966) pointed out. His role theory of religious experience has proved a powerful heuristic device to analyze both contemporary and historical cases, and can be considered as a contribution to a cultural psychology of religion (Belzen 1996b).

Examples

Before closing, let us take a brief look at some examples of research on religion, performed along cultural psychological lines. We shall consider work from different countries and in different religious traditions.

(a)   The Belgian psychologist of religion Vergote has applied Freudian-Lacanian and Winnicottian psychoanalytic thoughts and cultural psychological reasoning in general in extended research on religion. His work is characterized by an – among psychologists! – remarkably unusual interdisciplinary approach: he draws on cultural anthropology, history and sociology, psychoanalysis and philosophy. When confronted with the task to define his object of study, he does not commit the fallacy of trying to develop a psychological definition of religion, but he turns to cultural sciences, especially to anthropology. Accordingly, the task for psychology of religion is to develop or to make use of an approach that will yield insight into the psychic processes that are involved in and determined by this culturally given religion. Next, there is no pretension of studying "religion" in general (whatever that may be), but an in-depth analysis of some concrete phenomenon, belonging to a particular religious form of life (be it stigmata, worship of ancestors, or whatever). Usually, Vergote's publications deal only with aspects of the Christian faith in its Roman Catholic version – even more concretely: from the Belgian context. In one of his main publications, he attempts a study of "belief," which he considers to be one of the most important elements in and specific for the Christian faith. Before starting his psychological research, he offers a brief account of what "to believe" means in Christianity (1983/1997, pp. 187–191). Proceeding in this way, he has removed himself far from any effort to write a psychology of religion in general: as he is not writing on religion in general, he is, in that volume, not even writing on the Christian religion in general, but only on one of its aspects: faith. As in his better-known *Guilt and Desire* (1978/1988), he defends the position that "by nature" the human being is neither religious nor irreligious; the human being can only become a religious or irreligious person, because of culturally available religious meanings: "what is studied by psychology is the effect of psychic archeology on the process by which the individual appropriates the symbolic system of religion" (1983/1997, p. 26).

Cultural Psychology of Religion

It is psychology's task to bring to light (latent) meanings and motivations in experienced religion, and to investigate how these relate organically to each other and form the structure of personal religiosity. Therefore, it just as revealing to study the process by which a person develops into an unbeliever, as to study the oscillations between belief and unbelief.

(b)   Research on a mystically oriented Christian spirituality in the Netherlands may count as another example of a cultural psychological approach to religion. As Belzen (2003) has tried to point out, the notion of conversion as adhered to by *bevindelijken*, orthodox-mystical believers belonging to the Calvinistic tradition, may well be interpreted with the aid of categories of social constructionism, especially in its "rhetorical-responsive" version. As in many non-western countries, but also with several more or less traditional religious groups in the West – where religion is a major shaping force in various, sometimes even almost all, domains of private and public life, and where people more often than not fail to distinguish between the two – *bevindelijke* believers have "embodied" (Bourdieu) knowledge "of the third kind" (Shotter) about their religion. *Bevindelijke* identity does not just consist in membership in some church, in affirming specific theological doctrines, in joining an "inner circle" or even in being able to account for one's religious experiences in a certain stylized way, but predominantly in an all-pervading "style," belonging to a specific "life form" (Wittgenstein), displaying itself in and through the body. Whereas Vergote has also worked with standardized instruments like Osgood-scales, Belzen utilized very diverse empirical strategies, including dozens of observations made during attendance at church services, observations and conversations on the occasion of visits to feast days (mission conferences, book fairs, training courses, political assemblies); numerous encounters with people, in the street, after church, at their homes, sometimes just "small talk," sometimes in the form of semi-structured interviews (in some cases even with a tape-recorder on the table); analysis of ego-documents, novels, spiritual authors and scholarly publications on *bevindelijken*; reading their newspapers, visiting them on Internet. In short: anything that might help a person to "get in touch" (Shotter 1992). In Chapter 9 we shall take a closer look at this research.

(c)   Similarly, Much and Mahapatra (1995) have combined anthropological methods and psychological reasoning in their study of a *Kalasi* (a possession oracle in the Hindu tradition) of Oressa, a state on the eastern coast of India. They show the interplay of meanings in the constitution of the life form of the woman they present in their case study, and consider her role as a possession oracle from the point of view of personal meanings and values, of social statuses or positions, and of local cultural symbolic contexts. In their analysis, they focus upon the cultural discourse that accommodates the role and status of a possession oracle, and upon the semiotic skills of the oracle herself as she transforms herself from her ordinary persona to a "moving divinity" (*Thakura chalanti*). During the times of transformation and possession (and at those times only!), *Kalasis* are expected to speak and behave in ways different from normally acceptable social behavior.

The resulting behavior is, however, a patterned and meaningful symbolic deviation from the norm, and not a random inhibition. There clearly are norms for behavior while possessed. *Kalasis* are held to have special powers when possessed by the Goddess. Their actions and speech are understood as her actions and speech, and their special powers under possession are viewed as attributes of the Goddess. According to Much and Mahapatra (1995, p. 76) the discourse of the oracle (*hokum*) is a socially shared illusion wherein participants have the experience of *darshan*: a vision of visions (or objects) who are special conduits of divinity, during which they can receive personal attention and advice directly from the Goddess. (As such, the hokum is not particularly different from other kinds of socially shared illusions in Western or Indian cultures, like psychotherapy, academic symposia or business meetings.) The authors point out that it is not the "supernatural" aspect of the hokum which makes it an illusion, but rather its socially constituted facticity, without which it would not be experienced as meaningful in the way that it is. Reflecting on their research, Much and Mahapatra come up with an interesting suggestion for psychological theory: from a cultural psychological point of view, personality patterns – dispositions, patterns of knowing and feeling, awareness and response – are aptly considered skills. A neonate enters the social world with a certain range of potentials, some universal or widely shared, others particular to a subset of individuals. Which of these potentials are cultivated or not, and in which way, depends to a large extent on cultural contexts of learning, knowing and performing. The marginalized or even pathologized potentials of one culture may be recognized talents, and so developed into socially and personally adaptive skills, in cultural contexts where these skills are accepted, where they can be cultivated in well-organized institutionalized forms, and where they are integrated with local social structures and cultural goals. Cases in point would be the various contemplative, mystical and ecstatic skills valued, taught and cultivated in South Asia but ignored and generally pathologized by mainstream contemporary western society.

Closing Words

As I shall try to argue also in Chapter 7, cultural psychology seems well prepared to correct one of the oldest and most widespread flaws in the psychology of religion, i.e. forgetting to focus, at least at some point, on religion as a phenomenon of culture. Cultural psychology may serve as a remedy here, as it enables us to do justice to the cultural impact of the phenomena under consideration: a cultural psychological approach takes into account the specific form of life (Wittgenstein) in which subjects are involved. I must grant that in so doing the results obtained are not valid for every person and/or group in every religion, but it is exactly this sort of aspiration that should be abolished from psychology (not just in psychology of religion)! As there is no such thing as religion-in-general, but only specific forms of life going by the same label "religious," and as psychology should not strive for insight into presumably basic elements of psychic functioning valid for all subjects, regardless of time and place, the psychology of religion should try to detect how a specific religious form of life constitutes, involves and regulates the psychic functioning of its adherents. The psychology of religion will have a future and will have the possibility to formulate meaningful results and interpretations by selecting specific phenomenon from religious forms of life, taking account of their particular psychic impact and using concepts and methods from cultural psychological theory.

Next to this, cultural psychology promises to be a valuable addition and corrective to other psychological approaches that already focus on religion as a cultural phenomenon but that tend to jump to conclusions no scientific analysis of religion could ever reach. An interesting example is the increasing attention to both the neurological and cognitive basis of religious functioning (cf., e.g., Andresen 2001; Cohen 2007). One finds results from this type of research used in both reductionistic and in apologetic reasoning (cf., e.g., Newberg et al. 2001). Authors from these approaches stress either the brain or the mind in their explanations of religion. However – and I am not doing justice to the literature on this topic (for an introductory review, cf. Reich 2004) – people seem to forget that even these are never more than the necessary preconditions for the specifics of human functioning and are not sufficient conditions themselves. If we can discover that some parts of the brain are more vital to religious functioning than others (Ramachandran and Blakeslee 1998), we still could not conclude that these parts are responsible for religious functioning. The impact of acculturation always remains and that is one of the main issues for a cultural psychological approach, particularly as regards its application to religion. Likewise, if evidence appears that religion has developed for evolutionary purposes (Guthrie 1993; Boyer 2001; Kirkpatrick 2005), it still remains for psychologists to find out by which means any given specific religion shapes the religious life of contemporary subjects. Also, when cognitive scientists show that also *in religione* the mind functions as it is predetermined to do (Andresen 2001; Slone 2004), is that not a bit trivial? How could we, after more than a century of reflection and research in the psychology of religion, expect otherwise? Of course, the mind will allow for the development of only certain religious ideas and practices, and facilitate these, hinder others; and of course scientific knowledge about the working of the mind must be taken into account in a comprehensive theory of religion (to which the whole of the psychology of religion will only be able to contribute modestly).

What will always remain an impossibility is the ability to judge the ultimate existential and ontological value of any kind of religion on the basis of scientific work. In addition to the fact that scientific knowledge is provisional by definition, in principle science can never be turned into an attack on or into an apologetic device on behalf of any religion. That brain and mind are involved in religious functioning is trivial, that they alone determine the form, content and modality of individual religious functioning or of religion as a cultural phenomenon is an unsound conclusion. But neurobiological approaches and cognitive psychology can help assess, and can join together with cultural psychology to detect and depict via an analysis of the interlacement of religion and psychic functioning what is specific to religious forms of life. We should take care not to repeat a kind of nature–nurture debate:

obviously, in all psychic functioning brain and mind are involved; they enable, shape and limit what human beings can and cannot do, but they do not determine all and everything. If we want to know more about a cultural phenomenon like religion, cultural psychology is a legitimate way, perhaps even the royal road, to try to find out more about its relationship to psychic functioning.

Different psychological approaches may be employed to try to analyze religious persons and phenomena. Although some may be more apt than others, each must remain modest: each will always offer only a partial perspective on the phenomenon under scrutiny. Yet in this way and in their own right the different psychological approaches to religion will do what their very name requires of them: use the instruments of psychology to find out more about religion, one of the most complex elements of human cultures.

Chapter 4
The Way Out of Contemporary Debates on the Object of the Discipline

Introduction

As should be well known, virtually all the founding fathers of psychology contributed something to the subdiscipline presently called psychology of religion. However, in spite of its lengthy history, this psychology of religion is a problematic enterprise and many of its basic questions – e.g., What kind of scholarship, if any, is it? What is its place in academia? What it is about? – still await answers. To some observers, research on religion is a field of applied psychology (Strien 1990): what is known from other branches of psychology can be used to analyze religion. Others, however, strongly opposed to this view, argue that psychology of religion belongs to theoretical psychology (Ouwerkerk 1986; Vergote 1983/1997). To them, religiosity is a test of the scope of more general psychological theories: Are these psychologies able to deal with religiosity? Can they take account of the special relationship the person is involved in, for instance, when praying, when speaking words into a void, addressing "someone" from whom no answer is expected, yet claiming that this moment fills life with meaning? As with other significant psychological research focusing on a specific domain (e.g., art, literature, sport, war and peace), there is no clear institutional unity among people involved in psychology of religion: they are found in departments of philosophy, psychiatry, anthropology, religious studies and in the various specialized departments of psychology. As seems to be the case within the numerous branches of psychology, there is no agreement on basic questions among psychologists of religion. There is not even a consensus as to what the field should consider as its very object, "religion," and no consensus as to what kind of psychology should be employed or developed to analyze religion. Of course, this need not be a reason for lamentations, on the contrary: discussions and controversy can be very fruitful. Yet, one might become suspicious when witnessing some of these discussions. Although many contemporary authors are scrupulously trying to be as neutral as possible, in their research, valuable as it is, religion is often not much more than a variable whose impact can be established with regard to coping, psychotherapy and many other psychological themes (cf., e.g., Paloutzian and Kirkpatrick 1995). As soon as it comes to a more theoretical approach, discussions on religion appear to be obscured more often than not by the all-too-personal suppositions of the participants.

J.A. Belzen, *Towards Cultural Psychology of Religion: Principles, Approaches, Applications*,
DOI 10.1007/978-90-481-3491-5_4, © Springer Science+Business Media B.V. 2010

Time and again, it is apparent that it is the author's personal stand toward religion that is being legitimated by his psychological "research," or that what the researcher privately considers to be the most appealing religion, also turns out as having the most positive psychological qualifications. To mention just a few examples: in the analyses by the atheist Sigmund Freud, religion is shown to be a collective neurosis, an infantile longing for the father, and other such "disqualifications" believers did not like to hear (Freud 1907/1959, 1913/1964, 1927/1961). Contrary, in the perspective of the very religious Gordon Allport, a unifying philosophy of life became the final criterion for a fully developed personality, religion being a "search for a value underlying all things, and as such [...] the most comprehensive of all the possible philosophies of life" (1937, p. 214). Likewise, psychological publications arguing for the (at least, relative) health of mystics, despite their frequent psychiatric symptoms, are often authored by Roman Catholics (e.g., in the journal *Études Carmelitaines*) in whose tradition mysticism is valued (as much as it is distrusted in some Protestant traditions within Christianity). Quite a number of publications have tried to argue that criticism of religion, as, e.g., formulated by the early psychoanalytic tradition, had not so much been false as limited: it would be true of "neurotic" religiosity only, not of all and especially not of "healthy" religiosity.[1] When the theologian and psychologist Daniel Batson (Batson and Ventis 1982) proposed an elaboration and improvement of Allport's classic distinction of extrinsic and intrinsic religiosity by adding a third type, this so-called quest-religiosity got away with sympathetic characteristics and proved to be rather identical with Batson's own liberal Protestantism (cf., e.g., Hood and Morris 1985; Derks 1990; Slik 1992). Examples like these could be multiplied. Of course, research inspired by a positive stand towards religion has helped to balance sweeping statements by critics and has added further nuances to the discussion. Besides, every scholar in any field may have a hidden agenda. Yet, it is debatable whether such agendas sometimes prevented progress in the psychology of religion.

Debates on the Object of the Psychology of Religion: Tema Con Variazoni?

One of the more recent discussions among psychologists of religion in Europe, with some echoes in the USA, has been about the question how the object of the discipline should be conceived of. The start of the discussion was reported in the *Proceedings of the 3rd Symposium for European Psychologists of Religion* (Belzen and Lans 1986), in which reviewers considered this discussion to be especially valuable (cf. Deconchy 1987; Stollberg and Wienold 1987; Hutsebaut 1986; Godin 1987; Visser 1987; for later contributions to the discussion, cf. Lans 1991b; Vergote 1993,

---

[1] Cf. the excellent historical exposé by Nase and Scharfenberg (1977) in which they characterize a second phase of psychoanalytical publishing on religion as "psychoanalysis as means to purify religion" (of its non-essential, criticizable elements); cf. also Belzen 1997c.

1995; Malony 1997; Beit-Hallahmi 1993; McDargh 1993).[2] In these discussions, heterogeneous motives can be detected. One colleague, for instance, explicitly stated that orienting itself towards the kind of psychology conducted in western psychological laboratories, is the only way for the psychology of religion to survive (Lans 1986). And since religion seems not to be a popular topic for those in charge in these laboratories, it would be wise and advisable to advance "meaning-giving behavior" as the object of the psychology of religion in order to obtain research funds and academic positions. Moreover, just as psychology would attempt to "develop general theories from particular observations" by "making inferences about common factors," the appropriate object for the psychology of religion should be the "search for meaning," whether religious or not (Lans 1986, pp. 79–80). Indeed, this position seems to be concordant with much of the psychology found in main-stream western "laboratories." Although the opponent in the discussion perhaps only spoke for a minority in the field, it is interesting to note that his position seems to be much closer to what might be called "cultural psychology" (cf. Vergote 1986). In this chapter, I will not try to renew this discussion, but to take a step back, as it were, and reflect primarily on some of the basic positions that can be distinguished with regard to the object of this psychological (sub)discipline. In comparison to the psychology of other specific domains (like sports or the arts), discussions about its subject matter are rather prevalent in psychology of religion. One may wonder what kinds of motives may be involved: Could it be that these discussions reflect implicit religious a priori's regarding the nature of the human being? After exploring this question, I shall argue that psychological analyses of religiosity might well be further advanced when approached from a religiously neutral cultural-psychological perspective.

No one can do without "pragmatic arguments" (Lans 1986, p. 80) and strategies – there need be no dispute about that. However, it does seem that by following the proposal to take "meaning giving" as the object of the (sub)discipline, psychologists of religion are just choosing another variation within the same tradition that has been prevalent since the time of Immanuel Kant (1724–1804). As is well known, Kant limited the competence of theoretical reason: it cannot get beyond sensory perception (*Begriffe ohne Anschauung sind leer*; constructs without perception are empty). Although we are forced to make orderly connections between the constructs of reason, this higher form of thinking (*Vernunft*) has only an ordering ability; it transcends ordinary knowing, but its ideas – for example, soul, world, God – are regulative, not constitutive, and, not registering anything, they do not contribute to our knowledge of reality. Thus criticizing rationalism *à la* Descartes and Leibniz, Kant undermined

---

[2]Another recent discussion on the object of psychology of religion originated in the USA (Heelas and Woodhead 2005; Wuthnow 1998, 2001; Zinnbauer et al. 1997). The issue was (and is) whether spirituality should be or become regarded as the object, or whether it should at least be including in the definition of the object of the discipline (Pargament 1999; Stifoss-Hanssen 1999). In division 36 of the American Psychological Association, the division for the 'psychology of religion,' a proposal was even made to change the name of the division to 'psychology of religion and spirituality'. That proposal was not accepted. Some years later, however, the supporters of the proposal started with APA a new journal entitled *Psychology of Religion and Spirituality* (since 2009). This primarily American discussion will be joined in chapter 6.

much of the theological reasoning of his time. Although to him it remained necessary to *think* (postulate) God, there could be no knowledge *about* God. Yet Kant tried – for whatever reason (as his famous utterance suggests: his old house servant Lampe needed a God to believe in) – to give theology a new foundation: no longer in theoretical reason, but in practical reason. For moral consciousness, the idea "God" is a necessary condition. (When ethical conduct is not possible to its fullest extent, because of "evil" in this world, it is necessary to postulate a [future] world in which this will be possible. This world Kant called the "Kingdom of Heavens" and therefore he considered it necessary to postulate, next to freedom, both the soul's immortality and God's existence as guarantees for morality.) God is a necessary and a priori postulate, not of theoretical but of practical reason, and is "saved" in this way, as Kant's dictum so nicely summarizes: "Ich mußte das Wissen aufheben, um zum Glauben Platz zu bekommen"("I had to remove knowledge in order to create space for faith"; Kant 1787/1956, "Vorrede").

Similarly, and with even more impact, the philosopher Friedrich Schleiermacher (1768–1834), searched for a new and secure basis for religion. Some consider him to be the father of modern psychology of religion (Berg 1958; Popp-Baier 1998; Vergote 1983/1997), as he tried to anchor religion in the person's psychic constitution. To him, Kant's solution was still too much affected by the style of the Enlightenment – freedom might be necessary for practical reason to guarantee morality, but not religion. Religion is found elsewhere: it arises from "the heart," from "feeling." Religiosity has a province of its own in the heart, "eine eigene Provinz im Gemüte." It is neither knowledge nor conduct, but the sense of infinity, found in every person's soul; it is the contemplation of the universe, found as much in ourselves as in the world. Religiosity is grounded in the person's awareness of existence in the world, it is the consciousness of being dependent ("ein schlechthinniges Abhängigkeitsgefühl," Schleiermacher (1799/1958), p. 39). Together with William James' classic text *The Varieties of Religious Experience* (1902/1958), Schleiermacher's philosophy inaugurated a tradition in the psychology of religion, dominant until today (cf. Hood 1995), focusing on "religious experience" and founding religion in emotion.

According to James (cf. the subtitle of his book: "A study in human nature"), the human being's nature is religious: it can be analyzed by studying religious experiences, what he conceives of as inner experience – the kernel and source of all religion ("the immediate personal communication of the founders of a religion with the divine," James 1902/1982, p. 42). Other aspects of religion – ideas, rituals, institutions – are secondary to this source. James explicitly combated what he called the "medical materialism" of his day. Adherents of that point of view, James argued, thought that they could disqualify religion because it sprang from (disordered) emotion. Although James admitted this "psychopathic" source, he refused to take this as the criterion of its value. As with art, and many other fields rooted in emotion, James asked: where does it lead to, what are its results, its fruits? And he concluded that, indeed: "the religious emotion adds something positive to the subject's understanding of life. It offers him a new source of strength" (p. 54). Rudolf Otto (1869–1937), with his equally classic volume *The Idea of the Holy* (1917/1976), situated himself in the same tradition. Although he belonged, epistemologically, to the neo-Kantian camp around the turn of the century, he too wanted to avoid what he considered a reduction of religion either to ethics or to rational thought. He postulated a specific emotion that he called "the numinous" (from the Latin *numen*: the divine, or the divine power) which he considered to be a "category *sui generis*." After analyzing the numinous experience elaborately, Otto concluded that its emotional scheme is a formal a priori of man's affectivity, analogous to the Kantian a priori of reason. As a result of this emotional structure, the human being is endowed with the sense of the Holy, in addition to being endowed with the categories of reason. Therefore, religion belongs to human nature.

When today some colleagues suggest that a person's search for meaning – that is, the innate tendency to make sense of an unceasingly, undifferentiated sensory input – would be the source and psychological kernel of religiosity, they are again founding religion in the person's psychic constitution, this time not in emotion, but in some cognitive faculty. This seems to be simply a variation of the tradition presented above, a tradition that has become dominant since the nineteenth century with the work of Darwin and his followers, who gave impetus to the idea of inherent sources of motivation, cognition and behavior. This tradition, suppressing the older empiricist tradition, ranging from the ancient Greeks to Hume (1711–1776) and Berkeley (1685–1753), postulated "instincts" as the explanation for people being religious. Thus Le Bon (1903), at the turn of the previous century, proposed a "religious sentiment" and McDougall (1909) understood religion to be an outgrowth of what he called the instincts of curiosity, fear and subjection. To these the latter added the three "religious emotions" of admiration, awe and reverence. L. L. Bernard (1924), who administered the death blow to this tradition by finding in his review of the literature 5,684 instincts (of which 93 were theorized to underlie religion), claimed that those who saw an instinctual basis for religion were naive with respect to heredity, and usually did not know that religion as they conceived it, was not universal, as biology would have it. Yet, even if the word instinct remains unspoken today, it still lurks in the background in some conceptions (as, for example, in the wake of Allport's (1950) "religious sentiment" and in discussions on "spirituality").

The proposal to conceive of religion as founded in a more general human "meaning-giving" behavior, is a variation within this "innate program" and articulated previously by another German scholar at the turn of the last century, Ernst Troeltsch (1865–1923), whose methodological reflections have been very influential in early *Religionswissenschaft* and psychology of religion alike (Troeltsch 1905). Next to Kant's a priori's of scientific, ethical and teleological-esthetical *Vernunft*, he postulated a "religious a priori": a capability to recognize truth, even within the confusing diversity of contemporary opinions. This potential of consciousness is actualized in concrete evaluations of religious phenomena. The religious a priori is independent of the other Kantian a priori's, in the same way as religion cannot be deduced from logic, ethics or esthetics. Perhaps purposively unclear about the status and qualities of his postulated a priori, Troeltsch instigated a wide discussion among philosophers and psychologists on religion (cf., e.g., Spranger 1910/1974). According to his student Süskind, however, the purpose of his thought was to integrate religion as a necessary and essential function of mental life into the system of the *Vernunft*, and to safeguard

58   The Way Out of Contemporary Debates on the Object of the Discipline

its normality (Süskind 1914, p. 5). Troeltsch had a major influence on Paul Tillich (1886–1965), one of the most powerful religious thinkers of the twentieth century, who for his part promoted an ongoing dialogue between theology and psychology (cf. Tillich 1952; Homans 1968). The type of reasoning as instigated by Troeltsch seems to fit remarkably well with theological interests to present religion as universal and inherent to human nature.

Defensive Motives?

Whatever opinion one may have of the variations people have put forward in this line of thought, defensive motives seem to be involved. With someone like Schleiermacher this is clear enough even from the title of his publication: *Über die Religion; Reden an die Gebildeten unter ihren Verächtern* (On Religion; Speeches to Its Cultured Despisers 1799/1958); many of the thinkers mentioned thus far started as theologians, as in a later era many psychologists of religion did; several authors in the wake of Troeltsch (e.g. Kalweit 1908) tried to use his reasoning to argue for the natural superiority of Christianity. Moreover, against the many criticisms that have been brought forward against particular forms of religion, and facing secularization and decline of church membership, quite a number of psychologists of religion obviously try to safeguard religion: Allport developed his distinction between 'extrinsic' and 'intrinsic' religion (Allport 1960) only when research indicated that religiosity correlated positively with ethical prejudices (cf. Allport 1962, p. 130). His differentiation restored peace of mind: "intrinsic" religion did not show the – initially disturbing – correlation with prejudice. For Batson, however, "intrinsic" religiosity comes too close to evangelical fundamentalism – his "quest" type would not be characterized by what he perceives as the former's vices. Likewise, an increasing number of publications on mental health and psychotherapy try to show that, contrary to the (only assumed?) disinterest of many psychologists, it is a failure to neglect or even oppose religion; these publications try to show what positive relationships (can) exist between religion and mental health, and how religion can be a beneficial factor in psychotherapy (Bhugra 1996; Corbet 1996; Randour 1993; Shafranske 1996a; Richards and Bergin 1997, 2000, 2004; Pargament 1997, 2007; Pargament et al. 1992; Sperry 2001; Sperry and Shafranske 2005).[3]

The same defensive reasoning is found in the debate briefly reviewed before: when religion is founded in human nature,[4] as with Lans' proposal to take "meaning-giving behavior" as the object of psychology of religion. An older example would, of course,

---

[3] Beit-Hallahmi (1992, 1993) is offering parallel criticisms of psychology of religion as being a defensive enterprise, but – to my judgment – his argument is often ad hominem.

[4] Usually, here as with Allport's theory of the personality, this viewpoint is the result of (implicit) theological a priori's – viewing the human being as God's creature and the relatedness with God as belonging inherently to human nature, only to be repressed at considerable (also psycho-social) costs – going back to Augustine's famous neo-Platonian adage "Fecisti nos ad Te...": "Thou [God] hath created us to Thee and our heart is restless in us until it rests in Thee" (*Confessiones*, Book I, 1, 3).

Defensive Motives? 59

be C.G. Jung's (1938/1969) founding religion in the collective unconsciousness; a rather recent one, is Jones' assertion that "being human [is] knowing God" (Jones 1996). This (theological) assumption can have odd implications such as, e.g., calling unbelievers nevertheless religious, or assuming that non-religious persons would be less developed personalities. Certainly contrary to the intentions, it might end as a very reductionistic enterprise, e.g., when in the wake of the earlier discussion in sociology of religion on substantial versus functional definitions of religion,[5] some psychologists of religion seem to redefine their object in order to call even attending a rock concert a modern type of, or equivalent to, going to a church service (Reich 1990). When apparently, there is no religion, some theoreticians nevertheless speak of "implicit" or "invisible" religion. An earlier exponent of this reasoning was Erich Fromm, who defined religion as: "any system of thought and action shared by a group which gives the individual a frame of orientation and an object of devotion" (Fromm 1950, p. 26). He himself showed the rather absurd consequences of this viewpoint, considering even the passion for money and sex or the desire for hygienic purity as instances of religion. Stretching the concept of religion in this way, these psychologists of religion might be in danger of losing their empirical object. With some theologians, that draw more on psychoanalytic object-relations theories, one encounters, e.g., the identification of 'faith' with a more general phenomenon like trust or confidence, considered to be indispensable for the human process of self-development (cf., e.g., Crocket 2007; McDargh 1983; Santner 2001). To some, religion and psychotherapy then almost become the same, both promoting personal integration by offering 'good relationships' with (a) god or a therapist respectively (cf., e.g., Guntrip 1969; for a more general *exposé*, cf. Eigen 1981, 1998).

Quite apart from the *content* of any discussion on the broadness or narrowness of the conceptualization of religion, the *strategy* of explaining religion by searching for a corresponding psychological feature and by assuming that people are religious because of that characteristic of human nature seems to have no equivalent anymore in any psychology of a distinct field. No longer do psychologists of, e.g., music, art, or sport try to explain music etc. by a plea to human nature, or to pretend that everyone is musical or artistic, and that therefore people are ("implicitly" or "invisibly") athletic even if they never perform any kind of sport and even if they abhor sport. In psychology of religion, however, this kind of argument can still be found. Clearly, in these discussions, more is at stake than just the search for psychological insight.

Yet, whatever personal reasons some psychologists of religion may have for this kind of reasoning, they stay within the bounds of mainstream psychology. That seems for its part to be inflicted with dominant western religious thought (not to be identified with Christian theology as such!). This way of thinking is visible in dualisms

---

[5] A classic functional definition of religion is the one by Yinger: "a system of beliefs and practices by means of which a group of people struggle with the ultimate problems of human life" (1970, p. 7); a well-known defender of the opposed view is Peter Berger, who states: "substantive definitions of religion generally include only such meanings and meaning-complexes as refer to transcendent entities in the conventional sense – God, gods, supernatural beings and worlds, or such metaempirical entities as, say, the *ma'at* of the ancient Egyptians or the Hindu law of *karma*" (1974, pp. 127–128).

such as mind/body, person/world – all going back to religiously articulated notions of the soul as substantial, immaterial and immortal. Regardless of whether it is with or without support from a religious or theological tradition that regards the human being as the lord of creation, mainstream psychology seems to make the individual the center of the world; and its established modes of discourse invite us to treat people as possessive individualism suggests, that is, as possessing all their psychological characteristics within themselves and owing nothing to society for them (Shotter 1989).

Although it should probably be admitted that implicit theoretical assumptions unavoidably affect any psychological theorizing, one may nevertheless ask whether it would not be worthwhile to strive for a religiously neutral starting point for the (sub) discipline and to drop assumptions about human nature being inherently religious.[6] Could cultural psychology help to achieve this? Could a reorientation towards the interdisciplinary part of its own history be of any use to the psychology of religion? Before considering a possible answer, let me first expand on the meaning of cultural psychology.

The Cultural Psychological Approach: A New Vista?

In all honesty, and to repeat: although it can claim precursors like Vico and Herder (cf. Jahoda 1993), it is still not easy to say in a few words, what cultural psychology is, as Clifford Geertz concluded when reviewing Jerome Bruner's last book (Bruner 1997; Geertz 1997). Cultural psychology consists in, or is compatible with, a variety of schools (sub)disciplines and several branches of theoretical psychology. (Instructive outlines are by now readily available: Cole 1996; Shore 1996; Kitayama and Cohen 2007; Markus et al. 1996; Valsiner and Rosa 2007; cf. also Goldberger and Veroff 1995; Matsumoto 1994b, 1996; Ratner 1991; Shweder 1991.) As with so many challenging approaches, cultural psychology is still working on its own identity, and it is easier to indicate what it is opposed to (or what it is not), than to say what it positively stands for (that is, what it is). But let me attempt a preliminary circumscription and mention a few of its elements. Stated rather simply, cultural psychology does not search inside the human being to investigate belief, feeling, reasoning and behavior,

---

[6] To be clear: I do not assert that every psychologist of religion has the "defense of religion" as her or his program, or starts from religious assumptions as dealt with in this essay. Evidently, there are people publishing on, e.g. mental health and/or psychotherapy, who strive to stay strictly within a psychological framework and who make no suggestions on a religious level to patients (cf., e.g., Rizzuto 1996; Strean 1994). Yet, in many related publications it is evident that at least one of the goals is to counterbalance (vulgarized psychological) views of religion as being neurotic, a hazard to mental health, etc. One should also note, however, that very often patients themselves try to draw the therapist into some kind of religious discussion, i.e. they want "more" than "just" psychotherapy (cf. Kehoe and Gutheil 1993). The same trends could be witnessed within other fields in psychology of religion.

but rather tries to understand how the specific form of life the person is embedded in, constitutes and constructs feelings, thoughts and conduct. Cultural psychologists try to counterbalance the prevailing bias in psychology according to which psychological phenomena have their origin in intra-individual processes. They stress that psychological phenomena – such as attitudes, emotions, motives, perceptual outlook, forms of reasoning, memory and so on – are not just shaped by a surrounding culture, but are constituted by and rooted in particular cultural interactions. Culturally different settings require different activities, leading to different (cognitive) abilities. Thus, to refer to just one example, it was found that arithmetic problem-solving goes on differently, leading to different results, in different situations: for example, Lave et al. (1984) found that whereas 98% of problems were correctly solved by subjects when engaged in grocery shopping, only 59% of an equal kind of questions were answered correctly by the same subjects when tested in a classroom. They argue further, that problem-solving is not a disembodied mental activity, but belongs to, and is specific to, the kind of situation the subject is involved in. Likewise, emotions are not just the same ones, differing in degree across cultures: they are different in different cultures, i.e. some emotions exist in some cultures and not in other ones. Emotions are characterized by beliefs, judgments, and desires – the content of which are not natural, but are determined by the systems of cultural belief, value and mores of particular communities. They are not natural responses elicited by natural features that a situation may possess, but socio-culturally determined patterns of experience and expression which are acquired and subsequently feature in specifically social situations (Armon-Jones 1986). Research in cross-cultural psychology has produced abundantly striking examples of this kind.

Accepting that culture is a major shaping force in people's self-definition, conduct and experience, requires a different kind of research than is usual in mainstream psychology of religion. The particular religious form of life the human being is embedded in, can then no longer be neglected, in favor of searching for some presumed inherent and invariable psychic structures. On the contrary, as is clear from the example of grocery shopping, it is necessary to study people *engaging* in their particular form of life, not to take them out of it, by submitting them to experiments, tests or questionnaires in the "laboratory." Accordingly, researchers have to turn to participant observation, analysis of personal documents, interview and other ecologically valid techniques. Further, it becomes necessary to study not the isolated individual, but also the beliefs, values and rules that are prevalent in a particular situation, together with the patterns of social relatedness and interaction that characterize that situation. In any case, it appears erroneous to try to study the "individual mind" as such.

To be more concrete, when analyzing different types of religiosity, one could consider employing several recent developments, compatible with a cultural psychological approach. Having discussed some examples of such possibilities in the previous chapter already, let us here consider an illustration from yet another psychological tradition: in order to assess the impact of the individual life history and its dynamic aspects for instance, psychoanalytic approaches that stress the importance of the local symbolic system might prove valuable (Clément and Kakar 1993; Kakar 1982; Vergote 1978/1988).

In some psychoanalytic circles – notably in France and in those that orient themselves towards developments there – there is an awareness of the impact of culture that seems contrary to much vulgarized psychoanalytic reasoning found so often. There is recognition that supra-individual entities like societies and/or entire cultures are not just repeating the phases and mechanisms that psychoanalytic theorizing claims to have discovered when studying patients. Instead, structurally informed analysts emphasize the importance of what Lacan called the "symbolic order" or the *discours de l'Autre*. This symbolic order preexists the individual and will persist when the individual has left it. Yet, the individual is already represented in this order before birth, even if only by the name that will be given. Lacan clearly gave primacy to cultural order when he invented his dictum: "man talks, yet because the symbol has made him man" (1966, p. 242). Psychic development is the result of culture: there is no natural – in the sense of innately preconceived – growth, according to Lacan. The structure of the psyche as such (not just its culturally variable contents) is dependent on culture, on forces from "outside." The constitution of the subject, the "psychic birth" (after natural birth) is dependent on (awareness of the separateness of) "other" (usually the mother); in order to achieve a first – imaginary – image of itself, the child (in the so-called "mirror-phase") needs someone else to pass down this image. Most important for cultural psychology: self-consciousness, in Lacan's view, only emerges thanks to language: it is because of identification with the "discourse of the other" that the human being becomes a participant in culture, able to say "I" and – later – to speak in its own name. Subjectivity is constituted and marked by cultural givens. Because of the entrance into the cultural symbolic order (preeminently language), needs are transformed into desires, which are therefore not naturally given, but a product of culture. In this sense, it is impossible to conceive of a human instinct that would not be marked by cultural references that define it. Even sexual instincts are never merely natural forces: the strata of meanings deposited in them invariably condition the strategies of satisfaction as well as the pitfalls of suffering and discontent. That human beings desire, and the way in which they want to satisfy that desire, is the consequence of cultural signifiers that direct human desire. Thus, similarly as Freud defined the drive as psychic *labor* because of the intrinsic unity with the corporeal, also culture imposes labor – it shapes the psychic realm.

Also Ricoeur (1965/1970) tried to show extensively that "desire" cannot be conceived of without an "Other," and that Freud developed his second topical model precisely because of his realization that libido is confronted with a non-libidinal variable, which manifests itself as culture (p. 188). Although it must be admitted that in this branch of psychoanalysis, emphasis is perhaps one-sided leaning towards language, stories and symbols; there is recognition of the cultural embeddedness of the individual life-history, and awareness that for a psychological understanding of meaningful action and experience it is therefore necessary to apply a double perspective: the perspective of the meaning shared by a cultural community in general as well as that of the personal meaning which can only be understood in terms of the individual life history. Even a deviation can be thus interrogated as to its meaning, since in deviating from the surrounding order it can be seen as a manifestation of the psychic conflict underlying it. I deliberately say "can be" since not every deviation points to psychopathology; and, on the other hand, the (apparent) absence of conflict need not indicate psychic health. Psychology cannot say a thing in advance about a person's health and sickness, and will only make statements after having examined a concrete individual against the background of his culture and life history.

Religion and the Perspective of Cultural Psychology: Closing Remarks

A cultural psychological perspective might be helpful to the psychology of religion in a number of ways. First of all, this perspective allows recognition of religiosity as intrinsically cultural in nature. In the same way as there can be no private language, there exists no private religiosity: it is always constituted by, modeled after, and maintained through (repeated) commitment to culturally pre-given arrangements, conventions and agreements. It is exactly one of the paradoxes studied by cultural psychology, that people can feel most personally authentic (for example, in religious conversion) when at the same time adhering to distinct cultural patterns. Second, this perspective is compatible with the recognition of the multiplicity of religious forms. As soon as one gives up trying to collect everything religious in one single essential definition and admits that the various forms of religiosity share "family resemblances" (Wittgenstein), psychologists of religion might draw advantage from the results of, e.g., anthropological theorizing. Here, and in *Religionswissenschaft* in general, it is recognized that it is fruitless to speak of religion as if it were always one and the same phenomenon; these scholars speak about *religions*, in the plural, as also becomes clear from the names of the discipline of their departments: "History of religions." Further, in the wake of Wittgenstein (1953), philosophers have increasingly conceptualized religion as a "language game" belonging to a distinguished "form of life," which is to be understood as a framework which sustains and makes possible a certain way of thinking, feeling, perceiving, and acting, but that does not offer a code of conduct which can be exhaustively spelled out in accordance with a given system of classification (cf., e.g., Brümmer 1991; High 1967; Hudson 1968; Kerr 1986; Nielsen 1982; Phillips 1991, 1993; Vroom 1988). Religiosity is not identical with (experiencing) a certain emotion, with knowing a certain creed, with following a particular moral, and it is especially not identical with membership of a certain organization (Glock and Stark 1965). Third, this perspective helps to make discussions on the definition of religion superfluous for psychologists. In discussions of the object of psychology of religion, it will be wise to apply the classical distinction between the "formal" and "material" object of any scholarly discipline – the formal object being the specific perspective of the discipline; the material object being the (variable) phenomenon that happens to be investigated. (To recur to a well-known Heideggerian example: the perspectives of a biologist and of a dealer in wood are quite different when looking at, e.g., the same tree.) For psychologists, it is appropriate to leave the definition of religion as a material object for their research to experts on culture, either to participants in or to scholars on that culture. To assess what characterizes a religion in a particular context, is not the task of psychologists, but of experts on culture(s) like anthropologists, historians or even theologians; to define "religion(s)" should be reserved to that specific scholarship of *Religionswissenschaft* (cf. also Pollack 1995). There is no need for an additional, psychological determination (or even explanation) of what religion "is." Past efforts seem to have been obscured all too often by (unreflected?) theological a priori's.[7] There is a need, however, for ongoing reflection on the formal object, on what kind of psychology is required in order to investigate a phenomenon as religiosity. Fourth, analyzing religiosity from these presumptions will mean trying to find or develop a psychology that will be able to deal with the specific religious phenomenon one wishes to investigate, as opposed to trying to force an alien psychology on phenomena or populations that just don't fit. (As happens, for example, when one tries to find a quest-orientation next to intrinsic and extrinsic ones (cf. Batson and Ventis 1982), or a literal, anti-literal, and mythological religiosity (cf. Hunt 1972; Lans 1991a) in populations other than the ones these differentiations were derived from. As has been stated often enough, scales assessing these kinds of differences may not find psychological structures, but simply measure acquaintance with linguistic convention.) Finally, recognizing that religiosity varies across time and subcultures also allows the researcher to take more seriously the various indigenous psychologies of religion that sometimes prove to be quite elaborated, for example, in mystical traditions.

Recognizing, then, that religion is first and foremost a cultural phenomenon, and that religiosity, as its subjective-personal counterpart, is (i) a multi-dimensional phenomenon constituted by specific religious (sub)cultures, about whose features and functions disciplines other than psychological disciplines can provide information; (ii) involving all kinds of psychic functions (instead of being rooted in a single psychological function); this may give an impetus to psychological analyses of religion.

In the psychology of religion, not much of a cultural psychological approach has been handed down until now (cf. Belzen 1997b). Where people have worked with, for example, ideas from narrative psychology, it has usually not been within a cultural psychological framework (cf., e.g., Day 1993). On the other hand, as religion can hardly be neglected when taking culture seriously, one does now again find articles and research on religion reported by psychologists who have no connection to what is called or organized under the label of "psychology of religion" (cf., e.g., Kakar 1982, 1991; Much and Mahapatra 1995; Obeyesekere 1981). As indicated already, one of the opponents in the discussion quoted previously does hold a position that is compatible with cultural psychology. Although this Belgian psychologist

---

[7] It should be pointed out that the very term "religion" is impregnated with Christian meaning, as it was created within Christianity in order to reflect on its own status and history. Today, it is increasingly realized that even the employment of the term may impair understanding of other "religions" (Feil 1986).

of religion usually does not present himself explicitly as a "cultural psychologist" when conceptualizing religion, Vergote (1983/1997, p. 21) does go back to an anthropologist like Clifford Geertz, who is widely quoted among other cultural psychologists. Vergote has a definite interdisciplinary orientation as becomes clear from his – for a psychologist remarkably broad – reception of social scientific and historical studies, and from his cross-cultural research (Vergote and Tamayo 1980). In the wake of Lacan, he conceives of religion as belonging to the symbolic order, and as such capable of inscription into psychic life. Like all cultural realities, religion exacts the labor of sublimation that organizes the joys and pleasures in which the instincts can find satisfaction (Vergote 1978/1988). Yet for him, as seems to be the case with Lacan, religion remains predominately conceptualized on a cognitive level with little attention to the non-verbal reality of religious culture. In addition, he has also been criticized for writing on religion as such or on Christianity in general, although restricting his studies mainly to Belgium, which is not even representative of Roman Catholicism in Europe. Be this as it may, Vergote's rather solitary perspective in the psychology of religion could certainly be enlarged with the help of notions and methods as they are being developed under the label of cultural psychology.

The aims of this chapter have been modest again. Although not dominant, a cultural-psychological approach is neither alien, nor entirely new to the psychology of religion. Moreover, the plea is for a modest stand as psychologists: when leaving the "safe" bastion of the "laboratory" and leaving behind the ambition to develop an all-embracing psychology or indeed to determine a single psychic function that could explain all and every religion, it may prove necessary to be instructed by other disciplines, in order to be able – with the help of different psychologies – to gain some psychological understanding of people in different (sub)cultures. (In the same way that narrative psychology might be of less use when analyzing the tribal religion of Trobriand Islanders, an account from the perspective of Bourdieu – see Chapter 3 – may fail to understand a conversion to an American "new religious movement.") Religion as a cultural phenomenon is always more than any necessarily partial psychological perspective can conceive of. And even religiosity, as its subjective-personal counterpart, is too (sub)culturally heterogeneous to be explained by one single psychological theory.[8] Acknowledging cultural pluralism, equally pluralistic cultural psychologies may be instrumental in analyzing the "varieties [plural!] of religious experience" (James 1902/1982). A cultural perspective does not claim to solve all the questions debated by psychologists of religion, but at least it seems to make discussions on the definition of the (material) object of the discipline superfluous. In the same way as kindred disciplines like sociology are not trying to develop their own definitions of "culture," but fruitfully work with concepts

---

[8] There is more to religiosity than being "reinforced behavior" (Skinner 1953), sometimes it may be a way to "human excellence" (James 1902/1982) or to "wholeness" (Jung 1938/1969), but at other times it proves to be "infantile wish fulfillment" (Freud 1913/1964, 1927/1961) or at best a "coping device" (Pargament 1990) – all these and other notions may reveal at least as much about their authors as about the religion they claim to study.

taken over from anthropology (Knorr Cetina and Grathoff 1988), cultural psychology relocates the difficulty of defining religion to where it belongs: with the cultural participants and with the cultural sciences. Psychology should be happy not to be called upon to define religion, but only to study its psychological aspects. After a century of psychology of religion, it proves to be difficult enough already to decide how to do that.

Part II
Approaches

Chapter 5
Methodological Issues

Towards Another Paradigm in Psychology of Religion

This chapter on methodology takes a meta-perspective on methods and techniques employed in the psychology of religion, especially in research. So it shall not focus upon specific methods or techniques, but offer theoretical reflections on the use of them in psychological research on religion. The focus will be upon two major methodological mainstreams in psychology: the empirical-analytical and the hermeneutical orientation, often roughly identified as quantitative and qualitative. Despite their call for a new multidisciplinary paradigm in religion, the review by Emmons and Paloutzian (2003) while focused upon new *topics* in the psychology of religion is not far distanced *methodologically* from the older measurement paradigm they argued has been replaced. This is partly why Wulff (2003) suggests it may be time to "start over." However, if we simply acknowledge the range of what is available in modern psychologies, also in variants of cultural psychology, we need less to start over and can recognize what methods are appropriate and when. Thus, I shall first say something about the different types of research practiced in the psychology of religion, then proceed with a discussion of the methodological mainstreams in psychology, and end with notes on the principles of hermeneutical research, especially as they apply to the psychology of religion. Let's start with some preliminary remarks.

The Relationship Between Psychology of Religion and General Psychology

Psychology of religion is a broad field. There is no generally accepted definition of the discipline or a common understanding of its boundaries. Opinions upon what belongs to the discipline are divided, sometimes even contested (Vergote 1993, 1995). To a large extent this is the consequence of the fact that there is no common understanding among psychologists of religion of either of its constituent terms, psychology and religion. The current debate within psychology of religion over definitional issues is well documented (Hill et al. 2000). Likewise, within general psychology the notion that it is a unitary discipline with a single methodological

J.A. Belzen, *Towards Cultural Psychology of Religion: Principles, Approaches, Applications,*   69
DOI 10.1007/978-90-481-3491-5_5, © Springer Science+Business Media B.V. 2010

focus has proven to be illusory at best (Koch and Leary 1985). Thus there is no need to try to offer yet another set of definitions of either psychology or religion. It is best to take a broad perspective of the field, and accept at least three circumscriptions of what psychological research on religion is or does. First, it investigates how psychic functioning manifests itself within a religious domain. Psychic functioning is a neutral term that includes but is not restricted to such psychological terms as cognition, motivation and emotion. Second, psychology of religion tries to research how religion becomes part of a person's psychic make-up. Third, it explores the psychic components in a range of religious phenomena.

These circumscriptions overlap, but are not identical. Research along the first circumscription usually starts from some psychological function or variable, and tries to detect whether, and to what extent, it has some impact on a person's religiosity. Frequently this research offers a kind of additional validation for research obtained in other than religious persons or groups, e.g. when the researcher asks whether religious activity improves life satisfaction (Ayele et al. 1999), when it is asked to what extent religious denomination may be regarded as a symptom-formation factor of depression (Braam et al. 2000), or how religion functions as a coping mechanism (Pargament 1997, 2007). The second kind of research focuses on the process by which a person becomes and remains religious (or not): like other cultural skills, religious functioning has to be acquired, both by a child born into a religiously active family and by a person committing her or himself to a (new) religious tradition or community. How this may come about, which factors facilitate or hinder processes of religious acculturation, conversion or maturing are typical research questions in the second kind of research just distinguished (Rambo 1993; Tamminen 1991). Research along the third line will focus even more directly on some religious phenomenon or another and try to analyze which psychic factors, next to a variety of other factors, have been influential, expressing themselves in the occurrence or development of the phenomenon under scrutiny (whether it is a mystical experience, religious art, liturgy, pilgrimage, autobiography, leadership, a corpus of religious doctrine, etc.).

These different types of research have different aims, and therefore employ different methods. No single method cuts across all types of research nor is any single method privileged (Rosenau 1992; Roth 1987). They also differ in the extent to which they collaborate with other disciplines to analyze religious phenomena or in the extent to which they proceed in an interdisciplinary fashion. The first type of research often limits itself to using or adapting standard research methods from mainstream psychology (like questionnaires, scales, tests, and sometimes experiments). It also tends to employ concepts established in mainstream psychology and applies them to religious phenomena. The second type of research includes research methods from a broader social scientific range, including methods more common to sociology and anthropology (like interview, observation, ethnographies, biographical analysis). The third type of research relies heavily on data and insights from disciplines like history, theology, literature and cultural studies. In all three kinds, however, the focus is on psychic processes at work in the object of research, whether a contemporary individual or group, a person or constellation from the past, or a product of religious activity. Therefore, the angle of interpretation is psychological in nature and is the very reason why such diverse kinds of research belong to the psychological approach to religion in the broad sense appropriate to a multilevel interdisciplinary paradigm.

Evidently, not all of this work is equally central to the development of general psychology. Psychology remains fragmented and far from a unitary discipline even after 100 years (Koch and Leary 1985). Despite the efforts of prestigious journals to insist on the experimental manipulation of measured variables, statistically analyzed as a hallmark of a scientific psychology, this restriction or preference is philosophically unsupportable and is rather part of psychology's inability to secure itself a place among the natural sciences despite what has playfully been identified since the birth of psychology in America as "physics envy" (Coon 1992). Laboratory experimental psychology began only a little later than in other natural sciences yet it has failed to achieve a cumulative body knowledge that parallels the achievements of the natural sciences (Robinson 1995, p. 4). As Wittgenstein noted in this regard, "The confusion and barrenness of psychology is not to be explained by calling it a 'young science' [...] for in psychology are experimental methods and conceptual confusion" (1958, p. 232). As with the field of psychology in general, some parts of psychology of religion are closer to the core of the discipline than other parts. The core of the discipline of psychology may be regarded as the effort to develop insight into, and therefore to formulate, validated theory about human psychic functioning. For the psychology of religion we should add, "also in religious matters." After more than a century of work in the psychology of religion, it has sufficiently shown that the psychic processes involved in religion are the same as the ones involved in other-than-religious functioning. Thus, the strong claim is that psychology of religion in not about psychic factors that would be at work in religious phenomena only. Neither is the psychology of religion proper a "religious psychology." Such a psychology would be part of or derived from a faith tradition or from religious teachings. Hindu, Buddhist or Christian psychologies would be specific derivatives of these traditions and only valid for participants of such traditions. Academic psychology as it has developed mainly in the West, however, does not call upon any religious concept, does not require a religious belief, but strives to work in an objectifying way, i.e., to proceed along lines that are understandable and repeatable for anyone with the appropriate psychological training – for better or for worse, which should be explicitly stated, for proceeding in this way Western science can arrive at only a very limited understanding of reality.

It is readily to be seen, then, that within the psychology of religion few theories have been formulated that derive from within this subdiscipline itself. Psychology of religion works with and takes over theories, methods and techniques from general psychology and either adapts these so as to be able to investigate religious phenomena or applies them in research on religious phenomena. Therefore, psychology of religion is not a core discipline of psychology in general (like social psychology, personality theory, developmental psychology, and – according to some – psychoanalysis), but a field of interest to which more general psychological insights are being applied. Even founding fathers of the discipline like Freud, Hall, James or Allport did not derive their psychological theories by specifically dealing

with religion, but rather illustrated their theories by applying them or – more seldom
– adapting them to religion. Although the latter (adapting existing psychological
theory to enable it to deal with religion) has happened (e.g., Rizzuto 1979; Vergote
1978/1988), the largest part of psychology of religion is application to a religious
phenomenon of either psychological theory (e.g. Freud 1928/1961; Pargament
1997) or of methods and techniques (e.g. Hill and Hood 1999; Hood 2001).[1] As a
consequence, psychology of religion does not have theories, methods or techniques
of its own, but utilizes basically the ones that are in use in psychology at large.
Indeed, it is difficult to conceive how a theory, method or technique unique to this
subfield of psychology of religion might appear.

The Role of Philosophical Presuppositions

Research questions in psychology of religion depend on the model of the human being
adhered to in different kinds of psychology. One often finds traces of this model in
the metaphors used within a certain type of psychology (cf. also Leary 1990). A model
of man has no ontological pretensions. To see the human being as, e.g., an information
processing system analogous to a computer does not entail that the human being is
a computer. Such a model helps to describe and analyze certain aspects of human
action, experience and behavior: it formulates the basic categories to be used to study
such aspects, and from the model can be derived which kinds of research methods
should be used to study the aspect under scrutiny. One of the consequences is that
the model determines which aspect of psychic reality will be studied. However, a
common error is that aspects envisaged by the model are taken as the whole (reductionism), or that the metaphorical quality of the model is forgotten (reification).

If one agrees that the object of psychology is variable across history and culture,
psychology cannot ignore the perspectives of neighboring disciplines like
biology, physiology, sociology, history, anthropology and other social sciences
(Belzen 1997b; Robinson 1995, pp. 3–5). Yet not all types of psychology can or need
deal with all aspects that can be distinguished in the psychic functioning of the
human being. As hinted at briefly in Chapter 2, psychological theories can be classified according to the levels of complexity that they take into account and hence
which methods are appropriate for that level. As one moves from mechanistic, to
organistic, and personalistic or hermeneutic levels there is a mounting complexity
as a result of the increasing historico-cultural determinacy of *both* the object and
the results of the research. The first type of theory studies the human being just the
same as all other reality simply as a mechanism. Higher level interpretations such as

---

[1]One should bear in mind that the field of psychology of religion is much larger than psychological
research on religion. Also dealing as a psychologist with religiousness in numerous practical
situations (e.g., psychotherapy) may contain elements of psychology of religion, and especially
the huge (historicizing) literature reflecting on the psychology of religion (e.g. Belzen 2000a;
Wulff 1997) should be considered as an integral part of the field.

the personalistic level presuppose lower levels. However, the lower levels do not necessarily presuppose the higher levels. To claim to explain a higher level exhaustively by a lower level is reductionism. Methodologically, to restrict study of higher levels to the methods and procedures appropriate to lower levels begs the issue in favor an apparent reductionism.

Personalistic theories remain close to extra-scientific, everyday knowledge about reality or what is often identified as folk psychology (Christensen and Turner 1993). They tend to reduce the complexity of the research phenomena as little as possible. Behavioristic learning-psychology and computational cognitive psychology belong to lower levels of theorizing. Theories like Gibson's or Piaget's belong to the organistic level; cultural psychological approaches like social constructionism or rhetorical psychology figure on a personalistic level. Organistic theories share with mechanistic theories the tendency to disregard as much as possible of the historical and cultural determinacy of human reality. In extreme cases they claim to have found universal principles that apply across history and cultures. On the other hand, in hermeneutic psychologies, common in postmodern theories, such claims are not simply undesirable, but challenged as an impossibility (Rosenau 1992). The higher the level of the structuring of a theory is, the more important is the factor of human consciousness, history, and culture. In behaviorism consciousness could be regarded as irrelevant, but in personalistic psychologies this is impossible. Cognitive psychology has yet to find a consistent model to appropriate consciousness and human experience (Varela et al. 1997).

In fields of psychology dealing with highly variable actions and experiences like courting, consumer behavior, or religion, theories on a high level of structuring should be preferred for the maximum in explanatory power. Theories on a lower level would be necessarily false if taken as fully explanatory. As partial explanations they may be valid, but as they exclude higher aspects that a researcher may want to explore, they remain insufficient. Psychologies on a high level of structuring must be interdisciplinary. Other than the proposal by Emmons and Paloutzian (2003), a truly multilevel interdisciplinary paradigm needs to integrate knowledge from other fields as well as to be sensitive to the level of modeling used to adequately approach and interpret the activities and experiences they wish to study. Because of the complexity of the phenomena studied, such psychologies are necessarily pluralistic. There will always be several psychological perspectives possible on the same phenomena. There may even be pluralistic possibilities on the same level of structuring of theories. Hermeneutics cannot exclude measurement any more than experimentation can exclude narrative analysis.

Two Methodological Mainstreams in General Psychology

In psychology two methodological mainstreams can be distinguished: an empirical-analytical one and a hermeneutical one (cf. Terwee 1990). These are often, not quite correctly, also identified as quantitative and qualitative respectively. Let us take a brief look at each.

The empirical-analytical mainstream is rooted in two major positions in the philosophy of science during the first decades of the twentieth century: logical positivism and critical rationalism. Philosophers in Vienna (Austria, Europe) belonging to the current of logical positivism tried in the 1920s to find a secure basis for scientific knowledge. They searched for a criterion to distinguish meaningful language from metaphysical, non-meaningful language. They thought they had found the demarcation in the principle of verification: only propositions that can be verified by facts should count as meaningful (cf. Wittgenstein 1921/1981). One of the presuppositions was that it would be possible to approach reality without a theoretical frame of reference. By means of a theoretically neutral language the scientist would be able to observe what is the case. On such a secure basis it should be possible to inductively arrive at general propositions of a law-like character. (If on a number of occasions it has been observed that a crow is black, never white, by induction one can conclude from this multiple singular proposition that all crows are black, a universal proposition.) In order to make psychology a "real science" (and to break away from disciplines deemed suspect like philosophy and theology), many psychologists in the twentieth century enthusiastically joined this position. Behaviorists, for example, restricted themselves to registering objectively measurable connections between stimuli and responses with animals, confident that more complex actions by humans would be explained similarly in some future. Detecting the laws of learning in a "laboratory" got a high priority. The ideal became to be able to explain (and predict) human behavior by means of the laws thus found.

Most philosophers of science, however, reject logical positivism in its strict form. Karl Popper (1902–1994) formulated the objections (1934/1959) as follows: all observation and description is theory-laden; there exists no possibility to attain secure propositions, the principle of induction does not hold, and verification of general propositions is impossible. Science begins with problems, according to Popper, for the solution of which theories have to be designed, and only afterwards are relevant observations and "facts" sought. Testing of theories by means of basic propositions (derived from direct observation) is possible to some extent, but those basic propositions are always formulated in language from a certain frame of reference and have a conventional character. One can use them as a "preliminary," but it is always possible to re-open the discussion about them when new theoretical reflections or observations are introduced. Accepting singular basic propositions allows for falsification, but not for verification: general propositions apply to an infinite domain, within which a falsification can always occur. Therefore, the only valid logical reasoning is deduction: from general propositions to less general, or even singular, propositions. From general propositions one can derive logical consequences: if those consequences do not occur, the general propositions is false; if they do occur, the proposition might be true. Demarcation in the critical rationalistic way as outlined by Popper means to distinguish whether propositions are scientific or non-scientific, not whether they are meaningful or not. Where theories or hypotheses find their inspiration, where ideas come from, is not relevant to Popper: the so-called *context of discovery* is left out of consideration; what matters is the *context of justification*: is the resulting proposition (or body of coherent propositions, i.e. a theory) falsifiable or not?

Within psychology both of these philosophies have had their influence, although logical positivism has probably been much more influential. Psychologists still write journal articles containing hypotheses to be tested and (with the editorial bias against the null hypothesis anticipated) are happy to submit manuscripts with evidence consistent with their theory (verification). For measurement-based psychologists within this verificationist current, the experiment is tantamount to their identity as "empirical scientists."

The logical-empirical approach, heir to both verificationist and falsificationist positions can be outlined as follows:

1. Research is conducted according to the empirical cycle: assumptions are formulated as verifiable hypotheses, from which predictions can be derived. These predictions are tested in controlled experiments (preferred) or by means of systematic observation (assessed by appropriate statistical means).
2. Concepts employed in empirical research should be operationalized completely. This assures predictions are unambiguously linked to concepts, allowing replication by others (Groot 1961/1969).
3. Results of empirical research are statistically evaluated. If an appropriate significance level is attained, the null hypothesis is rejected and the hypothesis counts as empirically supported. Thus, the probability that the hypothesis from which the prediction was derived is true, is increased.
4. The correctness of predictions can be verified, e.g. by statistical means applied to controlled experimental conditions. Psychology, like other natural sciences, seeks truths that can be assessed objectively by these means. As Smith (2001, pp. 191–192) notes, "Science is the body of facts about the natural world that controlled experiments require us to believe, together with the logical extrapolations from those facts."

Later philosophers and historians of science have pointed out that the course of science is not as rational as both Popper and the logical positivists thought. Scientists are not really interested in falsifying their theories; they instead have a tendency to confirm them. They work within certain research traditions (paradigms in the sense of Kuhn 1962, or research programs in the sense of Lakatos 1978) that are only abolished during scientific "revolutions." During the second half of the twentieth century, philosophical and scientific reflection on science has incorporated much more empirical-historical knowledge about the actual development of scientific ideas, programs and communities, paying a good deal of attention to human factors (like creativity, rivalry, the impact of funding and of finances in general) on the enterprise of science. Specific to the psychology of religion, Wulff (2003, pp. 26–28) has documented the fact that much of the material in the review by Emmons and Paloutzian (2003) comes from Templeton funding. Likewise, Hood (2000) has documented the influence of a few individuals on both the history of psychology in America and in the publication of articles in such flagship journals as the *Journal for the Scientific Study of Religion*. From a more hermeneutical perspective, it is now pointed out that it is impossible to formulate timeless criteria for rationality and scientific progress, as both logical positivism and critical rationalism thought would be possible (cf., e.g. Toulmin 1960, 1990).

The other major methodological current in psychology is hermeneutics. It includes a range of qualitative methods with the central focus on meaning. Hermeneutics is an old tradition, focusing on how to interpret texts (esp. sacred texts like the Bible). Friedrich Schleiermacher (1768–1834), whom many consider to be the father of psychology of religion, first systematically outlined hermeneutical reasoning. It has developed into a much more embracing philosophical approach, from which principles for research in the social and human sciences have been derived. One seeks not to predict and control, but to understand. The hermeneutical method as outlined by Gadamer (1960/1986) can be summarized as follows:

1. Exploration within a hermeneutical circle: interpretation begins on the basis of preliminary, intuitive understanding of the whole. This guides the understanding of the parts, leading to a judgment about the whole. This can be tested anew on a study of the parts. This is a cyclic process that never ends. It may entail the rejection of the initial intuition as based upon insights achieved in the process of interpretation. Understanding is therefore always finite, limited, and provisional.
2. The discovery of internal relationships: one looks for meaningful relationships between actions and occurrences. External relationships (like correlations or law-like relationships sought in analytically oriented empirical research) are insufficient to reveal meaning.
3. A focus upon individual cases: emphasis is on the understanding of individual cases, whether this understanding can be generalized or not. The unique is sought, not simply generalized across cases.
4. The merging of horizons: there is a difference between the knowledge or understanding of the researcher or interpreter and the subject of study. When understanding increases, the discrepancy between both horizons diminishes.
5. Application: all understanding is in the present. Written texts and human narratives are taken seriously in their claim to truth. These claims are applied in the present situation. Truth is always contextual and in time.

In psychology, hermeneutics as a research methodology has been championed by Gauld and Shotter (1977). According to some authors, psychology at present is a "changing discipline," turning away from its former emphasis on laboratory studies, experimental design, statistical analysis and an epistemology based on a particular conception of the natural sciences, where the empirical-analytical approach is appropriate. Psychology would become more "ecologically valid" (Neisser 1976) by conducting more "real world" studies. This move can be observed on several levels (Smith et al. 2003). First, psychology has become more open to research on a range of previously neglected areas, which are central to the psychology of everyday life (cf., e.g., the many studies on the self or the increase in studies on autobiographic memory). Second, there is greater openness to different types of data-collection, with a growing number of researchers and authors employing a variety of approaches going by names such as narrative, semiotic, critical, feminist and ecological psychology, that are all indebted to hermeneutical thinking. In these circles there is a preference for methods and techniques like "grounded theory" (Glaser and Strauss 1967), ethnomethodology, field studies, case studies and for so-called qualitative research in general. Psychoanalytical research is also given added scientific respect when its hermeneutical nature is acknowledged. Third, more studies are attempting to include appropriate participant groups, moving beyond the student population from which most "subjects" for experimental psychology have been taken.

In psychology of religion explicit efforts to introduce and to foster hermeneutical approaches are rather recent (cf. e.g. Belzen 1997a), although parts of the substantial psychoanalytic literature in psychology of religion may be considered to be hermeneutical in nature, at least to some extent.

The choice between empirical-analytical versus hermeneutical methods is not only, or not primarily, based on the object of research, but on the kind of knowledge aimed at.

Hermeneutical Research as Empirical Psychology

Modern psychology has co-opted the term empirical and reduced it to measurement, statistical analysis and experimentation. Many psychologists refuse to accept psychoanalysis, phenomenology, or other forms of qualitative research as "scientific" because they would not be "empirical." To assuage this claim, I focus upon the presuppositions supporting the methodological procedure involved in hermeneutical research.

1. The human world (which is the focus of the social sciences) is viewed as structured by co-constructed meaning (cf. e.g., Bruner 1990). Those meanings connected to thinking, talking, feeling, wanting and acting as well as to the objectivations of human praxis (like texts, the arts, architecture etc.) cannot be observed by "objective" instruments. The exploration of realities structured by meaning is in need of interpretative approaches. Their formulation can be made by the researchers alone, or in collaboration with the research participants. The development and reflection of the interpretation(s) should be methodically controlled.

2. The human world is regarded as possessing a process-character: meaning changes and must be co-constructed by the participants over and over again; this process is open-ended (participants do not just re-construct meaning or produce "fixed narratives once and for all") (Flick et al. 2000).

3. There is a return to experience in the original, Aristotelian sense. The Latin "experientia" is the translation of the Greek "empereia." The word "empirical" has been co-opted to the methodological-technical practices of the "sciences" in the specific understanding of "science" which has risen in and since Modern Times (Robinson 1995). The original Aristotelean sense implies also a return to "data" in the original sense of the word. (This word is derived from the Latin "datum": that which is given, versus "factum": that which is made.) Therefore, along with recognition of the central role of language and discourse, there is a preference to work with experience in the real world as opposed to experimental laboratory contexts. Hermeneutical research does not try to "bring about" experience in a controlled laboratory setting, but proceeds from what is "given"

already (e.g. autobiographies, letters, observations in real-life situations, and narratives provided by interviews).

4. Research is seen as a process, as a set of dynamic interactions, with openness for research participants, situations, and methods (cf. Appelsmeyer et al. 1997). Research participants are left as much as possible in their ordinary situation and way of functioning; they are not taken out of their "world" into a laboratory; nor are they submitted to experiments, questionnaires or other instruments in control of the researcher only. In hermeneutical research, nothing is fixed a priori; there is no reliance on one method only (in fact, sometimes a method has to be invented or designed as the research evolves). Research is empirical to the extent it is driven by the facts of experience and of the world as it appears to the subject.

5. Research participants are accepted as authoritative about their own experiences in their own right. Researchers try to be open to participants' perspectives and try to avoid translating the subjects' perspectives into the perspective of the researcher or into that of a given theory. They enter into an active dialogue with participants, often returning to them with the results of the investigation in order to discuss them.

6. Researchers not only attempt at nomothetic knowledge (about what "is always" the case, recurring across particular situations), but also at idiographic knowledge (about what "once was"). Nomothetic knowledge is ideally formulated in law-like propositions, idiographic knowledge is not. Idiographic knowledge should not be equated with $N = 1$ methodology or with case studies. According to Windelband (1894/1904), who introduced this distinction, while idiographic knowledge might be knowledge of single persons, it might also be knowledge "of an entire folk, [of] the peculiarity of a language, religion or legal system, of a product of literature, of art or of science" (translation by Lamiell 2003, p. 161).

7. Hermeneutical research tends to be reflective: researchers are reflecting throughout the investigation on what they are doing and on their own role throughout the research.

8. Hermeneutical research has an inclination towards case studies focusing on *how* or *what* questions, as distinguished from *why* questions (cf., e.g. Yin 1989). Hermeneutical research does not focus upon questions of causality.

9. Hermeneutical research is frequently oriented towards treating lives and cultural phenomena as texts to be interpreted, and models itself after literary theory. Accordingly, empirical data such as transcriptions of interviews, notes from ethnographic fieldwork, historical documents are employed.

10. Hermeneutical research yields a different style of reporting than objectivist, positivist social science and does not parody the style of the natural sciences. Whereas in the latter, the tested hypotheses, tables and figures speak for themselves (and only need to be presented, not to be written), the style of a hermeneutic researcher is not like that of an external privileged reporter. Data and theory need to be woven into a literate text, and many authors from the qualitative humanistic tradition feel they should perhaps turn to the tools of the novelist and the artist to report their findings.

How to Assess Qualitative Research

Hermeneutical, qualitative research relies on a different foundation and proceeds from a different orientation than quantitative research modeled after the natural sciences. The most important difference lies in the role assigned to the researcher. In quantitative research this role is minimized or neutralized. The researcher uses objective procedures and seeks generalized laws independent of the particular researcher. In qualitative research the researcher's approach and attitude towards the object of research are made part of the research process itself: reflection on that role becomes an instrument and the relationship with the research participants is regarded as a dialogue. This has consequences for the interpretation of criteria for quantitative research like validity, reliability, objectivity, representation and generalizability.

Instead of face-, expert-, criterion-, predictive-, known-groups-, and construct-validity, different kinds of validity apply to qualitative research. These include:

1. Ecological validation: validity in the natural life form of the research participants. Participants' life forms should be respected and integrated in the research procedure. Therefore, methods like participatory observation, interviews, group discussion, and document analysis are preferred as they allow the inclusion of the life form in the analysis and interpretation of the data.
2. Communicative validation: the effort to control the interpretation of the results by turning again to the research participants, or to other representatives from or experts on the life form the participants belong to.
3. Cumulative validation: the combination of the interpretation of the results with those from previous investigations or from other investigations by different researchers or the combination with investigations employing other methods and techniques (also called "triangulation").

A higher validity will be achieved when data are generated close to the social field, without being pre-determined by a frame of reference, when the meaning systems of the participants are taken into account, when methods are open and flexible, and when a successive extension of the research basis to include extreme cases is possible. Psychology thus becomes a human science, not simply a natural science.

For reliability, alternative methods of assessment have not really been designed. Qualitative researchers make a plea for the arrangement and presentation of the often very extensive and unsystematic data in such a way that other researchers may be convinced of the plausibility of their interpretations. Certainty is not achieved but is replaced by the acceptance of the best possible interpretation, which ultimately remains a human judgment. (This, of course, is also true in quantitative research.)

Unlike the natural sciences, in the human sciences no objectivity exists in the sense that results would be attainable independent of the researcher and the specific situation in which they were gathered. Here, objectivity is often interpreted as inter-individual reliability or verification, meaning that under ceteris-paribus conditions other researchers would attain the same empirical results. An important notion also is that objectivity is achieved by the relevance of the research object.

Transparence is regarded as more relevant than objectivity, and is understood as bringing the research process into the open instead of chasing an unattainable ideal of neutralizing the interaction between researcher and research participant.

Instead of statistical representativeness, hermeneutical research is concerned with the typical: it tries to establish types (ideal types, extreme types, prototypes, relevant types), which implies that sampling is done according to theoretical-systematical considerations, and not according to chance. Establishing types does not mean reducing complex states of affairs to single variables or constellations of variables; rather hermeneutics attempts to work in a holistic manner, "true to reality." Generalization is achieved by presenting typical cases (not by stochastic cases) and especially by intensive-subjective elucidation of validity.

On the Psychology of Religion

Religion and personal religiosity are complex phenomena; they are not of a steady but rather of a process-like character. In addition, sectarian and cult forms of religion are often of a controversial nature, while many who identify themselves as spiritual but not religious subscribe to a wide range of beliefs that challenge both religion and science (Hood 2003a). Hermeneutical approaches seem particularly apt for investigating the diverse manifestations on a level as high as possible in structuring, i.e. as close as possible to the everyday, "real" world experience of being religious. Experiments in a classic sense have hardly ever been conducted in psychology of religion (although some quasi-experimental studies have been published, cf. Darley and Batson 1973; Hood 2001), as in experiments one strives for control of all variables but the one(s) to be manipulated. This leads to a highly artificial situation (typically this type research is carried out in a "laboratory," as opposed to the "lifeworld") and has been given privileged status by those who consider psychology to be more like the natural sciences than the humanities. In correlational studies, surveys, tests and standardized scales are widely used and again gain a privileged status. In fact they virtually define the "old" measurement paradigm in the psychology of religion (Gorsuch 1984). However, the privileged status of measurement is challenged by qualitative researchers. Hermeneutical approaches acknowledge that measurement generates numbers and scores, but what they or the statistically analyzed data mean to the person who filled out the questionnaire is not clear at all. Although the use of such methods may have its rationale for certain research questions, hermeneutically oriented researchers feel they should turn to alternative methods and techniques in order to get insight into the particularities of the meaning of religion in the lives of individuals and groups.

Already in the first decennia of psychology of religion, quite a few authors have called for a turn (and quite a number in fact did turn) to what is now called "qualitative research methods." By now, several handbooks on such research have gone beyond first editions (e.g. Denzin and Lincoln 2000; Patton 2002). There is software to assist in the collection and analysis of material (e.g. QSR International, n.d.).

In general, however, researchers active in the empirical-analytical tradition of the psychology of religion have tried to line up with developments in mainstream psychology, and have used primarily quantitative methods (cf. Spilka et al. 2003). Similarly, while Emmons and Paloutzian (2003) have identified the new paradigm for the psychology of religion as both interdisciplinary and multilevel, the actual studies they review are largely measurement-based studies linked to the new positive psychology and to conservative religion (cf. Wulff 2003). Yet advanced measurement and statistical techniques such as structural equation modeling and confirmatory factor analysis only firmly advance the old measurement paradigm. To take seriously the call for a paradigm shift will not necessarily move psychology of religion into mainstream psychology, which is itself measurement and laboratory based. It would, however, appropriately remind researchers of the limits to measurement and laboratory research, and demand that they create and employ methods appropriate to their object of study. In the psychology of religion many of these methods will necessarily be hermeneutical.

Recently, some authors have made cautious efforts to employ or design methods that would allow them to "get in touch" with the religious phenomena they want to study (frequently phenomena that can't be approached with standardized methods and techniques). Examples include research on serpent handlers in Southern Appalachia in the USA (Hood 1998; Williamson 2000), on mystical experience with a Dutch ultra-Calvinistic minority resistant to all social scientific research (Belzen 2003), on the religious interpretations of everyday life (including one's own biography) among evangelical charismatics in Germany (Popp-Baier 1998), or on the diversity in the use of language among adolescent and young Belgian adults' accounts of moral and religious experience (Day 2002). None of these studies are measurement based nor do they yield data susceptible to sophisticated statistical analyses. Yet they point to the paradigm shift that Emmons and Paloutzian (2003) call for and which this chapter on methodological issues in the psychology of religion hopes to facilitate.

Chapter 6
When Psychology Turns to Spirituality

Recommendations for Research

Research on Research: A Metapsychological Perspective

Over the last few years, spirituality has been mentioned as a topic for psychological research, especially for the psychology of religion (cf., e.g., Paloutzian and Park 2005). Some colleagues even go so far as to declare the study of spirituality to be the core business of the psychology of religion, as from a psychological perspective spirituality would be the essence of religion. In this there is an orientation towards the so-called market (cf. Carrette and King 2005), which is not always wise and not always beneficial to our discipline. Since the so-called Enlightenment, religion has been a popular topic to criticize, and in many aspects correctly so. Within psychology, after an initial period in which all the founding fathers dealt with religion as a subject typical for the human being, the topic has become something of a taboo theme, usually out of disinterest or because psychologists no longer had the courage to talk about it (Farberow 1963). Craving for respect by the scientific community, it seemed to many psychologists wise no longer to do any research on religion. Many colleagues of the latter type are more than happy nowadays to notice that contrary to the great expectations of leading sociologists of religion, religion did not become extinct and is even returning to the headlines of the news, albeit in ways and for reasons that most people would never have wanted to become witnesses of (see, e.g., the religious or at least religiously legitimized terrorism covered in the media). The way out for many seems to be to talk no longer about religion or religiosity, but about spirituality. Spirituality would not have the negative connotations that religion and religiosity for many people have. However, it is doubtful whether we gain much by employing other words; indeed it is doubtful whether psychology has ever gained anything by orienting itself on any market other than its own striving toward insight into what the psychic realm is and how it can be investigated (cf. Fox and Prilleltensky 1997). Evidently, psychology is always practiced within a certain context, a context with creates, facilitates and conditions all research and training, but handing over to what any "market" urges psychologists to do research on, has never been a fruitful strategy. It only increases the number of projects and publications in which people with a degree in psychology are involved, but it does in no way lead to increase in

J.A. Belzen, *Towards Cultural Psychology of Religion: Principles, Approaches, Applications*,   83
DOI 10.1007/978-90-481-3491-5_6, © Springer Science+Business Media B.V. 2010

psychological insight, as not everything that someone with a degree in psychology does, is by itself psychological.

To avoid possible misunderstanding, it should be stressed that this plea for psychology's agenda being set by psychologists (or at least also by psychologists) does not mean to suggest that spirituality should not be studied by psychologists, on the contrary. Nor is the implication that psychologists of religion should not try to get their share of what is available as opportunities for funding of their research, etc. It is the balance between wanting to strive to increase psychological insight on the one hand and being determined by non-psychological forces on the other, be these forces pro- or anti-religious that should be kept in mind. More specifically, one should remember that spirituality has always already been an object of research for psychologists of religion, that there is nothing really new here, and that much of the present parlance about spirituality, also within psychology and psychology of religion, is (1) just a function of a wider trend in society to regard religion as "bad," but spirituality as "good" (Popp-Baier 2010); and (2) not about spirituality at all. In order to explain this closer, we need to take a step back, or take a bird's eye view, so to say; in other words, we must transcend the hurly-burly of much of contemporary psychological research and try to reflect on it.

The present chapter will, therefore, try to make psychological research as such the object of inquiry and ask questions about its purpose, its possibilities, restrictions, and conditions. Offering a couple of preliminary considerations, a number of controversial propositions will be put forward, but so be it: as scholars we want to learn and to be instructed, and this usually is achieved better by being confronted and meeting resistance than by being affirmed and by listening to repetitions.

To speak from the perspective of psychology, understood as the academic effort to understand human psychic functioning, is distinct from speaking from any spiritual perspective. This is an important issue to keep in mind, as most of the present literature and most of the activities (like workshops, seminars, training and what have you) under the combined labels of psychology and spirituality are indeed either spiritual in nature, or serving a spiritual purpose. More specifically, the present chapter speaks from the tradition that is called "psychology of religion," one of the oldest fields within psychology at large. Although spirituality and religion are certainly not to be identified (some of their differences will be elaborated in a moment), psychology of religion constitutes a tradition to which belong theoretical and methodological considerations that are indispensable if one aspires to study spirituality from a psychological perspective.

When psychology turns to spirituality, it turns to very diverse areas of human conduct, in the same way as when it turns to labor, the arts, sports, sexuality, war, etc. as fields of human activity, which can also be explored with the means of psychology. In doing this, psychology tries to investigate spirituality as scientifically as possible, striving to be neutral in its approach to the object and do to justice to it. Psychology as such is not in favor of spirituality, nor is it against spirituality, psychology does not try to foster spirituality, nor does it try to destroy spirituality, even though each and all of these motives may have been some of the reasons why individual psychologists have chosen topics from this area for their research.

In principle, psychology as a scientific discipline is neutral with regard to spirituality, in the same way as it is neutral towards labor, the arts or sports as such. Also, the results from psychological research on spirituality may be used in totally opposite ways, in the same way as the results of medical research can be used in totally opposite ways (e.g. to provoke or to prevent abortion). As the psychology of religion is, in general, not a religious practice (although it may be practiced for [anti-]religious reasons), the psychology of spirituality likewise is itself no spirituality nor to be approached from a spiritual perspective.

This said, it may and should be also said that psychology as such is not value-neutral at all; in general it is probably correct to say that most of psychology is committed to promoting human welfare. However, two points should not be forgotten here: (1) there is no consensus as to what human welfare is; human welfare is not a psychological subject, it is not defined by psychology; psychology may only assess and explain how psychic functioning is involved in it. Thus, to be concrete, if human welfare were defined in such a way as to include being free from all spirituality, psychology as such would have no counterarguments, and it might well be used to try to find out how to eliminate spirituality from people's lives (as happened in the past, under Communist dictatorship in Eastern-Europe, with atheistic psychological research on religion, cf. Kääriäinen 1989). In other words, and again: psychology cannot take a stand itself as to the evaluation of spirituality in a more embracing sense, and its own evaluation of spirituality will always be bound by values of a non-psychological nature. (2) Psychology should also realize that there may be other and higher values in life than human welfare; especially in the fields of religion and spirituality. (One should not forget that values that are self-evident to many psychologists today [like democracy, freedom of intellectual, artistic, political and religious expression, separation of science and religion, and many others] are rather recent Western inventions, not shared worldwide and not to be imposed in a George Bush-like way.) We shall come back to the issue later, but it may be stated a priori that the striving for value-neutrality and to do justice to the object is one of the most difficult goals to achieve in scholarship; it is never fully achieved, always remains an ideal, an ideal that should prevent us from making too quick a judgment.

Psychology Does Not Define Spirituality

As a consequence, and as should be clear, it is not psychology's task to come up with its own definition of spirituality. Just as it is not the task of psychology to define domains like labor, art and sports, but to investigate and try to explain and understand the human involvement in labor, art and sports, it is not psychology's task to define spirituality. Psychology turns to spirituality, a domain pointed out and defined other than by psychologists, be this "other" a common understanding in a certain society, a particular commissioner or another scholarly discipline. Yet, this does not mean that there is no obligation for psychology to point out what it is going to investigate when it turns to spirituality. Here we encounter a big problem: it is a struggle, although not a struggle specific to psychology, to define what spirituality "is." Outside of psychology, there exists an enormous literature on the definition of spirituality; and a number of psychologists have even been tempted to try to contribute to this literature (cf. Zinnbauer et al. 1999; Miller and Thoresen 2003). As there is no need for a psychological definition of spirituality per se, these colleagues will not be joined here. On the contrary, when one studies the literature, one is likely to come to the conclusion that it is a dead end to try to come up with one single definition of spirituality. The range of phenomena in the human world called "spiritual" comprises such diverse and contrasting forms of conduct that it seems in vain to try to catch them all into one, comprising conceptualization. There exist forms of human conduct that may count as spiritual, even as acts of spiritual heroism to one group, but are abhorred by other groups. Opposing practices range from engaging in "sacred sex" by some to celibacy by others, from working for world peace to violence including terrorism. To try to capture them all into one single definition obscures more than it illuminates, or leaves us at best with rather empty circumscriptions.

This does not mean that such circumscriptions are without any value, but, as psychology has to be spiritually neutral, it cannot itself judge whether any single act of human conduct is spiritual or not. To the extent that psychology would want to serve the perspective and/or purposes of any particular spirituality, or of any particular commissioner, it could disregard, disapprove or even condemn whatever conduct this commissioner wants it to do (as would be the case if a psychologist only accepts or investigates as spirituality what, for instance, a Christian church considers to be spirituality). To the extent a psychologist wishes to refrain from any spiritual judgment herself, she will have to accept as spiritual whatever her research participants tell her they consider to be spiritual. Between these two extremes any concrete psychological project oscillates. As in any context there is always some understanding of what should and could be considered as spiritual, however circumstantial that understanding may be, here the limited value of a certain circumscription of spirituality comes in: as psychology in general studies human conduct, it may consider as spirituality any *operationalization of commitment to Transcendence* ('transcendence' understood in the sense more or less lined out by the philosopher Karl Jaspers). Research participants may be involved in the most diverse forms of conduct, but only if they themselves circumscribe their acts as resulting from commitment to what they consider to be Transcendence, should a psychologist consider their acts as spiritual. Hence, the same activity – e.g., engaging in sex, shouting, violence – may be spiritual to some, but not to others, who may even condemn such activity as utterly non-spiritual, pleading for the exact opposite – e.g., refraining from sex, silence, pacifism – as spiritual. What matters, is not what the research participant is involved in, but whether she performs her conduct out of commitment to what she considers to be Transcendence. It should immediately be granted that this circumscription does not solve all conceptual problems, but that is not its aim; it only wants to help psychologists get out of the dilemma of accepting a too narrow understanding of spiritually versus having no idea at all what they are talking about.

As for decades in the scientific study of religion there have been debates about substantive versus functional definitions of religion (Platvoet and Molendijk 1999),

Psychology Does Not Define Spirituality

it would make little sense to repeat such debates, only now concerning spirituality. Although no one has been able to ever define religion in a way that is satisfactory to all scholars of religion, we now have at least the distinction between religion and religiosity, the general understanding being that religion refers to a macro-cultural entity and religiosity to the correlated human functioning on a personal level. Studying religiosity we can, therefore, usually relate it to some more or less clear tradition, group or organization. While this is not impossible with spirituality, it is less easy, especially in the so-called West in recent decades. While there is a high correlation between religiosity and religion, this needs not be the case with spirituality and religion. While religions always presuppose and prescribe spirituality, spirituality does not necessarily presuppose religion.

It should be clear by now that spirituality is not the same as the macro-cultural phenomenon that religion is, but is not the same as religiosity either. Spirituality, as I have tried to circumscribe here, refers to human conduct, to practices, to acts and activities. As such, it only overlaps with religiosity. Some religious persons are also spiritual: they perform acts and activities because of their religion; but some religious persons are not at all or hardly spiritual. (Someone who is a member of a religious organization, who believes certain things, but does not engage in any activity because of her of his commitment to Transcendence [whether a religious activity or not], will hardly be called spiritual; with such a person, one could still investigate the genesis and development of her images of god, the structure and functioning of the belief system, etc., but not of her spirituality.) It is clear that all religions presuppose and prescribe spirituality: they want their adherents to live, to behave and to *be* in certain ways; but it is also clear that individual members of religions do not always live that way, or sometimes do not live that way at all. Thus, when inventing diagrams or formulas to explain the relationship of religiosity and spirituality, one should not ask whether religiosity includes spirituality or the other way round, but realize that they are like partly overlapping circles. Therefore, if persons do not belong to any religious tradition and if they even deny being religious, they might still call themselves spiritual, but only if they can point to their practice of certain acts and activities because of their commitment to Transcendence.

This way of conceptualization, sensitive to diversity as it may be, does not solve all problems. It especially leaves open the question of what Transcendence is: should we accept anything research participants come up with, or are there clear limits here? There seem to be at least some limits. Whereas someone could claim they go for a walk in the forest for spiritual reasons (so not, or not only, to relax or because of health reasons, but also because she, e.g., venerates Nature), or could claim to go to work not only because of the inherent satisfaction or because of the money earned with the job, but also because she sees this as a service to Humanity, it would be hard for anyone to claim to be involved in activities for spiritual reasons when his surrounding society regards them as criminal. Note: the clumsy phrasing "it would be hard" is deliberate, as it is not impossible to be for spiritual reasons involved in activities that others may condemn as criminal. The examples that may be found with violence – the events of 9/11 are a clear example – show how difficult or even ultimately impossible it will be to come to a common agreement.

To repeat: what the reasoning presented here is intended to achieve is to help psychologists to avoid taking a spiritual stance themselves. As there exists no spirituality in general but only specific spiritual conduct, psychologists should listen to their research subjects, and accept what they point out in their lives as spiritual, albeit not in a naïve way. Spirituality as such does not exist, only concrete forms of spirituality: practices, acts and activities performed by human subjects as operationalizations of their being committed to whatever they regard as Transcendence. It is the individual motivation and legitimation – always bound by context – that make an act spiritual, not the act itself. Therefore, psychologists wishing to investigate spirituality (a word which we now realize refers to a non-concept) are usually hardly in need of discussions such as the one we have been involved in briefly here: they can turn to human subjects involved in specific forms of conduct considered spiritual and they can start to work from there. So, the proposal is to refrain from talking about spirituality and to continue to talk about spiritual acts and activities, not all of which psychology can even strive to investigate. Psychology can, however, do research on specific examples of spiritual involvement and on its results. Before trying to make some recommendations for concrete research, let us shortly reflect on what type of psychological research might be employed here.

What Type of Psychology Do We Need in Order to Approach Spiritual Acts and Activities?

Immediately following up on the above, two major areas of research within psychology need to be distinguished. Psychology can contribute to research on contemporary subjects, their behavior and experiences, but it can also contribute to research on the outcome of such behavior and experiences. It is an error to think that only contemporary subjects could be the object of psychological research. The psychology of the arts, for example, not only deals with presently living artists, but also with great works of art that have stayed with us as the result of past artistic activity, whether it be painting, poetry, music, architecture or whatever. Considerable knowledge or at least perspectives from psychology can be drawn upon when interpreting a work of art: one might ask what motivated the artist, what kind of person she is or has been, how her object relations may express themselves in the work, what intrapsychic conflicts it reveals or manifests; one can also inquire into the effects of the work of art on the observer, etc. The same can be done when it comes to lasting products of religious and/or spiritual involvement. A large part of the psychological approach employed within religious studies is already pursuing this track (Capps and Dittes 1990; Haartman 2004; Homans 1989; Jung 1967/2003; Kripall 1995; Rollins 1999); and some psychologists of religion try to take such an approach to the lives of past or present religious persons too (Belzen and Geels 2008), but among psychologists they are a minority. This possibility should be mentioned explicitly, however, as it could also be practiced with products resulting from spiritual activities.

An oeuvre like Krishnamurti's or John Heider's, persons one cannot easily call religious, could be approached in this way (cf. e.g., Kripall 2008). Having mentioned this type of research, let us continue to consider which kind of psychological approach is to be preferred when studying contemporary subjects.

As indicated already, in the case of spiritual acts and activities we are dealing with the results of commitment to Transcendence. Commitment is engaging; it is not something that comes about just like that; it does not come about easily and it is not easy to sustain. This is precisely what the literature of the otherwise heterogeneous spiritual traditions tells us: they conceive of spirituality as a path, as a time-consuming process, full of ups and downs. Although it might be possible to isolate a single experience or act, the perspective any psychology typically takes to understand it, is that of a process. Even an isolated experience or act a psychologist would try to understand in part out of the biographical context of the person involved. Studying processes requires a longitudinal approach, also in psychology. Preferably a psychologist would employ such theories, concepts and research instruments that are sensitive to cultural specifics and that are dynamic, in order to detect, follow and analyze the struggles and vicissitudes of the individual-biographical process in which the particular act or experience is embedded and of which it is an inherent and constitutive element.

The challenging and indeed one of the most basic questions is whether psychology can contribute anything to the understanding of spiritual acts and activities as such. Psychology of spirituality shares this challenge with the psychology of religion.[1] Let us therefore briefly turn to psychology of religion, in order to learn and apply our findings to the psychology of spirituality. To try to develop a psychology of religion only makes sense under certain conditions: if we think – or are made to think, this awkward phrase will be explained soon – that there is something specific to religion, to the diversity of all the phenomena being referred to, correctly or not, as religious. If religion were only a matter of "being integrated in a group," only of "giving meaning," of "coping with existential issues," psychology of religion would be a sub-field of social psychology, of cognitive psychology, of existential psychology. But perhaps there is something specific to religion? Perhaps it is a specific segment of culture, involving human beings in other ways than other segments do? The question is then, What is this specificity and can psychology contribute to its assessment, exploration and explanation? If we did not assume there was something specific to religion, there would be no need to develop any psychology of religion, for then psychology of religion would only be repeating psychological research on religious subjects, coming up with results that have been attained already, and are therefore quite superfluous. Before we continue, two remarks, one short, one a bit longer.

---

[1] I shall refrain from adding every time the all too tiresome "and/or spirituality" in this paragraph. Most of what I shall say here about psychology of religion pertains to psychology of spirituality too, and where there are differences, I shall make them explicit.

Hidden Agendas in the Psychology of Religion and Spirituality

First, much of the so-called psychology of religion is indeed precisely doing nothing more than this: it just doubles psychological research done elsewhere already and does not come up with anything new or with any insights of its own. As such, this is not a problem: there may be good reasons to apply existing psychological research to subjects, events and contexts that are called religious, repeating and confirming what psychologists know already from other and previous research. But perhaps that would thereby offer interesting insights to religious populations or commissioners of such research on religion, as it introduces to them a psychological perspective on phenomena or on an entire field of existence ultimately relevant to them. Such research and insights would typically lead to books with titles such as "Psychology for Theologians," or "Psychology for Spiritual Leaders" (Blattner et al. 1992, 1993; Klessmann 2004; Watts 2002; Watts et al. 2002). There is nothing wrong with books like these: the aim here is not to criticize them; the point is, that it is an "introduction" to psychology employing examples from a domain that this specific readership wants to read about (i.e., religion); it does not expand existing psychology nor does it lead to treatises about the specificity of religion (and/or spirituality). On this point, the view presented here departs from the otherwise excellent albeit critical remarks David Funder (2002) makes in his commentary on a number of recent articles in the psychology of religion: he too sees psychology of religion as a field of application of existing psychological devices to the domain of religion, but he refuses to acknowledge the psychology of religion as a distinctive sub-field. Risking criticism for struggling about words only, the present view defends the existence of the psychology of religion, but as a separate field of application, just like there are so many other fields of application in psychology. The psychology of religion is important, because religion is so important, both on the level of the individual and on the level of society or even on a global level. Psychology of religion is not important because it would be a necessary part of the systematics of psychology. Any psychology may be valid, even without turning explicitly to the study of religious phenomena; however, it will be hard to get around turning to religious phenomena if one wants to come up with an embracing psychological view of the human being.

The second remark is related to the first: psychology, like all scholarship, always functions in a context, functions thanks to possibilities provided by that context, but is also limited by that context. To give one obvious example: that the largest percentage of psychologists is in one way or another involved in clinical psychology does not indicate that this is the core or even the most important part of psychology; it only indicates that this is the segment in society where most psychologists are able to find employment. It is not because it is central to the discipline, but because of the relevance to society that clinical psychology has become so large. As indicated, there is nothing wrong with this, just as there is also nothing wrong with other segments of society, like churches or theological seminaries, wishing to teach about and to explore the psychological aspects of the Christian religion. Much of the psychology of religion has come into existence precisely because of the possibilities for psychological work provided by this kind of "commissioner," to call them that for the moment. Being employed by a Christian organization does not necessarily imply producing a psychology that is necessarily biased towards any Christian position, although that may often be and has been the case (Miller and Delaney 2005; Roberts and Talbot 1997): obviously, a psychologist may wish to serve the interests of his employer; there is as such not much of a problem with this. Things become more problematic, however, if the "commissioner," Christian or not, interferes with the psychological work, if she or he tolerates certain types of research only, if she or he even allows only certain results and ideas. In such a case, the professional and even personal integrity of the psychologist might be at stake (and it would hopefully result in her or him changing to another employer).

This case might be clear and easy; but things become much more complex if the effort to come up with certain results and reasoning is not the result of external pressure on the psychologist, but because she is under a personal and subjective urge to do so, an urge she may be unaware of herself. Such a desire may well stem from a particular religious involvement, from a particular religious worldview or philosophy, or from sympathy for a certain religion, be this sympathy reflected or not. Throughout its entire history, the psychology of religion has been heavily influenced by what seemed to be Christian ideas. This was not the result of the research subjects almost without exception being Christians, but because of a priori's on the part of the researchers themselves: very often they were Christians, very often they tried to scientifically "prove" the truth of Christianity. Even those who tried to get away from such simplistic desires, very often remained convinced of at least the cultural superiority of Christianity. Up until the present day, there is a large group of colleagues affiliated with the psychology of religion, who would like to use psychology to instigate and foster religion, usually Christianity, with other people (Belzen 2004b). Even in a profane clinical setting, like e.g. psychotherapy, they would like to employ religious language, ideas and rituals – very often well intended, hoping to help their clients (Miller 2002; Pargament 2007; Richards and Bergin 1997; Wong, and Fry 1998). Although some would like to deny that they are trying to evangelize, one might have doubts here: how could one really "neutrally" employ language, ideas or rituals from a religion one does not believe in, to help a client? Even if the claim is that therapists should work with the resources that are available from the client's background, it is hard to image therapists of this (usually evangelical) orientation praying in a Muslim way with a client from, e.g., a Moroccan background. But to the extent psychologists are open about their reasons for blending psychology and religion in treatment, and to the extent they are doing this in a setting where a client knows she can expect this, one need perhaps not to be too critical about this kind of practice.

It is not this more or less open blending of religion and psychology that we are dealing with here. The concern is more with the hidden religious and spiritual agendas one encounters so often in psychology, especially in the psychology of religion (and in all likelihood also in future psychologies of spirituality). Just a brief word by way of explanation. Throughout the entire twentieth century, one witnessed, especially in Europe, psychology of religion becoming more profane: many researchers left all specific Christian apologetics behind, but stuck to a position that "religion is better than no religion," they would assume e.g. that being religious is better, in whatever way, than not being religious. Even if they would admit that for psychology as a science, it is impossible to confirm the theological truth of any belief system, they would reason that being religious is better for mental health, usually on the basis of the old a priori that the human being is religious by nature. As is not the intention to set out on a historical tour, we shall not go into this any further, but examples abound: from Hall and Leuba wanting to update Christianity by means of psychology, through James whose *Varieties* are a plea for the assumption that man is religious by nature, through Gordon Allport who wished to defend religion against the accusation of being correlated with prejudice, up to the present day. The suspicion seems justified that in the present interest in spirituality by many psychologists, whether they call themselves psychologists of religion or otherwise, there lurks a similar apologetic desire, be it in still less religious terminology, or perhaps one should say, be it in still better disguise.

Without going really into the history of the psychology of religion, one can draw on it to make this suspicion clear. One of the ways in which previous generations tried to "prove" by means of psychology that "religion is good" – of course, things were phrased more subtly than can be done here now – is by basing it in human nature, e.g. in human cognition or in meaning giving, drawing on an old metaphysical tradition ranging from Kant's necessary postulates of practical reason to Troeltsch's a priori's (Belzen 1999a). Far clearer even: for decades psychologists have sided with Rudolf Otto (1917/1976), who claimed that there is a specific religious emotion. In contradiction to James (1902/2002), who had stated that religious emotions are only religious because of their being directed towards a religious object or because of their functioning in a religious context, Otto and his followers claimed that there exists a separate, independent and unique emotion that would be religious in nature. Of course, it is possible to conduct psychological research on the basis of such an assumption; and some years ago, in Germany, even an elaborate statistical report concluded again, or anew, that such a religious emotion exists and can be distinguished from other emotions (Beile 1998). When one sets out with an assumption, the assumption usually returns and is confirmed. But how necessary is the assumption? How valid is it? The suspicion seems justified that the same is happening with regard to spirituality today.

Another example: for decades, while quarreling over the definition of religion, religiously inspired psychologists and other empirical researchers have been (over) stretching the meaning of the term, apparently to include all and everyone under their definition of religion and under their assumption of humans being religious by nature. Thus, even where no religious activity or religious inclination was found anymore, and even when subjects would deny being religious, researchers would still claim or at least suggest that they are, as attending a rock concert, flocking to Lenin's mausoleum, or even being attached to money would be "religious" too. With this type of reasoning, psychology – and any other branch of scholarship pretending to do research on religion – does not gain anything: it blurs concepts, it loses the phenomena it claims to be investigating, and in the end we don't learn anything about any specificity whichever form of religion may have. (And one should be reminded that no other sub-discipline in psychology is trapped in this kind of rather bizarre reasoning: if people are not engaged in sports, if they are not performing any artistic activity, no psychologist sets out to call them sportsmen or artists. But in psychology of religion, due to peculiar religious a priori's, numerous researchers and authors want to find religion and spirituality even with people that don't care about religion or about anything transcendent.)

At present, we seem to be witnessing a similar apologetic move with regard to spirituality: some psychologists suggest that spirituality is part of human nature. All human beings, so they claim, are spiritual; this may manifest itself in religiosity, but not necessarily. (Hence we seem to encounter a further step towards secularization: no longer is everyone called religious, everyone is now called spiritual.) Defenders of this position employ different types of reasoning. Remaining in the quantitative-statistical tradition, Piedmont (1999) comes to the conclusion that spirituality is a factor of human personality, just like the so-called Big Five would be. Reasoning from a trans-personal position, Helminiak (1996) defines as spiritual the inherent tendency towards growth in the human mind – attending to this innate capacity would result in spiritual-ity. It sounds quite paradoxical and illogical: for even without spirituality, a human being is still spiritual, according to Helminiak. The objection to this reasoning should be the same as the objection towards overstretching the concept of religion (or of being religious) and of wanting to found religion (or religiosity) in human nature: (1) there is no necessity for the assumption; (2) we don't learn anything about the speci-ficity of any form of spirituality in this way. Rather, two proposals or suggestions could be made: (1) psychologists should refrain from making assumptions with regard to human nature; they would do better to realize that there is no human nature as such, but that it arises from its being embedded in a human culture, from the human being treated in a particular way (Shotter and Gergen 1989); one might then assume the human being can *become* either spiritual or not (and every modality between these two), but not that it is spiritual by nature and from birth onward; (2) psychology should try to contribute to the exploration and explanation of *specific* forms of spiri-tuality. By analyzing particular spiritual acts and activities, and by comparing them to such acts and activities that seem to be functionally equivalent, we might be able to detect something of the surplus meaning a spiritual act or activity may have for the persons involved.

The Specificity of Religious and Spiritual Conduct

Let us return to the major issue: Can psychology contribute anything to the assess-ment, exploration and explanation of the specificity of religious and spiritual acts and activities? Such a contribution would truly constitute a systematic, as distin-guished from a pragmatic, argument in favor of a separate sub-discipline called the psychology of religion and/or spirituality. What is that specificity? Can psychology say anything about it?

Spirituality clearly is a cultural phenomenon: it consists in all kinds of acts and activities on which subjects bestow a certain meaning derived from their being embedded in a certain spiritual tradition. It is the type of meaning bestowed that makes a certain act spiritual, not the bestowing of meaning itself. As with religion, national identity, the arts, sports and countless other "fields" (in the sense of Bourdieu 1993) that human beings engage themselves in, it is the field that is specific, not the human engagement therein. It is the structure and the nature of the field, of that cultural entity, with its specific values, convictions, conventions and morality and with its own ways of regulating human cognition, emotion, motivation and behavior that lead to the specificity of experiences and conduct, not anything inherent in the nature of the human being. If there would be anything in human nature that is of a religious or spiritual nature itself, we would need a different anthropology and psychology to account for it; we would move perhaps in the direction of parapsychology or, even perhaps more probably, in the direction of transpersonal psychologies. This is certainly a theoretically possible option, but as transpersonal psychology has not yet convinced psychology in general of its truth, it may be allowed to remain with more established types of psychology, conventional as this may be. To these types of psychology as we know them – one should realize that this psychology is a Western enterprise: in the East elaborate but radically different psychologies exist! (cf., e.g., Paranjpe 1998) – a religious motivation is not the same as an economic motivation, albeit not because different psychic processes would be involved, but because religion is not the same as economy; it is the particular nature of the different religions as cultural fields that evokes religious motivations. Therefore, religious motivations are motivations arising and functioning in a religious field. Also with regard to spirituality, the present hypothesis is that psychology cannot bring more to light about the difference between spiritual and non-spiritual activities than just this: a different meaning is bestowed, but the psychic processes involved are the same as in all meaning giving. So, once again: the various types of spirituality have a specificity of their own: they are different from other-than-spiritual acts and activities because they are related to something very specific, to whatever the persons involved consider to be Transcendence; therefore, the different types of spiritual acts and activities are not all alike and not all the same; being involved in Jihad is certainly not the same as trying to follow the eight fold path the Buddha spoke about; the phenomena of "conversion" are not the same even within one religious tradition (within Christianity, for example, there is a wide variety of different, sometimes even contradictory meanings of the concept and the act of conversion). However, the psychic processes involved are not specific to any spiritual act or activity.

This modest stand should *not* be understood in the sense that "therefore" there is nothing to detect for psychology, nor that there would be no need for a psychology of religion or of spirituality. On the contrary! One of the tasks of psychology is to help us to understand the particularities of human lives, also in the realms of religion and spirituality, and it needs to go a long way to do so. For the persons involved, what type of meaning they bestow, what type of interpretation they offer for their behavior and activities, is precisely what makes them who they are, and psychology should not

The Specificity of Religious and Spiritual Conduct

try to abstract from this, but try to understand the peculiarities thereof: it will teach us something both about the person involved and about the type of meaning she bestows. Human beings are not machines that would function the same way in whatever contexts they were placed. (Not even machines function the same way in all contexts; this whole way of phrasing, heir to Cartesian thought, is flawed, but it would lead us astray to enter into its criticism here.) Obviously, when someone entertains (or does not entertain) a commitment to Transcendence, it is the result of a historical process during which the subject has been introduced to one or several spiritual traditions or perhaps even only to elements thereof. But it is always the result of a process during which subjective-biographical factors, accessible to psychology, have played a role in the genesis, development and maintenance (or the lack of maintenance) of a particular commitment to Transcendence. If someone has not developed any such commitment, or if it has got lost, this does not mean that the person is psychologically impaired (which would be the logical consequence if we assume that human beings are spiritual by nature or that spiritual acts and activities exist by virtue of the existence of some specific psychic faculty or whatever; entertaining no relationship to Transcendence would then have to count as a defect, as not fully functioning).

Neither does the absence of spirituality imply that a person would be mentally less healthy, or less able to attribute meaning; nor does it mean this person would not endorse particular moral values, nor anything else that might disqualify a human being. The only thing we can say – and which is no psychological verdict as such – is that such a person apparently does not attribute spiritual meaning to anything or does not entertain spiritual values. About such values or about the desirability to entertain them, psychology knows nothing. Psychology can, however, contribute to achieve two important goals: it may help to explore (1) the genesis and development of commitment versus non-commitment (or apostasy) and try to find out whether it means a difference to the persons involved; (2) how entertaining one meaning is different from entertaining another meaning, thereby contributing significantly to the exploration of the kind of world a subject enters or lives in when oriented to this or that meaning. But psychology cannot conclude that the value orientation as such is defective nor that the individual-biographical factors responsible for the non-commitment to Transcendence defect every and all value orientation! To give just a simple example: one research subject, raised in a rather traditional protestant milieu, over the years developed an increasingly New Age-oriented spirituality. To her, remaining faithful to the Christian heritage proved impossible — among other factors, because of her father image; she experienced her father as weak, even as a loser, and with her obviously the appeal of the Christian image of God as a Father was insufficient to provide her with an image of God as a Father to whom one could have recourse, or who would be adorable, a strong helper, or whatever. For her, a personal god had to be rejected, precisely because the Christian doctrine she was introduced to presented such a god as a Father. Her struggle with her personal god image, however, did not prevent her at all from developing an alternative value orientation or a corresponding spirituality. Studying her case, we not only learn about her and her peculiarities, we also learn about the particularities of a part of the Christian religion, viz. about the opportunities offered to and difficulties bestowed upon believers by this religious tradition.

Recommendations for Empirical Research

There are many possibilities for a psychologist wanting to do research on a particular type of spirituality, on particular acts and activities resulting from someone's being committed to Transcendence. One can, for example, try to assess the relations between these activities and issues of interest like health, health behavior, well being, etc. The only footnotes to such research should be: (a) This is not very specific to psychology. Such questions may also be asked – and increasingly are being asked! – by insurance companies and politicians. The methods employed to answer such questions – typically questionnaires – are not specific to psychology either: they may also be employed by journalists, sociologists or political scientists. For research to be psychological, a more specifically psychological question and interpretation are necessary. (b) This sort of research is always in danger of becoming too instrumental: serving not only the interests of others-than-psychologists, but sometimes even losing the spiritual behavior as such out of sight. It is obvious that there is much more funding available for research that serves the interests of the health business, but psychologists should strive to also remain with the very object of their research, and explore spiritual acts and activities both for their own sake and for psychology's sake, not only because spirituality may be related to health issues. Although it should be granted that psychological research can hardly be conducted without employing a psychological theory (for exploration as such does not yet constitute psychological research), a science like psychology should always take its objects seriously, not reduce them, or at least not a priori, to the categories of some theory, nor to what can be dealt with by some particular type of research method. Let us therefore turn to some recommendations for empirical research, recommendations that should be taken to heart, even *before* considering which theory and which method to employ. As space is limited, just a few issues can be dealt with and those only briefly.

1. A first and very important recommendation for empirical research on spiritual acts and activities sounds so obvious but it all too often is *not* followed: go and study especially intensive cases! If one wants to study smoking behavior from a psychological perspective, there is little use turning to persons who at some point in their lives have smoked a cigarette; there is even little use addressing gentlemen who smoke a cigar on Christmas Eve once a year. If one wants to find out something about smoking, one must take smokers as subjects of inquiry, people that really smoke, who are addicted, who can tell what it means to smoke, to try to kick off, to start again, etc. Likewise, if one wants to study sports, one shouldn't turn to persons who have no physical exercise other than mounting the few steps to their front door; one would turn to persons who deliberately, frequently and intensively practice their branch of sports. If one wants to study criminality, one would go to a jail, join a gang, whatever, but not interrogate one's undergraduates. When one wants to study a form of spirituality, it is not much different: one should go and turn to people who really practice that type of spirituality! If one wants to study fasting as a spiritual activity, visiting a website advertising programs for losing weight, is not an obvious option. If one wants to study Franciscan spirituality,

talking to Franciscans seems a likely option. If one is trying to prove an assumption about all humans being spiritual, however, one will need to design a definition that holds true for all and everyone; one may then ask whomsoever for answers to one's questions (questions that will for sure *not* be understood if one dares to really approach all and everyone from all traditions and continents); and one will therefore run the risk of not garnering any information about any form of spirituality, like the Franciscan one, like the one of a sannyasin of Sri Ravi Shankar, or someone attending New Age oriented workshops, or what have you.

If one wants to study mysticism, which some people assume to be the core of all religion, one would turn to people who are following a mystical path. They are not easy to find, though. There has hardly ever been a mystic who showed off as being a mystic. One will have to search, win confidence, etc. And if one has found the persons one needs, it will be wise to pay attention to the particularities of the form of mysticism they are involved in. Otherwise one runs the risk of coming up with results that signify very little. To make just one comparison: take traveling. There are many forms of traveling. Assuming that there would be a common kernel to traveling, from which all traveling derives, its meaning is just that: it is an assumption, but it does not help to understand what it means to a person to travel. For it is clear that traveling by car, by boat or by airplane are quite different. Asking for a "common core experience" misses the point. Also designing or employing a statistically more sophisticated instrument is of little help. Take, for example, a well-known instrument like the Mysticism-Scale (Hood 1975). Perhaps it would be allowed to voice criticism of the M-scale in a playful image: Hood managed to get a rabbit out of his hat, but…, only after he himself put the rabbit in first! Hood wanted to find out whether there is a common core to all kinds of mysticism, which is a valid and relevant question, of course. He set out to answer it empirically (Hood 2003b) – quite correctly so. He designed an instrument to answer the question, tested it out, and lo and behold, a common core shows up – *but* the instrument was based on a conceptualization of mysticism, by Stace (1960), that *presupposes* a common core. So: Hood got a common core out of the empiricist's hat (the M-scale), so to say, but only after he put it (Stace's theory of a common core) in there beforehand. Or, phrased in less playful terms: the instrument used to verify Stace's conceptualization is not independent of Stace, but based on him. This criticism should be understood correctly: it is *not* claimed that this type of research should not be conducted. But as there exists no spirituality in general and as not everyone is spiritual, a psychologist needs to turn to a specific form of spirituality, find intensive and representative cases of it, and study these in depth (as Hood has been involved in more recently, see Hood and Williamson 2008; and as has been done, from very different perspectives by, e.g., Belzen 1999b; Cohen 2007; Geels 1997; Hijweege 2004; Popp-Baier 1998). Only afterwards could comparisons be made with equally carefully researched activities also called spiritual, to detect what similarities and differences exist.

Turning to intensive forms of the phenomenon one claims to study is not only a requisite from a phenomenological point of view: it is not only necessary to remain true to the object one intends to study, but also from a psychological point of view. The founding fathers of our discipline taught us to turn to the investigation of real, clear and exceptionally intense cases of spirituality, instead of looking for marginal forms, or residues of spirituality, with the largest possible sample. We need only remind the reader of the *Varieties* of William James (1902/2002), a study inaugurating the psychological study of both religiosity and spirituality, and until now the very bestseller of our sub-discipline. With the inaugurator of the psychoanalytic tradition, Freud, we find a similar plea: he suggested that in order to learn something significant, we have to study intensive cases, in which even the derailment of human subjectivity we sometimes encounter (in dreams, in the so-called Freudian slips and in clinical setting, cf. his metaphor of the "broken crystal," Freud 1933/1964) can teach us something about the human being in general. Also the name of Karl Jaspers (1917/1997) could be mentioned, a researcher and theoretician who even left us an elaborate methodological account of phenomenology and of psychopathology. In more recent decades approaches like those of the founding fathers have led to the development of contemporary methods and techniques employed under labels such as phenomenology, hermeneutics, "grounded theory," self-confrontation method, ethnomethodology, field studies, case studies, biographical research and so on, all of which seem indeed to be more suited to exploring domains that are characteristic of the human being such as spirituality. (Unless, again, one wishes to come up with definitions that are so empty that even other beings than humans can be categorized under them....).

2. As spiritual acts and activities always result from a subject's being embedded in a particular spiritual context or tradition, it is for the understanding of such acts and activities of vital interest to explore the respective contexts of meaning. Such an exploration is not psychological per se, but constitutes a necessary primary component of any psychological research on a spiritual phenomenon. The knowledge that the psychologist needs to draw upon is available from a multitude of sources, among them information provided by the particular spiritual tradition itself, but especially knowledge made available by other scholarly disciplines working on the same or similar spiritual phenomena – especially by other social sciences like history, sociology and anthropology. Psychological reports that aspire to leave the reader with a greater understanding of the spiritual phenomenon under scrutiny than before reading them, are by necessity interdisciplinary.

3. Next to obtaining information about the phenomenon under scrutiny, it is necessary to witness the phenomenon (if it is a publicly accessible phenomenon – which it usually is). Quite a number of research psychologists have been criticized for never having visited the sites where the phenomena they question their subjects about manifest themselves; some, sending out perhaps thousands of questionnaires, are even criticized for never even having spoken with their subjects. If it is allowed to exaggerate a bit with the following formulation, one could say that a psychologist who is disinclined to speak to people is a strange kind of figure; and a psychologist who is afraid of spiritual phenomena would make a strange kind of figure if she desires to become involved in the psychology of spirituality.

Criticisms like that just referred to should preferably never be possible of a psychologist of spirituality!

4. Be radically empirical: although this point could easily be subsumed under the previous one, it may be stressed that for a psychologist who wishes to understand the experience a subject is reporting on or to understand the meaning of the behavior he is witnessing, it is desirable to "get in touch" as close as possible with the experience or the behavior of the subject. To understand the meaning of a spiritual act, the psychologist will be well advised to conduct the act *herself*, even if she would perhaps not do this because she interprets it as an operationalization of commitment to Transcendence. It will need little explanation to see that a psychologist who has joined her subjects in meditation will come up with different results than a psychologist who does not know the experience of meditation and who perhaps only submitted respondents to a survey. (The latter will obtain answers that articulate opinions about meditation but will have only very limited access to the experience and the activity of meditation itself.) Psychologists will be well advised to go *radically empirical*: to get in touch with the phenomena they claim to investigate; and although there are clear limits to what a researcher may be able to get involved in, not only from an ethical point of view, it will be good, e.g., when doing research on followers of Amma, the hugging guru from Kerala (India), to go and be hugged by Amma, to go to India, to participate in the activities of her ashram, etc., to obtain at least some understanding of the spirituality of these people.

5. For anyone wanting to do research on issues that are intimate to the subjects involved, it is necessary to learn how to interact with the research participants. As all psychologists should know from their professional training, doing a research interview requires training: training in listening, training in holding back one's own opinion, training in not entering into any discussion. It should also be added: training in developing the appropriate attitude of fascination and respect, while keeping one's distance and perhaps even disapproving. Just as it requires training, at least for most psychologists and counselors in general, to be able to speak about sexuality without too much overt embarrassment, it requires training to be able to communicate about issues that may be equally intimate to the research participants and about issues or practices that can be equally non-understandable, disgusting or whatever to the researcher. Also, as we know from research on both sex and religion that many informants will not speak or not speak freely when encountering a person who is just asking questions, it is advisable that the researcher tries to get as close as possible to the subjects she is dealing with, in appearance, sometimes, in the way of speaking, sometimes, just to win confidence and have access to private opinions, feelings, activities. Of course, this is no recommendation to cheat one's research subjects; it is probably best, also ethically most appropriate, to not pretend to be or to be doing as the research participants are doing if this is not really the case. (Although it should be admitted, that it has been fortunate that on some occasions researchers did not reveal too much of themselves and let the subjects be uncorrected in their false assumptions about the researchers..., see, e.g. the classic on failed prophecy by Festinger et al. 1956.)

With this last recommendation we have returned to what has been stated at the beginning of this chapter: this is one of the most difficult aims to achieve for any researcher, but it should be considered a challenge and a professional duty especially for psychologists to be able to learn to speak to and deal with persons whose values they perhaps do not share and whose spiritual practices they perhaps even abhor. A psychologist is, or should be, interested in human beings; she should try to explore the subjectivity of her research participants, learn – in the same way one is trained to conduct psychotherapy – to listen, to be attentive, to find out what is psychologically relevant, all the while postponing private judgment. The difficulty is to not lose one's own standpoint, not to slip into relativism, not to enter into any discussion, but as in any psychological assessment, to get as close as possible while keeping distance. Although other researchers often have to achieve this too, psychologists more than any other researchers in the field of spirituality and religion are professionally trained in this. Let them excel in this psychological skill. Let them take the lead in scientific research on those phenomena that are most specific to and characteristic of human beings: religiosity and spirituality.

Chapter 7
The Question of the Specificity of Religion

A Methodological Excursus

> *Historical studies pursued by active practitioners of a discipline often suffer from a tendency to look for precursors of present day viewpoints or anticipations of current theoretical positions. That is quite understandable if one's primary engagement is with today's issues, but it does not make for very good history. Whether Wundt is cast aside because he offends current orthodoxy or whether he is admired because some of his ideas are seen as sympathetic to modern projects, the aim of the exercise remains justificationist, his name is used to justify situations that developed long after his death. This kind of historiography may have some ornamental or rhetorical value, but it remains trapped within the parameters of the present and therefore cannot supply what only good history can deliver, namely, an illumination of the present through its confrontation with the otherness of the past. In relation to the psychologies of today Wundt's psychology has a quality of otherness that is potentially its most valuable feature. Paying attention to this otherness just might enhance awareness of current biases and preconceptions.*

> (Danziger 2001a, p. 92)[1]

Introduction: Psychology and Its Methodology

Methodological questions seem endemic to psychology, as they are to the social sciences in general. The great philosopher of science Henri Poincaré observed: "The natural sciences talk about their results. The social scientists talk about their methods" (in Berelson and Steiner 1964, p. 14). Although methodology deals with the methods and techniques of empirical research, its issues do not derive from these methods and techniques as such, but from much more fundamental questions regarding the nature of psychology (and of scientific knowledge in general): what is the object of psychology? How can it be properly conceived? Which methods can be called upon or should be developed to explore the object of psychology? Can a

---

[1] This quotation from Danziger refers to Wundt but, as I hope to show, applies equally to James.

single method serve all of the various subfields of psychology? Is psychology a singular science or rather a pluriformity of scientific approaches that presently share little more than the name by which they go? Is psychology a science at all or is it, like history, literary theory, and philosophy, a branch of scholarship different from, but just as academic as, the natural sciences? After more than a century of theory and research psychologists still debate the approaches and paradigms proper to their fields of research. A common complaint has been that in so doing they have frequently defined the latter in terms of the former, that is they adapt their definition of psychology and its subject to what they can investigate with those methods at hand instead of following the old Aristotelian adage that methods should be designed according to the nature of the object to be investigated and – I would add – according to the questions one wants to answer. Until the present day this has resulted in publications on the "crisis in psychology" (one of the earliest being by Hans Driesch 1925) and in pleas to "rethink psychology" (Smith et al. 1995), including its methods (Smith et al. 1995/2003).

Many of these discussions are extensions of opposing trends in the philosophy of science dating from the turn of the twentieth century (see also Chapter 2). United by their opposition to methodological monism, which defends the idea of the unity of scientific method amidst the diversity of subjects under scientific investigation, divergent thinkers nevertheless introduced similar methodological dichotomies in order to claim scholarly-scientific status for the humanities. The philosopher of life (*Lebensphilosoph*) Wilhelm Dilthey (1833–1911) identified understanding and explanation as the approaches of these respective branches of scholarship: when investigating humans and their culture, he claimed, observation alone is not sufficient. We also need to grasp thoughts and motives, which must be discovered by trying to go through them ourselves. We must make inferences about inner states, as opposed to external, observable behavior, by imagining ourselves in the position of the agents. Such a method of understanding Dilthey declared to be basic to all of the humanities. Neo-Kantian thinkers like Wilhelm Windelband (1848–1915) and Heinrich Rickert (1863–1936) likewise refused to model research in human sciences like history and psychology, on Galilean research procedures used by natural sciences like physics or physiology, with their strong emphasis on formulating hypotheses in a mathematical language about law-like uniformities that could be tested experimentally. They stressed instead that the different aims and subjects of scientific research call for different methods (Belzen 2001b; Leezenberg and Vries 2001; Pollmann 1999). Windelband distinguished nomothetic knowledge (knowledge of what "is always" the case across particular situations) from idiographic knowledge (about what "once was"). Nomothetic knowledge is ideally formulated in law-like propositions while idiographic knowledge is not. Corresponding dichotomies have been introduced under such labels as quantitative versus qualitative research methods. It is important to note, however, that present methodological debates in psychology are not merely reiterations or simple continuations of earlier controversies. For instance, idiographic knowledge should not be equated either with what is nowadays referred to as N = 1 methodology or with case studies. The validity or even possibility of this kind of knowledge is still doubted by many contemporary psychologists, even if they

Introduction: Psychology and Its Methodology

allow for so-called qualitative methods. Likewise, Dilthey's (1910) dichotomy between the *Naturwissenschaften* (natural sciences) and *Geisteswissenschaften* (human sciences) has not only been highly influential in psychology, but also had its precursor in this field: Wilhelm Wundt (1832–1920) – today usually only remembered as the founding father of experimental psychology – distinguished another, even more important branch of psychology which he called *Völkerpsychologie* to which he devoted the larger part of his energy and contributed numerous publications, including a ten-volume work by that title between 1900 and 1920.[2]

Current discussions might benefit from taking a look at earlier methodological debates. They often show that in addition to similarities and continuities – which raises the question whether there has been much progress in psychology – there are important deviations from positions defended by the founding fathers of psychology as an academic discipline. Rather than arguing for or against certain methods and techniques in psychology, considering their initial positions may help us to realize what psychology seems to have lost and may result in a challenge to return to its foundations and to take up parts of that unfinished program. Psychology of religion in particular is a branch of psychology well suited and perhaps in need of just such an exercise, as it has recently been characterized as a "field in crisis" (Wulff 2003). According to David Wulff, who probably has the best overview of the field, psychology of religion needs to ask itself; "Is it time to start over?" Religion is a subject that almost every founding father of psychology (Wulff 1997) has addressed, but it has suffered from the loss of investigative breadth of psychology in general and virtually vanished from the field altogether with the rise of behaviorism and the experiment as favored method, even in research on topics that seemed to exclude experimentation (Hood and Belzen 2005). Embarrassment about the subject is also a major reason why psychologists have neglected religion as a research topic (Ragan et al. 1980; Shafranske 1996b). Now that religion and spirituality are once again topics of popular interest in the United States and even in much more secularized Europe, psychology – especially clinical psychology – is rediscovering its interest in the subject too. A rapidly increasing number of publications, symposia and other organizational developments testify to this trend (Belzen 2002a). On the other hand, the psychology of religion is only just large enough a field within psychology to exemplify a number of enduring, general methodological debates.[3]

---

[2]*Völkerpsychologie* should not be translated as "folk psychology," as it usually is, but perhaps rather as cultural psychology (see Danziger 2001a), although – as shall be pointed out later – Wundt's conception differed strikingly from what is nowadays understood by that name. Throughout this chapter, I shall use the original German term to refer to this part of Wundt's psychology.

[3]A number of handbooks testify to the ongoing quarrels about empirical-analytical versus hermeneutical approaches, as well as about quantitative versus qualitative research methods (see Paloutzian and Park 2005). A recent German "introduction" to the psychology of religion (Henning et al. 2003) was unable to present matters pertaining to research methods in an integrated way and contains two different chapters on methods, one on quantitative methods (Wolfradt and Müller-Plath 2003), and one on qualitative methods (Popp-Baier 2003).

Let us examine, for example, the approach introduced and defended by William James (1842–1910), arguably the founding father of psychology in the USA. It is well known that he is widely referred to by psychologists, but his theory and method are hardly ever followed. This was evident on the centennial of the publication of his *Principles of Psychology* (1890), as it was even more clearly when in 2002 the centennial of his *The Varieties of Religious Experiences* (1902/2002) was celebrated at many conferences and symposia (Belzen 2006; Carrette 2005). It seems that James is dealt with more seriously within philosophy than psychology, however. For decades the *Varieties* has been important to psychologists of religion as James' celebrity legitimized religion as a topic for psychological research as an academic enterprise. But, even amongst the small group of researchers in the psychology of religion James did not have any real followers (Belzen 2005b). The *Varieties*, like most of James' work in psychology, has not generated a dynamic theory, created any specific method or technique, nor led to the development of a school in the sense of a coherent group of researchers or research projects drawing on the same inspiration, using the same theories and methods and working towards a common goal. It seems that the psychology of religion, like psychology in general, is doing little more than paying lip service to the honor and memory of that grand old man William James. This is a rather paradoxical state of affairs which, with regard to methodology, was nicely summarized some decades ago by James Dittes who wrote:

> [James'] psychology is not employed by the field, and, far more importantly, his spirit does not inspire it. If William James is honored as the "father" of the psychology of religion, it is in a very special sense, which can be interpreted in terms of ambivalence appropriate to the psychology of religion. He is revered as a great and distant hero but hardly heeded. He is the liberating Moses, who called down a plague on the houses of both the religious and the medical Establishment and who led the psychology of religion into independent existence. But his recommendations as to how that independent existence should be conducted are ignored as thoroughly as the builders of the golden calf ignored those of the law-giving Moses. (Dittes 1973, pp. 328–329)

Today, most of the psychology of religion contradicts William James' most essential convictions. Many practitioners still adhere to empiricism, objectivism and generalizability as the criterion of good scholarship in this field (Hood and Belzen 2005). Also, in those areas where psychology in general (though still too rarely within the psychology of religion) is developing and testing new methodological vistas, there is usually no longer any reference made to James and certainly not to his *Varieties*. As the *Varieties* is obviously compatible with qualitative, interpretive and hermeneutical methods (such as biographical analysis, N = 1 methodology, case studies and document analysis), I shall not deal with this issue any further. I will focus instead on the methodological debates his *Varieties* generated in Europe and concentrate on the remarkable objections (and alternatives) brought forward by Wilhelm Wundt, the founder of psychology as an academic discipline on the other side of the Atlantic.

Wundt Contra James

It is not generally known that Wundt devoted a substantial part of his work to the psychology of religion. His *Völkerpsychologie* contains three extensive volumes on the subject, entitled *Mythos und Religion* (*Völkerpsychologie* Volumes 4–6). In the preface to part I of this subproject (*Völkerpsychologie* Volume 4) he wrote that myth and religion are "surely those subjects of common life that more compellingly than others require to be dealt with psychologically" (Wundt 1905/1920, p. vi). Wundt thought it curious that although interest in these subjects was clearly increasing both within and outside the academy, psychologists were not researching them. This was not because they were busy with "more important and higher things," but because they were so involved with elementary, preliminary concerns (largely still overlapping with physiological ones) that they had no time to investigate the life of the soul itself in order to approach the complicated problems of the genesis of myth and religious development with psychology's newly acquired methods and perspectives (Wundt 1905/1920, p. v).

Wundt's statements are surprising in several respects and raise a number of questions. Was he not aware of James' *Varieties* (1902/2002), or other early works in the psychology of religion (such as those published by the "Clark-School" (Vandekemp 1992): Stanley Hall 1904; James Leuba 1896; Edwin Starbuck 1899) when he published his first edition of *Myth and Religion* (1905)? The answer to this question is highly likely to be negative; something else was probably at stake. For when Wundt published the second edition of *Myth and Religion* in 1910 he did not change or delete these sentences even though by that time the number of publications on the psychology of religion was rapidly increasing and even a professional psychological journal for the field had been founded in 1904 by Stanley Hall (1846–1924), another giant in the history of psychology. Moreover, the German translation of the *Varieties* appeared in 1907 and had instigated enormous interest in German-speaking countries; also in 1907 a German journal for the psychology of religion had been established (containing Sigmund Freud's (1907/1959) very first contribution to the field). It seems certain that something other than a lack of information or historical precision was the reason Wundt republished the same preface in the third (corrected and updated) edition of his *Myth and Religion*, Part I in 1920 because by then, religion had become one of the leading topics in psychology (see the regular announcements and reviews in the *Psychological Bulletin* of the time), and was attracting an ever-increasing number of practitioners, especially in Germany (Belzen 1996c). In this third edition Wundt did discuss James' contribution to the psychology of religion, but curiously without mentioning the *Varieties* at all and, even more surprisingly, he still failed to mention any other effort made in this field (including the establishment of a second German journal in 1914). Was Wundt not aware of approaches in the psychology of religion other than James'? As it is almost certain he was (he had even been formally invited to participate in an association for the discipline), why then did he neglect them? Finally, what kind of psychology of religion had he himself proposed?

Since the focus of this chapter is not the history of the psychology of religion, I shall not present a summary of Wundt's thought but review the methodological and conceptual debates on the psychology of religion at the time, debates that neither were nor are restricted to this branch of psychology. I submit that what was at stake in the discussion (or rather, lack of ample discussion) between James, Wundt and other pioneers in the field, were profound differences regarding the nature of psychology, its methodology and theoretical presuppositions. These differences continue to haunt psychology to the present. In order to understand and analyze these debates and substantiate those claims already made, we shall need to take into account some historical facts and developments. This historical contextualization serves an analytic purpose, however. I shall first review methodological aspects of the debates following the publication of the German edition of James' *Varieties* and then introduce some of the combatants. These past debates are astonishingly similar to those that present day psychologists are engaged in.

The Varieties in Germany

James owed the 1907 German translation and publication of his *Varieties* to theologian Georg Wobbermin (1869–1943), a systematic theologian interested in the scientific exploration of religion and affiliated with the prominent universities of Berlin and later, Göttingen. His own turn-of-the-century text was one of the earliest on theology's relationship to psychology (Wobbermin 1901). He became renowned for his efforts to introduce a "psychology-of-religion-circle" into theology (Klünker 1985). Although the *Varieties* was already well known in German-speaking Europe in its original English version, Wobbermin translated it into German hoping to further stimulate interest in the psychology of religion (Wobbermin 1907/1914, p. iv). In the foreword to the first edition Wobbermin acknowledged that the Americans had made the single most important contribution to the psychology of religion and he mentioned James' *Varieties* as their current masterpiece (Wobbermin 1907/1914, p. iv). From the perspective of the history of ideas, or perhaps more precisely from the perspective of the history of theology, he saw Friedrich Schleiermacher (1768–1834) and Albrecht Ritschl (1822–1889) as James' predecessors. He also mentioned the names of two Germans who were also engaged in the psychology of religion: Ernst Troeltsch and Gustav Theodor Ferdinand Franz Vorbrodt – Who were they?

Troeltsch (1865–1923) was a systematic theologian and a keen thinker in the philosophy and sociology of religion. His paper entitled: "Psychology and Epistemology in the Science of Religion" (Troeltsch 1905), has become quite well known and is quoted by numerous thinkers on the psychology of religion. In it, Troeltsch reflected on the foundations of the discipline and tried to answer the question whether and to what extent the psychology of religion can deal with truth.

The Varieties in Germany 107

He concluded that the psychology of religion is "only" an empirical discipline (that is, it can merely register and cluster phenomena), and that questions about truths within religion can only be solved by the philosophy of religion. Troeltsch's position became one of the twentieth century's dominant views. Despite his interest in psychology – demonstrated earlier in his reviews of books on the relationship between psychology and religion – Troeltsch did not truly belong to this field.

Vorbrodt (1860–1929) was a Protestant pastor with a strong interest in psychology which he expected to modernize theology and the church. His interests lay in reconceptualizing theological and religious themes in biological–psychological categories (Vorbrodt 1904). His efforts – due to his rather confused writing style – did not meet with much sympathy among reviewers. After he heard of efforts to conduct empirical research on religion by Americans and Frenchmen, he became one of the most active promoters of an empirically based psychology of religion in Germany (although he himself never conducted any empirical research). In addition to actively following foreign publications and reporting them to diverse theological (and sometimes also philosophical) audiences, he developed a number of activities to promote the field (e.g., in 1906 he taught the first course on the subject in Germany, and in 1907 he co-founded the German "Journal for the Psychology of Religion"). He also influenced several individuals who later made important contributions to the psychology of religion in Germany (for a broader treatment of Vorbrodt's activities and work, see Belzen 2001–2002).

In the preface to the German translation of James' *Varieties*, Wobbermin criticized Troeltsch only mildly, for as a theologian Wobbermin was primarily interested in the question of truth which, in his opinion, could not be clarified by psychology. The truth that matters in religion, he said, is absolute truth, that is, a truth which differs from that which comes into play in other forms of human perception. Since he believed that truth is fundamental to every religion, one cannot avoid it in the sciences of religion, to which the history of religions and psychology of religion belong; it must, in fact, be regarded as constitutive for the science of religion – "even though it must be emphasized fundamentally and from the beginning that the final, decisive answer can only be given by religion itself – that is only by faith as faith" (Wobbermin 1907/1914, p. xi). The psychology of religion was to be of limited use in this regard however; it could not determine by itself what is essentially and specifically religious in the phenomena it studied. Troeltsch, Wobbermin asserted, correctly understood and investigated this subject, but Vorbrodt, who held the opposite view (i.e., that psychological facts can indeed represent a criterion for epistemological or generally normative decision making), erred. Vorbrodt overestimated what psychology could accomplish. James, on the other hand, would have seen things as did Troeltsch and Wobbermin, and merely failed to state this with sufficient clarity. In his preface Wobbermin repeatedly stated that he did not unreservedly support everything in James' text (he even added a new subtitle to it), but he did regard it as sufficiently important and effective "in awakening an interest in reflections on [the] psychology of religion" to translate it into German (Wobbermin 1907/1914, p. iv).

Questionnaires and Statistics Versus Case-Studies

It was probably more than just this critique that caused Vorbrodt to engage James (and also indirectly Wobbermin) at length soon after in a place which does not seem entirely appropriate, the preface to the German edition of Starbuck's *Psychology of Religion* (1899; German: 1909). Vorbrodt contrasted Starbuck to James and judged the latter very harshly. In his opinion Starbuck's work represented a "completion, perhaps even the foundation [...] for James' abnormal psychology" (Vorbrodt 1909, p. ix). He admitted to being somewhat sharp in his characterization of James' *Varieties*, but commented that the significance of the *Varieties* was really only in the fact that James had such a widespread reputation in psychology and that he offered "sensation": a "number of deviant examples whose relevance impressed Germany's theologians, tired as they were of conventional rationalism" (Vorbrodt 1909, p. ix). Vorbrodt then stated his criticism of James (and of Wobbermin, who in Vorbrodt's opinion misinterpreted James) in a few sentences:

> That which James offers is at best a popular psychology of religious questions, partly reminiscent of Schleiermacher's oratorical romanticism. Wobbermin refers to this, but is in error when he takes the individualizing diversity of religious views in Schleiermacher's thought as reason to find something similar in James' book. James' *Varieties* refers to a randomly selected collection of experiences, Schleiermacher's systematic tendency is to unite the many links and forces of the universe into one: James particularly wishes to establish pluralistic idealism, a philosophical inclination, that lets his book on religion appear not so much as *psychological*, as Wobbermin pretends, but rather as *philosophical*. (Vorbrodt 1909, p. ix; italics original)

While this criticism still deals mainly with the history of ideas, Vorbrodt soon expresses a rather more methodological-psychological criticism. James, he claimed, did not want to carry out a comparative investigation of the types of religious experience, for

> [James] does not provide a systematic classification, nor does he close with a clear overview of the varieties. James is less concerned with uniformity [...] than with differences, and not with pathology – as Wobbermin and others erroneously assume – for conditions that appear to be of a pathological nature are, in James' opinion, certainly healthy and normal as variants of general experience. (Vorbrodt 1909, p. x)[4]

Vorbrodt then concludes that James must not be regarded as a psychologist of religion – an opinion opposite to that held by Wobbermin, who regarded the *Varieties* as the "main work" of Anglo-Saxon psychology of religion! Vorbrodt briefly inferred that Starbuck's, and not James', psychology of religion was the first true work in the psychology of religion presented to the German public (Vorbrodt 1909, p. x).

---

[4] This should be understood correctly: Vorbrodt does not attempt to protect James against Wobbermin and others' false interpretation. Vorbrodt meant that James failed to view a number of the case histories he selected as pathological. Wobbermin and others incorrectly interpret them as meaning that James was concerned with the analysis of abnormal phenomena, which accounts for Wobbermin's addition of the word "pathology" in the subtitle of his translation. That which Wobbermin recognized as pathological, James took as healthy, according to Vorbrodt.

Wobbermin naturally responded to the challenge. Just a year later he discussed Vorbrodt repeatedly in his article "The Current Status of Psychology of Religion" (Wobbermin 1910). For brevity's sake, I will only touch on these passages in passing. Wobbermin actually has very little to counter Vorbrodt's criticism. He provides no real arguments to support his assertion that James continues to offer the most stimulation and greatest advancement. Vorbrodt's criticism, Wobbermin asserted, is based on an overestimation of Starbuck's promising statistical investigations in the psychology of conversion and on an underestimation of the eminent psychological contents of James' *Varieties*. Wobbermin failed to indicate why he considered the *Varieties* to have eminent psychological content, however. He merely pointed out that James had already used empirical material gleaned from Starbuck (which in itself does not make the *Varieties* a psychological investigation), and that a German psychologist as esteemed as William Stern (1871–1938) had written: "the true value of the work is undoubtedly in its psychological content" (Stern 1909, p. 466). In this article, Wobbermin essentially added nothing to the arguments he put forth in his preface to James' book in favor of the *Varieties*. He commented, however, that Starbuck's book falsely bears the title "Religionspsychologie," since it is exclusively a study of conversion. His text clearly shows his preference for Leuba over Starbuck.

Methodological Preferences in the Psychology of Religion

One might wonder why Vorbrodt and Wobbermin, who were after all both theologians, were so much at odds in their evaluation of James' *Varieties,* among other things. I shall disregard here whether this was due to personal differences or whether their disagreements were related to differing theological viewpoints. I shall concentrate instead on the psychological aspects of the debate. It then seems that the two are separated by differing methodological preferences. Wobbermin was comprehensively educated and informed about psychology, but nonetheless did not develop into a psychologist. He never conducted empirical research in psychology and does not seem to have occupied himself with its research methods; he never published psychological interpretations of religious phenomena; his works on the psychology of religion, though interesting, remain almost exclusively on epistemological ground, wherein he proved himself to be a competent and systematic theologian. Furthermore, he remained largely active within theological circles. In some of these ways Vorbrodt was clearly different from Wobbermin, for he had actually set out to develop his own psychological approach, no matter of what nature or value it may have been. After he crossed paths with the empirical approach to the psychology of religion, he eagerly read its literature and studied its methods. He actively sought to work together with empiricists of various orientations outside theology and although he did not publish any empirical studies himself, he frequently reported on them in his essays on the psychology of religion and called for active participation in empirical projects (of which there were few in Germany at that time). Despite his erudition, he was not a systematic thinker like Wobbermin or Troeltsch. Perhaps partly due to his work as a pastor, he always paid close attention to the relevance of – as he called it – "applied psychology of religion"[5] to practical theology. If one were to schematize, one might summarize the contrast between Vorbrodt and Wobbermin as "empiricist versus theoretician."

While psychologists and social scientists generally like schematizations, classifications and typologies such as "empiricist" and "theoretician," these often fail to do justice to details. This is also the case here; while Vorbrodt was certainly more empirically oriented and informed than Wobbermin, he nevertheless did not become an empiricist in the general sense of the word. On the other hand, Wobbermin has often said that the psychology of religion is an empirical discipline (although he consistently pointed out that it could not be solely empirical). The fact that the *Varieties* was evaluated so differently by Vorbrodt and Wobbermin perhaps hinges less on the "empirical vs theoretical" issue than on *what* empirical research in the psychology of religion was supposed to look like. The root of their differences may therefore lie in a methodological difference such as that between James and Starbuck. Starbuck conducted his research by collecting questionnaires from persons who, he hoped, constituted a representative sample of general religious experience within a larger population. James, on the other hand, selected documents of a rather extreme nature (from, among other things, Starbuck's empirical data). Thus, his material is representative not so much of a population of individuals as of the phenomenon to be studied. Further, James was of the opinion that "phenomena are best understood when placed within their series, studied in their germ and in their overripe decay, and composed within their exaggerated and degenerated kindred" (James 1902/1982, p. 382). Finally, he utilized an analytic method unlike Starbuck's: where the latter chose a statistical approach (he coded the answers on his questionnaires into different categories, counted, calculated and presented his results in tabular and graphic form), James was considerably more hermeneutic. James quoted in detail from the selected document and added background information and commentary. Starbuck set out to determine the frequencies of the phenomena and their characteristics while James attempted to bring the phenomena themselves to his readers. He described and commented empathetically so as to enable his audience to develop a feel for the subject. Both authors worked descriptively – Starbuck statistically and James in a literary manner.[6] It is not known which

---

[5] By which he meant something approximating contemporary pastoral psychology; this however is only one of the areas to which the insights and results of the psychology of religion can be applied. Indeed, applications are not only possible within pastoral settings, but also in all sorts of applied psychology in general (e.g., health psychology, psychotherapy).

[6] James' method is more often characterized as "phenomenological" (see, e.g., Edie 1987), which is, however, somewhat problematic. The *Varieties* is certainly not phenomenological in the sense of phenomenological psychology as was developed in the twentieth century by, for example, Husserl, Merleau-Ponty, Bühler, Van den Berg, Rogers and many others (see Misiak and Sexton 1973). At best, the *Varieties* is phenomenological in the sense of being descriptive and "open-minded," something that might be called "proto-phenomenological" (see Wilshire 1968). Wulff (1997, p. 486) called the *Varieties* "a vicarious phenomenology." See also Spiegelberg (1972, 1982). In general, a great many contributions that offer nothing more than description are incorrectly labeled "phenomenological" nowadays.

Methodological Preferences in the Psychology of Religion

American Vorbrodt first read, but it is clear that the seemingly "exact" statistical method, as applied by the Clark school, impressed him considerably. As he understood it, the psychology of religion was practiced here in a way that would impress even those prejudiced in favor of natural science. In the case of James' more familiar style, he obviously sensed the theoretical and philosophical problems more clearly than in Starbuck's case. As mentioned earlier, he repeatedly tried to gain support for conducting empirical work by questionnaire. Wobbermin, on the other hand, seems to have been relatively unimpressed by Starbuck's work. Despite recognizing its value, he obviously did not regard it as highly as Vorbrodt. The *Varieties* was clearly more to his liking (although he in no way agreed with James' philosophy), and he regarded it as more suited to fostering the psychology of religion in Germany – his reason for translating and publishing it.

Thus the differing answers to the question of which methods and techniques should be employed in the psychology of religion are more likely an explanation for the various evaluations of the *Varieties* than an "empiricist vs theoretician"-type comparison of Vorbrodt and Wobbermin as such. Yet this is not a complete explanation either, for later years show that Vorbrodt distanced himself from the questionnaire method. As early as 1911 he wrote that Starbuck's method might be too leveling and that the questionnaire method supplied "artificially-induced testimony images" (Vorbrodt 1911, p. xii). Vorbrodt seems to have developed the view that questionnaires were not always the best possible method and that one might wish to give preference to other methods in the psychology of religion. Obviously this time influenced by the seminal Swiss psychologist Théodore Flournoy (1854–1920), he wrote that it was sometimes better to use "religious psychogrammes in the manner of medical histories [...] statements made more casually, picked up like observations of the stars" (by which he meant "factual materials offering themselves in history, biography, free forms of expression, unsought or undesired experiences"). He believed this all the more meaningful when

> the artificial inducement of religiosity, viz. questions posed and statements about it, are contradictory to its psychological nature as spontaneous appearance of phenomenon, and lead to certain psychic changes as in no other field; free observation, anamnesis, recording of religious facts should then be preferred. (Vorbrodt 1911, p. xii–xiii)

It is unclear why Vorbrodt changed his methodological preferences, but it seems certain that – despite the polemics with Wobbermin – it was not a change in his evaluation of the *Varieties* or of James in general which stimulated him to develop a stronger interest in – to use a modern expression – case studies like Flournoy's. In his preface to the German edition of Flournoy's texts Vorbrodt again expressed clear criticism of James, stating that while it was not wrong that Wobbermin demanded a transcendental psychology[7] to uncover the motives and powers of religious life, it had been none other than Flournoy (and therefore not James), who had

---

[7]A term about which Vorbrodt was somewhat disparaging, writing that it had "an uncomfortable ring of spiritualism" (Vorbrodt 1911, p. xv).

given an empirical foundation to this concern, as his own selection of Flournoy's case studies demonstrated. He also stated – and here too criticism of James can be discerned – that these case studies were cases of "normal piety" (Vorbrodt 1911, p. xv), "more or less normal cases" (p. xviii), while James worked with pathological material (see above). As late as 1918 Vorbrodt made much the same criticism of James and Wobbermin. James, he wrote, published his *Varieties*

> not for the sake of the psychology of religion, the latter was – as must be emphasized time and again – merely a side product of his idealistic pluralism, of which the reader of the German edition knows nothing[8] and which mattered more to James' in the *Varieties* than the oft-mentioned pragmatism. (Vorbrodt 1918, p. 439)

Historically, it is also possible that criticism of questionnaires as voiced by Stählin, a participant in Vorbrodt's 1906 course on the psychology of religion, caused him to change his methodological orientation.[9] Who was Stählin, and what did he have to say about methods in the psychology of religion?

Experiments Versus Questionnaires

Wilhelm Stählin (1883–1975) had initially trained to become a Protestant pastor, but his interest in the psychological analysis of religion led him to enroll in a doctoral program in psychology. He went to Würzburg to study with Oswald Külpe (1862–1915), who had been Wundt's first assistant in the Leipzig laboratory for experimental psychology. After being appointed professor in Würzburg, Külpe developed his own approach within experimental psychology, an approach in which Stählin was educated and which he introduced to the psychology of religion (Stählin 1914b), after defending an empirical-methodological study on the "psychology and statistics of metaphors" as a doctoral dissertation in 1913 which he published in the leading German psychological journal (Stählin 1914a).

Having conducted extensive statistical analyses himself, Stählin often criticized statistical work by other psychologists sharply and with great wit. In his excellent review of Starbuck's *Religionspsychologie* (1899/1909) Stählin highlights many positive aspects of the work. He generally agreed with Starbuck regarding the principles of the psychology of religion, for instance when the latter stated that

---

[8] Wobbermin omitted the relevant passage in the translation. He defended himself by pointing out that the *Varieties* was not dependent upon James' pluralistic metaphysics and that the omitted final chapter was more suggestive than explanatory. Additionally, James had "just approved" of Wobbermin's procedure (Wobbermin 1910, p. 535).

[9] Historically, it may also be that Vorbrodt's personal encounter with Flournoy at the International Conference of Psychology in Geneva (1909) so impressed him that he immersed himself in the latter's work and eventually decided to translate several of his works into German. These questions cannot be answered since the relevant sources are missing (neither Vorbrodt's personal papers nor correspondence with colleagues could be traced).

Experiments Versus Questionnaires

the psychology of religion should not use methods other than those used by general psychology – that its only prerequisite was the "fruitful working hypothesis" of the regularity of all psychic occurrences (Stählin 1910, pp. 7–8). Stählin is only moderately satisfied with other aspects of Starbuck's thinking, however. The latter's physiological investigations shed light on the role of religion in the development of the young, but for an understanding of religious life they are at best an illustration – not an explanation. Additionally, Stählin accuses Starbuck of many errors, both statistical and tabular (Stählin 1910, p. 6), of confusing coincidence and causality (when Starbuck asserted that religious awakening is an effect of sexual awakening; Stählin 1910, p. 2), of over-generalizing (since results probably apply only to a certain sector of persons questioned; Stählin 1910, p. 4), and of not giving more consideration to doubts about the questionnaire method.[10] Stählin also expressed doubts about many of those questioned (e.g., a boy just 7 years old), and reproached Starbuck for not considering that in the process of "conversion" one almost always adopts a religious way of thinking and seeing things, virtually excluding the likelihood of a faultless description of one's own former inner life (Stählin 1910, p. 5). After noting that Starbuck shows no empirical evidence for many supposed "facts" (e.g. the preparation of the conversion crisis in the subconscious), Stählin pursued a more general theme:

> The use of questionnaires and statistics in the psychology of religion has the greatest weakness in that this method never accesses more than certain external signs and symptoms,[11] while the next and most important task of psychology of religion must be the pressing analysis of the psychic facts themselves. A comprehensively designed effort would have to show whether published autobiographies of religious personalities would not, after all, offer more material than the unreliable reports of many who are wholly untrained in self-observation. (Stählin 1910, p. 7)

Stählin dealt increasingly critically with the questionnaire as a method in the psychology of religion in several other publications as well. According to him, psychology must include introspection ("observation of self"). In line with his contemporaries, he distinguished between the researchers' own self-observation and the information derived from other people's self-observation. The ideal situation is that in which researchers who have been critically trained to observe themselves combine these results with an analysis of others' self-observation. The less dogmatic or prejudiced the latter are, the better. Stählin (1911) points explicitly to the value of (what in contemporary language is called) unobtrusive measures (autobiographies, memoirs, diaries, letters, sermons, religious poetry and others). Next to this, he left room for interviews. Questionnaires, however, provide information of limited use (despite

---

[10] Stählin named three: a most weak talent for introspection (according to "experimental" psychologists of the day – a group which Stählin trained to join – this talent must be trained); an imperfect memory; and the suggestive effect of questionnaires.

[11] Two pages earlier Stählin formulated sharply: "Despite the opposite intention, often instead of real experiences only 'opinions' are reported" (Stählin 1910, p. 5). Stählin's criticisms are echoed in current methodological discussions (cf., e.g., Westerhof 1994).

generating large amounts of data): there is considerable doubt as to whether informants provide real and honest answers to written "questioning." Statistical analysis does indeed provide some guarantee against arbitrary conclusions, but it can never improve the poor quality of the data, and one can hardly draw psychologically significant conclusions from numbers. At best, questionnaires provide information about average religiosity in a certain population and are consequently more interesting to sociologists than to psychologists. There are too many flaws in the information derived by means of questionnaires: self-observation is insufficient (a point to which we will come in a moment), reports are often untrustworthy, formulations imprecise, side issues prevail over central processes and opinions rather than facts are articulated (Stählin 1912, p. 402).

Although Stählin allowed for the analysis of exceptionally intensive religiosity by means of case studies, he clearly changed his methodological orientation after he met Külpe. With regard to case study analysis, he preferred Flournoy to James' *Varieties*. He too considered the *Varieties* a book by a "philosopher" on the aberrations of religious consciousness. In French contributions to the psychology of religion, he perceived most notably the pitfalls of confusing intensive religiosity with mental illness or being mainly interested in abnormal phenomena (Stählin 1911, pp. 48–49).[12] During his training in Würzburg Stählin was instructed in what he learned to see as an ideal method to ask other people about their religious self-observation: the experiment. The word "experiment" was employed very differently from its contemporary usage in psychology, however. Essentially, it meant to deliberately produce the phenomena the researcher wants research participants to report by way of self-observation. In his 1912 article on questionnaires in the psychology of religion Stählin supplied nothing more than the fictive example of asking someone to attend a religious service and immediately afterwards questioning them about their impressions (Stählin 1912, p. 399). After his doctoral training in the psychological laboratory in Würzburg however, he reported on an experiment he himself had carried out. He had 25 people react to 227 quotations with religious content in order to find out: "how they were understood, facilitating or obstructing factors, which were best retained, how plastic language would be perceived and how it would work, to what deep impressions would connect and of what sort, and similar questions" (Stählin 1914b, p. 118). It was an experiment conducted in the tradition inaugurated by Wundt, a tradition of performing "experiments" very differently from what is nowadays understood by that term in psychology. In contrast to contemporary experiments, subjects then were not usually naïve regarding the actual object of research, they were not chosen randomly but deliberately, based on the extent to which they were trained in introspection, in order to gather a group which would report as faithfully as possible what went on internally when exposed to a stimulus. Stählin and others considered this most scientific, as the same procedure was

---

[12] Although Stählin did not mention them, he must have had authors like Ernest Murisier (1892, 1901) and Theodule Ribot (1884/1894, 1896/1903) in mind, representatives of the French psychopathological school in the psychology of religion.

The Genetic Approach Versus Experiments 115

used in a standardized way with all subjects and all reactions were noted (in later experiments even reaction times were measured).[13] In terms of what is now the common parlance of methods and techniques in psychology, this "experiment" clearly belonged to the so-called "qualitative" methods. As the German *Zeitschrift for Religionspsychologie* ('Journal for the Psychology of Religion') ceased publication in 1913, Stählin established the *Archiv für Religionspsychologie* ('Archive for the Psychology of Religion') in 1914 in order to foster this "exact-scientific" approach in the psychology of religion. He even founded an Association for the Psychology of Religion to support this new journal. (Well-known psychologists such as Kurt Koffka, Oswald Külpe, Harald Höffding, August Messer, and Théodore Flournoy served on the board of the journal and the association.)

The Genetic Approach Versus Experiments

As one would expect, the inaugurator of experimental psychology, Wilhelm Wundt, shared Stählin's criticism of the use of questionnaires in psychology. He sneeringly criticized "some French and American psychologists" who tried to gather self-observations by spreading out questionnaires and who thought they were doing scientific work of the same precision and value as the experiment (Wundt 1907, p. 359). He ridiculed them by imagining a situation in which pedagogues, teachers and other professionals distributed questionnaires to their pupils actually believing that they were doing "scientific work"; little did he know that, in fact, large parts of psychological research in the twentieth century would precisely follow this plan (see the preceding chapter)! In an article on the psychology of religion he spoke equally critically about "the so-called 'psychology of religion-method,' that is, a motley collection of statistics on ecstatic conditions" (Wundt 1911, p. 108), by which he may well have meant the work of the Clark School as published by Starbuck (1899/1909). In this same article Wundt also severely criticized James' *Varieties,* asserting that the American's testimonies of religious experiences "do not deserve in any way" the name of a psychology of religion nor that of psychology in a more general Jamesian sense (Wundt 1911, p. 103). Wundt explained why the cases James described lacked "just about everything [...] for a psychology of religion":

> Neither have the conditions under which the manifestations came into existence been determined, nor are the latter themselves subjected to a psychological analysis, since this in turn would only be possible based upon a determination of those conditions and of the relationships to other psychical processes. Among those conditions in this case the historical ones are of prime importance. (Wundt 1911, p. 106)

---

[13] This is the reason that Karl Girgensohn (1875–1925), who became the best known and most influential representative of the experimental approach in the psychology of religion, also considered the Freudian psychoanalytic situation as "experimental": everything the patient said during their "free association" was taken with equal seriousness. He found the experiments as performed in the Würzburg School more precise, however (Girgensohn 1921/1930, pp. 23–25).

116 The Question of the Specificity of Religion

According to Wundt, James himself did not regard the *Varieties* as a contribution to the psychology of religion but as examples that prepared for a more thorough exposition of his pragmatic philosophy of religion, an exposition he announced in the final chapter of his *Varieties*. (James had pointed out in other publications as well that his pragmatic philosophy was independent of his psychology.) Wobbermin thus made a grave error when he omitted the very chapter James considered the most important part of the *Varieties*, as it outlined and prepared his further philosophical treatise on religion (Wundt 1911, p. 94).[14] It seems to have been important to Wundt that people understand that the *Varieties* is not a psychological study, for it

> naturally shows major gaps since it only takes a limited number of occurrences into account, and it gives rise to the suspicion that it makes this selection based on criteria unrelated to psychology. (Wundt 1911, p. 107)

On the other hand, Wundt did not side with Stählin in the latter's preference for the experimental approach to psychology. As we have already noted, he completely ignored work by Stählin and other early psychologists of religion and did not criticize or even refer to it. Part of the reason for this must have been the serious methodological controversy between Wundt and the Würzburg School on the applications of the experiment and the nature of psychology. As noted, Stählin and later adherents to the experimental approach in the psychology of religion were trained in the tradition of the Würzburg School. This school differed from Wundt in that it considered experimental research on the so-called higher psychic processes, thinking being foremost among these, both possible and legitimate. Wundt, however, had stated almost from the outset of his involvement in psychology that experimentation was only applicable in the field of physiological psychology. Wundt conceived of a methodological plurality in psychology as he considered "the psychic" (*das Psychische*), psychology's object, to be found not only in individuals but also represented in products on the level of society (primarily among them language, myth and ethics/morality). In his *Methodology* (Part II of his *Logik*, Wundt 1883) he distinguished as "means, methods and principles of psychology": (1) the inner observation,[15] (2) the psychophysical experiment, (3) the comparative-psychological method, and (4) the historical-psychological method. It was just one of the many outlines Wundt gave of psychology and its methods, outlines that differed and sometimes contradicted substantially (Hoorn and Verhage 1980). Important here is that Wundt increasingly came to see psychology as both a natural and a human science and that he even regarded psychology as basic to *all* human sciences. It is also important to note however, that in so doing he held fast to his idea of one all-embracing psychology of which individual psychology (which he sometimes equated with experimental

---

[14] Apparently Wundt had not read Wobbermin's (1910) defense against this same reproach by Vorbrodt (1909), although Wobbermin had published his defense in a psychological, not a theological, journal.

[15] Wundt opposed this inner observation to self-observation, failing, however, to make the difference clear and to explain how the results of "inner observation" could be reported.

The Genetic Approach Versus Experiments 117

psychology) was only a minor part. The larger part, which he eventually came to declare the more important branch of the discipline, he called *Völkerpsychologie* (Wundt 1888).

As necessary background, we should remember that Wundt's philosophy was thoroughly collectivistic, not individualistic. It was collectivistic in two ways that are important for an understanding of his thinking about psychology. On the one hand, for Wundt social order and cultural products represent phenomena that cannot be explained in terms of individual psychology; on the other hand, culture is implicated in the individual psyche. An individual's psychic functioning cannot be understood without taking into account his or her "mental environment" (*geistige Umgebung*); an isolated individual mind cannot exist, it is an "abstraction" and as such "arbitrary" (Wundt, in Danziger 2001a, p. 85). In the introduction to the first volume of his *Völkerpsychologie*, Wundt wrote that the common view of psychology as the science that "investigates facts of immediate experience, as presented by the subjective consciousness" is too limited because it does not pursue an analysis of the phenomena that result from the mental interaction of a multitude of individuals. It was not Wundt's intention to plead for a kind of "applied" psychology, as for example, in applied psychoanalysis, where cultural products are explored for the role individual psychic processes have had in their production and maintenance. Wundt opposed the terminology of "applying" psychology (*Anwendung*) to culture in this way. Instead he advocated an extension (*Ausdehnung*) of psychology to the level of culture, which he conceived as a "theoretical science" (as opposed to an applied science; Wundt 1900/1997, pp. 241–242). In his view, sciences such as history, ethnology and other human sciences were "auxiliary" to *Völkerpsychologie*, which would uncover "the general psychic processes, underlying the development of human communities and the origin of common spiritual products of general value" (Wundt 1900/1997, p. 247). It was a rather ambitious program and one is justified in asking how much of it Wundt actually realized himself. Let us first return to his methodological discussion with the Würzburg School, however.

Wundt considered the experiment inadequate as a research method to investigate "higher psychic processes." His discussion with the Würzburgers dealt precisely with this issue: Külpe, Bühler and others were of the opinion that it was possible to investigate human thinking by means of experimentation. For Wundt however, the data for human thinking could not be revealed by individual scores in experimental designs, as if thinking was a feature of the individual human mind. Thinking could only be investigated in the context of the psychology of language, a natural subject for *Völkerpsychologie*, not for individual psychology. The disagreement between Wundt and the Würzburgers was fundamental: Wundt considered experimentation inadequate for the study of cultural phenomena. Unfortunately in his discussion with Karl Bühler (Bühler 1908, 1909) about the appropriateness of experimentation to investigate thinking, Wundt himself contributed to the reduction of this principally methodological debate to a discussion about methods only (Holzkamp 1980). He tried to show in detail that what Bühler did could not be properly called an "experiment"; Wundt (1907, 1908) called it, somewhat pejoratively, a "questioning-method" (*Ausfragemethode*). Neither Bühler nor Wundt elaborated more principal

118   The Question of the Specificity of Religion

viewpoints about psychology during these discussions. At this point we have enough material however, to answer our initial question as to why Wundt neglected work in the spirit of the Würzburg School within the psychology of religion.

To explicate and summarize: Wundt had three reasons for his opposition to the employment of the experiment in the psychology of religion. Firstly, but least importantly, he did not consider experiments as conducted by Stählin – inspired and supervised by adherents of the Würzburg School such as Karl Bühler and Karl Marbe (Stählin's promoter) – to be real experiments at all. Secondly, even if experiments to his liking had been utilized, Wundt would still have rejected the research as he considered the use of an individual psychological method (like the experiment) inappropriate to investigate higher psychic processes that rely on cultural phenomena. Finally, reversing the latter argument, Wundt believed religion was a subject of *Völkerpsychologie*, a domain which he wished to investigate with another method, a method he designated in different terms of which "genetic approach" or "historical-comparative method" have become best known. In order to better see these methods, we must briefly examine the outlines of his own psychology of religion.

Wundtian Psychology of Religion

Although quite a number of publications deal, sometimes extensively, with Wundt's *Völkerpsychologie* (see e.g. Danziger 2001a,b; Diriwächter 2004; Eckardt 1997; Oelze 1991; Schneider 1990), treatises on his substantial contributions to the psychology of religion are still lacking.[16] This chapter too cannot be exhaustive and will only deal with methodological aspects. For an understanding of Wundt's approach it is more instructive to turn again to the essay he devoted explicitly to the psychology of religion than to his three-volume project *Myth and Religion*. After criticizing others (foremost, as we have seen, William James), Wundt sketched his own "genetic" psychology of religion in this article. He began with a reminder of the difference between psychology and sciences of norm, sciences of value and metaphysics and asserted that it is not psychology's task to evaluate religion in any of these respects. Wundt observed that many scholars, even theologians, nevertheless sought to derive religion from a single source, whether ecstasy or revelation, belief in souls or ghosts, being impressed by phenomena of nature etc.; in contrast Wundt believed that "religion did not grow from a single root, but from many" (Wundt 1911, p. 113) and offered a remedy against this reductionist fallacy in the psychology of religion: 'whoever wants to investigate psychologically [religion's] origin, must penetrate into the totality of phenomena of religious life and explore the relationships of the separate factors to one another and to other domains of life' (Wundt 1911, p. 113). As religion is not an

---

[16] The otherwise excellent overview of the psychology of religion by Wulff (1997) deals with Wundt only in passing. Schneider (1990) deals only very descriptively, not always correctly, with Wundt's psychology of religion, comparing it more with the sociology of religion than with the psychology of religion.

individual product, it cannot be explored at the level of the individual: "Religion is just as language and morality a creation of the human community and is related intimately to those two" (Wundt 1911, p. 113). The psychology of religion is "in the first place" a part of *Völkerpsychologie* and as the individual presupposes the community, religion cannot be dealt with on the basis of individual experimental psychology. As *Völkerpsychologie* presupposes the history of the phenomena of common life, "the thesis that *Völkerpsychologie* has nothing to do with the history of religions, is methodologically on the same level as the [equally nonsensical] one that claims language, art and morality be independent of the historical development of these phenomena" (Wundt 1911, p. 114). According to Wundt, the only possibility is a genetic psychology of religion that would be achieved by studying: (a) religious development at various stages in an upwards direction (that is, purely historical); and (b) a sample of relevant phenomena by tracing its origins by virtue of its subsequent transitions. Procedure b Wundt regarded as a condition for procedure a, and therefore he pleaded for the psychological study of the development of prayer, ritual cleansing, funerals, conceptions of taboo, of the holy, etc., in order to answer the question "how religion in an objective sense originates and which are the subjective motives that may be concluded from these objective creations" (Wundt 1911, p. 115).

Having made these general remarks, Wundt continued polemically towards different opponents. "Taking out one of the separate elements of religion may be sufficient for the tendentious philosopher, who is not concerned with knowledge about religion itself, but only about the prevalence of his a priori. Yet this arbitrary, isolating contemplation cannot be called psychology of religion" – in all likelihood a sneer against William James who concentrated, according to Wundt, on pathological religious phenomena only. Equally polemically, Wundt defended himself against the objection that the phenomena he wanted to study belong to the history of religion and not to the psychology of religion, as the latter would deal with facts of individual consciousness independent of historical conditions. Wundt firstly pointed out that a validity that pertains to the "last elements of consciousness" like sensations, feelings, simple affects, is here erroneously being extended to "psychic products, that, as far as our experience goes, develop only under specific historical conditions" (Wundt 1911, p. 116). Secondly, it is the task of history to point out the development of different peoples, but psychology must demonstrate relationships to other religious ideas and how religious motives are connected to the general psychic make up of humans. (This may be sneer towards so-called "empirical" psychologists of religion like Starbuck and Stählin who employ individual-psychological methods in a subdomain of *Völkerpsychologie* like religion.) Wundt concluded: "there can be no psychology of religion without history of religions" (Wundt 1911, p. 116).

Problems with Wundt's *Völkerpsychologie*

The methodological debates on the psychology of religion, which followed the publication of the translation of James' groundbreaking *Varieties* (James 1902/2002) into German (James 1902/1907), seem to have become endemic (and not only to this branch of psychology). As those working in the psychology of religion do so with the same theoretical and methodological instrumentarium as psychology in general, one finds similar debates and quarrels over psychological methods and techniques as in psychology at large. Before we enter into a brief discussion of some of these, it may be informative to offer some thoughts on the reasons why Wundt's psychology of religion failed to make an impact.

Firstly a general point: as Wundt's psychology of religion is part of his *Völkerpsychologie*, the former shared the latter's sad fate. A number of commentators have dealt with Wundt's *Völkerpsychologie* and pointed out important flaws such as the vagueness of what he had in mind, changes in his ideas or even contradictions which cropped up during the long decades he worked on it, and the doubtful psychological nature of his own execution of the project. Even German scholars, able to read his original texts and devoting book-length treatises to Wundt's *Völkerpsychologie* (like Eckardt 1997; Oelze 1991; Schneider 1990), find it hard to understand what exactly he had in mind by *Völkerpsychologie*. In the preface to his first volume he points out that *Völkerpsychologie* – as the necessary addendum to "individual psychology" – should analyze "phenomena resulting from the mental interaction of a multiplicity of individuals" (Wundt 1900/1997, p. 241). In the next line he describes the task as "the investigation of the psychic processes bound to the living together of human beings" (Wundt 1900/1997, p. 241). He also points out, however, that "the phenomena of general (i.e., individual) psychology are socially determined" and that *Völkerpsychologie* should occupy itself mainly with those phenomena that "can be explained only on the basis of the general laws of psychic life," as already active in the individual (Wundt 1900/1997, p. 241). It is not easy to understand what Wundt meant by this or how he thought these tasks or descriptions could go together. Sometimes his argumentation sounds circular: if the psychic phenomena found with the individual depend on interaction within a certain culture, how can one use the "laws" of individual psychic functioning to explain the development of that culture? And if these "laws" are the same for both individual psychology and *Völkerpsychologie*, why is it then necessary to repeat, so to say, individual psychological research at the level of culture, as seems to be the task assigned to *Völkerpsychologie*? (See the description of *Völkerpsychologie* research's task just a few pages further: to investigate the psychic processes upon which rely the general development of human communities as well as the origin of common mental products of general value, Wundt 1900/1997, p. 247.) In the preface to the first volume Wundt points out that the objects of *Völkerpsychologie* (language, myth, morality) were originally studied exclusively by disciplines such as philology and history. What more does *Völkerpsychologie* offer compared to these disciplines? Wundt answered that the Völkerpsychologist provided a new perspective due to his training in experimental thinking and his eye for psychic factors and processes (Wundt 1900/1921, pp. v–vi). In reasoning this way, however, what distinguished him methodologically from the application (*Anwendung*) of depth psychology to culture made by Freud and other psychoanalysts, a procedure Wundt combated elsewhere?

That Wundt changed his mind repeatedly during his long career is hardly criticism of such a great thinker. It does not, however, make it easier to understand what he

Problems with Wundt's *Völkerpsychologie*

wanted to say or to summarize his ideas. To give just one striking example: although Wundt consequently gave the different volumes of his *Völkerpsychologie* the subtitle "an investigation of the developmental laws of language, myth and morality," he never dealt with morality in the *Völkerpsychologie* itself. He simply referred to *Ethik*, a book he had published quite a number of years before he began writing his *Völkerpsychologie* (Wundt 1886). Is it possible that his thought regarding the place of ethics within *Völkerpsychologie* had not changed over the course of 35 years? Or did he – contrary to the subtitle – no longer regard ethics as part of the project? (Curiously, Volume 2 was devoted to art, and Volumes 7 through 10 to society, culture and history.) Additionally, whereas in the early years his remarks on *Völkerpsychologie* stressed that the realms of culture and history were formative to psychology (that is, of psychic functioning and therefore of psychology as the science of psychic functioning), in his last years Wundt seemed to be committing the methodological error he had earlier so instantly warned against: that is, to seek to explain developments in culture and history by means of psychological laws rather than the other way around.

Furthermore, to many observers, both then and now, it remains unclear what kind of psychology Wundt contributed to with his *Völkerpsychologie*. When taking examples from his psychology of religion for instance, we encounter lengthy chapters on "myth-building fantasy," "belief in souls and sorcery cults" and "cults of animals, ancestors and demons" (Volume 4, some 580 pages), on "the myth of nature," the "myth-fairy tale" and the "legend of the hero" (Volume 5, some 480 pages), on "the myth of gods" and on "religion" (Volume 6, some 550 pages) with no clarity as to what is psychological in this account of historical and cultural phenomena. Wundt used no psychological principle to arrange and to expose the bulk of material, no psychological perspective to analyze it, and no psychological conclusion was drawn at the end of his lengthy treatise. One would expect the final chapter of Volume 6 (Chapter 6 of the subproject *Myth and Religion*) to be a résumé of his results and insights into the psychology of religion. Instead the chapter offers (1) an account of conceptions of the afterlife and of belief in immortality, (2) a description of religious cults, and (3) a treatise on "the essence of religion," a subject he himself earlier clearly assigned to the philosophy of religion (Wundt 1911). This last treatise is then divided into (1) religion as a psychological problem, (2) the metaphysical and ethical roots of religion, and (3) the current and future state of religion. In "Religion as a Psychological Problem" we again find no results, but rather a programmatic text in which Wundt points out anew that religion needs to be studied from a völkerpsychological perspective and that pragmatic philosophers err. As noted above, Wundt does not mention James' *Varieties* even once here, although he contests the method of "selected cases" (upon which James based his work) as an approach that has nothing to say about the origin of religion, its development or its meaning in "contemporary culture" – tasks Wundt apparently assigned to the psychology of religion. Yet hardly any psychologist of religion – then or now – would agree that these issues should be dealt with by the psychology of religion. To psychologists of religion, the final task assigned by Wundt to the discipline would probably seem more appropriately handled within historical scholarship, not within psychology: "to show how philosophical ideas have developed from religious symbols and how they have affected the transformation of those symbols" (Wundt 1915, pp. 529–530). Even if we could understand in general what Wundt wanted with his völkerpsychological approach to religion, it remains difficult to find any substantial psychology in his extensive writings on the subject. In Volume 8 of the *Völkerpsychologie* (on society), he claims to have dealt in earlier volumes with the psychological properties of shamans and priests, but when we go back to the volumes to which he refers, we do not find a psychological treatise but only a description, an historical account. So what did Wundt mean by having dealt in a völkerpsychological way with a cultural product such as religion? If we were to take examples from other areas of *Völkerpsychologie*, we would end up with similar questions and problems. It is hardly surprising that a contemporary critic like the linguist Hermann Paul (1846–1921), who was well acquainted with *Völkerpsychologie* and who had already discussed work by the earlier investigators in the field of *Völkerpsychologie* Lazarus and Steinthal (Eckardt 1997), wrote: "We ask: which are the psychological laws that Wundt derived from his observation of language? I have to admit that I have looked for them in vain" (Paul 1910, p. 321).

To bring this first, more general point to a close, I should perhaps indicate some of the non-specific characteristics that may be responsible for the fact that Wundt's *Völkerpsychologie* has had so little impact. It seems that the project has been an elite enterprise: none of Wundt's many doctoral students has ever received a völkerpsychological topic for his dissertation, apparently Wundt deemed only himself capable of doing *Völkerpsychologie* (Kusch 1999). This certainly hindered the spread of the approach among psychologists at the time. Apparently, at the end of his life even Wundt realized that *Völkerpsychologie* – despite his ten volumes on the topic – remained a "future science" that had not accomplished all too much during his lifetime. Furthermore, the project seems to have been much too ambitious. Wundt wrote as if other human sciences would be merely auxiliary to *Völkerpsychologie*: history, ethnology and other disciplines may furnish data, but this would then have to be arranged and interpreted by a Völkerpsychologist (Wundt 1918, p. xi). What this Völkerpsychologist had to offer, however, remains unclear, as we have seen. Yet by formulating his argument this way and because of his polemical style in general, Wundt did not pave the way for his *Völkerpsychologie* among practitioners of other human sciences who felt he was degrading them rather than treating them as equal partners. *Völkerpsychologie* increasingly manoeuvred Wundt into an isolated position (Oelze 1991, pp. 22–23). Finally, it may well be that Wundt's *Völkerpsychologie* was an old project from the days before he started his work in psychology. In his autobiography Wundt relates that he had initially intended to write a comparative history of religions (Wundt 1920, p. 199), a project he characterized at the end of his long life as "actually völkerpsychological" (p. 200).

There are other possible reasons for the weak impact of Wundt's *Völkerpsychologie* (Oelze 1991, pp. 5–6), but as they are even less specific to the psychology of religion than those we have dealt with already I shall refrain from going into them. Instead, let us take a brief look at some less personal but more methodological issues that were responsible for the fact that Wundt's approach did not become a guiding light

Problems with Wundt's *Völkerpsychologie* 123

for the psychology of religion. Foremost among these – and this is a point that applies equally to the "psychology" of his "adversary" William James – is the narrowing of psychology in the decades after the deaths of these founding fathers. As is well known and does not need to be recounted here, to many psychologists the pluriformity in their field presented a "crisis"; and they have looked for ways to unify their discipline. From their perspective a unified science is in need of a unified methodology and the one they adopted was modeled after the more prestigious natural sciences. So instead of following James' and Wundt's pleas for methodological pluralism, psychology at large turned to methodological monism (which, it should be stressed, is *not* the same as a methodical monism) that tended to disregard James' more hermeneutic approach and Wundt's essentially qualitative "experiments," adopting experimental procedure as developed in the natural sciences supplemented by psychometric tests and standardized questionnaires which are then analyzed by means of explanatory statistics. The dominant methodology in psychology consists of (Cahan and White 1992):

1. Methodological behaviorism: laboratory studies of perceptual and learning mechanisms as the basis for a unified science of psychology.
2. Reliance on experimental procedures that take 'collective subjects' (groups of people) as the basis for inferences about individual psychological processes.
3. The use of inferential statistics applied to group data, as, for example, in correlational studies based on psychometric tests or analysis of variance procedures applied to classical treatment-control experiments.

With regard to methodology, methods and techniques in psychology, James and Wundt both lost: their approaches did not prevail, but – despite criticisms voiced by observers like Stählin – were repressed by the approach exemplified by researchers like Starbuck who proceeding rather a-theoretically, measured variables and analyzed them statistically.[17]

---

[17] This is not to say that there have not been methodical followers of Wundt and James, or more precisely, psychologists who were heavily influenced by them. However, the psychological school closest to Wundt flourished in the former Soviet Union, isolated from the West, where their ideas were received only slowly (see Vygotsky 1930/1971; 1934/1987; 1978; Luria 1971, 1976, 1979, 1981; Leontiev 1978, 1981). Incidentally, there have been US psychologists (especially in the early days, when many went for training to Germany) with sympathies for Völkerpsychologie. Cole (1996, p. 35) notes the example of Charles Judd (1926), an educational psychologist who wrote a book on social psychology (his rather erroneous translation of Völkerpsychologie). He explicitly followed Wundt when he argued that language, tools, number systems, the alphabet, etc. are forms of accumulated social capital developed historically. Newborns must adapt to social institutions and practices; individual minds are actually formed by the process of socialization. Consequently, social psychology cannot be based on properties of the individual mind, but must be an independent science, employing methods from anthropology, sociology and linguistics. James, influencing other pragmatic thinkers like Mead (1934) and Dewey (1938/1963), typically had more followers from *sociological* social psychology (using qualitative methods such as symbolic interactionism and ethnomethodology) than *psychological* social psychology (using quantitative experimental methods). On the distinction between these two social psychologies, see Strycker (1977).

Wundt's more specific, non-individualistic, völkerpsychological approach was also fairly quickly forgotten. Culture was not deemed an object for psychological research and if it were it would be treated as an object to which psychological insights could be applied; that culture is constitutive of and regulating meaningful human action is an insight usually abstracted from in general psychology. Psychologists usually neglect Max Weber, another founding father of a psychologizing social science, and his insight that humans are suspended in webs of significance they spin themselves. Instead, the universality of "laws" obtained by general psychology are generally claimed not just across contexts, but across the entire species as well (Cole 1996, p. 31). In psychological publications culture is accorded a distinctly minor role: if it appears at all it refers to cultural difference. Even when general psychologists do acknowledge the influence of culture they assume this works through universal mechanisms, which are the real object of psychological interest: "The main force in general psychology is the idea of a central processing device. The processor, it is imagined, stands over and above, or transcends, all the stuff upon which it operates. It engages all the stuff of culture, context, task and stimulus materials as its content" (Shweder 1991, p. 80). In the psychology of religion one recognizes a preoccupation with individuals extracted from their culture, in the almost exclusive focus on (private) religiosity, and in the almost total neglect of religion as a topic for research in the psychology of religion. Indeed – probably out of fear of committing a reductionistic fallacy regarding (ontological) truth claims that are inherent in all religions – many, perhaps even most, psychologists of religion defend the position that they can only investigate religiosity, the individual-personal correlate of a certain religion into which the individual is socialized, and not religion as such. This however, should be questioned, especially in light of the early debates on methodology in the psychology of religion just reviewed.

Ongoing Debates, Regained Perspectives

A reappraisal of and reorientation towards early perspectives in the field may be vital to the psychology of religion. Wundt's plea for a cultural psychology seems particularly relevant. Granted, Wundt's own contributions to what he called *Völkerpsychologie* may be flawed and he may have hindered this branch of psychology at least as much as he advanced it, but his general theoretical and methodological insights still hold. Expressed in contemporary terms: all conditions and determinants of psychic functioning, whether limitative (such as psychophysical makeup or social and geographical conditions), operative (such as acquired, learned activities), or normative (such as rules and norms), are always cultural-historically variable and therefore all "higher psychic functions" are constituted, facilitated and regulated by cultural processes (see also Part I of this book). One of the problems with Wundt's *Völkerpsychologie* is its lack of appropriate theories and concepts. Wundt did not have specific theoretical tools to conceptualize the relationships between psychic functioning and culture. In recounting the histories of languages, societies, religions, etc., he did not come much

Ongoing Debates, Regained Perspectives 125

further than concluding that "psychic factors have played a role," without having determined these factors and their precise impact. When he started his project he did not have any other "fundamental concepts of *Völkerpsychologie*" at his disposal than "folk spirit and folk soul," "prehistory and history," "individual and society" (Wundt 1900/1921, introduction, Part II). A century later we now have more precise and useful theories and concepts such as "activity," (symbolic) "action," "dialogical self" and "mediation" (Boesch 1991; Cole 1995; Eckensberger 1995; Hermans and Kempen 1993; Ratner 1996), there is work on autobiographical memory, on narratives, and on discursive psychology, etc. (Crawford and Valsiner 1999; Belzen 2004a; Wang and Brockmeier 2002). Yet still very much in the spirit of Wundt's *Völkerpsychologie* contemporary cultural psychological work also stresses that cultural patterns of acting, thinking and experiencing are created, adopted and promulgated by a number of individuals jointly. Such patterns are supra-individual (social) rather than individual, and they are artifactual rather than natural. Psychological phenomena are therefore cultural insofar as they are social artefacts, i.e., insofar as their content, mode of operation and dynamic relationships are socially created and shared by a number of individuals and are integrated with other social artefacts (Ratner 2002, p. 9). A religious phenomenon, e.g. conversion, has different meanings within different subgroups of each religion as it is the result of certain patterns of religious practice which relate to sometimes very different religious doctrines and rituals; it may even not be found in some religious (sub)groups at all (Belzen 2004a; Hijweege 2004; Popp-Baier 1998). In cultural psychology the *meaning* of some form of action (or thought or experience) is typically central rather than the action as such (which could be, and in fact often is, studied by other social and human sciences too).

Although Wundt was perhaps too dismissive of the psychology of religion in his day; nevertheless, much of his critique is still valid. Essentially his reproach was twofold: psychology of religion reduces its object to religiosity; and it does not generate significant results. The two points are related. Clearly there are a great number of people interested in a psychological approach to religion: the enormous current production of popular literature, seminars, workshops etc. – often strongly psychologizing in nature – on religion, spirituality, esotericism and so on testifies to this. On a more academic level, there is a growing interest on the part of religious institutions and professionals in what psychology has to say. (In fact, most professorships and other academic positions reserved for the psychology of religion are found in departments for religious studies and theology, rather than in departments of psychology.) However, people from these disciplines are often very disappointed by what the psychology of religion in a proper sense [18] has to offer (Nørager 1996).[19]

---

[18] The psychology of religion should be distinguished from religious psychology, which is a psychology inherent to religious traditions (e.g. Buddhism), from pastoral psychology, religious psychotherapy, and from other forms of psychology serving religious aims or purposes. In principle, the psychology of religion is a scholarly-analytical perspective on religion, neutral towards its object of investigation (see Belzen 1995–1996).

[19] In this article the Danish scholar of religion Troels Nørager refers to reactions by students of religion at the University of Aarhus (Denmark) after taking a course on the psychology of religion.

This disappointment with the psychology of religion seems to be endemic to the field: even as the field was in its infancy observers complained that the psychology of religion would have very little to say about religion itself and would be primarily concerned with its acceptance by other psychologists, proving itself equally "scientific" by performing experiments, using statistics, but neglecting its very object of research (Belzen 2004b). Indeed, it is remarkable that much of what is being done by those assigned specifically to the discipline digresses from what is regarded to be mainstream psychology: both teaching and research in the psychology of religion at departments for religious studies are more often than not along psychoanalytic lines (see, e.g., Capps 2001; Jones 1991, 1996; Jonte-Pace 2003; Jonte-Pace and Parsons 2001). Psychological monographs on explicitly religious phenomena or on religious subjects are seldom published by psychologists, but are written by practitioners of the field with a background in psychiatry or the history of religions (see, e.g., Carroll 2002; Cohen 2007; Geels 1991; Kripall 1995; Meissner 1992, 1997), and are often more readable than most introductions to the psychology of religion in a narrow sense (see, e.g., Argyle 2000; Spilka et al. 2003). It is striking that in several recent general scholarly works on religion as a phenomenon, the authors explicitly turn to psychological theories and research but hardly quote anything from the psychology of religion in a strict sense (Boyer 2001; Cohen 2007; Guthrie 1993). In a way, these anthropological thinkers on religion seem to continue Wundt's initial program: they explicitly work interdisciplinarily on religion, employing insights from current psychology but remaining outside the scope of both mainstream psychology in general and mainstream psychology of religion.

Psychologists of religion working within the institutional setting of a psychological department naturally orient themselves as much as possible to the style and requirements of mainstream psychology. There is nothing wrong with this strategy, but it runs the risk of contributing to the dubious relevance of the psychology of religion.[20] The reason for this is that the subdiscipline shares the strengths and weaknesses of psychology in general: to the extent that the psychology of religion is part of psychology in general, criticism of the mother-discipline is likewise pertinent to the subdiscipline too. Indeed, if the psychology of religion is merely repeating psychological research on religious populations it is in danger of only drawing conclusions that have already been reached by researchers on other populations. In other words, by proceeding along that path the psychology of religion is not doing anything wrong, but not doing anything particularly right either. Such psychological research may be conducted in a methodically correct way: known psychological mechanisms, distinctions and variables may be recognized in religious subjects, psychological theories may apply in religious contexts too. All of this is certainly informative, but to a critical observer it may seem trivial. The psychology of

---

[20] Psychologists of religion may be well advised not to be too concerned about their (non-) centrality to mainstream psychology: virtually none of the founding fathers of both psychology in general and of the psychology of religion (like Hall, James, Freud or Wundt) specifically, and even further, almost no other later significant contributor to the field (such as Allport, Fromm, Jaspers or Maslow) would be considered mainstream by contemporary psychology.

religion obviously cannot but employ theories, methods and techniques from psychology in general, but if it only functions as an additional validation or example for such theories, methods and techniques its value is rather limited.[21] If some element of psychology is known to be valid knowledge, one can a priori assume it is valid for religious populations and contexts too. The pressing question, however, is whether the psychology of religion does not have a more important (albeit, more difficult) task: focusing on its classic object, i.e., on religion. The ideal task for the psychology of religion would be to provide additional knowledge about religion, from a psychological perspective. The psychology of religion should therefore consider as one of its prime tasks the discovery and depiction of what is specific about religion: that religious subjects are embedded in religious groups and communities is obvious, that many processes as explored in social psychology and sociology will be found with such groups and communities is equally trivial. The question as to whether there is any difference between membership in a religious group versus membership in non-religious groups is not a trivial one however. Does the religious character of a group add something significant for its members? If it does, what is the nature of that "surplus"-meaning membership in a religious group may have? If – as e.g. being stated in Christianity – the deity is a person and if being a Christian means entertaining a relationship to a personal God, the relationship to that God will probably display many characteristics that psychologists have discerned about interpersonal relationships in general. Yet, the relationship to (a) God is not entirely identical to a relationship to anyone else, not even to an absent lover, a relative, etc.: the Christian God is not a person in the sense other human beings are persons. What then is the difference between a relationship to God and that to any other person; if that difference can be discovered and explored, does it have any psychological meaning for and impact on the subject involved, and how can that be investigated and conceptualized? What kind of reality is it in which a religiously devoted person is involved? From a psychological perspective how is it different from and similar to fairy tales, fantasy, myth, delusion, ideology and so on? If the psychology of religion is able to come up with answers to questions like these it will contribute significantly to both psychological knowledge and to knowledge about religion(s).

Returning to classic texts is not always a way out of a crisis and merely repeating them never is, for the context in which they functioned and would need to function again are constantly changing. However – as pointed out by Danziger in the lengthy quotation at the beginning of this chapter – for psychology there may be ample reason to reconsider the theoretical and methodological debates from the days of its inception. As the psychology of religion seems to be in crisis (Wulff 2003), Danziger's remark may be equally true for this subdiscipline of psychology in general. While no publication in the psychology of religion has ever equaled James'

---

[21] One should note that no psychological theory has ever been formulated on the basis of research on religion. As is logical and correct, the psychology of religion has always used extant psychological theories, methods and techniques.

Varieties in public or scholarly appeal, there may be – despite Stählin's, Vorbrodt's and Wundt's criticisms – good reasons to take another look at this founding father's theories and methodology in order to fertilize present-day psychology of religion. Now that cultural psychology is slowly becoming a clearly audible voice within psychology at large, offering theories and concepts as well as methods and techniques to analyze the relationship between human psychic functioning and culture, it may be equally wise to take another look – despite its flaws – at Wundt's plea to take religion, not just religiosity, seriously as an object for cultural psychological inquiry. Before religiosity can develop in the life of any individual human, religion is first encountered as a cultural phenomenon. Conceiving religion as an element of culture may enable psychologists to participate in the analysis of religion, e.g. in the search for any specificity the religious "form of life" (Wittgenstein) may have with regard to the subjectivity of those involved in that religious form of life.

Chapter 8
A Cultural Psychological Promise to the Study of Religiosity: Background and Context of the "Dialogical Self"

An obvious conclusion to be derived from the previous chapter could be formulated thus: When we, like Wundt, understand religion as an element of culture, we need concepts and units of analysis that will enable us to investigate the nexus between a certain culture (or cultural context) and the person. Wundt himself did not yet dispose of them; but they have now become available with such concepts as activity, action, habitus, and also narrative or "story." The theorizing about the "dialogical self" as initiated by Hermans and Kempen may count as an example as well. Their work – which has been well received by the international cultural psychology "movement" (Hermans 1999a, b, 2001a, b, 2002, 2003; Hermans and Dimaggio 2007; Valsiner 2001) – is promising for a cultural psychological analysis of religion. It is particularly interesting to take a closer look at this body of theory, as its development sustains historical relationships with the psychology of religion. The dialogical self may be regarded as a belated result of a much older Dutch initiative to integrate cultural psychology and psychology of religion, which led to the establishment of a department for the psychology of culture and religion at Nijmegen, in the Netherlands, in 1956 (although the roots of the initiative reach back to the founding years of psychology in general in the Netherlands). As well as this, it catches up with a stand that has become fundamental to all psychologies of religion for a long time: psychological research on religion must be performed from a secular perspective (cf. Belzen 2001c). To corroborate these claims, it is necessary to draw substantially on historical information as well as on information about recent developments. I shall therefore present a mixture of historical and systematic argumentation.

The Dialogical Self

One of the attractive aspects of the concept of the dialogical self as developed by Hermans and Kempen (1993) is that it is both firmly rooted in classical European traditions in psychology and compatible with contemporary discussions within international, nowadays USA-dominated, psychology. The concept of the dialogical self is the result of an ongoing reception of and conversation with authors as diverse as Heidegger and Merleau-Ponty as representatives of phenomenological thought,

J.A. Belzen, *Towards Cultural Psychology of Religion: Principles, Approaches, Applications*, DOI 10.1007/978-90-481-3491-5_8, © Springer Science+Business Media B.V. 2010

James and Mead as representatives of American pragmatism, and Sarbin and the Gergens as representatives of such contemporary movements as social constructionism and narrative psychology. The compatibility with developments presently taking place in philosophy, literary theory and in various segments of interpretative psychologies is evident, as is made clear in *The Dialogical Self* and numerous other publications by Hermans and Kempen (Hermans and Kempen 1993, 1998; Hermans et al. 1993), as well as in publications by other authors (McAdams 1999; Fogel 1993). In their effort to conceive of the human person as a multiplex and changing, context-dependent, embodied self, Hermans and Kempen clearly contribute to a cultural psychology as it is presently developing at various places and with different branches, but also as it had a long tradition at Nijmegen, where both authors have been studying and working for some 40 years. The diversity of influences and sources manifest in their work has always been a feature – both a strength and a burden – of the Nijmegen tradition in cultural psychology. But first let us briefly consider the concept itself.

Hermans and Kempen propose an idea of the self as a multiplicity of relatively autonomous *I* positions in an imaginal landscape. Drawing on Sarbin's (1986a) proposal for a narrative psychology, assuming that in the self-narrative a single author tells a story about herself as actor, Hermans and Kempen conceive of the self as polyphonic: one and the same individual lives, or can live, in a multiplicity of worlds, with each world having its own author telling a story relatively independent of the authors of the other worlds. At times the various authors may even enter into a dialogue with one another. Moreover the self, conceptualized in analogy with a polyphonic novel, also has the capacity to integrate the notions of imaginative narratives and dialogues. In their idea of the self, Hermans and Kempen no longer stipulate – in contrast to James and Mead – an overarching *I*, which would organize the several constituents of the *me*. Instead, the spatial character of the self leads to the supposition of a decentralized multiplicity of *I* positions that function as relatively independent authors, telling their stories about their respective *me*'s as actors (Hermans and Kempen 1993). In their initial publication on the dialogical self, the authors point out three ways in which their conception differs from much of the received view in the West. First, in contrast to a conception of the self as individualistic, the *I* moves, in an imaginal space, from one position to another, from which different or even contrasting views of the world are possible. Second, the dialogical self is "social," which does not mean that a self-contained individual enters into social interactions with other outside people, but that other people occupy positions in the multi-voiced self. The other person is a position the *I* can occupy and that creates an alternative perspective on the world (including the self). Finally, the conception of the dialogical self opposes the ideal of the self as a centralized equilibrium structure. Hermans and Kempen do not stipulate the self as the center of control: The different *I* positions in the self represent different anchor points, which – depending on the nature of the interaction – may organize the other *I* positions at a given point in time (Hermans et al. 1992).

Having sketched the dialogical self, I shall try to show the importance of the concept within contemporary cultural psychology and especially its importance to

The Origin of the Idea of Cultural Psychology

a culturally sensitive psychology of religion. A brief historical exploration of the concept's intellectual context will lead me to the conclusion that the dialogical self is both a late realization of, and a final breakthrough within, a program for cultural psychology and the psychology of religion already called for well before World War II. We shall start by asking where the interest at Nijmegen in a culturally sensitive psychology found its inspiration – leading to the establishment of a rather unique professorial chair in 1956 and later to a department of cultural psychology. In a second return to the past, we shall try to understand the equally uncommon Nijmegen desire to combine cultural psychology with the psychology of religion. In the next part of the chapter, I shall contextualize the developments some more and draw on the previous information in order to support my conclusion.

The Origin of the Idea of Cultural Psychology

The idea of establishing a professorial chair in cultural psychology came from F.J.Th. Rutten (1899–1980), the man who built up the psychology department at Nijmegen. We need to take at least three factors into consideration if we want to understand his motivation: (a) His professional training; (b) His personal context, personality and style; (c) His vision of psychology.

Professional Training

In 1931, Rutten was appointed to teach psychology in a context of educational sciences, with the aim of training Roman Catholic teachers. It was a position in which he succeeded his teacher in psychology, F.J.M.A. Roels (1887–1962), whose assistant he had been for a number of years. In those days, empirical psychology was still a rare subject at Dutch universities. Theoretical, or philosophical, psychology had been taught for decades by some professors of philosophy, but the introduction and establishment of psychology as a separate, empirically working discipline was a late one, especially in comparison with neighboring countries. In fact Roels seems to have been the first person to be appointed as a full-time professor of psychology only at a Dutch university, i.e., at Utrecht University in 1918.[1]

At the Roman Catholic University in Nijmegen (est. 1923) the priest J. Hoogveld (1878–1942) was responsible for pedagogics. He wanted to follow the example of

---

[1] To be historically correct and to use the proper terminology: Roels started out as an assistant to C. Winkler (1855–1941), Professor of Psychiatry and Neurology at Utrecht University. In 1916 he became a private teacher at the Faculty of Humanities and Philosophy. He was appointed "lecturer" at Utrecht in 1918, and "professor" in 1922. Since 1980, the lectureships at Dutch universities are called professorates. Neither function nor title exist anymore.

132   A Cultural Psychological Promise to the Study of Religiosity

the Catholic University in Leuven (Belgium) where psychology had been given a place on the pedagogics curriculum. He therefore recruited Roels – who had studied philosophy and psychology at Leuven with Michotte (1881–1965), a pupil of Wundt and Külpe – to become a part-time professor at Nijmegen University. Roels had a close colleague and friend in A.A. Grünbaum (1885–1932), who was born in Russia, worked in Germany and fled to the Netherlands at the outset of World War I where he was appointed honorary professor for developmental psychology at Utrecht University in 1928. He was one of the people who introduced the phenomenological movement to the Netherlands. In his work, one finds all kinds of anti-elementaristic themes as they were elaborated in Germany at the time: "Intentionality" (Brentano), "totality" (Gestalt psychology), "existence" (Husserl), and "understanding" of life out of life itself (Dilthey). Grünbaum developed an "organological" view of consciousness, i.e., the view that consciousness should be considered as a unity, which unity is the result of the human being's commitment to a concrete situation requiring action. Within the scientifically oriented psychology that was prevalent at the time, the consciousness of, for example, a blacksmith working on a piece of hot iron, would be described as a series of sensations, acts of attention and impulses of the will. But according to Grünbaum, such a description is artificial as it contradicts the experience of the blacksmith. Precisely because he is involved in making something, "the whole complex of sensations, feelings and impulses is carried by the experience of the situation as a whole, in which there is no separation between an 'I' that is reacting and an environment that is influencing the 'I'" (Grünbaum 1928, p. 13). The blacksmith does not see separate sensations, which are to be followed by impulses of the will, but a horseshoe that does not yet have the shape he wants it to have.

Roels was strongly influenced by the views propagated by Grünbaum. He too stressed that the person is a unity. The unlife-like character of experimental psychology was a result of its preoccupation – in line with Cartesian dualism – with consciousness. Roels agreed with William Stern (1917) that the basic principle of reality is not the fact that there are psychic and physical phenomena, but that there are concrete persons: "The immediate experience teaches that the human being is a 'unitas multiplex': very divers elements unite in him" (Roels 1918, p. 25). Consciousness should not be regarded as isolated from activity, nor from the "outside" world. Therefore Roels considered Watson's (1913) definition of psychology as the study of behavior to be equally one-sided, for Watson remained within Cartesian dualism, only this time focusing on the body. In Roels's view the only adequate definition of psychology could be "the study of the human being as a psychophysical unity."

Roels was far more than just a theoretician, however. He had a very practical orientation and wanted to apply psychology in the search for solutions to all kinds of daily problems. In his opinion applied psychology was as "necessary as bread" (1918, p. 13). But in a notable text from 1928 he had to conclude that the psychology of his day had hardly anything to offer when it came to answering practical questions. He stated that applied psychology, or "psychotechnics", in his terminology, was impossible without cultural psychology. Psychotechnics only registers the

The Origin of the Idea of Cultural Psychology 133

elements out of which psychical phenomena are constructed (Roels 1928, p. 82). Gestalt psychology had shown, according to Roels, that the whole cannot be constructed by addition of the elements. Consequently he saw it as cultural psychology's task to regard phenomena as "constituting moments of a meaningful whole" (1928, p. 88). This much needed firm cultural psychological basis was almost entirely lacking, not only with regard to pedagogical psychology, but also with regard to the psychology of worldviews, social psychology, and economic psychology.

Personal Background

Rutten acquired his interest in cultural psychology from his teacher and promoter, Roels, who requested that Rutten be appointed at the Catholic University. They published together and almost immediately after the defense of Rutten's dissertation Roels took his leave from Nijmegen, thereby creating the possibility to appoint Rutten as his successor. Rutten's study *The Transition of the Agrarian Popular Type into the Industrial Popular One* (1947) testifies to his continuing interest in cultural psychological questions. According to Harry Kempen, who – like Hubert Hermans – had been a student of Rutten, this study must also have had a personal-autobiographical background. Rutten came from the very rural, traditional Limburg (in the south of the Netherlands), which in those days was a rather undeveloped area. For his academic training, he moved to Utrecht (a major university city in the middle of the country), and then to the French-speaking university in Leuven (Belgium). The then substantial differences between these settings may have brought the importance of the relationship between culture and behavior to his attention. Like Roels, Rutten was interested in developing psychologies of the different subcultures to be found in the Netherlands. In order to apply psychology practically, exploration of the different worlds of subjects had to be undertaken. These were the worlds of the dockworker, peasant, and academic, and also of the different milieus within religiously divers segments of society. When, in later years, he traveled to the USA, he was struck by the very different style of approach taken by his colleagues there (Rutten 1954). He seems to have realized that the differences between European and American psychology were not simply the consequence of different scientific considerations, but that the different settings gave rise to different psychologies.

Vision of Psychology

Rutten's sensibility to different contexts and cultures/subcultures also made him realize – to use a Heideggerian phrase – the *seinsgebunden* character of knowledge, also of scientific knowledge. (One could perhaps translate this phrase into English as something like: "determined by being": it refers to "situatedness" as referred to by different thinkers nowadays.) Consequently Rutten strove for an open-minded psychology, one that would be all-round and inclusive, not restricted to one or only a few approaches. According to people who knew Rutten intimately, this striving must have been deeply characteristic of him. He questioned fundamentally several trends he perceived in modern Western culture: the rationalism that had invaded all segments of life, the increasing individualism, and the decline of mythical sensitivity. In his view, psychology should help to balance these trends. He subscribed wholeheartedly to the aims the American Psychological Association had formulated for the discipline, but realized that the application of psychology "as a means of promoting human welfare" required at least a supplement to developments in contemporary psychology. The psychology he encountered in the USA struck him as being very "narrow" (Rutten 1954). Rutten, contrarily, was interested in the development of a kind of *psychologia universalis*, in transcending locally valid knowledge (a goal we would at present probably no longer subscribe to). Cultural psychology should serve this interest, and from the beginning of the 1950s onwards he started – despite resistance from various sides – to lobby for a professorial chair in the subject. On behalf of future generations of students, he intended to keep psychology in "his" institute broad and diverse. When in the 1960s psychology in the Netherlands turned almost completely towards American inspired operationalization and the employment of statistics, Rutten must have been just as pleased with his assistants and successors who went to Tolmin and Coombs in the USA, as he was with those who traveled to India and Thailand to explore Hindu and Buddhist lifestyles and spirituality (cf. Fortmann 1968).[2]

The Combination of Cultural Psychology and the Psychology of Religion[3]

The professor holding the chair Rutten created in cultural psychology had to pay, it was initially formulated, "special attention to the psychology of religion." The question is whether Roels and Rutten had already conceived of the psychology of religion as necessarily conducted from the perspective of cultural psychology, or whether the combination had something to do with the first professor to hold this chair.

---

[2] In 1975, when at his former institute operationalism and testing of hypotheses had become dominant too, Rutten published a short article, in which he recommends psychologists to read "great literature" (philosophers, poets, novelists). He wrote that as psychologists, we "… are captured in a certain historical way of thinking. The professional language we have been taught, and the methods and techniques that we have learned to handle, orient the way in which we perceive behavior. There is real danger that the expertise we have gained will hinder new developments. We are constantly forced to struggle to get hold of *and* to overcome the doctrinary conformism required by any training" (Rutten 1975, p. 391).

[3] For broader accounts of the institutional development of the psychology of religion in the Netherlands: cf. Belzen (2002b, 2007, 2009b).

The Combination of Cultural Psychology and the Psychology of Religion 135

Let us briefly consider the first possibility. In general the psychology of religion received virtually no attention from Dutch Roman Catholics before World War II, and when it did, the attention was deeply distrustful (cf. Belzen 2001c). The first to speak positively about the subject, even in the sense of defending the subject, and calling for a Catholic institute for the subdiscipline, was – again – Roels. The psychology of religion had been led astray, in his opinion, by "wrong friends, Protestant theology and positivistic philosophy" (Roels 1919–1920, p. 343); and Roman Catholics should not leave the subject to them. Yet, at the time (1919), he expected from a psychology of religion mainly "contributions to apologetics": Catholics would be able, for example, to point out how gratifying the liturgy is to the soul, or how "insane" it is to compare ritual with obsessive neurosis. But Roels did not get his way. It was years before the psychology of religion was again spoken of in Dutch Roman Catholic circles.[4]

In 1937 Rutten gave a lecture at a meeting of the Roman Catholic Society for Thomistic Philosophy on "the domain of psychology of religion." In this methodological exposé Rutten clearly distinguishes a religious or theological, perspective from a psychological one. According to Rutten both perspectives are legitimate, theology searching for the religious value and truth of the phenomena, and psychology investigating their psychical aspects and conditions. Scientific research into religious phenomena can never call upon supernatural factors to explain them; the work of "grace" cannot be made visible in a psychological investigation, but cannot be denied either. As far as scientific psychology is concerned, it has to work with the conceptual and methodical instruments of psychology in general. (Although Rutten, like Roels (1919/1920), denies that psychological experiments – as conducted by the German psychologist of religion, K. Girgensohn (1921/1930) who applied *Külpean* techniques in his research – could be employed.) Methodologically, psychology is neutral, according to Rutten, also when it investigates religion. On the other hand (and he calls this a "perplexing fact"), the psychology of religion can, in his opinion, only be performed by a psychologist who is religious himself, as it will be necessary to participate intentionally in the phenomena under research in order to understand their significance. In this thoughtful text, Rutten makes only a few remarks that could be interpreted as being inspired by a cultural psychological perspective: "To the extent that certain forms of behavior as expressions of persons, each with their own disposition and development, coincide with certain circumstances of time and place, they are subject to empirical-psychological laws" (Rutten 1937, p. 10).

---

[4] In his text on cultural psychology, some ten years later, Roels devotes only a small remark to religion: "A beginning has hardly been made with a psychology of worldviews, that is, a psychology that explores the psychic-spiritual structures or inner attitudes, from which different types of worldviews stem" (1928, p. 88). This sounds rather casual, unlike his earlier plea for the subdiscipline. But one cannot infer from this quotation that he had abandoned the apologetic aims he pursued with the psychology of religion: The 1919 text was addressed to a Roman Catholic audience; and the passage from 1928 comes from a publication by the Psychological Laboratory at the religiously neutral State University of Utrecht. To what "psychology of worldviews" Roels is referring here remains unclear. Perhaps to Jaspers (1922)?

By "circumstances of time and place" Rutten did not only mean factors that could be experimentally manipulated. He also mentioned "forms of religion handed down" and the "peculiarities of an epoch." These phrases *could* be understood as a reference to a cultural and historical context, although the text as such is certainly not conceived from a cultural psychological perspective. Unlike Roels's text, Rutten's is not a plea for an apologetic use of a psychology of religion, although he does clearly point out that such a psychology can be of great value for pastoral care (Rutten 1937, pp. 33–34).

As should be clear, neither Roels nor Rutten were very outspoken about the desirability of a cultural psychological approach to the psychology of religion. It is doubtful, therefore, whether they were acquainted with Wundt's thesis that "religion is not a topic for individual psychology, but for cultural psychology" (Wundt 1915, p. 513).[5] Therefore, the reason for Rutten to combine his older interests in both cultural psychology and the psychology of religion may – the second possibility – have been of a more trivial nature. Several years after his lecture on the psychology of religion, he supervised a doctoral dissertation on prayer, a project by Han Fortmann (1912–1970), a Roman Catholic priest who had studied classical languages and psychology. After he obtained his doctoral degree in 1945, Fortmann became involved in Roman Catholic youth work, also on a national-organizational level, and he was one of the editors of *Dux*, a periodical primarily oriented towards youth work, but which was read by a much broader audience. Fortmann published over a hundred articles in *Dux*, on such subjects as education for the citizenhood, the development of faith, the will, fantasy, conscience, sexuality, and so on.

Over the years, he maintained contact with Rutten (as can be inferred from their correspondence, which is now in the archives of the psychology department at Nijmegen). At the beginning of the 1950s, Rutten became Minister of State for Education and the Sciences. In the mid-1950s, Fortmann joined a group of modern-minded Roman Catholics who wanted to change Catholic morals and customs with respect to sexuality. One of the group's members was the internationally renowned phenomenologist F.J.J. Buytendijk (1887–1974), who became president of the Catholic Central Society of Mental Health. In a historiography (Westhoff 1996), prominent members of this society are referred to as "liberators." They were deeply concerned with the mental health of Catholics, and perceived many spiritual problems to be caused by, or at least related to, mental health problems. At the time, the Roman Catholic leadership was suspicious of psychiatry, psychotherapy, and mental health care, and in later years the legendary "pastoral commission" had to work in

---

[5] It is possible of course that they had read this work, or that Roels had become aware of this part of Wundt's theorizing via his teacher Michotte in Leuven, who had been working at the Leipzig laboratory in 1906, precisely at the time when Wundt was working on his cultural psychology, which he considered a natural complement to his earlier, experimental work in psychology. According to Wundt, psychology would have to be plural. Psychology can only turn to experiment as an auxiliary method if it seeks to examine the "elementary psychic processes"; but if it seeks to study the higher psychic processes it has to consult other sciences for orientation (Wundt 1900–1909). Wundt's own suggestion was that psychologists should consult history (see Chapters 2 and 7).

secret, as it was perceived as being almost subversive (Suèr 1969). When in the mid-1950s Rutten returned to his professorial work at Nijmegen, his former student Fortmann must have seemed the ideal person to perform a couple of tasks Rutten perceived to be meanwhile highly necessary: (a) Fortmann had broad interests and would contribute to Rutten's ideal of keeping psychology open-minded and interactive with such related fields of knowledge as anthropology and history; (b) he was able to contribute to the promotion of human welfare by taking from a psychological perspective a critical stance toward developments in society at large; and (c) as a Roman Catholic priest who had written a psychological dissertation on a religious topic, he would be able to develop a psychology of religion. The task Rutten assigned to Fortmann was a broad, and in some ways hybrid, one: "Cultural psychology with special attention to the psychology of religion," which very soon proved to be too large for the part-time post Fortmann was offered in 1956: just 3 years later, the professorship was changed into a full-time position for "general and comparative psychology of culture and religion." It is irrelevant to follow the history of the professorship and its department here; for the purpose of our analysis, I only need to focus on the kind of cultural psychology Fortmann tried to develop.

Cultural Psychology: Program and Preliminary Achievements

To anticipate the end of the story: Fortmann has never been able to fully meet the assigned task as he interpreted it, perhaps partly because he passed away at a relatively young age (he was only 57 when he died in 1970). The two domains – cultural psychology and the psychology of religion – only gradually merged in his work, and never became truly synthesized. This is most evident from his *Introduction to Cultural Psychology* (1971), in which he pays almost no attention to the psychology of religion; and in his work on the psychology of religion, on which he published more than he did on cultural psychology, there is not much written from a cultural perspective. Although the subtitle of his main work, *Als ziende de Onzienlijke* (1964–1968), is "A cultural-psychological study on religious perception and so-called religious projection," it is more a programmatic phrase than the realization of a project. In this four-volume work, Fortmann takes a stand in the debate on religious projection as it was happening in the Netherlands at the turn of the 1960s. He provides summaries of the positions taken by important contributors to the debate (and also of the forerunners, such as Marx, Freud, and others); and from a phenomenologically informed viewpoint he argues that there exists no "projection" in the sense of projecting something "inner" onto something "outer." To give a brief characterization: *Als ziende de onzienlijke* is an in-depth treatment of its subject, yet primarily on a theoretical level, taking into consideration notions from several disciplines (including theology); however, it seldom deals explicitly with culture and devotes only limited attention to such cultural anthropologists as Levy-Bruhl and Lévi-Strauss; moreover, Part IIIB (Volume 4) is entirely devoted to the relationship between mental health and religion, yet essentially from a non-cultural-psychological perspective.

(Thus in that sense, the volume is indeed in line with Rutten's wish for a psychological critique of contemporary culture, but not with Fortmann's own developing insight into the predominant importance of culture for the constitution and regulation of human experience and action.)

In his major works on cultural psychology and the psychology of religion, one sees Fortmann continuing his work, preparing his project of integrating both fields, and collecting material for a future program. His broad orientation prevented him from adopting a single perspective or only a few perspectives; he tried to become acquainted from several angles with many approaches and with literature that might prove useful for a future cultural psychology of religion. When he started out, there was little that he could orient himself on: The older psychology of religion as developed in the USA hardly fitted into his cultural psychological interests; the German psychology of religion had become almost extinct after World War II, and the experimental methodology of its most important pre-War representative, Girgensohn, was not considered applicable; about the psychoanalytic psychology of religion Fortmann was, and remained, somewhat suspicious. His discontent with the existing psychology of religion may have encouraged him to adopt a new approach: a cultural psychological one. But then again, what types of cultural psychology could he have relied on in those days? According to Harry Kempen, who became Fortmann's first assistant in the field of cultural psychology (and *not* that of the psychology of religion), it was mainly non-psychological theory that Fortmann had to turn to. From psychoanalysis there was only the society-oriented work of the older Freud, Jung, and the Frankfurt School. Then, from cultural anthropology, there was the "culture and personality" school, with work from such authors as Benedict, Hallowell, Kardiner, the Kluckhohns, Linton, Margaret Mead, and the Whitings. Finally, the older Durkheim was a sociological source of inspiration. Whereas the early Durkheim conceived of society as a "thing" that exists exterior to the individual (and that should not therefore be studied from a psychological perspective), the older Durkheim abandoned this sociologism and realized that society exists only in and through individuals. The mediating concept between actor and society became "collective representations," a forerunner of the contemporary concept of "social representations" (Moscovici). In his later years, as is clear from his posthumously published *Introduction to Cultural Psychology* (1971), Fortmann also proved himself to be an early Dutch recipient of the – in those days primarily French – structuralist movement in psychoanalysis (Lacan) and literary theory (Barthes).

A mild critique on Fortmann's work is that much of his theory-oriented writing bears the character of summaries of important publications; it is as though he were collecting the stones to build a structure, for which he may have had some kind of architectural design. However, this design – his not all too explicit view of a cultural psychology of religion – was not well understood, and after his death, his department split up into three sections (cultural psychology, the psychology of religion, and pastoral psychology) that were integrated neither theoretically nor practically. Psychologists of religion in the department oriented themselves either on sociology and social psychology, or on clinical psychology. To a large extent cultural psychologists continued to orient themselves on Fortmann's style: they read widely,

Cultural Psychology: Program and Preliminary Achievements

were theoretically pluriform, but in order to get research going (and completed), they usually had to limit themselves to the perspective of some theoretical "hero," or to the application of standard methods and techniques. The number of theoretical approaches drawn upon at the department of cultural psychology increased, however, by adding to Fortmann's reading the following:

- Social behaviorism and the sociology of behavior, notably "social learning theory," an approach that perceives cultural processes from the perspective of behaviorist and neo-behaviorist learning and decision-making laws
- Psychoanalysis as employed by leftist theorists, starting less from drive theory and the Id, and focusing instead on I and Superego processes (Althusser, Foucault)
- Symbolic interactionism, a branch of psychology inspired by George Herbert Mead and developed by sociologists
- Cognitive psychology and cognitive anthropology which reminds cognitive psychology – which is always in danger of conceiving of the subject as "buried in thought" – of the existence of sociocultural systems as reservoirs from which actors derive their information and "input"
- Russian cultural-historical psychology, as developed by Vygotsky and Luria, and in later years by Bruner, Cole, Scribner, Wertsch, and others, and stating – in line with Wundt – that all higher processes of the mind are mediated by culture
- Social constructionism, as seminally formulated by Berger and Luckmann and later eloquently defended and developed by Gergen, Sarbin, and others

At the department, it was Harry Kempen in particular who continued to explore contemporary psychology and other bodies of theory, in search of approaches that could contribute to a future synthesis of cultural psychology, a synthesis that was not likely to develop in the way that theorizing took place at the department of cultural psychology. Instigated by Fortmann, and ideologically bound by the vacant professorial chair in cultural psychology and the psychology of religion (a chair that was to be divided at the beginning of the 1980s, as no-one could be found who would be acceptable to both cultural psychologists and psychologists of religion), the several sections of the department remained loosely connected. Input from a relative outsider was needed to achieve a theoretical breakthrough. This person was Hubert Hermans, an old friend and colleague of Harry Kempen, and also a student of both Rutten and Fortmann, who had been granted a professorship in personality psychology in another department. Hermans's strategy differed from Kempen's: he published easily and widely; influenced by the same phenomenological orientation (among others Merleau-Ponty), inherited from Buytendijk and Fortmann, he developed an original approach based on his successful work on motivational psychology (Hermans 1967, 1971; cf. also Hermans 1970). He conceived of the self as motivated by a number of coherent but diverse values, an idea he worked out empirically by constructing an elegant research technique: The Self-Confrontation Method (Hermans 1974, 1981; Hermans and Hermans-Jansen 1995). The friendship and ongoing dialogue between Hermans and Kempen led to the development of the idea of the dialogical self, which is clearly compatible with, and a contribution to, cultural psychology: for whatever the values may be around which a self is organized, they are derived from some cultural context, and are developed in interaction with other persons from that context. Hermans and Kempen conceive of the self as evoked by culture, as structured by elements from culture, and as multiplex and changing because of a personal history within a culture at a certain socio-historical stage. Elegantly adopting several theories from cultural psychology, and combining these with phenomenologically inspired self-psychology as initiated by William James (1890) and with Bakthinian ideas (Bakthin 1929/1973), they present the self as a multiplicity of voices, as a decentralized multiplicity of *I* positions, telling stories about their respective *me*'s.

As my aim is not to present their theory at length here, but merely to provide some systematic reflections on it, let me proceed to point out in which ways Hermans and Kempen's thinking is in line with, and is part of the line started by, Rutten and Fortmann; and, even more importantly, in which way it is a further development of this line. I shall deal with these two aspects under the headers: "Deconfessionalizing of the psychology of religion" and: "Toward a cultural psychology of religion." In this account, we shall be confronted with another clear example of the cultural embeddedness of psychological science, traditionally a topic high on the agenda of cultural psychology's research (cf. Hume 1997; Danziger 1990, 1997; Knorr Cetina 1999; Moscovici 1988; Valsinger and VanderVeer 2000).

Conclusions

Deconfessionalizing of the Psychology of Religion

The Roman Catholic University in Nijmegen was founded with the explicit aim of providing an academic training that would not be dominated by positivistic thinking and would not contradict Roman Catholic teaching. The reasoning was that as the natural sciences, and the philosophy of life many people (not only academics) derived from it, had – from Galileo to Darwin – seemed to be a series of attacks on the Catholic philosophy of life, students had to be protected. Psychology – which was becoming experimental and scientific at that time, orienting itself on the natural sciences and emancipating itself from philosophy – was regarded with deep suspicion. When Rutten was appointed professor of empirical psychology, the Bishop of Den Bosch (Mgr. Diepen) who was responsible for the University, summoned Rutten and demanded that he explain how he would proceed. Rutten could not really reassure the Bishop, who told him to beware, as he was still young and inexperienced, and forbade him to discuss such topics as free will in his lectures. Mgr. Diepen promised Rutten he would pray for the outcome of so risky an enterprise as lectures on empirical psychology (Abma 1983, p. 36). However, as we have seen, Rutten, while being a devout Catholic, did not develop his psychology on the basis of Roman Catholic philosophy, but empirically. He tried to create a kind of "free space" for psychology, even if it turned to religious phenomena: psychology would not be able to make judgments

Conclusions

141

regarding the value or truth of religious phenomena, but to the extent that they are human phenomena, they could be investigated by psychology. The theological factor of grace could not be denied by psychology, as that factor did not belong to its perspective; yet, to safeguard religious phenomena from hostile psychological analysis, Rutten declared it necessary that the psychologist of religion be a religious person. Therefore, and although psychology in general would be "methodically without confession," the psychology of religion had to remain reserved for religious, Roman Catholic psychologists only. In that way the results of the psychology of religion would also be helpful for such religious activities as pastoral work and spiritual direction. Roels had defended a similar position earlier, but in comparison with Roels, Rutten took a more liberal stance: for him, the psychology of religion was no longer primarily an apologetic instrument in defense of Roman Catholicism, but only a potential source of general insight, useful to the ministry.

Fortmann made a further distinction: he separated the psychology of religion from pastoral psychology, recruiting different staff members for these divergent fields. With Fortmann, the psychology of religion became a kind of neutral research into religiosity, the personal-human counterpart of religion. Fortmann kept in line with Rutten, however, in his use of psychology for criticizing defective manifestations of Catholic religiosity (but not of Catholic religion in general) and for elevating Catholic spirituality. Also, being a priest and working at a Roman Catholic university before the great secularization of the Netherlands, the topics he dealt with were Catholic ones and he was clearly recognizable as a religious Roman Catholic author. The psychology of religion was more or less a Catholic enterprise within secular psychology at Nijmegen.[6] In the period after Fortmann, this remained the character of the psychology of religion at Nijmegen for a long time (the department was even known as the "Catholic corner" of the building), not least because most staff members were, or had been, clergy. Increasingly, however, it was presented as an interest in religion in general. In many publications from the psychologists of religion at Nijmegen a mildly apologetic undertone remained audible: in the days of disinterest in, or even contempt for, religion as a topic for psychological research, they strove to keep religion as a topic on psychology's agenda, using clinical-psychological argumentation. Reasoning was based on the a priori that religion is an inherent part of, and therefore benevolent to, human nature. Although staff members no longer tried to use psychology to elevate Catholic customs and spirituality (as since the 1970s these had no longer been dominant, and sometimes no longer even visible in society at large), they did use the supposedly neutral terminology of psychology to show how religion can be positively related to mental health and what impact religious and other values may have in psychotherapy; they tried to detect favorable conditions for faith development, and showed that new religious movements need

---

[6] Of course, Roman Catholic influences on the psychology at Nijmegen can also be detected in the strong interest in phenomenological psychology, a psychology that tried to be not natural-scientific in nature, and therefore according to many Catholic psychologists, would be more apt for investigating the psyche. Relations between Catholicism and phenomenology can be clearly pointed out in the work of such well-known Nijmegen professors as Strasser and Buytendijk.

not be a hazard to mental health. Funding for their research mainly came from Catholic sources, etc. The general attitude was that, admittedly, religion can be a monster, but that – appropriately understood and practiced –it can also enhance human existence. In other words, in line with developments in society at large, there had been a steady deconfessionalization at the Nijmegen department of the psychology of religion since the days of Roels: Rutten freed empirical psychology methodologically from Catholic patronizing and softened its apologetic aims; Fortmann strove for a psychology of religion that would be a neutral enterprise of research, although he remained focused on Roman Catholic topics; after Fortmann, non-Catholic topics were investigated as well, and although the benevolent inclination toward religion was still dominant, efforts were made to participate in ordinary, psychological research which was not religiously bound, also to be financed by non-religious sources and to be published in non-religious media.

It is only with the concept of the dialogical self, however, that an original perspective has been developed that is not religiously motivated or legitimated, that can be applied within the research on religious and non-religious topics alike, and that, most importantly, no longer presupposes any superiority to being personally religious. The dialogical self acknowledges that human beings live in multiple social worlds, inhabited by both "actual" and "imaginary" others, persons known both from the past, and from the multiple stories we live by. If a person is religious, or at least acquainted with some kind of religion, he or she may entertain relationships with gods, spirits, saints, and/or religious authorities, and may conduct a dialogue with them, and they may all be part of a narrative construction of the world (Hermans and Kempen 1993; Hermans and Hermans-Jansen 2003). It is important to realize, however, that the concept of the dialogical self does not presuppose that relationships with religious "others" should in any way be part of the self; such a presupposition would be a theological a priori, and theological reasoning or evaluation is alien to the dialogical self as a psychological concept.

Toward a Cultural Psychology of Religion

As will be understood by now, the dialogical self is the first original Nijmegen contribution to cultural psychological reasoning. Based on theories and concepts that used to be in vogue in Nijmegen psychology, it formulates an original and elegant insight into the relationship between self and culture. Informed by a cultural psychological heritage, it opposes the idea of a unified, separate, and centralized self. It presents the self as being evoked and structured by a diversified cultural setting, and views the self as an ensemble of relationships with "actual" as well as "imagined" others, from different realms: From history, from one's personal past, but also from a mythical past or some spiritual realm. A person may maintain relationships with persons actually met, but also with persons known from stories, television, or pictures or statues in a temple or other religious meeting place. Therefore, Hermans and Kempen represent the self as an embodied multiplicity of

Conclusions

143

I positions in stories, made possible and available by cultural contexts. To the extent that a person is religious, or is familiar with religious discourse and practices, she or he will be acquainted with stories about gods, spirits, and saints; in other words, such a person will be familiar with religious signifiers, with whom she or he may or may not interact. Whether, why, and to what extent one or several relationships with religious signifiers constitute an essential part of one's narrative construction of the world, what their place is in the more general organization of the self, and why, when, and how such *I* positions will develop and where they will be moved to, are empirical questions that will be examined by a psychology of religion drawing on the theory of the dialogical self. Any psychology of religion employing the theory of the dialogical self will be a culturally sensitive psychology of religion, and therefore an example of the kind of a cultural psychology of religion Fortmann aimed at.[7] I therefore conclude that this theory is a breakthrough in two related ways: (1) it is the first original Nijmegen contribution to cultural psychology; and (2) it is an integration of cultural psychology and the psychology of religion, which had been separated since Fortmann's death. The theory of the dialogical self is a worthy tribute to the heritage of Hermans and Kempen's old teachers: Rutten and Fortmann – the initiators of cultural psychology in the Netherlands.

---

[7] For a correct understanding, one should differentiate clearly the employment of the theorizing about the dialogical self from the employment of just the Self-Confrontation Method as developed by Hermans earlier. The use of the Self-Confrontation Method as such does not make an investigation a psychological one (it may be used in theological research too, cf. Putman 1988), and is not necessarily associated with a cultural psychological perspective. Research from the perspective of the dialogical self, however, will always also be an exploration of a subject's personal culture, as I hope to show more concretely in an empirical study reported in Chapter 11.

Part III
Applications

Chapter 9
Religion as Embodiment

Cultural-Psychological Concepts and Methods in the Study of Conversion Among "Bevindelijken"[1]

Psychology of Religion and Cultural Analysis

Some years ago, Meredith B. McGuire, then president of the Society for the Scientific Study of Religion (SSSR), tried to call the attention of sociology and psychology of religion to the human body (McGuire 1990). In an eloquent presidential address, she claimed that the social sciences of religion "could be transformed" if the notion that humans are embodied would be taken seriously. In particular, she pointed out the body's importance (a) in self-experience and self's experience of others; (b) in the production and reflection of social meanings; (c) as the subject and object of power relations. McGuire's essay testifies to the growing awareness in contemporary general sociology and psychology of the impact of culture on human functioning, including religiosity. Deplorably, McGuire has not found much of a reception in the psychology of religion. At about the same time, in an invited essay in the opening volume of the newly established *The International Journal for the Psychology of Religion* (IJPR), Richard Hutch (1991) similarly called attention to the issue of embodiment. He showed that the body has been neglected both as an object of study and as "a researcher's best tool" (p. 196). Attention to embodiment, Hutch (1991) claims, could foster a comprehensive theoretical reconstruction of the psychology of religion that works beyond ethnocentric limitations. But if one goes through the following volumes both of the *JSSR* and the *IJPR*, one finds no echoes of McGuire's or Hutch's plea. For the development of theory and research in the discipline, this is to be deplored. Theory, however, is not an end in itself. In any scholarship, also in the scientific study of religion, new theories, concepts and methods will only count as progress when they demonstrate an improved access to and understanding of the phenomena to be analyzed, when they enable research of

---

[1] *Bevindelijken* refers to a group of "experience-oriented" religious people in the Netherlands that is being described in the text. I know of no English word that captures the meaning and current connotations of this term and therefore prefer to use the original word, as is customary in studies in anthropology and history of religions.

J.A. Belzen, *Towards Cultural Psychology of Religion: Principles, Approaches, Applications*, DOI 10.1007/978-90-481-3491-5_9, © Springer Science+Business Media B.V. 2010

phenomena that were considered unapproachable, or when they make visible hitherto unknown (aspects of) phenomena. Therefore, theorizing about "embodiment" will have to prove its value in its empirical application: what can it add to the exploration and understanding of religion(s)?

Like all cultural phenomena, religions are multifarious and multiplex, not to be explained by one single scientific discipline, but neither to be approached by one single theory or method within a branch of scholarship. Simple as this sounds, it is still not a common realization. In particular psychology – and to the extent that it, rightly, orients itself on this discipline, this criticism pertains to psychology of religion as well, see the previous chapters – suffers from a lack of attention to the specificity of its objects. The main reason for this is the adherence to the so-called dogma of the "psychic unity of mankind." In psychology (of religion), there is little realization that many results from research are valid only "for the time being" (Gomperts 1992), and that psychologists are usually writing contemporary "history" (Gergen 1973), not discovering perennial laws of an unchanging human mind. As a result, many psychologically intriguing phenomena in past and present, are either not being approached by psychology at all, or they are tailored down to what current methods and concepts can deal with. From a methodological perspective (which in academic psychological training is often typically reduced to statistics only), this is a fundamental fault. As should be evident, this is a criticism of a general feature of the discipline, not of individual researchers who – because of lack of time and resources – are all too often forced to conduct research with whatever means their training provided them with. Neither am I claiming to proclaim anything "new"; on the contrary, the plea is for an application of the "old" Aristotelian insight: that methods should be designed according to the nature of the object to be investigated and – I would add – according to the questions one wants to answer. When this chapter calls upon other concepts and methods than those employed by current psychology of religion, there is no intention to present these as superior or as a substitute to all that has been done in this field so far. Rather, the intent is to broaden the scope of psychology of religion, to enlarge the range of phenomena with which it can deal, and to contribute to a more appropriate understanding of some religious phenomena. (Certainly not of all! Every object of research should be allowed to call for its own approach.)

It is not just for the sake of theory, therefore, but because of being involved in empirical research on a religious minority and the resulting need for an appropriate conceptual framework that I turned to the "various theoretical approaches" McGuire and Hutch draw on. Some of these are also being presented under the admittedly still diffuse label of "cultural psychology." Here, one finds not only a recognition of the pluriformity of human conduct, a pluriformity which calls for equally pluriform psychologies to account for it, but also an increasing realization of culture's necessity and inescapability in evoking, facilitating and structuring human subjectivity and functioning. Accordingly, methodologies and concepts are being developed in different corners of cultural psychology to investigate and conceptualize the relationships between culture and personality. Having said this, I should immediately stress

The *Bevindelijke* Tradition

that what is at stake is something other than an elaboration of the common sense notion that "everything is cultural" in the sense that everything has a cultural context. The point is far more radical, and has been aphoristically expressed by Clifford Geertz: "There is no such thing as human nature independent of culture" (1973, p. 49). The viewpoint, therefore, is also very different from that of the older "culture and personality" school, as developed, for example, by Franz Boas and Margaret Mead. In the latter school, Western psychology (at the time, it was usually simplified psychoanalysis) was placed at the heart of the enterprise and researchers tried to find corroborations or at least equivalents of personality traits such as were supposed to exist in the West. (In a way, this is still part of the program of the so-called "cross-cultural" psychology.) Subsequent schools have developed under the names of "psychological anthropology" and "ethnopsychology" that come closer to what is nowadays increasingly called "cultural psychology" (Voestermans 1992).

What all of these traditions have done is show the deficiencies of mainstream Western psychology. Criticizing existing psychology (which has been done ever since the discipline established its independence), however, does not necessarily mean having an alternative. It is only in recent years that several approaches are being developed that seem promising for the rise of a different psychology (and social science). First of all, these contemporary approaches realize that we are not just dealing with "them" but also with "us": they no longer deal with "foreign" cultures only. Research in the (briefly mentioned) traditions has shown that the ways in which human beings perceive, categorize or reason are not processes deducible from any human machinery or "hardware," but reflect and depend upon cultural self-definitions. This also pertains, therefore, to the Western researchers themselves. So cultural psychology, unlike the other traditions mentioned, often tries to understand how any (also Western) human conduct is being constituted by "culture." Secondly, this implies a stronger emphasis on the interwovenness of human bodies with cultural regulating systems. To quote an aphorism by Geertz again: "Culture, rather than being added on, so to speak, to a finished or virtually finished animal, was ingredient, and centrally ingredient, in the production of that animal itself" (1973, p. 47). We will turn to this issue of the importance of the body in a moment. Thirdly, our taking cultural psychological claims seriously may, indeed, as McGuire (1990) expected, lead to a transformation of the psychology of religion. But first, let us turn to our empirical object.

The *Bevindelijke* Tradition

Research on a Dutch religious minority led to the search for an appropriate cognitive and empirical *instrumentarium* which this chapter reflects. One of the Calvinistic traditions in the Netherlands is known by the term *bevindelijken* (Dekker and Peters 1989; Hijweege 2004). This term, which does not belong to ordinary Dutch, is hard to translate and functions as a *terminus technicus*. At its root *bevinding*, an old word

150   Religion as Embodiment

for "experience," is to be understood as: experience of the spiritual process through which the soul passes in its "hidden friendship" (cf. Ps. 25:14, RSV) with God. Ignoring here an assortment of theological distinctions, one might designate the *bevindelijke* tradition as focusing on subjective spiritual experience; and even though these believers themselves, for theological reasons, abhor the word "mysticism," theologians and scientists of religion have often depicted the tradition as a mystical one (Belzen 2003; Beumer 1993; Brienen 2003; Quispel 1976). Although this characterization is not sufficient, let us first look at what is meant by their focusing on experience.

Besides discussions and conflicts about, among other themes, the doctrine and organization of the Church or its relation to the political world and the alien "world" in general, etc., Western Christianity has an unbroken tradition which is particularly focused on what one could call "interiorization." Ignoring many differentiations here, one can say that the concern of many mystics and spiritual authors has primarily been the cultivation of a heartfelt personal life of faith. Although many of them have also been very active in (church) politics and, conversely, many a reorganization was based on spiritual ideals, their primary aim was to interiorize the truth confessed, to appropriate, to experience and to live that truth in their lives. Rather than dogmatic expositions, one finds in this tradition treatises on spiritual virtues, prayer, growth in faith, the shape of a life that is well-pleasing to God, etc. (cf., e.g. Aalders 1980). To mention just one example and simultaneously the book which, beside the Bible, has been the most widely read in the West, let me refer to *The Imitation of Christ* by Thomas à Kempis. When the Reformation of the sixteenth century also found acceptance in the Low Countries (equaling roughly now The Netherlands and Belgium) and the majority of the Protestant inhabitants organized their church along Calvinistic lines, representatives of a spiritual movement in the seventeenth century insisted on a *further reformation*: needed beyond church reform was a reformation of the heart. *Pietas*, practical piety, must be cultivated. To be rejected was a lukewarm middle class life within a mainline church, even though it had been organizationally reformed. Formalism and fossilization had to be combated. This demand is similar to that which is presented in pietistic circles. The reception of German, French, and above all English pietistic (Puritan) authors led, in the seventeenth century, among a series of other factors, to a variant of pietism peculiar to The Netherlands (Heppe 1879/1979), with representative figures like Voetius, Teelinck, Lodenstein, who along with internationally better known men like Bunyan, Whitefield and (later) Spurgeon, are still being read in certain Reformed circles today (Hof 1987).

In The Netherlands one naturally finds a broad spectrum of spiritual currents and also among the "Reformed" (Calvinists adhering to different churches that all use the adjective "reformed" in their name) there are a number of very distinct types of piety. And of course, there are other protestant groups like Pentecostals and Evangelicals strongly focusing on subjective experience, equally characterized by a somewhat literal understanding of the Bible. These should be well distinguished from the *bevindelijken*, however. For up until now the believers who and the groups

Bevindelijke Spirituality: Am I Converted ...?

which strongly identify with the main representatives of the *Further Reformation* are a clearly recognizable minority. These people, who today number approximately 250,000 (the Dutch population being about 14 million citizens), are to be found in different (Calvinistic) churches; the *bevindelijke* tradition is not identical with specific churches, although some churches (e.g. the "Old Reformed Church," cf. Tennekes 1969) may have a higher percentage of *bevindelijke* congregations (parishes) and individuals than other churches, e.g. the Dutch Reformed Church. They have their own schools, socio-economic organizations, press, media, travel agencies, a political party (with two seats in Parliament equaling about 1.3% of the votes), etc. Also as individuals they can often be easily recognized as members of this community: they usually dress in black, or at least in very dark clothes; women may not wear slacks, avoid the use of makeup, wear their hair in a bun; working on Sundays is taboo (as is riding a bicycle or going out visiting, etc.). They relate antithetically to contemporary culture: television is rejected as well as medical insurance, birth control practices, sports and many other things. In their public recognizability they remind one in many respects of certain orthodox Jewish communities or of groups like the Mennonites in Ontario. (Although they may not like this comparison, it is not meant to be pejorative or to stigmatize them at all. I am only trying to convey an impression of the nature of the – in many respects respectable – subculture with which we are dealing.) The theologian VanderMeiden, a former adherent of the tradition, published a "portrait" of these communities, a portrait that is intended for a broad public and is generally recognized (also by the *bevindelijken* themselves). He points out that the demand for the interiorization of religion – which in his opinion is justified – as it was put forward by the Further Reformation, pietism, and many other spiritual movements, has – like any other demand that as such is proper – often led and still leads to one-sidednesses. According to VanderMeiden, the *bevindelijke* spirituality is "still exactly as pious and genuinely experiential [as in its original phase, JAB], still faces the world much as outsiders, is still exactly as focused on heaven and as powerfully fascinated with the stirrings of the soul more than by the earth, which has been designated as the place of the saving action of God" (VanderMeiden 1981, p. 101; my translation). Let us take a somewhat closer look at some of the elements of the spirituality of this circle, although we have only a very few (inadequate) words at our disposal for this purpose. (VanderMeiden devoted an entire book to the project.)

Bevindelijke Spirituality: Am I Converted ...?

These believers have often been described as the "heavy ones." The reference is to their seriousness or to the gravity with which they take all the things of (the) life (of faith), the fear of sin and of hell above all. Their theology and spirituality is centered on *election* and *conversion*. "Many are called but few are chosen" (Matt. 22:14). Conversion is viewed as a process, not so much as a once-and-for-all,

152

or repeated, act. It is the work of God in his chosen ones. The elect person must be converted (by God) and repent (avoid the world and sin). Conversion as an act of God, though in principle it is a once-and-for-all event, must be confirmed afresh over and over in life. The converted is "placed on a road:"[2] he gains knowledge of his sin, learns to see that he has fled from God, indeed even hated Him, has betrayed His love, and transgressed the commandments. He learns to see that he is incapable of keeping God's commandments, incapable of changing himself, let alone of improving himself. He learns to see himself as a sinner who not only cannot change himself but also does not *want* to change at all: he is recalcitrant, flees from God, even when he outwardly puts on a pious front .... He learns to accept that only God can convert him back to God, that an intervention of grace must come into his life, from the outside, to change him. Just as the Heidelberg Catechism teaches: elect sinners, once they have begun to receive this knowledge of *sin*, move forward to *redemption*, which is the unilateral work of the Holy Spirit within them, in order to arrive at the end at the station of *gratitude;* that is, *if* the "grave" believers of the "further" or "second" reformation type, ever get that far.... For those who think that grace is at work in them, who think they see a small cloud of salvation, must be on their guard: are they not fooling themselves? Are they not being deceived by the devil? Are they not rocking themselves in the cradle of a false security? Are they not steering themselves, "while harboring an imaginary heaven in their heart," straight to hell? Did not the apostle say: "Examine yourselves to see whether you are holding to your faith" (2 Cor. 13:5)? These and numerous other Bible verses are cited and pondered as favorites. One learns to examine oneself, to make distinctions between countless kinds of Christians (nominal Christians, Christians-in-word, camp followers, Sunday Christians, talk-Christians, baptized citizens of the world, etc.), to distinguish the many stations of the spiritual life (also in their own life), to distinguish the many forms in which a person can know Christ (as surety, as high priest, as advocate, and many more).

Really and truly, these people are "grave"; they are "troubled" (which they distinguish as a spiritual stage before conversion) over their salvation; they transpose everything in life into the key of the absolute. VanderMeiden writes:

> Laughter is not forbidden, but for a person who has discovered his wretched condition, laughter finally dies except when eternity beckons and smiles at him. The face, the clothing, the gait (especially on Sundays) – all this is burdened by the leaden weight of a human fate,

---

[2] Although one can hardly do so in a translation, in the next sentences I will try to convey a little of the style of the *bevindelijken,* using their rather rhetorical terminology. I will deliberately avoid gender neutral language, which they would abhor as opposing the "divinely ordained creation order of male headship." In many respects, the *bevindelijken* are strictly conservative; even their language, called the "language of Canaan," is old-fashioned, rooted in a – to their understanding: irreplaceable – Bible translation from the seventeenth century and in authors from the Further Reformation. Many of the distinguishing characteristics of the group fall outside the scope of this article; in the text I focus on their spirituality, which, for lack of space, I can only describe in part. Some more information in English on the group and its spirituality can be found in Belzen (2003).

Bevindelijke Spirituality: Am I Converted ...?

the burden of being or not-being elect and of the necessity of conversion. This fundamental question: "am I elect and hence can I be converted?" injects immense seriousness into a person's life. It is a weightier question than all other questions in life: weightier than all the social and political problems combined. The "grave ones" get up with it in the morning and go to bed with it at night. In "grave" circles one frequently hears the familiar greeting: "How are you?" interpreted as follows: "How are you doing spiritually; have you made progress on the road of salvation; do you already know whether you are elect, called, born-again, converted, justified or sanctified? And can you detect these progressive steps in yourself?" (1981, p. 40)

Thus they examine themselves – and others. For "spiritual conversation" is highly valued. Over and over, in *bevindelijke* circles, conversation will touch upon the spiritual life, allusions are made to it, biblical or other religious phrases are used. All of life is permeated by religious elements in such a way that much of what an outsider would regard as religious is not experienced that way at all by the people in question. For them, activities become religious in the strict sense only when they are performed with a religious intention, for example when, after repeatedly talking about God and his work during the day, these people come together explicitly for this purpose in the evening. For aside from the (often triple) Sunday services there are numerous occasions in these circles where people meet for less formal "house-gatherings" ("conventicles"), where they talk about "God's Word" (the Bible) and especially about the *praxis pietatis*: where they tell stories about what "the Lord has wrought in the lives of individuals" (Schram 1983). Partly these stories are borrowed from books published in their own circles (conversion stories; spiritual autobiographies); partly they are also presented by the participants about and by themselves. At least, *if* there are those who are bold enough to testify that they are converted or at least that they can observe or have observed the workings of the Spirit in their life! This takes courage both before God and before oneself as well as before the others. For, in the first place, these people do not want to commit the sin of appropriating for themselves what has not been granted to them by God. And, in the second place, they will have to expose themselves to the criticism or at least the looks and questions of others who are present and who must first be persuaded before they will acknowledge that a given person is in fact converted. With the help of what they know – from sermons, personal accounts, stories, and from books of their great authorities, the "old writers" of the Further Reformation – about the heights and depths of the spiritual life and with the help of what is known about the life and conduct of the person in question, the narrator is made to understand how people rate her or him spiritually. Hence there is reason to be on one's guard ...

As may be clear, in many respects the *bevindelijken* do not have a theology that would be different from "mainline" (if there is such a thing) Protestantism (compare with, e.g. McKim 1992). It is their spirituality, their "operationalization" (Belzen 1996a) and experience of Protestant (i.e. Calvinist) principles in daily life that makes them different. Their spirituality is centered on conversion, which is a highly ambiguous, even controversial, topic. Controversial – not in the sense that there would be theological debate about it, but in the sense of the recognition among individual believers. On the one hand, people are being confronted time and again with the call to repent: in church services, in literature, and also in private discussions the necessity of conversion is spoken of continuously. On the other hand, great emphasis is laid on the human *im*possibility to convert her- or himself: it is God's (highly exceptional) work in the elect ones. To claim without warrant that one is converted would be one of the greatest possible sins. Therefore, and paradoxically, an individual account of conversion is very exceptional; it is distrusted and only accepted (if ever) after extensive "testing" (often by informal authorities, i.e. not by theologians or church leaders, but by, say, the leaders of conventicle meetings). Although there have always been a few people who were accepted by many (never by everyone) as converted, and who were held in high esteem, in recent years their number has dwindled. (*Bevindelijke* theological interpretation: the Spirit is not working among us anymore, we are approaching the last days.) But even these acknowledged converts would never claim to be or boast of being converted; they would tell about their spiritual struggles, of hoping and of despairing, of the ups and downs in their spiritual life. Especially people going to conventicle meetings (a similarly decreasing number), but also regular churchgoers are even recognizable without special dress (which is often a traditional type of costume). Their way of walking, looking, their vocabulary, their intonation – it is all peculiarly characteristic of a "true *bevindelijke.*"

Pressing down upon the life of these people is the deadweight of the idea of being guilty and of having to submit, with complete justification, to the punishments God sends down on them. They reject vaccination and health insurance, for example, since sickness is interpreted as being sent by God whose will one ought not to resist, nor should one seek to escape the consequences of God's wrath by taking out insurance. In all things, both in their personal life and in events on a larger scale, these people discern the hand of (especially a punitive), God. The following quotations from a variety of sources illustrate this point.

One of our informants told us about his religious socialization:

> I was three years old when I broke my thighbone; in the same year I got diphtheria and became seriously ill. My mother, who is a "changed" person,[3] always saw this as a warning. Until I left home and certainly till I was twenty, she kept telling me that I should change my way of behavior for I must be a wicked person for the Lord to send me so may calls of conscience at such an early age. Time and again she warned me, for I would go to hell, if I did not change my behavior.

During the great flood which struck The Netherlands in the winter of 1994–1995, the *Reformatorisch Dagblad,* a newspaper of the *bevindelijke* school, editorialized as follows:

> The floods which threaten the houses and properties of many of our compatriots and fellow parishioners call upon us, now that the Lord's Day is approaching, to bring the

---

[3] That is a person in whose life God has "wrought a change."

Obstacles to Empirical Research

prevailing distress into the worship services with all due sobriety. The need to humble ourselves and to return to Almighty God is spelled out for us in Jeremiah 5:20ff. May this message break down our delusions of autonomy and awaken us out of our blindness and deafness, so that we may see the hand and hear the voice of the Lord. (*Reformatorisch Dagblad,* February 3, 1995)

The hog cholera which swept the hog industry in the southern part of the Netherlands in 1997–1998 also struck farmers who as Christian believers belong to the *bevindelijke* tradition. One of them is an elder with the "Old Reformed Church" in The Netherlands. In a newspaper article he is quoted as saying: "With this epidemic the Lord is demonstrating the powerlessness of humans. God rules: that is a reality which should humble us." He also has reasons of principle for not inoculating his pigs:

Man cannot banish any illness. That, after all, is perfectly clear, isn't it? Despite all the measures which have been taken, the epidemic is steadily assuming more severe forms. The Lord is still stretching out his hand and showing man his powerlessness. (Berge 1997, p. 17)

Obstacles to Empirical Research

Trying to conduct any psychological investigation into these people's spirituality is not an easy undertaking. Besides difficulties one may have to deal with in general when intimately exploring people's religiosity or when investigating any (new) religious movement that relates antithetically to "the modern world" (including especially the psychology of religion: researching without taking into account God's action!), the paradoxical nature of *bevindelijke* conversion plays tricks on the researcher. Dealing with religious topics is strictly reserved for religious discourse itself (whether in church or conventicle, by a minister or an elder, or in private spiritual conversations). Someone who does not express himself in this way and in this context will not have access to these people's religiosity. Passing out questionnaires, therefore, would be useless: they would not be returned. Sending out interviewers seems to be of little use either, as *bevindelijken* will not consent to being interviewed, or will avoid talking about what exactly is their experience of, or with, conversion. Moreover, it would take hard training for the interviewer to learn to talk and behave in the proper way, a task almost certain to fail. Trying to carry out observations is likely to turn out to be a very embarrassing experience, both for the observer and the observed. Church services may be visited publicly, although it may happen that one – especially when it is clear one is not coming for reasons of personal piety – is firmly invited to leave the church or even the church area! And even if one stays to attend a worship service, one will only witness what any published or tape-recorded sermon could yield as a result: the singing of psalms (in a translation and a melody from the seventeenth century; no musical instruments), some announcements on church activities, some long prayers (about 15 min each) and a very long sermon (about 60 min), in an archaic language,

156   Religion as Embodiment

telling the listeners they are doomed eternally unless they are converted. Even fellow researchers in this project who have been studying this group for a long time (in some cases, amounting to several years) felt extremely uneasy in such a situation, for it is apparent that even in relatively moderate circles the visitors/researchers are not welcome. Such observations do not yield much insight into private spirituality, into experience of, or with, conversion.

Obviously, these obstacles to empirical research are not altogether unique to dealing with the *bevindelijken*. However, since psychologists are usually interested in experience, in private affairs and subjective states and reports, people all too often conclude that psychological research into *bevindelijke* conversion is an impossibility. Besides theological and other scholarly research from an "inside" perspective (Brienen 1978, 1986, 1989; Florijn 1991; Graafland 1991; Harinck 1980; Jong et al. 1992; Ketterij 1972), there have been some studies from a social scientific "outside" perspective by historians and sociologists (Beumer 1993; Dekker and Peters 1989; Janse 1985; Vellenga 1994; Lieburg 1991; Zwemer 1992), but – to my knowledge – hardly ever by psychologists.[4] Nevertheless, experiences incurred in a long-standing project (Belzen 1989b, 1990, 1991b, c) on "*bevindelijke* spirituality" do not entirely accord with this view. Together with several (changing) others, I have tried to get as close to *bevindelijke* conversion as seemed possible without, however, ever becoming "one of them," without any inside experience of their religiosity of my own. Therefore, the empirical results that I draw on in this chapter, and that have also been used in the above introduction to the group and its spirituality, have not been collected in any standardized, straightforward way. Besides this, they are very diverse, including dozens of observations made during attendance at church services, observations and conversations on the occasion of visits to feast days (mission conferences, book fairs, training courses, political assemblies); numerous encounters with people, in the street, after church, at their homes, sometimes just "small talk," sometimes in the form of semi-structured interviews (in some cases even with a tape-recorder on the table); analysis of ego-documents, novels, spiritual authors and scholarly publications on *bevindelijken*; reading their newspapers, visiting them on the Internet (which some of them do indeed use!). In short: anything that might help a person to "get in touch" (Shotter 1992). (Compare the methods Festinger employed in his classic study *When prophesy fails* (1956). Note, however, that no "participant observation" in the strict sense was used in this research with the *bevindelijken*: I did not really "participate"; cf. also Hood's (1998) approach in order to get access to and win the confidence of the "serpent-handlers" for a contemporary example of the creative ways one must sometimes adopt in order to obtain any results at all.)

---

[4] Even an application I made for a grant for student research was initially (1992) criticized by reviewers of the Netherlands Organization for Scientific Research: I should have realized that this group is too closed to be investigated, especially about conversion.... Meanwhile, the student successfully defended her doctoral dissertation: Hijweege (2004).

Variants of Cultural Psychology

To what extent can psychology be of any help in understanding this *bevindelijke* spirituality? Generally, and in accordance with a metaphysical tradition that is powerful in the West, psychology pursues what is presumed to be the case for, or to be the basis elements of, all human psychic functioning. Typically, no attention is paid to "culture," whether contemporary or historical; particularities are to be excluded. Cognitivist approaches – created in tandem with computer technology (Sampson, p. 601) – for example, usually center on a mind that is a kind of abstract calculating device dwelling inside the head of an individual and conducting its operations on symbolic representations of the outside world. The embeddedness of human beings in history, society and culture is excluded by such an approach in order to focus on the mind's intrinsic processes and structure. Although voices criticizing this approach have become more frequent and louder in recent years, this picture still holds true for the major part of psychology, also in its analysis of religion. Rambo (1992), author of a synthetically designed psychological model of conversion, writes, "Psychologists [of religion, JAB] typically do not address the context of religious conversion because their emphasis is on the individual. Until recently they tended to focus on issues that ignored or downplayed cultural and social variables" (p. 164). Although Rambo is clearly aware of the importance of context, in his monograph (1993) he can hardly quote from any empirical study that realizes the impact of culture in conversion. It is not likely that such psychological studies – worthwhile as they may be in themselves – will be of great help when it comes to an adequate psychological conceptualization of the specific characteristics of *bevindelijke* spirituality. Moreover, most psychological studies on conversion have studied conversion *to* a new faith or *to* a new religious group (not necessarily a "new [usually meaning: non-Western] religious movement," but new to the individual concerned). Clearly, conversion *to* a new group is not what is at stake in the case of the *bevindelijke* conversion. One cannot even say it is a (new) commitment to a formerly held faith, as a "true *bevindelijke*" believer is already very committed, yet the more committed (s)he is, the less likely it is that (s)he will claim or consider her or himself to be converted. Besides, and importantly: conversions to the *bevindelijken* as a group are not known at all; although people do change their membership in churches, they – already *bevindelijk* – remain within the same tradition.

A current approach in psychology that does strive to give appropriate attention to the fact that humans are cultural beings is Social Constructionism (cf., e.g., Cushmann 1990; Gergen 1985; Harré 1986; Sarbin and Kitsuse 1994). In its different variants, it is one of the most powerful factions of a cultural psychology (Voestermans 1992; Sampson 1996). Social constructionism strives to replace interest in psychological processes within individuals – common fare in experimental social psychology – with concerns for interdependencies, jointly determined outcomes, "joint action." The attempt to identify emotions, for example, is regarded as obfuscating. Social constructionists point out that emotional discourse gains its meaning not from its (assumed), relationship to an inner world (of dispositions, drives, instincts, traits), but from the way it figures in patterns of cultural relationships.[5] "Communities generate conventional modes of relating; patterns of action within these relationships are often given labels. Some forms of action – by current Western standards – are said to indicate emotions" (Gergen 1994, p. 222). A much quoted research study by Averill (1982) shows that a person is not "motivated" or "incited to action" by emotions, but rather, one *does* emotions, or participates in them (as one would, say, on a stage, as narrative psychologist Sarbin (1986a) points out). Following Austin's (1962) analysis of speech acts, one can say that the performative value of an utterance, say, with regard to someone's spiritual state, is derived from its position within some extended pattern of relationships. Using Wittgensteinian (1953) terminology, Gergen (1994) argues that utterances may be seen as constituents of more extended forms of life, which may include both actions (other than verbal) and objects or environments. Gestures and facial expressions, for example, contribute to the context which renders speech meaningful, given its status as a particular kind of performative.

The "rhetorical-responsive" version of social constructionism as articulated by John Shotter (1993a, b) emphasizes and elaborates precisely this last point. Unlike earlier approaches which focused on events within the inner dynamics of the individual psyche or on events within the already determined characteristics of the external world, Shotter attends to events within the contingent flow of continuous communicative interaction between human beings. Shotter agrees with Harré (1992) that meanings, and even cognitive abilities (Shotter 1993a, p. 7), are being formed in what people say and do, rather than existing already, well-formed sources of actions and utterances, but he stresses that this is always done in relating to others. If human beings are to be perceived as speaking authoritatively, they have to acquire the capacity to respond to others should the latter challenge the claims made. Speaking to and with others, in the various forms of "talk," is always also rhetorical: the aim is to "move" others to action, to believe, to change their perception or opinion, etc. Shotter stresses that one accounts for one's actions in terms understood by members of the social reality of which one is a part. Contrary to earlier approaches, his focus is on the unordered "hurly-burly" or "bustle" side (Wittgenstein 1980) of everyday social life (Shotter 1993b). What is embodied in this conversational background of human life is a special kind of knowledge, unvoiced in psychology thus far: namely how to *be* a person of this or that particular kind according to the culture into which one develops as a child (Shotter 1993a, p. 19). This is a knowledge that does not need be – probably even cannot be – finalized or

---

[5] A related current similar to discursive psychology is even more outspoken in this regard. Regarding discourse as the characteristic feature of human life, Harré and Stearns (1995) state that there is no central processor (Shweder 1991), or any such mechanism as assumed by the "old" cognitive psychology. Psychology should not search for that. It should rather disclose the structure of the discursive productions in which psychological phenomena are immanent and seek to discover how the various cognitive skills needed to accomplish the tasks that psychology studies are acquired, developed, integrated and employed. Resisting any (neuropsychological) reductionism, they apodictically write: "There is nothing in the human universe except active brains and symbolic manipulations" (Harré and Stearns 1995, p. 2).

formalized in a set of statements before it can be applied. It is neither theoretical knowledge ("knowing that") for it is knowledge-in-practice; nor a skill or craft ("knowing-how"), for it is joint knowledge, knowledge held in common with others. It is a third kind of knowledge that cannot be reduced to either of the other two. It is "the kind of knowledge one has from within a situation, a group, social institution, or society; it is what we might call a 'knowing-from'" (Shotter 1993a, p. 19). It is the "practical-moral knowledge" Bernstein (1983) spoke about.

These reflections seem particularly useful for the analysis of what is involved in *bevindelijke* spirituality. For being a converted person or – more precisely – being someone about whom fellow believers think she or he may be converted has to do with this third kind of knowledge. It is not – or not just! – a matter of being able to give a theologically correct account of one's conversion, nor of expressing oneself in the appropriate terminology. Difficult as that would be, all this could be attained by a researcher of the *bevindelijken* too. She or he would, however, still lack "inside" knowledge. For what is at stake is a knowledge that one has as a socially competent and accepted member of the *bevindelijke* culture. So, although a *bevindelijke* believer may not be able to reflectively articulate the nature of this "knowledge" as an inner, mental representation, according to questions asked about conversion and spirituality in a more general sense, she or he can nonetheless call upon it as a practical resource in framing appropriate answers. Although a *bevindelijke* will not be able to list the criteria why and when any believer should or may be assumed to be converted – since according to popularized versions of theological doctrine, no one can know or judge upon someone's being converted, a straightforward question on this would be totally out of order – there is very often a high degree of agreement among *bevindelijken* as to the spiritual state of some of their fellow believers.

While acknowledging the importance of narratives as shaping and expressing human subjectivity (Belzen 1996b), social constructionism calls attention to "narration" (Gergen) or to "words in their speaking" (Shotter). As pointed out earlier, an account of *bevindelijke* conversion will only be accepted if – correct content and phrasing being assured – all kinds of characteristics of the speaker that may seem irrelevant to outsiders (like dress, body posture, pitch of voice, glance, facial appearance, breathing; but to some extent also features like geographical, family and educational background) correspond with the expectancies of the *bevindelijke* listeners. Indeed, it is very hard to be "recognized" as being converted, and almost impossible to convert *to* this tradition!

Body, Culture and Religion

The characteristics just cited, by way of examples, call attention to the eminent importance of the body for a psychological understanding of the *bevindelijke* tradition. In scholarly, say, theological, reflections on the *bevindelijken*, the importance of the correct account of conversion is stressed. Without denying this, I would like to reflect on embodiment, a theme increasingly recognized as being of central importance to cultural psychology, as it refers to the recognition of humans being socialized into both a linguistic and a bodily community of practices such that what is said and the embodied quality of how it is said are simultaneously engendered and inextricably intertwined (Sampson 1996).[6] One should think in this connection of seemingly "simple" examples (how human mouths, lips, lungs, vocal chords are socialized to form the sounds appropriate to spoken language), but also of complex bodily practices (how to stand and move, how to comport oneself through various circumstances and situations in life). As introduced briefly in Chapter 3, Bourdieu's concept of the *habitus* is illuminating here and can serve as a supplement to social constructionist considerations.[7] Bourdieu describes *habitus* as "a system of lasting, transposable dispositions which, integrating past experiences, functions at every moment as a matrix of perceptions, appreciations and actions and makes possible the achievement of infinitely diversified tasks" (Bourdieu 1977, p. 82) or as "a set of historical relations 'deposited' within individual bodies in the form of mental and corporeal schemata of perception, appreciation, and action" (Bourdieu and Wacquant 1992, p. 16).[8]

Bourdieu tends to unite in the concept of the *habitus* what Westerners usually separate: body and discourse, as they go together in, say, the articulatory style of a

---

[6]Criticisms of the neglect of the body in psychology, indeed in Western thought in general, have been offered by philosophical anthropologists and phenomenologists like Nietzsche, Heidegger and Merleau-Ponty (for instructive reviews, see e.g., Csordas 1990; Merwe and Voestermans 1995; Stam 1998; Voestermans and Verheggen 2007). In fact, good reasons may be put forward to argue that human beings can understand and think as they do because our more abstract understandings are grounded in preconceptual embodied structures (Lakoff and Johnson 1980; Johnson 1987). A contribution from evolutionary biology to these reflections is provided by Sheets-Johnstone: she points out that major abstract concepts (including notions of death, numbers, agency, etc.) derive from an original corporeal logos. Suggesting that the roots of human thinking lie in the hominid body, she asserts: "meanings are generated by an animal's bodily comportment, movement and orientation [...] semanticity is a built-in of bodily life" (Sheets-Johnstone, in Sampson 1996, p. 618). Cf. also Sacks (1990) who describes how bodily activities evoke a self (p. 46). It would take me too far afield to develop these ideas here. For one of the rare – strongly Lacanian psychoanalytically oriented – attempts at conceptualizing the interwovenness of the human body and culture in psychology-of-religion research, cf. Vergote (1978/1988); also cf. O'Connor (1998).

[7]In fact, it is a matter of discussion whether social constructionism is in fact sufficiently sensitive to the embodied aspects of human life (cf. Baerveldt and Voestermans 1996; Sampson 1996).

[8]Bourdieu's (typically French) writing is not easy to read, not even in translation. Let us take just one more look at a description of what he means: "[...] the principle generating and unifying all practices, the system of inseparably cognitive and evaluative structures which organizes one's vision of the world in accordance with the objective structures of a determinate state of the social world: this principle is nothing other than the *socially informed body*, with its tastes and distastes, its compulsions and repulsions, with, in a word, all its *senses*, that is to say, not only the traditional five senses – which escape the structuring action of social determinism – but also the sense of necessity and the sense of duty, the sense of direction and the sense of reality, the sense of balance and the sense of beauty, common sense and the sense of the sacred, tactical sense and the sense of responsibility, business sense and the sense of propriety, the sense of humor and the sense of absurdity, moral sense and the sense of practicality, and so on" (1977, p. 124, emphasis in original).

Body, Culture and Religion

social class – or, for that matter, of a religious tradition like the *bevindelijken* – noting how a group's very lifestyle becomes embodied. Discourse should not then, in a Bourdieuian sense, be understood as being of a solely linguistic character; on the contrary, it is a *praxis*, and it even includes ideologies, class characterizations and politics. Although these can be distinguished on a societal or cultural level, they do not exist in the abstract or disembodied. Domination, for example, is an embodied reality; submission is most often not a deliberate act of conscious concession to anyone's force, but is "lodged deep inside the socialized body. In truth it expresses the 'somatization of social relations of domination' (…) an imprisonment effected via the body" (Bourdieu and Wacquant 1992, pp. 24, 172). Bourdieu suggests that the actual body is molded to carry within its very tissues and muscles the story of a given ideology.

Notions of embodiment, like the *habitus*, are important since they allow us to overcome the old conceptual separation of subject and world that has been haunting psychology for so long. Whereas the body might be conceived as an individual entity, embodiment cannot: because embodiment is about culture, about "world," not only about material worlds, but also about possible worlds. Thanks to embodiment, human beings are able to engage in the world so as to fashion semblances and configure social worlds, in short, we are able to symbolize. For an understanding of what is significant about embodiment for social religious life, it may be useful to remind ourselves of work done by Goffman (1951) who pointed out that symbols of class status carry both categorial and expressive significance. The categorial significance is concerned with matters of denoting or claiming identity; the second significance expresses the style of life or point of view of the person concerned (cf. Radley 1996). The dark clothes of a *bevindelijke*, the stony face, the grave look, the walk with a stoop, the dragging speech – these and other embodied characteristics do not just identify a person as a member of the *bevindelijke* tradition. They are also the expression of a way of life; they portray the conception of a human being who knows that the "pleasures of the world" are treacherous, is bowed down by the realization that (s)he will be doomed because of her or his sins, who knows that (s)he is totally dependent on grace, something for which a person can only humbly wait. The "socially informed body" (Bourdieu) is in these cases the medium individuals employ to display things that matter to each other, and how they matter. Such displays are not to be confused with non-verbal communication; they are expressive forms that do more than communicate ideas about selves in abstraction (Radley 1996, p. 562). Such displays are "enactments with the body that symbolize certain ways of being, that make certain social worlds appear" (p. 566).

With other religions, or probably more correctly, with other traditions within a certain religion, being a believer may have to do with membership in some church, with affirming specific theological doctrines, with joining an "inner circle" or even with being able to account for one's religious experiences in a certain stylized way (e.g., with evangelicals) and with alterations in behavior. All of this is not specific enough to characterize what being a *bevindelijke* is or may be. Being a *bevindelijke* has to do with an all-pervading "style," belonging to a specific "life form" (Wittgenstein), displaying itself in and through the body. Knowing the doctrine, frequenting the conventicles, or being able to tell about her or his spiritual experiences in the required way, would not, on this basis alone, be accepted by *bevindelijken* as proof of being a "true" believer, let alone "converted." And, conversely, if a believer's body expresses experiential-subjective knowledge about misery, redemption, and gratitude, if the face is marked by the struggle with God, if the voice is characterized by the afflictions endured, if body and clothing express the knowledge of being dependent on grace, then even a theologically doubtful way of talking about spiritual experiences will be accepted. No *bevindelijke* will ever claim to be converted or talk about her or his conversion, but the more the body reveals the "experiences with the Lord" this tradition induces and requires, the more easily one's fellow believers will judge someone to be converted (or at least to be a person "who is being visited by the Lord"). Better than being elected as elder to the congregation, it is the "countenance, conversation, and clothing" (as one of the group's "winged expressions" has it) that must bear public testimony to a person's inner spiritual state. Since what matters for the *bevindelijke* is not only the acceptance of a new doctrine and membership in a different denomination, but an inclusive style as a component of an integral "life form," it is understandable that a person not born and socialized in it will hardly qualify for acceptance as a believer in this religious subculture. It is similarly understandable that almost no conversions to the *bevindelijke* subculture are known to occur.

Concluding Comments

Bringing the body (back?) to the psychology of religion may transform the discipline, Hutch (1991) and McGuire (1990) claimed. Affirming as I do the importance for psychology of religion of dealing with the theme, or perspective, of embodiment, I would like to make a perhaps less ambitious but certainly no less encompassing assertion: attention to the body must be embedded in and is necessary from within a culture-psychological perspective. Attention to embodiment (although very important!) is not only a requisite for enabling the study of religion to participate in new theoretical developments in psychology;[9] it is also necessary, for at least three reasons, from the perspective of empirical research.

1. In our society, a society which is rapidly becoming more heterogeneous and pluriform, "religion" is not always, everywhere, and for everyone the same, nor does it mean the same. This is becoming consistently more clear to Western

---

[9] For the psychology of religion, coming to an understanding with these new theoretical developments will be the more fruitful since their representatives are much less averse to religion than earlier generations of psychologists tended to be. Authors such as Boesch (1983, 1991, 2000, 2005), Gergen (1993, 1994), Much and Mahapatra (1995), Obeyesekere (1985), Sampson (1996) and Scheibe (1998) , while not counted – even by themselves – as practitioners of the psychology of religion, do in fact again include in their work a consideration of a variety of religious phenomena.

psychologists as well. Inasmuch as every religion produces religious experiences and behavioral dispositions of its own, it is of eminent importance to examine how a given religion (as a cultural phenomenon) "works" psychologically: how it transmits, generates, facilitates these experiences and dispositions and makes them function.

2. All psychological characteristics are incarnated and habitually organized. Deep-rooted practices, needs, and emotions are anchored in the body and often only to a limited extent accessible to reflection. A cognitive viewpoint, therefore, is too limited for empirical research: aside from having instruments for "measuring" explicit (i.e. carefully considered) meaning-bestowal, ideas and views (even with reference to oneself), one must employ or develop experience-near techniques to be able to examine obstinate, unreflected, patterned behaviors in primary relationships (Voestermans and Verheggen 2007).

3. In this manner, the scope of the psychology of religion can be broadened. Not only people able and willing to cooperate in tests, questionnaire-research, and experiments but also an array of minorities will in this way become accessible to research. Although criticism of psychology as being based on white middle class students has been around for decades, numerous research projects in the psychology of religion are still based on this category (Batson et al. 1993; Loewenthal 1995, p. 152). Also in many conversions to so-called new religious movements the "test-persons" concerned came from this segment of society. Socially less advantaged and less well educated people, however, are frequently not accessible to the "pen and pencil" research practice that has become standard. In addition, minorities which for religious reasons may not be accessible to questionnaires and other quantifying methods may in this manner be involved in the research as well. An empirical phenomenon like a *bevindelijke* conversion may thus be studied by psychology nevertheless.

Chapter 10
Religion, Culture and Psychopathology

Cultural-Psychological Reflections on Religion in a Case of Manslaughter in the Netherlands

At the start, a case: During one of the religious gatherings which for some time had been taking place in the evening at the home of farmer Martin Schroevers in the Dutch village of Betuwe, Schroevers killed his own farmhand Peter, inasmuch as the latter was thought to be possessed by the devil.[1] Approximately a dozen persons – men, women, and children – were present at the scene, some of whom horribly maimed and mutilated the body. Martin was thereupon proclaimed the Messiah and taken in triumphal procession by his psalm-singing adherents from Betuwe, where he lived, to Diedenhoven, where he was acclaimed by his mother and his brothers as God's Chosen One. Early in the morning Martin, along with his adherents, returned to Betuwe, where he was arrested by the police and brought to prison. Three other involved persons were taken to psychiatric institutions, to which Martin was later transferred as well.

Just what happened here? Was it murder? A case of mental illness? If so, what did religion or religious notions have to do with it?

Introduction: The Necessity of a Multiple Perspective

The connections between mental illness and religion are numerous and complex, as well as controversial (Akthar and Parens 2001; Boehnlein 2000; Clarke 2001; Kaiser 2007; Koenig 1998; Loewenthal 2007; Plante and Sherman 2001; Utsch 2005). Many people may even raise an eyebrow when mental illness is associated with religion at all. What, for example, does the attempt by renunciation to reach Nirvana or to lead a Christian life have to do with an *illness* of the soul? Why should kneeling five times a day with one's face toward Mecca while reciting prayers be considered pathological? Or must one then from time to time go to a physician when a young man or woman, deeply religious and anxious not to sin, decides to stop speaking, mindful of the saying that; "One who guards his tongue

---

[1] All names of persons involved have been changed (also the name of the village). Evidently, quotations have been translated.

J.A. Belzen, *Towards Cultural Psychology of Religion: Principles, Approaches, Applications*, DOI 10.1007/978-90-481-3491-5_10, © Springer Science+Business Media B.V. 2010

and does not err in speech can also control his whole body"? Should we in such cases perhaps actually be startled, except when the person in question wants to become a Carthusian monk? In this last case, is psycho-pathologically fueled skepticism inappropriate since we are dealing here with an ancient and venerable tradition? Should we instead distrust the so-called "new religious movements"? These questions are difficult. They are hard to answer not only because the state of affairs to which they pertain is so complex, but also because the questions themselves are hard to formulate. By the nature of the questions or the manner in which they are stated one can already often easily discover which and whose interests the questioner represents. If someone asks how one should judge the behavior of a person who closes her eyes, folds her hands, and – either silently or out loud – begins to speak to a person whom she has never either seen or heard and from whom she does not expect to hear an answer but with whom she nevertheless claims to maintain an intimate personal relationship – it is probable that the questioner is associated with some form of critique of religion. If, however, he enters upon a discussion of the care of the mentally ill as it has been organized by the churches, the wind is bound to blow in some other direction.

It is nonetheless useful to pose the one question as well as the other and thereby address various aspects or possibilities of relating mental illness to religion. As is the case with virtually every basic set of problems, the questions are not easy to formulate, let alone answer unambiguously. With questions such as these, therefore, the reward of the discussion usually seems to consist, not in being able to give *the* answer, but in being able to uncover and take note of several additional aspects of the problems in question. Progress does not lie in the answer but in differentiating appropriate questions. That is how things still stand after approximately a century of research in, and reflection on, mental illness and religion. Whereas in the circles of cronies, in the press or in politics, the watchwords are often ever so reassuringly unequivocal, in so-called professional circles (similarly reassuring?) ambiguity is accepted: the connections between mental illness and religion are manifold, and branch out in all directions; that which is hypothetically possible can also be found empirically. Religion can be both the root and the expression of mental illness, but it can also be a defense against it, a means of healing, a final refuge, a method and way of dealing with the illness (cf. Batson et al. 1993; Hood et al. 2009; Schumaker 1992). What in the meantime has also become clear, however, is that both concepts, "mental illness" (and "mental health") and "religion" are far too diffuse or multidimensional to be simply placed in relation to each other.

We can already tell from this extremely sketchy characterization of the pertinent results that the relations between mental illness and religion can in any case no longer be conceptualized from the perspective of a causal connection between them. People have also found that, perhaps especially in view of the kinds of knowing, experiencing, and behaving which up until a couple of decades ago were called "pathological," the desire to *explain* is inadequate in large areas of the psychological sciences. Psychic dysfunction cannot be explained in terms of "causes" which one can "treat" in the sense of eliminating them in order thereby to restore "normal" psychic functioning. And even if one is able to identify "causes," or to put it more

Introduction: The Necessity of a Multiple Perspective

cautiously, factors which have contributed to an illness, one can never manipulate these factors as though they were variables, but must look for ways to deal with and manage the situation one has encountered. Nor do we read any longer today about "religion" (whatever we are to understand by the word) as the "cause" of "mental illness": central in current discussions is the question of religion as a "coping system" (cf. Pargament 1990; Pargament et al. 1992). In the last several centuries in the West the search for explanations was *the* paradigm for scientific research. The "mechanization of the world picture" (Dijksterhuis 1986), the success of the natural sciences and the related achievements of technology have for a long time marginalized every worldview other than that of the natural sciences as inferior. There have nevertheless always been thinkers who pointed out that the practice of causal thinking belongs to a specific worldview, and that there are other worldviews (or attempts at interpreting the world), which are frequently as adequate or even more so. They have stated as their position that distinct phenomena (or entire blocks of reality) require, for the purpose of discussing them, distinct ways of thinking. Numerous distinctions and descriptions of the various kinds of thinking have been proposed. Probably the best known alternative to "explanation," one that has come down to us in a tradition put forward by W. Dilthey (1894/1964), is usually denominated as "understanding" or "interpretation". In a way which differs from "explanatory" natural sciences (which have proven their strength especially in the study of areas of reality that are independent of man), people in the "human sciences" attempt to "interpret" the products of culture. Literature, art, societal patterns of coherence as well as the various expressions of human consciousness, according to this tradition, require a totally different kind of "explanation" from that which is customary in the natural sciences.

Contemporary practitioners in the human sciences such as Clifford Geertz (1973) and Paul Ricoeur (1981) demand – especially where religion is concerned – a method (which they call, respectively, a "semiotic" and a "hermeneutic") which allows us to grasp the *rules* which control a given system of symbols or conventional practices. One cannot understand any text if one does not know the grammar of the language in which the text is couched; one cannot interpret any act without regard to the context and the language and concepts at the disposal of the actors. However helpful these distinctions may have been, they do not solve every issue. The moment human beings come into the picture, they become problematic. For humans are both "nature" and "culture," a situation in which the relation between the two may not be construed in such a way that the two parts alternate or that "culture" is attached or added to "nature". To function humanly is almost always both at once: being wholly dependent on and determined by nature and at the same time fully structured by culture and only intelligible in this light. Human functioning can always be considered and analyzed from a multiplicity of perspectives, although, to be sure, one can then debate the adequacy or the outcome of the different perspectives. To mention an example from the domain of the psychology of religion: one can examine what changes in brain activity can be registered during prayer, or under what conditions prayer makes its appearance, or also what prayer means to the prayer. Which of these inquiries one will carry out depends on the kind of psychological knowledge one prefers. As psychological inquiry they are all, along with others, conceivable. What is important is the realization that in the human sciences a multiplicity of perspectives are both possible and have in fact been developed.

Although in the last few decades it has been less influential in the academic world than the natural-scientific branch, on the "culture" side of psychology there nevertheless exists a whole series of approaches which present themselves under a variety of labels, such as, for example, "phenomenology," "symbolic interactionism," and "social constructionism". Noteworthy in this sector of psychology is also the turn towards language. Under the influence of such distinct psychoanalysts as Lacan or Schafer, it is increasingly realized that the so-called "self" has a linguistic structure and is a fictitious entity, constituted by words and ideas which do not refer back to a "real" world since signs, after all, are of a non-referential nature. As different as these divergent theoretical and methodical approaches may seem sometimes, they all have their roots in a common philosophical position which has developed, in the footsteps especially of Martin Heidegger, in the twentieth century. Central to this so-called "hermeneutic" is the notion that reality cannot be grasped "in itself" (Ricoeur 1965/1970). Whatever knowledge people may think they have of it, this knowledge is conditioned by – and hence limited to – the "situatedness" of the human condition; and in this context a prominent function is assigned to language (cf., e.g., O'Connor 1997). Unlike empiricists and positivists, hermeneutically oriented researchers do not assume that only the (natural) sciences will yield valid knowledge of reality. They are much more convinced that all insight, including their own, is subject to cultural-historical changes. Hermeneutically-oriented empirical research attempts to examine the meanings which were available to people in a specific situation and how they originated: that is, how people were able to perceive these meanings. Like the older phenomenologists, this kind of research highlights the intentions, plans, goals, and purposes which motivate individuals and groups; but more vigorously than in the case of the phenomenologists, this research takes account of the fact that *meaning* comes into being by the joint agency of actors so equipped, i.e. is *constructed*. As a result, the construction of meaning as well as the makeup of the constructing persons acquires an increasingly central place in this branch of research. Among the empirical psychologies one finds molded along these lines, besides discursive and dialogical approaches, a so-called narrative psychology. We will draw on this psychology in the analysis of the striking case of manslaughter mentioned above.

Narrative Psychology and Analysis of Religion

As with all approaches which are said to belong to the psychology of culture, with narrative psychology we find ourselves in the tracks of the "world hypothesis" or metaphysical mainstream which Stephen Pepper (1942) called "contextualism". In addition, Pepper distinguishes "animism," "formism," "mechanism," and "organicism" which were at one time derived from a characteristic basic metaphor. The basic metaphor of mechanicism, which is so dominant in the West, is the machine (e.g. a pump, a dynamo, a computer, etc.). The mechanicistic worldview makes natural events appear as the result of power transmissions. The goal of every natural scientist who works within the paradigms belonging to mechanicism is the search for causes of some kind. Mechanism also underlies many a theory in the field of psychology. (Cf. Freud's metaphor of the psyche as "psychic *apparatus*," the use of the telephone exchange and, later, of the computer as a metaphor in cognitive psychology.)

Contextualism as world hypothesis, on the other hand, does not look for causes and causal connections but for patterns of meaning. Its basic metaphor is the historical happening about which one can talk in various ways but which is always presented as a "story" in which different actors play distinct roles. Theodore Sarbin, probably the best known initiator of narrative psychology, follows this line of thought. With reference to developments in the philosophy of history and the meta-theory of psychoanalysis he argues that the story – the narrative – is a fruitful metaphor for psychology in the study and interpretation of human functioning. Concretely, and reduced to the smallest denominator, Sarbin defines his contribution to a narrative psychology as follows: "I propose the narratory principle: that human beings think, perceive, imagine, and make moral choices according to narrative structures" (1986a, p. 8). His further expositions contain approaches which may be relevant. Sarbin in fact points out that stories have a powerful influence on the development of *self-narratives*. He recalls the "Quixotic Principle" formulated by Levin (1970), which proceeds from the observation that readers construct an identity and a self-narrative from the books they have read. Putting it somewhat more cautiously, one may perhaps say that individuals (and probably also groups) construct an identity from various culturally available elements, among which, in any case, are various kinds of stories and imaginary figures which play a role in them. To the identity constructed and presented in each case belongs a story whose plot-structure puts the person in question and his surroundings in a narrative relationship from which the functional direction is taken. A simple example: one who understands and/or presents herself as "mother" will act and react in a culturally predefined manner. This must not be understood too stereotypically. The fact that Sarbin, a role-theoretician in the past, is now doing narrative psychology shows theoretical progress: individuals do not copy static predefined roles, but function as they do in stories; nothing is precisely determined in advance but a direction is given. In the story of a (Western) mother it is probable that, on account of her taking care of her son, she is or was not (fully) employed outside the home; it is unlikely that it was she who taught him to play soccer. Paradoxes and special effects (say, in art) result precisely when the story departs from the stereotype; for example, if concerning an individual whom we know was an executioner in a concentration camp but also learn was a loving father and a highly sensitive violinist, or about a Catholic priest that he had fathered several children by different women. As a rule, such stories are the result of diverse elements (to which also the story and self-definitions of other persons belong) and are considered authentic when, though true to life, they are nevertheless not merely copies of it.

In the course of their lives people hear and assimilate stories which enable them to develop "schemes" which give direction to their experience and conduct – schemes with whose help they can then make sense out of a potential stimulation overload. To

170   Religion, Culture and Psychopathology

each developing story, and in every situation with which they are confronted, people bring an acquired catalog of "plots" which are used to make sense out of the story or situation (Mancuso and Sarbin 1983). Here lies a possibility of applying narrative psychology to religious phenomena. For, as was explained in Chapter 3, whatever religion may be besides this (defining religion is actually hard and highly controversial), it is in any case also a reservoir of verbal elements, stories, interpretations, prescriptions and commandments, each of which in their power to determine experience and conduct and in their legitimation possess narrative character.

If in what follows we attempt to apply these reflections to a case of religious manslaughter, it is in the first place to explore the possibilities and limits of the narrative-psychological approach. For this purpose we have selected a case which is rather extreme or – from another viewpoint – rather misguided, in the hope that here, as through a microscope, we can more easily gain access to questions which we could also raise in connection with other cases.

Kill the Devil: A Case of Religious Pathology?

It is not hard to imagine that the events in Betuwe furnished the usual sensation and that there was an uproar in the public media, especially when none of the people concerned were prosecuted, since the courts adopted the psychiatric verdict: "not responsible by reason of insanity". The reactions and the predominant part of this exciting story are irrelevant here, for our sole interest is to conceptualize from a cultural-psychological vantage point the religious dimension of the happenings as a whole. After all, it seems to deal with a case of religious psychopathology. The fact that this case – as stated above – is quite extreme may also be evident: subduing the devil at a religious gathering is certainly no common religious practice. Still, the killing of a human being as a matter of a religious conviction is not at all unknown, either in the world religions or in Western history. It would be irresponsible at any given time to speak of "illness" in such cases. But let us leave aside this complicating cross-cultural and cross-temporal question and, for the sake of simplicity, begin by agreeing with our colleagues of that day: prominent here was a case of psychic infection, or psychic induction in which the mental illness of an individual or individuals was passed on to (the majority of) a group. But first we want to consider what is meant by "religious insanity".

In this connection we can ignore the many publications in which the authors argue that religion as such is actually a form of mental illness, a collective illusion, an infantile phase of cultural history, etc., as well as those publications which, for whatever anthropological or religious reasons, presuppose that religion is a condition or mark of psychic health. In the more empirically based literature, which is concerned with the pertinent themes relative to the functioning of concrete individuals or groups, religion and mental illness are usually only brought into a descriptive connection. One can make a distinction between cases of mental illness in religious functionaries ("psychopathology in the clergy") and cases in which religious language (themes,

The Spiritual Background   171

ideas) or actions are a manifest aspect of the symptoms. In the second category fall
all those cases in which, say, someone believes he is Jesus Christ. Also, the first category can easily be imagined; a possible example would be a priest who is subject to
compulsive behaviors in the area of sex. A third obvious category can be found in the
– somewhat older – literature: the publications in which the authors examine the question whether and to what extent religious conceptions and practices play a role in the
onset of illness. As we noted above, this question (concerning a causal connection)
has almost never in recent years been put in those terms, since all sorts of factors may
in a given case have contributed to illness and almost always did contribute to it.
There is hardly ever a single cause of mental illness; and thus therapy is usually aimed
at influencing the conditions involved so that the patient can function again without
inflicting evident damage on himself and/or others. Like so many other factors, religion, in whatever form it is present, can play a role in illness. A distinction between
"pathogenetic" and "pathoplastic" does not help much at this point either. Also, the
boundaries between the categories listed above are not watertight: in the example
cited for the first category, did not the obligation to be celibate play a role in the life
of this man? In the case of the person who imagined himself to be Jesus Christ, an
overly intense and overly investigative identification with the faith-model may be a
factor; perhaps he also belonged to a religious group which passionately desired to
live the life of Christian discipleship and was too late to counteract the derailments of
its members? In each individual case one could try to explore whether and how a
certain type of religion plays any role in the life of the patient. After being approached
from angles that were either hostile to religion or apologetically, the subject "religion
and mental illness" has been absent from the literature for years (Neeleman and
Persand 1995). Only more recently have certain authors made a plea, not only in
religious but also in psychiatric periodicals, for the position that religion and spirituality should no longer (out of inappropriate disinterest or out of fear of stirring up a
sensitive topic) be left unexamined but should rather be explored (cf., e.g. Boehnlein
2000; Koenig 1998; Shafranske 1996b; Sims 1994).

   In our case model we seem to be dealing with a connection between religion and
mental illness of the second category: the symptoms of the victims of the psychic
infection were religiously colored. At least this was the unanimous view of psychiatric professionals at the time, whether they wrote their assessment in the service
of the state or as employees of confessional institutions. Still, the latter were highly
uncomfortable with the whole matter, the role of religion in this offense was
strongly disputed in the public media, and one senses doubt in the judgment of the
confessional psychiatrists.

The Spiritual Background

The incident occurred in 1900, among adherents to the *bevindelijke* spirituality we
encountered in the last chapter. In this case, they were as a small group living
amidst a Roman Catholic majority of the population, only a few years after a larger

split had shaken up the largest Dutch Protestant church. The Catholic press immediately seized upon the incident as a point of attack against the Protestant religion as such, indicating that this is what happens when people leave the Catholic Church ...

> How many of these peculiar apostles and prophets has the world not already seen since the Reformers threw their principle of free Bible study as a dangerous bomb in the midst of the Christian Church! From that moment on everyone, learned or unlearned, clever or dumb or wise in their own eyes, could explain the dark passages of Scripture. What devastations has not the arbitrary interpretation of Scripture brought about! What blindness and confusion, what fanaticism, madness, and crimes has it not produced!

In the press of the so-called Reformed who had broken away from the larger Protestant church of the Netherlands such accusations were rejected out of hand: yes, the incident concerned Reformed Protestants, but they were not genuinely Reformed; rather, they constituted a sect which was still addicted to a variety of pagan elements. Involved here was not "true" but "false" religion. (About the various reactions to the case, inter alia in the press, see Belzen 1998a.) Reformed psychiatrists, however, could not so easily apply this distinction between true and false religion to mental illness. They had too often seen believers – doubtless from "sound," "non-sectarian" Reformed congregations – become mentally ill, who then spouted all kinds of religious notions. On the other hand, in the case in question there were too many elements present from standard Reformed spirituality to dismiss the patients "merely" as "different," "unsound," "sectarian," etc. Motivated by an obviously similar interest to the Reformed press to protect their own religion from attacks, confessional psychiatrists all too eagerly took over the arguments from the prevailing psychiatry which was then oriented to the natural sciences: mental illness is the result of a disturbance in the physical substratum and usually conditioned by heredity. Confessional psychiatry – from which, because of its "belief" in the "soul," something else could have been expected – had hardly any feeling for the psychic components of meaning in the case (Belzen 1989a). On the other hand, they too had no concepts at their disposal for considering the role of religion as anything other than a relevant or non-relevant "cause". But what kind of (elements from) Reformed spirituality are we talking about in this case? To answer this question we must make a brief historical digression.

As we saw in Chapter 9, conversion is a big issue to *bevindelijken*: being "converted" or not is at the heart of their spirituality. Hardly anyone dares to claim to be converted, believers are hesitant to accept even the most devout believer as converted. (Often evasive phrases about such persons are being used: they will be designated as "being changed," someone in whose life "the Lord's hand has become visible.") But *if* a person is genuinely converted, people are all the more eager to listen to him or her in order to experience first hand how the Holy Spirit has dealt and is still dealing with this person. Once recognized as being truly converted, this person will become a spiritual authority whom people from other local churches will seek out, in order to hear his report, to experience the work being done in him and to talk with him. With admiration, perhaps even with a touch of envy (though this would be sinful) and with gratitude these people will listen to the "spiritual

The Events in Betuwe 173

person" whose authority in time will not only apply in spiritual matters (he will judge whether another has similarly been "placed on the road" or whether his situation is otherwise), but which will also extend to other domains.

> In ultra-Reformed churches and groups "spiritual persons" tend to have authority. They decide who can come to the Lord's Supper and who cannot. They will tell you what can and what cannot be done, and also what should and what should not be done. This authority encompasses virtually the whole of life: from the question how the liturgy should be arranged and how the minister should preach to the question whether one may take out fire insurance and whether one may go bathing (on Sundays, yes or no; in mixed company, yes or no). (Ruler 1971, p. 34)

Whether these "converts" still find themselves, with their judgments, within the (original) Reformed tradition no longer plays a role. "What these spiritual persons say is 'the truth.' It is the will of God," says Ruler (p. 35), a very spiritual theologian who is close to these people but who, despite his sympathy, has pointed to the danger that people's dependence on these authorities can also lead to uncontrolled tyranny.

The Events in Betuwe

The believers in our Betuwe case all belonged to this "grave" Reformed modality. The village of Betuwe is located in a predominantly Roman Catholic area. The protestants of Betuwe formed one church congregation with those of the neighboring village of Altforst, which was composed of two parties of which the participants in the Betuwe drama constituted the conservative wing. Their dissatisfaction with the direction pursued by the pastor in the early 1990s of the nineteenth century went so far that at the time when the official worship services were held, they had their own gatherings at which someone of their own group, a certain Oswald Suurdeeg, was the leader. But when in the mid-1990s another, more conservative pastor came, these meetings were suspended and these people were again among the most devout members of the church. They were zealous in participating in the life of the church, and zealous in reading the Bible and in praying. In their spare time, for their own edification and instruction, they read religious books which they shared amongst themselves, inter alia those of Bunyan and other books containing (allegorical) accounts of devils who attacked and then left people alone again. One of these writings, for example, bore the title (translated) *The heart of man as the temple of God or the abode of the devil*, and was illustrated with fantastic images.

A good friendship developed between Suurdeeg and Martin Schroevers, resulting in many a spiritual conversation. Early in 1900 one of Martin Schroevers' brothers fell ill with the flu. This man, Art Schroevers, was unmarried and still lived at home with his widowed mother. Along with the high fever came hallucinations. Art had horrible visions and saw very strange things. Among other things he reported was the story of how he lay stretched out on the edge of hell and that God raised him up again. The story swiftly went around that Art had repented of his sins, so that relatives and acquaintances came streaming in from every direction.

"People wanted to witness the grace that had befallen him," says the report which the Reformed psychiatrist, L. Bouman, drew up on the events (1901, p. 108). Martin, the owner of a neighboring farm, frequently visited his brother. Everyone, especially the members of the family, was deeply impressed by what took place in the sickroom and became very thoughtful. At first it was only Art who experienced something astonishing. He related, for example, how he saw his mug full of water even though he had drunk from it; that he heard voices which commanded him to sing and to pray. Later, other people saw and heard amazing things. (The family included, in addition to the mother and Art, four brothers and three sisters, several of whom also became infected with the flu.) One day, during Art's illness, the relatives and some friends had again been sitting together and reading a passage of Scripture. Suddenly, they saw, one after another, the devil. And at other gatherings they repeatedly saw apparitions and heard strange noises, as several later related to the psychiatrists and to the police (cf. the reports of Ruysch 1900; and Bouman 1901). Subsequent to these events, the relatives lapsed into a state of agitation; at night they were afraid to fall asleep. Often, they barely slept at all.

In the meantime, other amazing things happened. In May of the previous year, one of the Schroevers brothers, John, had gone away since there had been much conflict over his intention to marry a Catholic girl. Although he had not yet joined the girl's church, he had gone along with her to a Catholic mass several times and had several talks with the Catholic priest. Since in May 1899 he had moved in with a relative of his fiancée, he rarely visited his mother and, when he did, it was only very briefly. During Art's illness, however, he came more frequently and did not leave the sickroom; he repeatedly stood immobilized for an hour without saying a word, so that the others marveled. One time he suddenly began to shout, "Art, Art," whereupon he stood for several minutes in silence and then started to cry out again. Everyone in the house had rushed to the bedroom to witness the event. Some visitors were also there; the younger girls began to cry, but Art had interrupted them saying, "It does not matter at all, John. I am willing to die for you."

Everyone belonging to this wing of the church congregation was convinced that great things were happening in the Schroevers family. Another person, one who enjoyed a great reputation in the church community, viz. Mrs. Soontjes, was of this same opinion, which, as a result of the respect people felt for her judgment in religious matters, contributed significantly to the reinforcement of the conviction of the others. It was reported that both brothers had become "strangers in worldly matters"; and people dropped by to gain a personal impression. Only the pastor maintained an attitude of reserve. After one visit he was reported to have said, "I want to hope that something good will come from all this," and to have finally advised people to leave the patient alone. This was impossible, however, for from every direction fellow believers came to visit and people hardly slept anymore. Even the animals in the barn were left untended: people thought they saw the devil emerge from the bodies of some of them; they began to prophesy and to wait for the coming of Christ.

In the meantime similar scenes were being played out in the house of Martin, who was recovering from his flu. There, too, people observed remarkable phenomena, as was confirmed by John and Art who were likewise sufficiently recovered to

The Events in Betuwe

175

visit Martin. On the first of February, Martin told his mother that a great change was occurring in him. People thought he was talking about his conversion. Among the people who came to visit him were two sisters, Ella and Maria Laven, 17 and 22 years old respectively. On the evening of the second of February, Maria had a long talk with Martin. On her way home she felt relieved, experiencing freedom and forgiveness. Unable to sleep, she wanted to see Martin again to share with him the great mercy of which she was the recipient. To that end she suggested to her sister Ella, around 1 a.m., that she return with her to Martin's place, that she might also be delivered from the devil. Once there, she asked Martin to drive the devil out of Ella and he, in turn, blew on her mouth and into her nostrils. Ella became very agitated. When Martin sensed that the devil did not simply want to leave, he summoned his farmhand Peter, the maid, and his children to come and help him. The farmhand delayed his appearance, however, calling, "I have nothing to do with this whole mess". Martin then ordered him to hold up the chamberpot so that Ella could spit out the devil into it. Then Martin held Ella's eyes shut, hit her in the face, and asked, "Do you feel this?" Ella answered: "No" (Ruysch 1900, p. 89). What happened next she did not really know, she saw Peter falling over, "struck down by the hand of God". Then the devil came out of her eyes and mouth; she saw flames and heard a roar. She thought that the devil passed out of her and into Peter. At that moment she felt immensely relieved. Ella recalled in her conversation with Ruysch that Martin and the others stamped on Peter and hit his dead body till blood flowed out of it. Then she began to feel happy and everyone was in high spirits. They had triumphed over the devil. They sang: praise God, the devil is defeated! Singing, they went in procession to the neighboring village where Martin's mother lived, in order to bring her the happy news.

Early in the morning Martin, who had stayed at home, went to his neighbors and said, "Shake hands with Christ! I have been sanctified; I have crushed the head of Satan." A little later Suurdeeg appeared, and the two of them took the road to Martin's mother. One of Martin's married brothers later reported to the psychiatrist, Dr. Bouman, that he and his wife had been aroused by one of his younger brothers (who still lived with their mother at home). They must come and see the miracle that had happened. The devil had been slain, and Martin was letting them know that they should immediately come to see it.

> We hadn't yet eaten anything. My wife and I immediately went to mother where we found Martin and Suurdeeg. They talked without stopping and no one dared to ask any questions. Especially Martin, whom I saw covered with blood, was extremely agitated. The sisters had lost their heads. We should all follow him, said Martin. He talked without stopping and I did not dare to contradict him because I did not know what was going on. I wanted to stay at home because my animals had not yet been fed. Martin and Suurdeeg said: "We are entering the millennium; the animals do not have to be fed; you are not going home." At that point I therefore let my animals alone and followed them. (Bouman 1901, p. 112)

When they returned to Betuwe, singing psalms along the way, the police met them and arrested Martin. No one offered any resistance, for Martin assured them that the authorities could not do him any harm and that he would be back home very shortly. He told his followers: "Sing, children; they are putting handcuffs on the

Lord Jesus Christ." When they came past Mrs. Soontjes' house and she stopped the procession, one of the fellow believers of the conservative wing which had meanwhile joined them, turned to her in doubt about the whole thing, but she answered: "Everything is in order." On hearing this, they went on to Martin's house where they found even the maid singing psalms. This reinforced the conviction that a miracle had occurred: that Martin's wife and children sang was understandable but since even the maid was filled with joy, there must have been a real miracle.

In Martin's house people joined them and continued the celebration. Every time they heard a sound on the street they sprang from their seats, ready to welcome Martin home. People sang, they prayed, they again cast out the devil, until gradually the group dispersed, since one or the other, making excuses, was fetched by relatives. On the next day Ruysch, asked to come over by the police, started his investigations and the two Laven sisters (who had meanwhile returned home where people completely believed the rest of their stories), were taken, like Martin and Suurdeeg before them, to a psychiatric institution. In the events which had occurred Ruysch saw something different from what the participants themselves believed: not a work of God, nor any heresy leading to criminal behavior (as the Catholic inhabitants of Betuwe viewed it), but *insanity*. His medical interpretation was to become dominant and, as a result, neither Martin nor the others were judicially prosecuted.

The Role of Religion

Ruysch, along with his Reformed colleagues, disputed the opinion – advanced especially in the Roman Catholic press – that it was the religion of the participants which caused the Betuwe drama. Among Reformed psychiatrists, this argumentation may also have been prompted by apologetic motives. But, if one takes the assignment of guilt and the matter of causation out of consideration, it remains plain that religion had something to do with the issue. But what and how? Religion was the "cultural context of meaning" (Much 1995) for the Schroevers family and the others involved. Such a context makes possible action and experience which is not accessible to those who have not been brought up in the same context. By means of an instilled symbolic system like religion, for example, people understand and construe the (natural, social, and – in some cases also – spiritual) world. In this connection, narrative psychology points especially to the relevance of stories. The stories of the grave Reformed spirituality which these believers had in common yielded meaning and experience, brought coherence to the group, and furthered the action in question: for a fairly long time, people in the conservative camp of the local Protestant church had been convinced that God was active amongst them, especially in the Schroevers family. Art was literally down on his bed, troubled over his sins, and summoned the others to conversion, since otherwise they would be lost for all eternity – all in accordance with the spirituality handed down to them. The desire "to be elect," which sprang from the grave Reformed tradition, and the grace manifested among them prompted the believers to come together and reinforced

The Role of Religion

their struggle for salvation, their analysis of the stirrings of their own souls, and their religious engagement. When, on the strength of this, Martin sensed a change occurring within himself, people gathered in the home of this spiritual man and sought to engage in edifying conversation with him. That people could not sleep out of anxiety over their sinful and lost condition, or on account of spiritual joy, and would possibly turn in the middle of the night to the pastor or some other spiritual leader is not unusual in this tradition; one can find such things in many conversion narratives. When Martin's hired man Peter then refused to have anything to do with the whole thing and showed himself recalcitrant, it was evident to this dualistic type of spirituality that he was an adversary, a devil, or a person possessed by the devil. To have been able to overcome him was a work of the grace of God. That God's chosen man trampled all over him is prefigured in Scripture: does it not say in the earliest messianic promise that Satan would be crushed (Gen. 3:15)?

After the occurrence of so many miracles in the preceding days, it did not greatly surprise the other believers when they were hauled out of bed with the news that something great had happened – that Martin had been chosen and that the devil had been overcome. The kingdom of God had come; one of them recalled that in the preceding week he had read repeatedly the closing chapter ("Maranatha", or "The Judgment of the Great Judge") in Koenraat Mel's *The Trumpets of Eternity and Various Sermons about Death, the Resurrection of the Dead, the Final Judgment, the World's End, Hell, Heaven and Eternity* (Amsterdam, 1752; translated title). An eschatological interpretation of the events at once spread: money was no longer necessary; animals no longer needed to be fed. Firing each other up, people sang psalms and fell into a state of spiritual ecstasy. When, on top of this, a doubter heard from Mrs. Soontjes ("who in religious matters had better insight than anyone else among us") that everything was in order, everyone was convinced that something very special was happening. People sang psalms, prayed, shouted jubilantly, forgave each other their sins and cleared old grievances out of their system. A few of them, while singing psalms, reviled the Catholic church and slandered the Pope; activity that is somewhat aggressive, to be sure, but quite in accordance with their teaching about "the whore of Babylon," which was the Catholic church. It must have done more than a little to stir up the angry reaction of local Catholics. But this resistance and the arrest by the police proved unable to shake their faith; they knew from Scripture that the gentiles rage and the kings of the earth set themselves against the Lord and his anointed (Ps. 2:1–2). Martin, like Jesus, was taken prisoner and Martin, like Jesus, would keep his promise and return soon. For everything that happened these believers had available to them a Bible verse or religious phrase; everything was explicable to them in terms of the Scriptures, by which they structured their experience and conduct. One must not underestimate the importance of religious concepts in this or other cases. The moment a myth, whether of a religious kind or not, "becomes part of the fabric of a civilization's system of beliefs, it guides thought and action, and thus it inevitably militates against the introduction of alternative metaphors," writes Sarbin (1992, p. 325) in an initial essay which applies his narrative-psychological perspectives to "unwanted conduct".

These considerations do not, of course, "explain" the events; that is not why they are presented. Nor is it in any way appropriate, therefore, to break with the psychiatrists of that day and make religion responsible for what happened or fault it in other ways. Yet, it will be well to remember that the psychiatric explanation ("illness") is only one possible interpretation (a relatively new one, from a historical viewpoint) and that at other times, and in other social contexts, the whole event would be viewed and treated differently. Many a viewpoint (e.g. that a stone falls down because it wants to get to its natural habitat, cf. Kuhn 1962; or that there is a crop failure because of a witch in the village, etc.) may not be at all plausible to a Western person in the late-twentieth century, but this can hardly be an argument against the viewpoint in question. Surely we may always proceed from the premise that for the interpretation of a given state of affairs, several perspectives can be applied. To understand an outbreak of war, for example, one must consider economic, military, social-political and numerous other aspects as well. A phenomenon such as mysticism can be analyzed from historical, sociological, medical-psychological and many other vantage points. Even within a single perspective one can highlight various aspects. A narrative-psychological approach, for example, is only one possible psychological point of entry among several which could be applied in the Betuwe case. A less cultural-psychological analysis, but one that proceeds more along individual lines, could discuss Martin's personal life history, which must have been very significant in this connection. Had he, a man who had married a wealthy widow with a farm of her own and who, despite his relatively youthful age, had already been made a church elder, perhaps been stirred to envy at the thought of the "great things" which had happened to his brothers, Art and John? Had there been rivalry among them? Had there been tensions between him and his hired man, Peter, before the events in question? What was the role played by the fact that two young women had such high regard for him, treating him as a religious authority and even visiting him at night? Was it perhaps his wish to show himself off when something "great" had also happened to him? All these and similar questions are doubtless possible and relevant, but cannot be answered because the sources for such analysis are not available. In any case, they may not entice us into making a "wild analysis".

Different perspectives can often coexist amicably inasmuch as they deal with distinct aspects and function on different levels. Erikson's psychological analysis of the young Luther, for example, in no way undermines the believing view that this man was an instrument of God. Theological and/or religious interpretations do not really exclude psychological and/or psychiatric interpretations. Still, there may be tension between the two. To stay with the case before us: psychology cannot of course decide whether Martin was "genuinely" converted or not. Nor can it in any way judge the theological correctness of the doctrine of election. But it can, and perhaps should, pose questions to a spirituality which tells people that they are damned for all eternity, that hell awaits them, that a worm is to be considered more fortunate than they are, since it cannot be "lost" (etc.). That all people are sinners in need of the grace of God may indeed be theologically correct, but can one also defend (psychologically, anthropologically or even pastorally), the practice of instilling such an extremely negative self-image? It may be spiritually desirable for a person to allow himself to be imbued with the reality of sin and to want to experience this truth existentially, but does that mean that all spontaneous joviality must

The Role of Religion 179

be nipped in the bud with questions like, "What do you have to laugh about? Don't you know what awaits you in the hereafter?"

These questions are hard to answer and require the joint reflection of psychologists and theologians (or religious leaders). In the case under consideration, as stated at the beginning of our reflections, the decision is simple: What happened here was not normal; it could not and cannot be religiously justified. No psychologist can judge whether somebody is a messiah and someone else is possessed, but the official religious community immediately rejected these "delusions". From a Reformed viewpoint, this cannot be justified and is contrary to the teaching. But were people who represented the church and theology not equally eager to distance themselves from the event because the case was so degenerate and depraved? Because there was a death? Again, there was of course something really wrong here and Reformed spirituality cannot be held responsible for a homicide. But at what point did things go wrong? At what point did the desired self-analysis of Art become sick? When did the reading of conversion stories, the conduct of edifying conversations, praying, singing, etc., go too far? When did the worthwhile become delusional? It may by now be clear that – whether in the domain of spirituality or elsewhere – the boundaries between mental illness and mental health are extremely hard to draw. Remember that, in the case under consideration, at his last visit the pastor, who was otherwise uninvolved, though he was not exactly thrilled, did not undertake any action beyond this and clearly as yet took no notice of mental illness. Or take an even stronger example: when in the morning Martin and Suurdeeg also went to visit Martin's mother and reported the "great things" that had occurred, the local constable went there, but being caught up in the general excitement – despite the blood stains on Martin's hands and clothing – he did nothing. He even accompanied the group back to Betuwe and when his colleagues there wanted to arrest Martin, he first remained quietly in his vehicle. Not until his colleagues (who, meanwhile, had presumably seen the corpse), explicitly demanded that he help them, did he begin to move (cf. Bouman 1901, p. 112). Had this man perhaps also been "infected" by this mental illness?

Or did the whole affair, the stories and the actions – despite the excitement – (still?) not fall outside the Reformed framework? Was the policeman, who was perhaps Reformed himself, familiar with the frame of reference?[2] Was that why he, like the other Reformed folk, could not recognize that something absurd or even criminal was happening or had happened here? All of these are questions to which in this case we will probably never know the answers. But the questions are not limited to this case; they evoke the entire complex of the problems of culture and psychopathology, to which a psycho(patho)-logical critique of spirituality could also belong. It is not my intention to develop such a critique here, inasmuch as it lies outside the scope of this essay, whose sole purpose has been to point to the significance of narrative for psychological analysis.

---

[2] It proved impossible to find out to which church the policeman belonged.

Chapter 11
Psychopathology and Religion

A Psychobiographical Analysis

The Role of Autobiography in Psychology

When psychology turns to autobiographies, it does not do so to examine the situations described in them or to reconstruct particular events or points in time; such research, interesting as it may be, is usually left to historians. Nor does psychology delve into the existent or non-existent literary qualities of an autobiography, or into the genre of autobiography as such; this is the realm of literary theorists. When psychology avails itself of autobiographies, it does so by asking psychological questions and from a psychological perspective. The most important argument for doing this is usually that working with autobiographical texts, in whatever form (they certainly need not be limited to published autobiographies but may include texts written at the explicit request of the researcher, diaries, and many other forms of autobiographical data; cf. Bruner 1990, e.g.), is the most effective way of gathering information for certain kinds of questioning. If the researcher is interested in studying the development of someone's identity, for example, hardly a better method can be devised than to ask the research participant to provide at regular intervals a text that is as subjective and personal as possible. Even when psychologists look at existing autobiographies, published or not, they do so in order to find answers to systematic psychological questions concerning such factors as psycho-social development, parent–child binding, and social relationships in general, guilt and shame, experience of sexuality, mental disorder, and many others. For the psychologist who is interested in religion, autobiographies may provide a great deal of information concerning the development of individual religiosity and the influence that certain forms of religion can have on the development of the personality.

Autobiographies can also serve as an important source of information for research on that which psychologists call "the self," since it is in an autobiography that an author presents herself. He presents himself in a certain way, telling us a story about himself and his life. In doing so the author usually draws an ideal picture of herself. Although the story itself need not be ideal in any way (and the author may be reporting it with quite a bit of shame), he paints a picture of himself which he hopes the reader will endorse. In this chapter I will attempt to employ several forms of psychology in order to interpret one particular autobiography,

---

J.A. Belzen, *Towards Cultural Psychology of Religion: Principles, Approaches, Applications*,   181
DOI 10.1007/978-90-481-3491-5_11, © Springer Science+Business Media B.V. 2010

again with a view to a theme that is relevant to the psychology of religion: the relationship between religion and mental health. Before introducing the autobiography, I would first like to sum up a bit of theoretical background.

Often the first reaction to the idea mentioned above – the autobiography as presentation of the self and the self as a narrative construction – is that of shock. Does this mean that a person's self or identity is "only" a story? Wouldn't it then be possible for someone to tell any manner of story about herself? People tell many different stories throughout their lives, and they also tell different versions to different listeners. If all those stories are what the self, or the selves, of a particular person are, where is the unity of that person? Let's deal briefly with these questions, mainly in order to avoid or rectify a number of misunderstandings.

As we have seen in preceding chapters, the self is fundamentally characterised, even constituted, by language and story. For the development and functioning of human self-awareness – regarded by many theoreticians, in line with Hegel, as precisely that which distinguishes the human being from the animal – language is of vital importance. Self-awareness, says Kojève (1947, pp. 163–168), presupposes that the human being, by using the personal pronoun "I," is able to locate himself as distinct from the world of objects and even from himself. So according to Kojève there is an intrinsic connection between self-awareness and language: in fact, there can be no self-awareness without language. The psychoanalyst Lacan (1966) would later speak of the "birth of the subject," referring to the process by which the child enters the symbolic order and in particular learns to handle and to conform to the language he encounters in his subculture. In order to speak about himself, a person must have developed the ability to objectify, which he does thanks to language. So language is a precondition that makes subjectivity possible, and not the other way round. There is not an essential subject who desires to make use of language; rather, the constitution of the subject presupposes language (Haute 1993, pp. 165–167). When the subject, once constituted by language, wants to know something or share something about herself, she must avail himself of language if she is to tell herself or others who she is; she must make an announcement concerning who she has become up to that point. "Up to that point" – for the human being is a historical creature: her life, between birth and death, is a history. That history can be expressed in different places and different ways. It can be imparted in the form of a story. If people are asked to indicate who they are, they will answer with some kind of life history. Indeed, human transience can only be expressed linguistically. To specify this linguistic structure, Ricoeur (1981, pp. 169–172) uses the term "narrativity". Man has a narrative structure by virtue of his historicity: he must relate history, especially his own history (Zwaal 1997, p. 100). This makes the self not only a product of the past but also an interpretation of the past.

In developing her own notion of herself, woman must rely on the stories that are passed on to her and that are absorbed by her, as it were, during socialization. Each story about ourselves is always already embedded in the continuing story of a particular cultural history. The possibilities for self-comprehension that we acquire and develop are themselves always products of a particular historical tradition that makes us its product (Heidegger 1927). Such stories, which inhabit and form our lives and make them possible, are first of all the stories that constitute the background of every notion within a certain culture. They are embodied not only in our views of humankind, the world and life itself, but also in art forms and rituals that are shared by all the participants in that particular culture. They are the archetypal stories from every culture, and we run across them in metaphors and expressions, films and plays, but also in functional symbols such as a cross or crucifix, the V-for-victory sign, in monuments and in symbols that are associated with commemorations as well as with holidays and festivals (Guignon 1998, p. 569). These are the stories that impart structure to the ordinary, mundane stories we experience and indulge in every day and give them meaning by making available a certain horizon of comprehension. Naturally such archetypal stories differ from culture to culture (and from subculture to subculture). The optimistic stories about the redemptive self from the United States (McAdams 2006) are very different from those about sacrifice and suffering that the Russians grow up with, and both are quite distinct from the archetypal stories about ritual suicide such as those told in Japan. Such fundamental differences can make the life patterns of one culture or subculture seem pointless in the eyes of another (just think of how the forms of Roman Catholic monastic life are perceived by certain Protestants). Secondly, the impact of stories can be found in the ordinary, everyday way that people communicate with each other. Whenever we engage in an ordinary conversation, we structure our stories according to the storytelling standard that is or is becoming generally accepted within our culture. In doing so, we often use narrative cues that inform the listener as to the kind of story she is about to hear. (An opening sentence such as "Once upon a time" calls for an entirely different kind of comprehension than "What rotten luck I had yesterday".) So we are very far from being able to tell any random story about ourselves (or even to consciously construct such a story); indeed, the ways in which the self can be articulated are subject to strict limitations that usually remain implicit. While language and story make the self possible, they also determine its limits.

In narrative psychology, such as that introduced by Sarbin and others (Sarbin 1986b,c, 1993; Sarbin and Kitsuse 1994; Sarbin and Scheibe 1983), these notions are expanded to cover broader parts of psychic functioning than the self alone. In one programmatic text, "The narrative as a root metaphor for psychology," Sarbin (1986b) introduces the "narratory principle": "human beings think, perceive, imagine, and make moral choices according to narrative structures" (p. 8). He sees emotions, for example, as inextricable from their social context. In his analysis he uses the image of a scene with many individuals in which the action of one participant functions as the focus for the following actions that are carried out by the person himself as well as by the other participants. (So emotions should never be studied as events that happen within a single individual.) According to narrative psychologists, however, it is not only emotions that are led by narrative plots; actions are, too. In listening to and telling stories there is an involvement in the actors and their adventures. Action is not only present *in* the story, however; it also *follows* from the story. The so-called Don Quixote principle states that people act in order to extend the plot of a particular story, especially when they imagine themselves to be the protagonist of that story. The Don Quixote principle refers to the practice of shaping one's identity by emulating stories. The central idea is that the narratives with which the cultural participants have become acquainted go on to determine their actions: they provide the characters, ideas, settings, instruments, and procedures that individuals and groups can use to give shape to their own activities.

The narrative approach directs attention to the interface between individual and collective functioning. It is an attempt to understand human functioning as culturally located: no matter what emotion or form of activity a person is about to display, it is seen as dependent on the stories, the plots and the roles from the culture or subculture in which the person grew up and in which she now happens to be functioning. Because there are always others present in the current situation, real or imagined, every act is an interactive occurrence, always directed at one or more others. And at different times and places the person will present versions of himself that deviate from each other to a greater or lesser extent. (Thus a life companion will be shown a self that is different and probably more private than a colleague, etc.) But no matter what stories are told about the self, they will all follow existing plots. For this reason, Hermans and Kempen (1993) – by analogy with Bakhtin (1929/1973) and using the terminology of James (1890) and Mead (1934) – present the self as a polyphonic novel: a person standing in a multiplicity of worlds in which a story about a "me" with an accompanying "I" can and must be told over and over again. Those stories can be relatively independent of each other (and sometimes even contrary to each other) and the "I's" of the different stories can even communicate with each other within the same self. There are different worlds with different stories told by different "Is" but there is no overarching "I" that organises and/or coordinates the different "me's" (see also Chapter 8). So the self is not one and undivided, not always and everywhere the same; it is plural and context-dependent, a decentralized multiplicity of "I" positions that function in dialogue like relatively independent authors. That is: they tell each other stories about their respective "me's" as actors.

According to an even older tenet of literary theory, every text – and therefore also the articulation of a self at a particular time and place – is a result of relations between texts, a product of intertextuality, a membrane into which elements are woven that had already been produced elsewhere in discontinuous form (cf. Sprinker 1980). So the dialogicity of the self presupposes much more than a conversation with whomever is present in the here and now, whether through direct eye contact or not. The articulation of the self, as it emerges at a certain time and place, does not sound like just one single voice; in such an articulation the resonances of other voices can be heard: the voices of the parents and significant others as well as the voices of collectives such as a social class, a professional group or a religious tradition. It is especially the social voices, such as those alluded to by Bakhtin (1929/1973), that have influence on what a person says, that determine what she *can* say in the first place, usually without being conscious of the fact. There are many personal, unique voices in the self, but there are also a number – perhaps a far greater number – of collective voices. So to repeat: people cannot tell any random story they choose in order to articulate who they are. The stories they tell, the meanings they construct, and the sense they impart are dependent on the interplay of various voices.

The Spiritual Autobiography as Source for the Psychology of Religion

Still other forms of psychology that are quite different from the possibly obvious narrative psychology offer other points of view that might be relevant in a study of a person's own life story. In this chapter I shall try to combine quite diverse forms of psychology to interpret a particular autobiography. Psychology at large is a very heterogeneous enterprise, with many differing approaches that sometimes even seem to contradict one another. In my opinion, this is no problem at all: reality, also the life of one particular individual, will always be richer than what any form of scholarship will have to say about it. To understand another person, psychologists will, by necessity, have to employ very diverse forms of insights and research techniques. Complications will be met along the way: recent psychological research shows that memories are not simply mirror reflections of the past. Rather, they are reproductions, and furthermore they are changeable (which of course does not apply to the past to which the memory refers). So notions about memory that depict it as something like a series of photographs or video recordings are incorrect: a remembrance is not stored in one place in the memory as if it were in a safe (in which all you would have to do to remember something would be to call the right photo or video to mind). In the words of a well-known memory psychologist, "memory is a process, not a depository" (Cermak 1989, p. 121). In addition, memories refer not only to the things that actually happened but also to fantasies, imaginings, stories, etc. So our remembrances are not only about an event that once took place but also about stories pertaining to that event and about stories pertaining to similar events. It is quite possible to think you are remembering an external event when in fact what you are remembering is a story.

The autobiographical memory is not fixed but in motion (Kotre 1995). It also has to do with the present and not only with the past. Yet once again we must beware of drawing incorrect conclusions: the process in question is not arbitrary, nor do individuals have it within their grasp. People do not consciously make or form their own memories to enable them to tell a certain story. Life experiences, etc., are not simply registered and stored but are selectively recorded (or forgotten) according to certain frameworks, only to be woven later on into the stories of who we are (cf. Scheibe 1998, p. 142). It will be important to remember this when studying an autobiography. In any case, it should be borne in mind that the general characteristics of the autobiographic subgenre of which the author is availing herself were not only involved in determining the shape of the story but were also active in the operation of the author's memory and in the selection, application, and interpretation of her memories.

The Spiritual Autobiography as Source for the Psychology of Religion

To avoid the impression that all we are interested in is abstract theorizing, let us turn our attention to an actual autobiography. We might wonder whether and to what extent someone's autobiography could provide insight into a possible relationship between religion and psychic functioning. With this question in mind we take up one of the oldest research traditions in the psychology of religion. The more specific question concerning the relationship between religion and mental health has always been a prominent one, and not only because of its presumed social relevance. Even the founding fathers of the field of psychology dealt with religion in terms of "healthy mindedness," "the sick soul" and "the divided self" (James 1902/2002) and made methical comparisons between religious rituals and obsessional neurosis (Freud 1907/1959). The animosity between psychologists and representatives of religious organizations has sometimes been bitter, but after more than a century of research and the formulation of theories a consensus seems to have been arrived at: it is almost impossible to make general statements. Religion may be (1) an expression of mental disorder; (2) a socializing and oppressive force, helping people cope with their life stresses and mental aberrations; (3) a protective agent for some mentally disturbed persons; (4) a therapy; (5) a hazard (Spilka et al. 2003). The relationship between religion and mental health can thus be structured in a variety of ways, and in any individual case it is good to consider what type of connection is at work. One interesting example is the case of an autobiography in which the "I" person tells how she was cured of a serious depression thanks to "religion" (a term that is far too broad and requires a more detailed explanation) but who, despite the book's clearly propagandistic intentions, was turned away by the very religious communities she wished to serve. The reasons for this rejection are certainly relevant but are not fundamental for the psychologist: her primary interest will be what motivated the author to write an autobiography and what psychic functions were involved, and among her questions will be those concerning the connection between religiosity and psychic functioning.

Let us first take a brief glance at the contents of the autobiography of Mrs. Reinsberg (1898). The title page states the following:

The conversion story of a fifty-year-old mortal,
afterwards
possessed by the devil at Veldwijk for two and a half years
and now redeemed and reborn in Jesus Christ,
her Redeemer and Savior,
Who will fulfill his purpose for her, now and forever.
By Mrs. Reinsberg, widow.
Published for the benefit of Veldwijk and for poor unfortunate patients.
At the expense of the author.
The Hague.
1898.[1]

---

[1] I will not weary the reader with too many quotes from her book, certainly not in a text that has been translated into English, which would fail to capture Mrs. Reinsberg's original language. When it is obvious that I am referring to her book, I will not keep repeating "Reinsberg, 1898" where a simple page number will suffice.

The author, Doetje Reinsberg-Ypes (1840–1900), was a woman from Amsterdam who had been institutionalized in the Veldwijk Christian Psychiatric Hospital in Ermelo from 1890 to 1892 with a diagnosis of "melancholia agitans" (which more or less corresponds to today's diagnosis of depression). Her document was of considerable length: 470 pages. She divided her publication into four "books" – or three, actually, since most of the fourth book consists of correspondence, some of it with more or less well-known Dutch theologians, and followed it with a Postscript and a Conclusion. The period of her stay at Veldwijk provides the structure for the history that Mrs. Reinsberg relates: the first book deals with her life before her stay at Veldwijk, the second has to do with her period in Ermelo, and in the third she talks about her life since leaving Veldwijk. The number of pages devoted to her period in Ermelo is the largest of the three narrative books. In the first book she tells that she was born in Leeuwarden, that she lost her father at an early age, and that after the death of her mother when she was over 17 years old she was taken in by her uncle. At the age of 20, she was more or less forced to go out on her own. She went to Amsterdam, where one of her sisters was already living. She had trouble finding her way in this city, but with the help of charitable Christians from diverse Protestant persuasions, and after a number of failed attempts, she finally found a position. She married a waiter, and after some time they opened their own café–restaurant–hotel. Although business was good, they were not able to escape adversity in other parts of their lives: she tells of the sickness and death of a few of their children. Sometime after her husband died she sold the hotel and apparently began living from the proceeds, enjoying a life of relative prosperity in Amsterdam with her three daughters. Yet things did not go well for long. She had had little to do with religion and the church for quite some time but now she resumed attending services. During one service she became ill. A process seems to have been set in motion which ultimately led to her being admitted to the Veldwijk "insane asylum" in Ermelo.

In the second book, Mrs. Reinsberg provides an elaborate account of how she was brought to Veldwijk and how she was received there. She recounts her daily life in the institution in great detail, describing how she was moved from one ward to another and finally how she left Veldwijk and Ermelo. In the third book she talks about going to live with her children in Baarn and later in The Hague. She describes making a journey, as it were, through various Christian church groups (almost all of them belonging to the Calvinist – *gereformeerde*: Reformed – denomination). This third book is not exclusively narrative, however. More than half of its pages are devoted to "reflections" of one sort or another with chapter titles such as "On false teachers in general" and "Concerning the just". It ends with an "Epilogue".

In her autobiography, Mrs. Reinsberg faithfully follows the structure of the "conversion story," a subgenre of the spiritual autobiography, which emerged in the Netherlands among the followers of the so-called *Nadere Reformatie* or Further Reformation. What follows is a brief discussion of these ideas.

Very few conversion stories are autobiographies. A large portion of them were written after the death of the protagonist and follow a tradition that goes back to the mediaeval "vitae". Those works contain a highly stylized story about the life of someone regarded as holy. "Religious autobiographies" have become popular mainly within certain Protestant circles. There is nothing strange in this: the Reformation put the individual faith experience in the foreground, and the question of salvation became a personal and individual one. (Compare Luther's famous question "wie krieg' ich einen gnädigen Gott?"; also compare Calvin's self-analysis in his *Institutes*.) With the elimination of confession the need arose for another form of religious reflection on one's life. According to Delany, who was one of the first to focus attention on the conversion story as a subgenre of the autobiography, the seventeenth century religious autobiographies written by Protestants were much more introspective than the objective accounts being written by Roman Catholic and Anglicans (Delany 1969, p. 4). The "spiritual autobiography" is a type of writing in which women are heavily represented, far more than in other types of writing. On the other hand, it is true that among the first general autobiographies, women were more likely to write about religious stirrings of the soul than men were. This was probably because religion was one of the domains in which women could write more or less freely (Pomerleau 1980, p. 28).

Recording one's personal conversion story is a phenomenon that occurred in the Netherlands mainly in the eighteenth century within the so-called conventicle system (Lieburg 1991). The conventicle system is usually associated with the *Nadere Reformatie*, a movement within Dutch Calvinism that took place in the seventeenth and eighteenth centuries under the influence of Scottish, English and, to a lesser degree, German Puritans and that strove to keep personal behavior and experiences within the norms of religious doctrine. "*Nadere*" – "further" – suggests that people had chosen not to content themselves with the external Reformation of the sixteenth century, the re-formation (reorganization) of the church as an institution, but felt that one's conduct and inner life should conform to the spiritual norm: the individual herself needed to be re-formed, changed, converted. That conversion would have to be internal as well as external: the believer would have to start living from a different orientation altogether and not simply adapt her outer behavior. Correct behavior as such does not provide a definite explanation of one's inner state; even an unconverted person can live a life that is outwardly exemplary. In the *Nadere Reformatie* of the Netherlands, the self-examination that can be found in almost all spiritual traditions became increasingly focused on whether one was "converted" or not (see also Chapter 9). According to Calvinist doctrine, being converted is an indication of being elected by God: "from eternity," before the foundations of the world, He was supposed to have determined who would be accepted by Him and who would be condemned, doomed. Because only a small number of persons were destined for election, the question of conversion was one of the most important in the life of the *Nadere Reformatie* believer – *the* most important, in fact, because the answer was decisive for one's eternal salvation or eternal damnation. The believers of the *Nadere Reformatie* tradition were intensely preoccupied with this question, and some still are up to the present day (cf. VanderMeiden 1981), not only during Sunday religious services but also at various private religious gatherings. These gatherings were called conventicles, where people spoke together about personal religious experiences and where such experiences were tested against the group

The Spiritual Autobiography as Source for the Psychology of Religion

norm, which was expressed in the books written by the so-called "old writers" – theologians from the time of the *Nadere Reformatie*.

Within the circles influenced by the *Nadere Reformatie* there was a custom of reading conversion stories that were regarded as authentic and were accepted within the group tradition. Gradually these writings began functioning as a norm, of course, with which the individual faith experience had to comply and on which many people modeled their personal religious behavior and inner life. Almost all such conversion stories have a comparable structure. Although the authors of the spiritual autobiographies of the seventeenth, eighteenth and particularly the nineteenth centuries will not have read Augustine's *Confessions* as a rule, almost all of them follow the outline it provides. This runs as follows: the author first paints a picture of his own life up to his conversion. This period will have been spent inside or outside Christian circles, when one was still "separated from God". A great deal of attention is then given to the moment (or the process: it may have been a journey lasting a number of years) and the circumstances of the "conversion" (or, to be more theologically correct, the fact of having been converted by God's intervention in one's life). The story is concluded by an account, sometimes lengthy, sometimes not, of the period since the conversion: the "new" life, devoted to the service of God, which may have its own problems and temptations but nevertheless takes place in His sight. If it is not an autobiographical conversion story, this is often followed by an extensive description of the "pious" death of the protagonist. As in the case of Augustine, the religious biography or autobiography may sometimes end with one or more reflections of a general theological nature.

This basic narrative occurs in almost every conversion story. The writings belonging to the *Nadere Reformatie* tradition, however, exhibit a number of features that are present to a lesser degree in conversion stories from other Protestant circles. In fact, it should be possible to indicate what the most or least frequently occurring features are for each tradition and sub-tradition, and on the basis of this to determine the religious tradition behind every conversion story. Like any autobiography, the conversion story is not just an account of experiences and events but it is also a self-presentation: the author presents himself in a certain way and tries to induce the reader to accept that presentation as truthful. The image of himself that the author chooses to evoke in others thus forms a second aim of the story in addition to the basic narrative: he or she wants to be acknowledged as the person whom the reader will be apt to recognize from his knowledge of the master narrative. In so doing the author will be inclined to omit, or even forget, whatever is at variance with the basic narrative she is using, and will shape the information she conveys to conform with that narrative's pre-existing structure. Sometimes the author will even supply information from the basis narrative that may otherwise be missing. There is certainly no need to accuse such an author of lying, secrecy, hypocrisy or embellishment – as Freud did in reproaching the biographer (rather ungraciously, particularly for the father of psychoanalysis; letter to Arnold Zweig dated 31 May 1935, in: Freud 1960, p. 423). Human actions simply have manifold causes, as Freud himself taught us. In addition, the fact that we allow ourselves to be led by narratives is usually not a consciously pursued strategy but a consequence of socialization processes, most of which have not been subjected to reflection. The human being is guided not only by conscious and unconscious personal intentions in the psychoanalytical sense, which only concern the individual life in the short term, but he is also guided by unconscious long- and medium-term factors such as genetic and historical-social factors. Among the latter are language and stories; they structure human subjectivity, and without them human subjectivity would neither exist nor be able to articulate itself.

The very title of Mrs. Reinsberg's book has all the hallmarks of conversion stories from the realm of Dutch Protestantism. The division of the work into four books also fully corresponds to the basic narrative that applies to the whole genre. She calls her life prior to her stay at Ermelo that of "a mortal without God". The second phase of her life comprises the conversion as it took place during her psychiatric period; the most extensive part of her writing is devoted to this account. In the third book she discusses the four plus years that she had been allowed to live as "someone redeemed by Christ Jesus," and in the fourth book she ends with a series of reflections of a more general nature. The structural similarity with pietistic conversion stories could not be greater.

Orienting ourselves to this genre also helps us to understand the incongruities in Mrs. Reinsberg's story. For example, she says several times that before her conversion she did not have or was not aware of any religious life, and that she had "nothing to do with religion". This is strongly formulated on the very first page of the "preface" to her book: "Although I did not know any passages from the Bible before the age of four, the Spirit of God now lets me speak from God's Word," etc. For an empiricist like a historian or a psychologist it is impossible to tell whether the Spirit of God did or did not let her speak from God's word. The first half of the sentence, however, might evoke some surprise: as we learn from her own book, Mrs. Reinsberg had by no means been without a religious upbringing, religious contacts, or religious habits. Yet her statement – with all respect to Freud – cannot be regarded as distorting, misleading, or anything else. This is where we see the themes from the present section being illustrated: it is entirely in keeping with the basic narrative of the pietistic conversion story that the author presents herself and experiences herself as someone who before her conversion was not at all religious or was even averse to religion. This does not mean that life had been entirely devoid of religion, but rather that the true "sanctifying" way of being religious had been absent up to that point. A person may have been baptized and may even have been more or less faithful in church attendance and in many other religious practices, but according to the pietistic tradition, especially the tradition inspired by the *Nadere Reformatie* in the Netherlands, that is not enough. Among these circles, as explained earlier, it was emphasized that in addition to a correct outward way of living there also had to be a correct interior condition and conviction. One had to be "converted," meaning someone whose first and primary inclination, from the depth of her heart and mind, was turned towards God, and whose entire life had become a witness to this new, converted state.

This will have to suffice as a very inadequate discussion of the "conversion story" genre.

The Narrative Construction of the Self

The human self is a dynamic and complex entity, full of contradiction and tension. The highly diverse types of psychology that have attempted to present this in terms of a concept place their emphasis in different areas. In modern theories, the self and identity – as parts of the more inclusive personality – are sometimes presented as a polymorphous and dialogical narrative. McAdams (1993) even speaks of a personal myth that each individual constructs in order to indicate who she or he is. Yet even this "myth" is not static. First and foremost, it is subject to change over time; and second, the story as told is dependent on the context in which it is told. Not only is the storyteller dependent on the possibilities supplied to him by the context as he constructs his story, but the presented self may also differ according to the "listeners" to whom it is told. Depending on the storyteller's situation, her perspective on her own past and anticipated future will produce a certain story. To paraphrase Hermans and Kempen (1993): the self is a text that is constantly being edited, not by a sovereign, central "I" authority but from a multitude of "I" positions, positions that can even interact with each other and with others (see Chapter 8). From this perspective, the question of Mrs. Reinsberg's "self" can be interpreted as: from which of her possible "I" positions is she speaking to her readers? What version of her "self" is being presented to them?

Mrs. Reinsberg talks about her life from the "I" position of someone who reached a point of conversion at a certain moment in mid-life. That position renders that life visible in a particular way – as every position does in its own manner. It allows a certain light to shine on the life and presents the "facts" from a particular perspective. But let us see whether her "I" position can be even more closely specified. Whereas in principle many "I" positions can be distinguished in each self (one of the meanings of the notion of the "multivoiced self"), each individual "I" position can also be investigated in terms of multiplicity of voices. This may mean trying to discover to what extent the story exhibits internal contradictions, lacunae, *Fehlleistungen*, and other characteristics. But because each person is a product of her own culture and history, "multiplicity of voices" can also refer to the sounds of other voices, such as the voice of a group, that can be heard in a particular individual voice (cf. Wertsch 1991).

At first glance, this closer definition of the "I" position from which Mrs. Reinsberg speaks to us in her book seems simple enough. After all, she describes herself in the title of her book as "now redeemed and reborn," and she calls her book a conversion story. So she is apparently speaking from the position and perspective of a converted person. True enough, except the designation is too simple and it does not go far enough in revealing the multiplicity of voices in Mrs. Reinsberg's spirituality, one of the aspects that make her story so interesting. For what (or who) is a converted person, and what is a conversion? There is considerable disagreement on this point, even in related religious circles. It is clear that in the case of Mrs. Reinsberg we are not dealing with conversion in the sense of switching to another religion, nor are we dealing primarily in the sense of switching

192   Psychopathology and Religion

to another community within the same religious tradition. In her case we are dealing with a form which Rambo (1993), in a commendable attempt to develop a non-theological typology, calls "intensification": "the revitalized commitment to a faith with which the convert had had previous affiliation, formal or informal."[2] For, despite Mrs. Reinsberg's repeated written claims, she certainly did not grow up without religious socialization. On the contrary, during her early Amsterdam years she became intensively involved in the kinds of religious experiences being practiced within the Réveil movement and other pietistic circles (of which the *bevindelijke* is only one, although one she was not acquainted with at that point). As indicated earlier, in constructing her life story, she follows the rhetorical strategies that are usually found in the published conversion stories of the *bevindelijke* circle of Calvinists, although her approach is perhaps too extreme and not very wise (for example, she denies having had any knowledge of the Bible at all). Besides this general structure there are many other structural features from the *bevindelijke* Calvinist conversion stories that can also be found in her account. One consists of the "pulsations" or "impressions" that she reports: the warnings and "voices" of God that urge the as yet unconverted person to abandon the sinful path she has been following up until now. Mrs. Reinsberg clearly says that she interprets several of the events in her life before the Ermelo period as God's intervention in her life. She has something that appears to have been a nervous breakdown after a small fire in the hotel and calls it "a serious warning," and she regards the sickness and death of her children as "God's voice for good or ill". She reports the death of her husband August Reinsberg in the chapter entitled "The Lord takes away my husband." Such incidents form a fixed part of the standard conversion discourse that pietists used to orient themselves when describing their conversions (Groenendijk 1993, p. 75). Their purpose was to show that there were indications that God was indeed "busy" with the narrator, that God was involved in the sinner's life – even those sinners who were not originally from pietistic circles. May we then conclude that the "I"-position from which she wrote her book reverberates with the Calvinistic-pietistic tradition? Without ever being able to respond with total certainty in a study such as this one, the answer must certainly be in the affirmative, although it should immediately be noted that this is not the last word on the subject. To substantiate the positive answer it can also be pointed out that not only did she align herself with this tradition but she also wanted to be recognized as a converted person. This is evident from the fact that she brought her book to the attention of a number of prominent Calvinist theologians.

Starting with her introduction to the Volten family, with whom Doetje received private nursing care in Ermelo during a transitional period between her stay in the insane asylum and her full discharge, Doetje gradually begins moving in a spiritually

---

[2] The other categories classified by Rambo (1993) are: apostasy or defection (becoming a nonbeliever), affiliation (when a previously unbelieving person joins a religious group), institutional transition (switching to another group within a particular religion) and tradition transition (switching to another religion) (pp. 12–14).

charismatic direction. This is the other collective tradition that can be heard in her individual voice, and the second spiritual qualification that we can apply to her "I" position: "charismatic". The content of this kind of spirituality is even more difficult to describe than that of Calvinistic pietism. Charismatic spirituality, even less than *bevindelijke* spirituality, is not tied to any particular church community – and certainly not during the time period we are dealing with here – although it was more likely to be found in some communities than others. It clearly overlapped with the forerunners of today's evangelical movement in the Netherlands, although a distinction should be made already – after the emergence of the Pentecostal movement in the stricter sense – at the beginning of the twentieth century. As in the case of the later evangelical "movement", and unlike the Calvinistic-pietistic tradition, it involved believers who did not seek spiritual nourishment exclusively in the church communities of which they were members, but who also attended (and provided financial support for) gatherings of other religious groups, read materials from many different circles, and participated in parachurch conferences and other activities. Theologically, the charismatic tradition shares most of the notions of mainstream conservative-orthodox Protestantism in the Netherlands (both the Calvinistic-pietistic and the Calvinistic-evangelical wings). It places its emphasis, however, on the functioning of the Holy Spirit in the life of the church and the individual believer, and maintains that the so-called charismata – the gifts of the Spirit – should function in the here and now just as they did in biblical times (this refers in particular to the more "spectacular" phenomena such as healings, glossolalia, and "miracles" of every variety).

The other religious voice that can be heard in the "I" position that Mrs. Reinsberg occupies as author is a charismatic-evangelical voice. This means at least two religious traditions can be identified in her presentation of herself, traditions that certainly have a great deal in common but are nevertheless interesting to differentiate in a detailed study like this one. The entwining of these traditions can be seen throughout Mrs. Reinsberg's book, even in the rhetorical structures and techniques. The personal conversion testimonies that are typical of those brought forward in charismatic circles differ somewhat from the published *bevindelijke* conversion stories, and the construction of the identity as a converted person is undertaken with slightly different rhetorical techniques. In the *bevindelijke*, Calvinistic-pietistic conversion story a clear time distinction is also made between "pre-" and "post-conversion," and the time and attendant circumstances of the conversion are delineated in great detail (while the decades occurring before the conversion are summarily dealt with, which is also the case with Mrs. Reinsberg). In the charismatic-evangelical testimonies, however, the contrast between life before and life after the conversion is depicted as much as possible in terms of a "non-religious" life versus a "religious" life. While *bevindelijke* conversion stories will speak of how a person, despite faithful church attendance, etc., was tormented by uncertainty about his own "condition" and did not dare take part in the Lord's Supper or pray a prayer such as the Lord's Prayer (all religious matters which betray pre-conversional familiarity), charismatic-evangelical testimonies will tell of how a person lived totally without God, without church, and without religion (or began living this way after having had a "Christian upbringing"). "Harlots and publicans" are the standard paradigms: people who are totally lost to sin to all intents and purposes, and then suddenly – preferably as forcefully as possible – converted, as if by a miracle. In Mrs. Reinsberg's story we see her working with this construction as well: she denies any knowledge of religious matters (although her own story sometimes contradicts this) and she discusses things as if she had never had anything to do with religion. For example, the title of the very last chapter in her book ("Decision") is "Prayer from the Holy Spirit, by grace, from someone who had never prayed before". It is precisely because her own account contradicts this that we can wonder whether an "average" charismatic-evangelical believer would have chosen such wording to tell her story. It's just a bit too extreme, and prompts us to further analysis.

After examining the constructivist aspect of Mrs. Reinsberg's conversion story in this section (among other points) we will begin a more functionalist analysis, for which we shall need quite different forms of psychological reasoning. For although the "how" of the construction of Mrs. Reinsberg's identity as a converted person is now clear to us, we are far from understanding the "why". Nor did the concepts of identity and self as they are used in this chapter give us sufficient reason to ask such a question. After reading Mrs. Reinsberg's conversion account as a story in this section – a narrative construction of her self – we can now start asking questions based on psychological theories that work with other approaches and that may help us understand why she wrote this book and why she wrote it in this way. In the voice that her "I" position, as author of her book, makes audible to us we can distinguish qualities such as tone or timbre in addition to the various collective positions and traditions. To give an obvious and probably recognizable example: Mrs. Reinsberg clearly paints herself as someone "special," someone who, after a difficult childhood, managed by dint of hard work to become a successful business-woman, and who, while still quite young, retired from her business to live from her private means like a woman of rank, moving in the better circles. She paints herself as someone who, after undergoing the requisite hardships in life, is blessed by God, someone who has special experiences with God and has been chosen by him to be his instrument in this world. She presents herself as someone who has a story to tell, a story that is so worthwhile that it should be heard by as many people as possible because they stand to profit from it. We may rightly ask ourselves what this tone means, what it refers to or what caused it. The identity presented by Mrs. Reinsberg is – as with every presentation of the self – a desired identity, and it exhibits all the standard problems that are part of the concept of identity. Identity as a narrative given is a text that obscures its own meaning, a meaning of longings that the author does not and usually cannot recognize (Ricoeur 1965/1970). So psychoanalysts such as Lacan point to the problematic status of the identity. According to Lacan, identity is a construct realized in the realm of reality that he called the "imaginary" and is followed by doubt and by suspicions concerning one's own understanding of self, while at the same time it is also the desperate antidote against internal fragmentation, conflictual longing, and threatening chaos (Rosenberg et al. 1992, pp. 41–42). Let us then briefly see whether there may have been inner needs in Doetje's life that caused her to write, and to write as she did.

Doetje's Psychic Energy: Self-psychological Reflections

Psychoanalytical perspectives can be worthwhile when used as heuristics and I shall try to use some of them as a complement to insights gained from working with approaches like narrative psychology employed so far. In a more extensive study it has been shown that the self psychology developed by Kohut in particular is useful for a closer exploration of Doetje's psychic energy (Belzen 2004a). Before discussing a few empirical facts, let us introduce some of Kohut's ideas, especially his reflections on narcissism as a form of psychic energy.

Freud identified a primary and a secondary narcissism. Primary narcissism develops after a brief period of autoeroticism. Initially the libidinal impulses do not focus on anything or anyone specific. The desire that the child experiences by sucking on its mother's breast is the same as the desire it experiences by sucking on its own hand. The child still experiences its mother's breast as part of the child itself (autoeroticism). The *Ich* marks the emergence of an object on which the libido can concentrate and attach itself: the beginning of narcissism (Freud 1914/1975, p. 377). So the term narcissism denoted the primary phase in which the child itself is the object of libidinal cathexis. Only after this does the phase develop in which the child is able to concentrate on an object outside and separate from itself; in this phase it becomes possible for the libido to attach itself to an object in the outside world. Freud saw a contrast between the *Ich*-libido and the later *Objekt*-libido. One emerges at the cost of the other. The more the libido attaches itself to objects in the outside world, the less energy will remain for the subject to focus on itself (Freud 1914/1975, p. 43). Even though narcissism, according to Freud, is never fully dissolved by the *Objektwahl* phase, he thinks the ideal is for the person to turn away from herself as much as possible and focus on the outside world.[3] When in a later phase the libido once again concentrates itself on the subject (and thereby withdraws its attention from objects in the outside world), the condition is known as regression, which Freud speaks of as secondary narcissism (Freud 1914/1975).

Kohut disagrees with Freud. He maintains that the *Ich*-libido (or narcissistic libido) and the *Objekt*-libido develop along separate but parallel lines. They should not be regarded as the extreme ends of the same continuum; rather, they both develop along separate continua from archaic to adult forms. So narcissism − including its manifestations after earliest infancy − should not necessarily be judged negatively. On the contrary, according to Kohut, narcissism (apart from pathological destruction) enables actions that are to be valued positively: it provides the energy that allows a person to be creative, to take pleasure in his work, to enjoy the achievements of himself and others, to pursue and realize ideals, etc. So narcissism is not to be defeated but transformed into an adult form. *Ich*-libido and

---

[3]Freud's reflections here are more or less consistent with the dominant religious reflections in the West that preach love of neighbor and regard attention paid to the self as sinful. Narcissism usually has a negative tone: it seems like a vogue word for selfishness. It should be pointed out, however, that this was not the meaning expressed in Freud's technical explanation.

Objekt-libido can go hand in hand, according to Kohut; they can focus on the same object (such as a possibly ideal love relationship). But narcissistic libido can also make possible the highest achievements in the artistic or humanitarian realm, such as those of Albert Schweitzer (Kohut in Moss 1977, p. 55). On the basis of an empathic analysis of patient transfer, Kohut maintained that besides the problems (standard in classical psychoanalysis) that are rooted in the Oedipal phase (when the child is faced with the task of forsaking his narcissistic desires and joining the existing whole, the culture that surrounds him), it is important to distinguish problems that have their roots in an earlier phase: in the phase of narcissism in which the "sense of self" develops.

According to Kohut, the self (for which he provides no unambiguous definition) comes into being through the sufficient, empathic mirroring of the child by the mother (or another primary caregiver; for the sake of convenience, however, we will continue to speak of the mother). The process by which the neonate becomes conscious of the separation from the mother is by its very nature difficult: the child must begin to realize that an outside world exists which is not subject to his wishes, and that the mother is not always available to him. For the neonate, who must rely on others for his survival, there is something life-threatening about this situation: if no one were to respond to his need for care, he would die. The child responds to this frustrating perception with the development of a certain hallucinatory desire, by which he tries to preserve the unity and completeness that have been lost. On the one hand he develops a grandiose image of himself (based on what has now become an aphorism: "I am perfect"), and on the other hand he forms the image of an almighty other, an idealized parent imago who is assigned to serve as guarantor of care and protection ("you are perfect, but I am part of you," Kohut 1971, p. 27). (According to Kohut this takes place among children between the ages of about 8 months and 3 years.) If the parent relates to the child with empathy, she thereby fulfils two functions that are necessary for the child: on the one hand by accepting the child's grandiose image of itself, by admiring the child and making him feel that he is indeed very special, and on the other hand by making herself available as an object of admiration. (In this way parents fulfill the so-called self-object function: they function as the first self-objects for the child.) What matters is not so much what the parents do as how they are: it is the quality of the interaction with the parents that is internalized by the child. If the parents fall short in this regard, the child will not be able to develop a normal, healthy "sense of self". He will continue to have doubts about himself and his self-worth, precisely because he was not mirrored, or not enough. He will have to go through life without a sufficiently crystallized sense of being "allowed to exist," of being "good enough," a feeling he can fall back on when he meets with adversity in life and from which he can continue to derive self-worth even in the face of failure. It is inevitable, however, that parents will not always respond fully to the needs of the child. According to Kohut that is neither necessary nor even desirable. By means of all sorts of small but non-traumatic frustrations, what he calls "transmuting internalization" can take place by which both necessary functions are gradually disconnected from the parents and absorbed into the self. The grandiose image of the self thereby becomes more realistic: from

Doetje's Psychic Energy: Self-psychological Reflections   197

exhibitionistic narcissism it becomes the "fuel for our ego-syntonic ambitions and purposes, for the enjoyment of our activities, and for important aspects of our self-esteem" (Kohut 1971, pp. 27–28). In the same way, the idealized parent imago is transformed into ideals to be pursued. The "grandiose self," the image of the self as grandiose,[4] is the first to become part of the nuclear self. This takes place between about the second and fourth years (Kohut 1977, p. 178). This self is mainly derived from the relationship with the mother. The "idealized parent imago" forms between the fourth and sixth years, during the Oedipal phase, and is derived from the relationship with both parents.

If the development of the child involves more than the "normal" traumatization (too difficult or too frequent experiences of a lack of empathic response, for example, or of divorce, disappointment and the like) the transformation of the two images (the self and the parent) will not occur; in such a situation they do not become integrated but continue to exist independently. If the grandiose self is traumatized in the midst of its development, the exhibitionistic narcissistic energy will not be able to reinvest itself in the grandiose self in modified form and the subject will ultimately be bereft of an adequate sense of self-esteem. If the idealizing narcissistic energy is traumatically disappointed in experiences with the idealized object it will revert to the idealized parent imago, thus depriving the subject's ideals of an adequate energy supply. Both images then retain psychic energy in repressed form or in a form that is separated from more realistic images; they will distort the development of the subject and prevent the later adult from acting and/or experiencing in a realistic way. The adult – each in his own way, of course, and to varying degrees – will remain tied to his (unconscious) delusions of grandeur and will act as if he were the center of the universe or will withdraw from everything because he is afraid that his extreme expectations will be disappointed. Or he will remain tied to the idealized parent imago and may spend his whole life looking for a parent substitute to which he can submit and with which he can identify, thereby sharing in the substitute's greatness but unable to stand on his own two feet. And if the expectations of such non-integrated self and object images are too badly disappointed, the adult may simply withdraw into the very early sub-representatives of self and object. His self and his world will then fall apart and fragment and the person will go insane (Pietzcker 1983, pp. 45–46). Usually things do not go this far, however. In most cases such a psychic decompensation does not occur, and the narcissistically vulnerable person is still able to do an excellent job of presenting an image of himself to the outside world as adjusted and even successful, although often at great psychic expense. And here it should be noted once again that narcissism and its expressions need not be pathological as such. If transformed, the pole of the self known as the "grandiose self" will supply the energy that the *Ich* needs for its activities. And the idealizing narcissism, in its transformed form, will make

---

[4] This is an example of Kohut's often inconsistent use of language: he uses the same word to refer to the image of the self as grandiose ("self") as to the self of which this image is a part.

possible such socially valued faculties as creativity, empathy, the ability to face one's own finiteness, humor and wisdom (Kohut 1966/1985, p. 111).

There are at least three indications that in the case of Mrs. Reinsberg we are dealing with a person who was narcissistically vulnerable or even suffered from a narcissistic personality disorder in Kohut's sense. I will touch briefly on the first two and discuss the third in greater detail. First of all, if a diagnosis of Doetje is attempted based on a modern psychopathological set of instruments such as the DSM (which is quite possible and has been tested by different raters, cf. Belzen 2004a), a narcissistic personality disorder can be confirmed. Second, counter-transference usually develops with readers of her book, which is an indication of such a disorder. Throughout her book, Mrs. Reinsberg somehow evokes feelings of boredom and resentment among those who seriously want to probe her story more deeply; we feel inclined to shut the book and stop reading. Kohut regards these kinds of feelings from a psychotherapeutic point of view ("counter-transference") as an important indication that we are dealing with a patient with narcissistic problems (Kohut 1971, p. 273). Third, the narcissistic personality disorder, which Kohut ranks fifth in his list of primary disorders,[5] seems plainly applicable to Doetje (Kohut 1977; Kohut and Wolf 1978). This disorder does not manifest itself in deviant behavior; the symptoms are rather hypochondria, a deeply rooted sense of emptiness and depression, a general feeling of unease, boredom, and emotional dullness. The ability to get any work done is often seriously inhibited. There is also an over sensitivity to personal offences, and the response to a suggested lack of empathy is fierce, often excessive rage (cf. Laan 1994).

From the daily entries in her medical file we can deduce that in Doetje's case at the time of her admission to Veldwijk there was indeed evidence of a preoccupation with her self-esteem. She experienced that self-esteem as nil: she was deeply sinful, it was "too late" for her, she felt "unworthy of everything; everyone is good but me" (Medical Dossier Veldwijk (MDV) 416, entry of 16 April 1890). These anxieties seem pre-oedipal in nature, since oedipal anxieties are experienced as attacks on the body or on physical integrity from some exterior source. They involve metaphors concerning external harm being done to cherished body parts (such as the eyes or the genitals); the most common example is perhaps castration anxiety. Pre-oedipal anxieties, on the other hand, manifest themselves as attacks on the self from within, sometimes committed by a persecutor (such as voices Doetje reports hearing), or by unbearable feelings of worthlessness (Gay 1989, p. 82). Pre-oedipal anxieties are often symbolized by an attack on the human face, that of the patient himself or of another person (Kohut 1979). Relevant in this regard is the very frequent mention in Doetje's medical file of the apparent aversion she had to her own face; she did not want anyone to see it and even kept it covered with a handkerchief. One entry states that "flying into a temper, (...) she gave one patient, who was talking excitedly, an

---

[5] In the secondary disorders, as opposed to the primary disorders, such reactions are regarded as responses by an in principle structurally undamaged self to the trials and tribulations of life.

Doetje's Psychic Energy: Self-psychological Reflections 199

unexpected slap in the face" (MDV 416, 4 October 1890). Mrs. Reinsberg herself writes many times of how she tried to hide her face as much as possible at the beginning of her stay at Veldwijk, sometimes by standing in a corner of the room.

As noted, Kohut makes a sharp distinction between problems that have their roots in the oedipal phase and problems that are rooted in the earlier narcissistic phase. (Freud also made this distinction, but he maintained that narcissistic problems could not be treated, which Kohut sees otherwise.) Kohut's differential diagnosis is based on the distinction he makes between the various kinds of transference that patients develop. Classical (neurotic) transference has to do with the problematic conflict concerning incestuous longings with regard to an object from one's childhood. The accompanying anxiety is related to threats of punishment or even physical neglect. The objects here are differentiated, however, and the problem is not situated in the self, which in this case already exhibits a fair amount of cohesion. In a person with a disorder that is rooted in the narcissistic phase, on the other hand, the anxiety is related to the self's awareness of its own vulnerability and tendency towards fragmentation. In these disorders the central problem is situated in the disturbed development of the narcissistic configurations, so that the self is deprived of narcissism's energy sources, causing an incapacity to maintain and regulate one's self-esteem (cf. Siegel 1996, p. 65). Thus the fear of disintegration is different in nature from the oedipal fear of loss of love, and according to Kohut it more closely resembles fear of death.

Doetje's frequent looking in the mirror could also be interpreted as fear of fragmentation. This could be dismissed as trivial, of course: she was ashamed of her face, after all, which was supposed to have been "too ugly, too thin". Perhaps she looked in the mirror because she wanted to make sure the face was still the same as before and needed to be covered by a handkerchief? This explanation is undeniable, although we may easily wonder why Doetje kept casting this self-tormenting glance in the mirror. Was something else being manifested there? With this in mind, let us briefly consult the reflections that the French psychoanalyst Jacques Lacan devoted to the narcissistic phase.

Lacan establishes an explicit relationship with the mythological figure from which the phenomenon derives its name. As in Ovid's story, narcissism supposedly has to do with being attracted to one's own mirror reflection (cf. Evans 1996, p. 120). Lacan therefore calls the phase in which this takes place (from about 6 to 18 months) the mirror phase ("stade du miroir," Lacan 1949/1977), a term that not only denotes an historical phase in the development of the child but also refers to the child's essentially libidinal relationship with the image of its own body (Lacan 1953, p. 14). The mirror phase has both an erotic and an aggressive element. Once the child begins consciously observing itself in the mirror, a double reaction is evoked. On the one hand the image demonstrates a unity that the child has not yet experienced as such; it is as if it were the promise of the future experience of fullness and unity. On the other hand, the image of unity confronts the feelings of fragmentation which until that moment are all the child has been able to experience; it still has no control over its limbs and its movements are still uncoordinated, and it becomes conscious of this by means of the image of unity with which it is confronted.

This contrast between the experience of the fragmented body and the unity provided by the mirror image results in anxiety, an anxiety which the child resolves by identifying with the image of itself in the mirror, which is the first step in the formation of the *Ich*. But this identification is also the beginning of alienation and doubt with regard to the child's own identity, something that will follow the subject throughout its entire life. After all, the child is identifying with something it is not; it is *not* the image in the mirror. So identifying with the image of oneself is *the* paradigm of the so-called imaginary order which the subject-in-progress has entered into. The imaginary order will continue to exist, to be sure, but in order not to remain permanently imprisoned within it the child must take the additional step of entering into the symbolic order by identifying with the identity that already exists in the world of symbols, cultural norms and values, and principally of language. The fear of fragmentation of the body – which can express itself in dreams and associations – manifests itself in a variety of images: castration, mutilation, being torn apart, disturbance, deterioration, debilitation, being devoured, bursting open, and the like (Lacan 1949/1977, p. 11).

By combining Kohut and Lacan, we can come to an understanding of the mirror phase as that in which the mother, as a reflecting surface, turns to the child, thereby making possible the emergence of the self. So when it was noted at Veldwijk that Doetje "frequently looks at her face in the mirror" (MDV 416, 17 April 1890), this could be an indication of the fragmentation anxiety she was experiencing, an anxiety which she resolved by constantly looking in the mirror to make sure she was still unified and not fragmented. This means the function served by Doetje's glance in the mirror may have been quite different from the function served by covering her face with a handkerchief, and should not too quickly be aligned with it. The glance in the mirror was reassuring for her. The mirror image met her deep wish to be complete, not to be fragmented. The function thus served by her mirror image would have been that of a self-object, as it is for most people (cf. Gay 1989, p. 152).

In a great many places in her book Mrs. Reinsberg describes emotions that can be unequivocally interpreted as "narcissistic rage" in the sense of Kohut's theory. This is a rage that is characterised by excessiveness: for people who are narcissistically vulnerable, a seemingly minor provocation can result in fierce outbursts of anger. Narcissistic rage always follows a narcissistic injury. It is the consequence of "the failure of the self-object environment to meet the child's need for optimal – not maximal, it should be stressed – empathic responses" (Kohut 1977, p. 116). The narcissistic injury goes hand in hand with feelings of humiliation on the part of the patient. He reacts to an actual or an anticipated injury by withdrawing in shame or responding with narcissistic rage. The rage arises because the self-object has been inadequate; it has failed to meet the expectations. Such narcissistic rage is characterised by the absence of any kind of empathy with regard to the person who has caused the injury. *Ich*-functions will then only serve as means and as rationalization in order to take revenge. Doetje shows this pattern quite frequently, yet we will have to limit ourselves to a single example.

After Doetje had lived with the Volten family for a while things began to go much better for her, both generally and according to her own gradually developing religious criteria. In terms of the structure that Mrs. Reinsberg used in her book, the event quoted below occurred when she had already been converted and had received the Holy Spirit. Although she was still frequently tormented by anxiety attacks and sometimes heard voices in her head, she had – according to her own insight – really begun to get somewhere. On a certain evening

> I put my sewing down and went downstairs to have a cup of coffee. That evening I spoke as the Spirit of God gave me utterance, and with fire, so that someone who was there told me, "Please, madam, be careful you are not sent back to Veldwijk."[6] (p. 159)

That was exactly the reaction Doetje could not tolerate: instead of winning admiration for her religious ardor and being recognized as someone blessed by God, she was reminded of her own fear of decompensating once again, the fear of losing the battle with her voices and having to be readmitted to an insane asylum, where the patients – at least as she came to see it – were in the clutches of the devil. The comment, well intended perhaps but utterly lacking in empathy, had been made by one of the family visitors (the Volten family, as the entire book attests, were much more cautious in their dealings with Doetje), and her reaction shows how hurt she felt and how much energy that hurt mobilized within her. The story continues:

> But suddenly I felt a wondrous power within me, and picking up the Bible and holding it aloft, I said, "As truly as this Bible is true, so assuredly will I never go back to Veldwijk." A holy tremor shook me when I said this. (p. 159)

Her frequently reported psychosomatic disorders, her unmanageable, attention-demanding behavior and her hypochondria – certainly when taken together – are also indications of a narcissistic personality disorder in Kohut's sense. They are indications of the fundamental weakness of the nuclear self, which can only preserve itself by means of a relationship with external self-objects in order to be reassured or admired. Let us attempt a closer examination of Doetje's self and any possible weaknesses it may have. An important instrument in this effort might be an analysis of the transfer Doetje establishes with her environment.

As already noted, Kohut recognized a so-called narcissistic transfer (later called a self-object transfer) in addition to the form of transfer already described by Freud. In narcissistic transfer, the patient does not respond to the psychotherapist as to persons from the oedipal phase (in such a case, the conflicts over power and authority are played out once again with the therapist), but treats the therapist as the self-object from an earlier phase, the narcissistic phase (here the patient experiences the therapist as part of himself, or himself as part of a greater whole). The problems that arise in this pre-oedipal phase have to do with the development of the self, with being one and being whole, with cohesion and self-esteem. Within this self-object transfer Kohut distinguished various forms that would also recur as elements in his theory of the self: if the patient treats the therapist as someone by whom she wants to be accepted, regarded as worthwhile or even admired, it is an indication of a

---

[6] That is, to be taken from foster care and admitted to the asylum once again.

reactivation of the untransformed or insufficiently transformed grandiose self from childhood. The grandiose self extends itself, as it were, to enclose the therapist, who then only exists to mirror the greatness of the patient's self. For this reason, this form of transfer is also called mirror transfer. If, on the other hand, the patient admires the therapist and ascribes to him all sorts of knowledge, skill and power, the idealized parent imago is being reactivated. In this case we are speaking of idealizing transfer. If the patient approaches the therapist as an equal to himself, as someone who is no different and in particular should be no different than the patient, the condition is called alter-ego transfer. For the patient it is apparently too threatening for the therapist to be a real other, but a "doubling" of himself is acceptable because this confirms and strengthens the desired fundamental unity (Uleyn 1986, pp. 55–56). These forms of transfer do not occur solely in therapeutic situations, however; they also function within all sorts of other relationships that are deemed important. For now, we will only examine the first and, in Doetje's case, most obvious form of transfer.

We have seen that Doetje wanted to be recognized as a special person by people whom she regarded as important, as someone who had been blessed by God and vigorously snatched from the hand of the devil, and who now had a mission to fulfill in the world. To be thus accepted was very important for her. Her book is full of examples of her desire to be affirmed and admired, but it also reveals the other side of the coin: her fear of failure and criticism. These characteristics can be found not only in her account of her stay in Ermelo and the years that followed: they are also evident in the little she shares about the previous years. For example, she says that in her youth she had a great fondness for beautiful clothes, and that she supposedly had "a terribly proud heart" (p. 9). But no matter how beautiful the clothes were, they did not assure her of being beautiful enough: "the more beautiful I was, the unhappier I felt" (p. 3). Writing about the period in the hotel, she says that she worked her fingers to the bone "so no one would complain. For as I always said, I'm more afraid of complaints than of death" (p. 21). Doetje gives the impression that she is very attached to things that will show her in a positive light, but her hunger seems insatiable. We see this pattern again in the religious "battle" she waged at Veldwijk: even though she was treated positively there by the personnel and by the chaplain, the Rev. Notten, and even though she was told many positive things from Christian doctrine (about mercy and love, that surely there is forgiveness for her, etc.), it was always difficult for her to accept it personally. She continued to hear critical "voices". Something in her made it impossible for her to believe that the message of Christian salvation might also apply to her. She was still afraid of being lost forever. She listened to biblical texts about hell with nothing but fear or tried not to hear them at all, etc. Apparently she had had an enormous, enduring, and unquenchable need for empathic responses from mirroring self-objects. Never able to believe in her own worth, she was driven to achieve that worth, and with it positive treatment by others, in another way: by earning it. From this pattern, now sufficiently well known, only one conclusion can be drawn in the light of self psychology: Doetje's grandiose self as part of her nuclear self was underdeveloped. Her normal need to be positively mirrored must have been traumatized in early childhood, so that the narcissistic grandiose self was never transformed into a self-object function that the subject could fulfill for herself but was split off and never integrated. Doetje must have suffered from a fundamental absence of faith in her own worth. She could only believe she was acceptable and worthwhile (and even then she could never fully believe it) if she could earn that recognition. Her share in what Kohut calls the "gleam in the eye of the mother" must have been quite inadequate.

Psychological Hypotheses and Empirical Historical Research

The historical facts available to us concerning Doetje's childhood corroborate the hypothesis, developed from psychology, that in Doetje there was clear evidence of a traumatized development of the grandiose self (and to a lesser degree of the development of the idealized parent imago). At the age when the grandiose self takes shape, Doetje must have had to endure disturbances in her need for empathic responses that were more serious than those at a slightly later age (when the parent imago develops). A great many diverse facts make it more than likely that Doetje's mother, Johanna Catharina (1806–1858), had not been able to give Doetje optimal attention during the childhood years that are so formative for psychic development. When Doetje was born her mother already had four small children to care for, and shortly before her birth she had lost a little daughter. When Doetje was just 1 year old Johanna Catharina became pregnant again, and 9 months later she had to begin nursing this new child. Only 15 months after that, when Doetje was just 3 years old, the next infant required attention. Two years later came the shock caused by the death of Mr. and Mrs. Ypes-Santée's youngest child, an event that, like the illness of sister Egbertina and the pregnancy that preceded it, must have prevented Johanna Catharina from being able to function as an optimal self-object for Doetje.

Mrs. Reinsberg's description of her childhood years is also in close agreement with the picture painted here. The first persons she mentions are not her mother and father; these do not come up until she talks about going to live with her uncle. The person in whom she apparently sought refuge was not her mother but the nanny. She sat with her in "a corner" and had a good cry when, at age three and a half, she came back from the nursery school for the first time, and it was the nanny who comforted her with fairy tales and other stories (p. 1). Had the little child already found it necessary to search for another hiding place and to seek solace in a fantasy world?

Even though Mrs. Reinsberg stylizes the description of her childhood for the sake of her plan to write a conversion story, and naturally presents it as a period of wickedness and unhappiness, it is still striking to read on some pages the repeated assertion that she felt so unhappy as a child. Through the loss of important others such as an elder brother and sister, and even her father (cf. later), the well-known feelings of guilt will not have been lacking. Greater than the problem of guilt, however, was that of shame (Mrs. Reinsberg often writes about feelings of shame but almost never about guilt) another indication of a self-psychological problem. The fact that she had been given the name of a little girl who had only recently died will also have had its consequences. Even though many children died in childbirth in the nineteenth century and the connection with a child may have been less intense than it is a hundred and 15 years later, the death of the first Doetje must have had an impact on the parents. After all, she was already 2 years old when she died. In such circumstances, parents suffer psychological loss for which they will try to find a replacement, often feeling compelled to prove to themselves and to the rest of the world that they are indeed able to bear a child and keep it alive (Agger 1988). Often the dead child becomes the representative of the parents' idealized hopes and fantasies, which are then imposed as expectations on the replacement. Not infrequently this leads to borderline or narcissistic disorders (Agger 1988, p. 24).[7]

The next child can never fulfill the idealized image of the one who died, however, and inevitably becomes a disappointment for the parents (Kernberg and Richards 1988). The mother in particular is often tormented by anxiety fantasies of the death of the "replacement child," which can leave the child with deep feelings of vulnerability and inadequacy. In the first pages of her book, Mrs. Reinsberg does indeed paint just such a picture of a child who is a constant disappointment, fails to meet expectations and therefore develops the corresponding feeling about herself. The narcissistic injury that arises from the chronic failure to satisfy the parents' expectations and live up to the idealized standard of the image of the deceased child leaves irrevocable traces: no attempt is adequate, no achievement satisfactory, no effort sufficient to compensate for the loss suffered by the parents. And we have seen how Doetje lived out this pattern in the way she diligently applied herself in the hotel and later applied herself "for the Lord". The burden of a replacement child also leaves a mark on her nuclear "sense of self". As a child, Doetje was not given the feeling that she was allowed to exist, that she was good enough and that she was accepted as she was. We will never know how the situation actually played itself out, but it cannot be doubted that the environment that was so important to her was less than optimal in meeting her rightful childish need to be mirrored. In her case, the traumatization of her sense of being someone, being a self (and being allowed to be a self) led to a gnawing doubt about her own self-worth, to a narcissistic disorder that expressed itself later in her life in an intense need to be admired by others whom she deemed important.

The formation of the idealized parent imago, usually with a great deal of impact from the father, takes place from the fourth to the 16 year of life. In Doetje's case it seems to have been much less traumatized than the early formation of the grandiose self. Her father disappeared without a trace when she was twelve, but at least until that time he was present (Belzen 2004a). An indication of the hypothesis that Doetje's formation of a grandiose self suffered much greater traumatization than that of the idealized parent imago can be taken from Kohut's comment that recovery from a narcissistic personality disorder is usually sought and found in the need and pole of the self that has been least traumatized and that has been able to compensate, as

---

[7] This is a well-known problem. Meissner (1997, p. 259) speaks of "the replacement-child syndrome" and cites a considerable amount of literature, from which it has been be shown that the syndrome played a role in the lives of such famous persons as Schliemann, Atatürk and Stendhal.

it were, for the defects on the other pole. Whether and to what extent Doetje recovered is a question that cannot be answered directly. Of course she was declared "recovered" when she was released from Veldwijk, but all we can deduce from this is that the reasons for her admission had been eliminated: Doetje was once again able to function in society, she could resume responsibility for her own life, live on her own, care for herself and occupy herself with her own affairs (such as the leasing and letting of buildings). When she left Veldwijk she no longer suffered from "melancholia agitans": she was no longer depressed. But what about her narcissistic personality disorder? Had that disappeared as well, or at least been transformed?

It's not likely. On the one hand it is clear that she had drawn strength from the idealizing transfer relationship that she had entered into with God. Thanks to what for her had become a living faith, she had acquired a perspective into which she could place her life and what had happened to her, including what had happened during her illness. The idealizing transfer relationship that she built with the Rev. Notten at Veldwijk gradually disappeared. In contemporary psychoanalysis, the development and gradual disappearance of such transfer relationships are usually seen as a good sign. According to Kohut, treatment involves the therapist making himself available to fulfill the self-object functions that were insufficiently performed by the parents. Thanks to the empathy that the therapist brings to the patient, a process of "transmuting internalization" can still begin and the patient can be helped to develop his own psychological structures, which makes continuous empathic availability of a self-object less necessary. But did this occur in the case of Doetje's relationship with Notten? It seems more likely that Notten, in functioning as a self-object (which he certainly did for Doetje), was simply substituted by God: Doetje found a "better" self-object and exchanged that for Notten. She continued to have great respect for Notten, but after she left Ermelo he became just another person with whom she was involved in a mirroring transfer relationship: he, too, was expected to admire her for all the great things she was doing. It looks very much as if Doetje's need to be admired did not decline but only increased, or at least became more apparent. Her need for idealized transference had already diminished in any case, as we have supposed, and apparently could be sufficiently fulfilled by the only object as such that we can find for the period in which she wrote her book. If it was indeed so – that God served as a self-object for Mrs. Reinsberg in an idealizing transfer relationship – we may take it as attesting to the plausibility of the supposition that the development of an idealized parent imago was apparently less traumatized. To have found God as self-object helped her reach a certain level in compensating for the defects in her grandiose self.

The research on which this section is based made use of psycho- and psychopathological instruments, even more so than in the previous section. After gaining insight into Doetje's illness and undertaking a preliminary exploration of her person on the basis of a modern classification system, we discovered it was mostly psychoanalytical theories and points of view that paved the way to a deeper understanding of the nature and context of, and possible reasons for, her psychic problems. Psychoanalysis posed questions concerning relationships in her childhood and youth and prompted a closer exploration of certain points in Doetje's biography (points we may not have brought up had we not been looking through psychoanalytical "glasses," at least not in this way) and urged to do additional historical research. This procedure may count as an illustration of the interdisciplinary approach outlined in Chapter 2, when we introduced psychohistory as an element of both psychological and historical scholarship. As explained there, the psychological viewpoints employed in the research discussed here have made two major contributions: first, they made it possible to place the scarce and sometimes disparate facts in a theoretically grounded connection; second, they functioned as a heuristic for empirical research, they urged for the finding of new data. Whether all the proposed interpretations that resulted are equally correct, or even plausible, remains to be seen, of course; we have indicated the methodological problems. Without the help of psychology and psychopathology, however, we would never have been able to develop a more nuanced story about Doetje Reinsberg-Ypes and about the different factors in her illness and recovery. Now we are approaching the moment at which we can answer the question why she wrote and published her autobiography, and what that may have had to do with her mental health, also as far as religion is concerned.

The Function of the Autobiography for Mrs. Reinsberg

Doetje seems to have been searching for a self-object. In her search for acceptance, affirmation and admiration, she tried to obtain from others what was denied to her earlier in life. It is here that the deepest reason for writing her book may be sought. With the previous discussion in mind, we should no longer find it difficult to realize that because of a defect in the development of her grandiose self Doetje was searching for admiration from mirroring self-objects. It is by no means certain, however, that her environment was able to meet her need in the way she so hoped. We have already noted that Doetje had been involved in a fair amount of church conflict in Baarn. She certainly will not have received the kind of appreciation she was yearning for there, and this may have been one of the motives (unconscious, of course) for switching church communities and finally leaving for The Hague. And it is quite conceivable that when empathic mirroring failed to materialize there too, Doetje came up with the idea of convincing her unwilling listeners by means of a powerful, voluminous witness: a book. If the people of The Hague did not want to believe her oral testimony, would not something spectacular like a book – written by a person who "used to be so ignorant," who "did not know God's Word" and "never read books herself" – serve to convince them? In any case, Mrs. Reinsberg does tell us that in The Hague it was "revealed" to her "by the Spirit of God (...) that it was God's will that this book be written" (p. 217). She, who had not been mirrored enough, found a – temporary? – strategy by mirroring herself: by writing a book that would become increasingly important for her, that she herself admired and that she would gradually even come to identify with the word of God, as she had also done with her testimony and her letters. The book would occupy more and more of her time. In the end she worked on it day and night. For her the last week before Pentecost 1897 was a battle "with Christ against Satan and his powers" (p. 433).

In the long run the book would function for her as the self-object with which she had had too few encounters in the outside world. By identifying with the self-made entity of her book she could still find the "wholeness" that she had not been able to experience within herself. The deficient inner completeness, the absence of a "sense of self," was symbolically compensated for in this way by the "perfect" book, desired and inspired by God (cf. Schönau 1991, pp. 12–14). So there was nothing accidental – indeed, it was a golden opportunity – about grabbing hold of the more or less socially accepted genre of conversion stories as a subgenre of the "autobiography," a genre in which narcissistic overtones have so often been demonstrated (Wysling 1982; Hansen-Löve 1986). The writing itself became important for Doetje. It was the means by which she came to feel that she actually was somebody, by which she kept the threat of fragmentation at a distance and tried to give herself what she had found deficient in others. For this reason the writing could not stop. When the book was finally finished, at least when she had related the story of her life up to the present moment so there was nothing left to tell, she continued to write a series of doctrinal chapters followed by an "epilogue". At the end of her "book IV" (containing the letters) she added a "postscript," relating what had happened with the manuscript of the book, and ending with a "conclusion". Even after the book had gone to press she kept on writing.

> And now one of these days the book will be published, eighteen sheets of which have already been printed. The rest is ready for the press, and right now I am adding the finishing touches so that the book, which I was directed to write by Almighty God, compelled by the love of Jesus Christ and filled with His Holy Spirit, will presently be ready. (p. 442)

As she came closer to the end of her book her verbal eruptions became longer and longer. The passages that no longer imparted any information but were simply a written form of "spiritual language" became more and more numerous; it is as if her nervousness was only increasing the longer she continued. That nervousness probably had to do with her fear that the book would be negatively received. After all, she had already had to accept the mildly worded rejection of the manuscript by the theologians Notten and De Savornin Lohman. In the long run she was prepared to give almost anything for the book – the presentation of herself – including her own financial resources. With great difficulty she had been able to find a printer, but not a publisher. The printer then told her that he would be happy to print the book if she would pay for the publishing herself, but that the manuscript first had to be made ready for the press (pp. 438–439). A person skilled in this area was then engaged, and in order to pay for the entire project Doetje even went so far as to sell her buildings in Amsterdam!

Religiosity in Relation to Mental Health

The book certainly did not bring Doetje what she had expected. It was not well received. An extensive study of its reception has shown that it was given no media coverage whatsoever (Belzen 2004a). Of the few copies found in Dutch libraries the pages are sometimes still uncut. There are several reasons for this lack of coverage for her book. One of them is the language, style and form, which did not fully comply with the Calvinist "conversion story" genre. Other reasons are her lack of authority to find acceptance for her story as well as the stigma of her psychiatric past (anyone who had been released from a psychiatric asylum – which was definitely a rare occurrence at the end of the nineteenth century! – had little chance of being taken seriously...).[8] There may also have been another factor in the explanation why the book was so badly received that the psychology of religion may shed light on: the psychic make-up of Mrs. Reinsberg's religiosity.

Religiosity, as the personal-subjective correlate of a particular form of religion, is part of a person's life, so naturally it shares in the person's ups and downs. Thus – to mention just one example from this extensive category – an image of God, the concept of God that an individual might have, is primarily dependent on his religious tradition and on the culturally and historically defined version that has been handed down to him, but it is also dependent on scores of factors in the individual's own life story. The image of God changes as the person grows older (or it doesn't, or it hardly changes at all, and this stagnation is also very significant). It can change under the influence of so-called "critical life incidents". It is dependent on important others such as parents or primary caregivers, figures of authority, mentors and other role models. Religiosity shares the dynamics – also the psychodynamics – of full life, whether it is the dynamics of groups or individuals. It is thus a function of what is referred to as personality or psychic make-up, or whatever we care to call it. In assessment or diagnosis it is quite possible to choose religiosity as a point of access for further exploration (provided one has sufficient knowledge of the form of religion to which the person belongs) and to obtain meaningful results. An analysis of the religiosity of an individual should, therefore, always take place against the background of a more comprehensive exploration of his psychic life, including the question of the person's so-called mental health. As we know, the criteria for mental health, or for the normal psychic life, are extremely difficult to determine. And even if they could be described as being ideal-typically, the question is still how to arrive at an assessment in an individual case. So how should we assess Doetje's mental health, including her religious functioning, at the time she was writing her book?

In a certain sense it seems simple enough: she was declared "recovered" upon her release; she no longer suffered from "melancholia agitans"; she could once again behave in an entirely "appropriate" way, could live on her own, etc. In that sense she was psychiatrically "normal". This does not tell us very much, however. In fact, at that time all it meant was that a person was no longer being institutionalized (and also nowadays it does not mean much more than that a person is not undergoing any other kind of psychiatric treatment). So let us try using yet another criterion – not in an effort to still declare Doetje "unhealthy" but to explore her psychic health. Let us consider the most famous of all descriptions of mental health, that of Sigmund Freud. He maintained that a person is mentally healthy if he is fit to work and to love.

---

[8] The psychiatric stigma will also have been the reason why the autobiography was "hushed up" in intimate circles and why the memory of Doetje herself has barely survived.

Vergote (1978/1988) added "to enjoy and to communicate" to these criteria, for use in religious psychopathology. Working, in the sense of making a living, is something Doetje never did again, but there was no financial necessity to do so. Would she have been fit to work? It's hard to say, simply because so many necessary data are missing. There seem few reasons to doubt that she would have been fit enough to do some work. Of course we do not know what the role of the daughters was in the move to The Hague (although we may well wonder whether the children had much of a say at all), but in any case it was an undertaking that she was able to perform quite well. She still traveled a bit and seemed to have been able to maintain several personal relationships. The writing and publishing of the book must also be regarded as a considerable achievement. But it is striking that she reports so little "enjoyment" in all this: whether she was able to derive very much pleasure or satisfaction from her restless activity is by no means certain. All her activities seem to have been inspired by the wish to convince her acquaintances, as well as herself, of her own "importance". The entire project seems to have been inspired by a need to be mirrored as an extraordinary person with extraordinary experiences, and suggests an unfulfilled passion. Was she able to love again? She certainly developed a form of love, for God and the church (in the general sense, not for any concrete congregation). Perhaps she was able to love her children again as well.

Mrs. Reinsberg impresses us as someone who did not maintain cordial relations with the people around her. Even though the conversion story genre more or less "allows" an author to be chiefly preoccupied with herself and not to paint portraits of others, it is still striking that Mrs. Reinsberg's book contains no articulation of warm feelings towards her children. Mrs. Reinsberg writes that while she was living in Baarn, and later in The Hague, she noticed a cooling within herself: despite the occasional improvement, the joy and "fire" had disappeared, and her main occupation was to fight a bitter battle "with the devil". According to Pietzcker (1983, p. 52), we can see this as an indication of the problem of the grandiose self: because of the fear that the outside world will react coldly and with rejection, the subject withdraws his psychic energy from the object and redirects it on himself. We can read that Mrs. Reinsberg writes of being "scared to death" of criticism, even before her period as a maid and hotelier. If we are indeed correct in our supposition that her grandiose self was not transformed, we may see further evidence of this in the insensitive, loveless way she related to her acquaintances. This also says something about her way of communicating. It is obvious that she was able to communicate; her book is full of evidence to that effect, and her letters and the book itself provide many examples of her communication skills. On the other hand, her form of "communication" was always very one-sided: other people served mainly as witnesses to whom she could tell her story, they served to be addressed. She wanted to speak *to* them, not *with* them. When she wrote to relations in Veldwijk it was mainly to show what great deeds she was supposed to have done. When she wrote to her brother it was to show off her faith; when she corresponded with Wisse and Kuyper it was to tell them how matters were to be viewed; and even when she answered a letter from Notten, she may indeed have responded to his comments but it was only to convince him that she was right. This is not the kind of communication that Vergote (1978/1988) had in mind.

Vergote also comments, by the way, that "objective" criteria, or "objective" handling of the criteria, is impossible. Mental health is not something that can be determined precisely, as if one were measuring it to within a few decimal points: "it is the style of how one relates to reality and society that is important. And that style represents the qualitative surplus value that eludes any objective rules" (Vergote 1978/1988, p. 29). It is precisely on this point of style, so difficult to quantify, that Mrs. Reinsberg raises questions regarding her psychic health, including her religiosity. Indeed, it is striking that she reports so few expressions of approval from Ermelo: the believers in Ermelo seem mainly to have been those who, clearly without premeditation or any systematic approach, introduced her to a new form of religious experience, or who reawakened the evangelical religiosity she may have been acquainted with during her first years in Amsterdam. For these Calvinist and evangelically-minded people in Ermelo, Doetje's religiosity as it developed during her period of home nursing must have seemed overwrought, something that reminded them too much of the psychiatric patient. They listened to Doetje as she became religious and (wisely?) did not contradict her, but neither did they react positively to some of her remarks, which were all too exaggerated for Calvinist ears. For example, when Doetje wrote a letter to her children for the first time she ended it with the comment "these letters are not only written with ink but are the true and living words of God," she showed it "to Miss Volten and Miss Juch [a friend of Mrs. Volten]. Miss Juch, that good, deaf lady, just sat there nodding her head as she read the letter, but she didn't say anything" (p. 157). Of course not, one might say. They must have been pleased that Doetje was apparently recovering, was undertaking positive activities such as re-establishing contact with her children, and was gradually becoming more independent, but they certainly will not have supported her claim to have written "words of God". The Calvinist reverence for the "word of God" is well known: this honorary title is reserved exclusively for the Bible as written text (and for the sermon in a church service as the spoken word). Despite all their esteem for the "old writers" no Calvinist would ever refer to a book by such an author from the *Nadere Reformatie* as the "word of God" or to an oral confession of faith as the "living words of God".

In view of the style of Doetje's behavior and in view of the nature of her conversion story, it is fair to wonder who would have agreed with her. Mrs. Reinsberg herself assures us that it did happen in the case of a single conversation during an accidental encounter (in which the reader must wait and see whether the impression she apparently made on her listeners as she describes it, and that either made them listen or silenced them, was always a positive one). That is, her work of witness did sometimes bear fruit. But insofar as she herself writes about it, it seems that in relationships of any duration she definitely did not receive much affirmation of her faith, her story, her convictions or her zeal. Perhaps this was also the reason why she left every congregation she ever joined, only to ultimately make a connection with unestablished groups such as the Salvation Army and the *Geloofsvereeniging der Volheid van Christus* (Religious Society of the Fullness of Christ), which were themselves marked by a style that was quite rapturous, certainly to the churches in the Netherlands at that time. Movements and groups that have yet to put down roots are usually not very selective with respect to their adherents; there is often a considerable turnover, and people and finances are needed to realize their often grandiose plans. Doetje, who clearly adopted elements from the spirituality of these groups, will certainly have felt at home there. But will the members, especially the leaders, have confirmed her in her religiosity, particularly in her religious claims? Because of its differently disposed pneumatological and ecclesiological views, the Religious Society, with its charismatic milieu, will probably not have denied that a believer could speak or write "true and living words of God". Doetje's insistence on being released from demonic possession, her view that healing comes by prayer alone, and her decision to present herself as a converted person are all elements to be found there, which she probably adopted from this milieu. Nevertheless, there is a suspicion that her relationship with the Religious Society did not remain optimal either. Even in these circles she may have come across as too exaggerated. Her way of associating with others was too aggressive, too deeply rooted in her need for self-assurance. There is a striking absence in her autobiography of names from these circles, and an absence of any mention of approval for writing her book. In many respects, the content of Doetje's religiosity does seem to agree with the form of Christianity advocated by these groups (aggressive witnessing, biblically fundamentalist views, fighting with established churches, rejection of doctrinal authority, experience as spiritual criterion, etc.), but somewhere there was a lingering difference. It is definitely not implausible that, in view of the psychiatric stigma (which may on the other hand have been less significant to the Religious Society than to members of established churches), she will have struck the members of this group as a "duplicate," to use an image from Rümke (1956/1981, p. 215) with respect to the phenomenological difference between psychic health and illness.

It might be supposed that Mrs. Reinsberg's religiosity was too dominated by her need as detected by self psychology. In the previous section we came to the conclusion that she must have had an enormous need for empathic responses from mirroring self-objects. Because she was not able to believe in her own worth, she was compelled to earn that worth, as it were, by way of effort and hard work. As is usually the case, we see this pattern pervade in her religious functioning as well. Of course she would have endorsed the message of grace, but rejoicing in grace and salvation was not what stood at the forefront of Doetje's religiosity. She worked herself to the bone, just as she did during her earlier period as a hotelier, restlessly active in her "fight" for God. It was not gratitude and joy but work and zeal – even doggedness – that were the hallmarks of her way of being religious. She was thus of the opinion (partly influenced by the ideas from the healing ideologies she had learned about, of course) that under no circumstances was she to call in medical help, but that "Christ alone sufficeth". It is evident from that story, from the account of the sale of the hotel, and from so many other passages that Mrs. Reinsberg's relationship with God was not one of gratefully receiving unearned love but of wresting answers to her prayers.

Religion and the Transformation of the Self

In the case of Doetje we can legitimately wonder to what extent her personality was transformed by, or under the influence of, religion. It is evident that she was changed by her conversion, that she had become "another person". Once again, whether and to what degree this was so in the religious-spiritual sense is something that science cannot judge. But we can wonder in what psychological sense she was changed. In that case, however, we need to be fully aware of the psychological theory within whose framework we are asking this question. Even a general term like personality change can point to very diverse things, such as a cognitive restructuring in the way information is processed, a modification of dynamic structures in the psychoanalytical sense or a demonstration of different behaviors according to the notion inspired by behaviorism. Religions usually demand change when conversion takes place. It is beyond doubt that Doetje was different after her stay at Ermelo. But is there also evidence of a personality change? By resorting to an increasingly popular personality model we can make differentiated assessments (McAdams 1994a,b, 2005). This model distinguishes three levels: (1) dispositions that are thought to be highly independent of context; the Big Five model from modern trait psychology[9] is situated here, but so is much of psychoanalysis; (2) personal "concerns" like contextual strategies, plans, goals; (3) identity, the life story from which people derive significance and meaning (and that, in addition to the related experiences, demonstrates an integration of the information from levels one and two). In terms of the third level it will be clear that Doetje changed dramatically: after her conversion, her identity, her self-presentation and the story she told about herself were completely different from what they had been before. In terms of a humanistic-psychologically inspired meaning of the word "personality," in which a great deal of attention is paid to self-definition and the experience of meaning – including the various views of the self, from James (1890) to Hermans and Kempen (1993) – there is clear evidence of a personality change in Doetje's case. This is also true with regard to the second level of the model. Doetje's behavior after her conversion exhibited a different orientation: her areas of interest changed, and the things to which she devoted herself were entirely different from those to which she devoted herself when she lived in Amsterdam. Her life had taken on completely different contours. As for the first level of the model, dispositions and psychoanalytically conceptualized structures, including the self, this is where we see the least change in the sense of personality psychology. The "self" found in psychoanalytical theories such as Kohut's means something different from the "self" in the tradition of psychology inaugurated by James. So let us look here as well, and in continuation of the reflections on Kohutian self psychology, for an answer to the question about Doetje's possible personality change: to what extent were her undeveloped narcissistic needs changed by her conversion?

We have already noted something relevant in this regard when we saw that Doetje's grandiose self had not undergone any transformation. But what about her idealized parent imago? After all, she did take God as her self-object. Establishing an idealized transfer relationship with God probably did have a certain restorative effect on the defects that existed at the other, grandiose, pole of herself, and the idealizing transfer helped her to keep going psychically. Whether the effect was

---

[9] These five are known by the acronym "OCEAN": openness to experience, conscientiousness, extraversion, agreeableness, neuroticism.

lasting and sufficient is something we do not know. We did comment earlier that at the time of her move from Baarn to The Hague, Mrs. Reinsberg reported increasing symptoms and made a more and more agitated impression. She also appeared to have arrived at the edge of the next psychic decompensation, which she was able to avoid only by means of retreating into herself, by herself (the writing of an autobiography being a textbook example). This is reason to express "concern" about how she will have fared after the publication of her book, certainly when it appeared not to have been enthusiastically received. The way she talks about the sale of her hotel shows that she was also relating to God in a highly imperative fashion: he *had to* listen to her prayers, he *had to* cure her when she became ill, the "miracle of the sale of the hotel" *had to* take place so the book could be paid for. Seen in this way, we can ask ourselves whether taking God as a self-object will have contributed very much to the transformation of Doetje's self. The answer is probably not all that positive, since God as self-object does not initiate the process of "transmuting internalization" that is so necessary for transformation. This process is set off by the non-traumatic shortcomings of those who serve as self-objects, whether a parent now or a therapist later on. By means of these non-traumatic shortcomings, the subject switches over to adopt and internalize the functions that the self-object had been fulfilling for him, and thus becomes less dependent on the empathic self-object. But in the faith experience of a believer like Mrs. Reinsberg, God does not fall short, does not "traumatize," so the relationship with Him does not spark a process of the internalization of self-object functions.

Whether religion in general can fulfill this function or not is the wrong question because it is too generally formulated. It has been sufficiently noted that as a concept "religion" is actually too inclusive; too much can be classified within it to be able to work with it analytically. The same is also true concerning the question just asked. Narcissism that has remained childlike can express itself in "religion," but transformed forms of narcissism can just as easily manifest themselves in religious activity. Religion as such, or a specific form of religion such as a Christian denomination or sub-denomination, does not "do" anything and bears no relation to psychic development or to something like mental health. It is religious symbols, especially practices, or better yet: it is persons involved in religion who sort out the effects. Doetje did not learn about any "new" religion (new for her) in Ermelo. Calvinism and evangelical Protestantism were not foreign to her; she had already come to know them in her childhood and early adolescence. So it was not the Calvinist doctrine, transformed into organizational structures at Veldwijk, that brought about the positive development within her; it were Calvinist and evangelically-minded people like the nursing staff, the Rev. Notten and the Volten family who, with patience that may or may not have been inspired or motivated by their Christian faith, offered Doetje the empathy she needed in order to recover psychically. In the same way, charismatic movements such as the Salvation Army and the Religious Society of the Fullness of Christ, with their emotional style that was still unusual in those days, also met Doetje's need for outward show. Her spirituality was not considered deviant in these circles; at least it was not out of the ordinary. The charismatic, freer spirituality that was advocated in the healing movement was the climate within which Doetje's narcissism may have been able to manifest itself more easily than in the more regulated church life of the Reformed Protestants and the Calvinists, just as forms of deviance are still more quickly interpreted spiritually in these circles than in the more mainstream churches. But this reasoning cannot be turned around; it cannot be said that these kinds of movements obstruct or reverse the development of narcissism, or that they induce deviance. Only members of such movements can do this, if at all.

The relationship between religion and mental health is a complicated one, and this is also true in the case of Mrs. Reinsberg. Schematic classifications can be useful, but they do not do justice to the richness of a full life. In the widely esteemed classification of possible relations presented by Spilka et al. (2003), a religious phenomenon can often be placed in several of the proposed categories. Religious expressions such as glossolalia, entering a monastic order, fasting, praying and so on may be the forms within which a psychic disorder manifests itself, but they may also be socializing and restraining factors with regard to mental disturbance. They may constitute a refuge and a therapeutic factor, but they may also represent a danger for a person's mental health. It is always important to check how individual religiosity is related to the cultural and subcultural "world" in which the person lives her life, and how it is structured within the person's broader psychic life. Now that we have traveled this long path with a single historical case, the relationship proves to be just as complicated as ever. Religion did play a role (albeit most likely a modest one) in the onset of Mrs. Reinsberg's illness, even if it was just as a vehicle by which she articulated her problems. Religion certainly played a role in her recovery as well. It provided a frame of reference that helped Doetje interpret her situation and symptoms and gradually to gain control over them again, and that enabled her to take up a new, independent life outside psychiatry. By developing faith in a loving and accessible God, Mrs. Reinsberg was given the opportunity to suppress her psychic problems and to socialize; on the other hand, her defective psychic health continued to manifest itself in her religiosity. Mrs. Reinsberg fits into every category of the classification proposed by Spilka et al. (2003). This makes the value of such classifications relative, but in principal heuristically useful. To understand something about a person's religiosity and its possible relationship with her mental health, no matter how structured, it is important to focus attention on the individual and to immerse oneself in her personal life story, as articulated in her autobiography.

Chapter 12
Religion and the Social Order

Psychological Factors in Dutch Pillarization, Especially Among the Calvinists

Introduction: "Pillarization"

In this final chapter we shall turn to a quite different approach within cultural psychology. We shall not inquire about the cultural part of psychic functioning of a group or an individual, but indulge in something that is more or less the opposite. We will address the psychic part in the development and the makeup of culture, or rather, of a selected subculture. We will turn again to the *gereformeerden* from the Netherlands, and try to understand how factors that might be conceptualized and explored by means of psychological theories and viewpoints have had an impact in their history. That history, in combination with that of several other groups in the Netherlands, has led to a social order, to a structure of society, that has been quite remarkable and for a long time has even been considered to be unique to the Netherlands. Although recent research has shown that the latter can no longer be maintained, so-called "pillarization" has been very characteristic of the Netherlands for the larger part of the twentieth century and continues to have effects to this day. Evidently, we first need to introduce the phenomenon.

History sometimes has a way of leaving strange tracks. When we consider the history of the European "university" phenomenon, we notice that the universities in the Netherlands do not really have a very long tradition. The oldest university (founded in 1425), "in the low countries on the sea" is in Leuven, located in what is now the Dutch-speaking part of Belgium. The first university in today's country of the Netherlands was founded in Leiden, and not until 1575. Stranger still may be the fact that the capital of the Netherlands could not be called a "university town" until the end of the nineteenth century. But remarkably, after 1880, Amsterdam suddenly found itself the home of two completely independent universities. The university that is now known as the University of Amsterdam traces its origins back to the *Athenaeum Illustre* ("illustrous school"), founded by the city authorities in 1632. Mainly devoted to medical teaching, this institution was not to become a municipal university until 1877, when it obtained the right to confer doctorates. Equal in status to the older so-called state universities, the University of Amsterdam is fully funded by the State and adopted its present name in the 1960s. During the same year, 1877, a number of Dutch Calvinists decided to found a Protestant university that would be unrelated to both the State and the churches. It was to be the *Vrije Universiteit* (Free University), opened to the public in 1880. This university was intended as a Christian institution, that is, a university based on Christian (in this case neo-Calvinist), principles and consequently resulting in a different sort of scholarship than that which was developing and being taught at the State universities. At this private, "special" university, a "special" – that is, Christian – scholarship would be pursued.

The fact that a religious group can have its own university at its disposal may seem, on the one hand, quite remarkable. Compare this to the situation in a neighboring country such as Germany, which at the end of the nineteenth century served as the model for academic education in the Netherlands. Not a single private university existed in Germany until the 1970s. On the other hand, the phenomenon of the private Dutch university is but a small piece of the mosaic known as the Netherlands that was forming during those years. For in the decades before and after the turn of the century the Netherlands evolved into a society divided into segments, each segment to a great extent autonomous and closed, and each held together by a religious and/or ideological background (also see Blom 2006; Rooy 2005). By the interbellum period, the Netherlands had become a nation of sub-societies: Protestant, liberal, Roman Catholic, socialist, and a few others. In the historiography and sociology of the past decades, this situation (which, by the way, did not occur in the Netherlands alone, but which did profoundly characterize this country for almost a century) has been frequently described and studied under the label *verzuiling* or "pillarization" (Blom and Talsma 2000; Becker 1993; Lijphart 1976; Post 1989; Velde and Verhage 1996). This term, which in itself imparts a specific interpretation and evaluation on the described phenomenon, suggests that Dutch society at that time had taken on the appearance of a classic Greek temple: just as the one roof is supported by many pillars, so the one country of the Netherlands was supported by many religious and ideological groups, each consisting of the full range of social strata. As will become clear, this is a rather euphemistic depiction of the situation at that time. In fact, numerous "complaints" about the system of pillarization were being voiced; it was said to be responsible for maintaining artificial social divisions, mutual stereotypes, and rivalries, and sometimes even conflicts between the different groups; and it was said to have given rise to the formation of in-group processes within the various pillars. Presently we will examine some of the results of the research that has been conducted on the system of pillarization (to continue to use this generally accepted term).

One striking feature of pillarization research, however, is that psychology is almost absent from the disciplines involved in the work. While sociologists, political scientists, and, at a somewhat later point, historians have produced whole cabinets full of literature related to pillarization, observations from the field of psychology are conspicuously absent. Even when considered from a general viewpoint, the dearth of psychological attention that has been paid to the subject is surprising. Regardless of whatever else may have been at work, the phenomenon known as "pillarization" was brought about by human beings and was a structure conceived and maintained by human beings, within which millions of people lived for decades.[1] Surely this is something that should have seized the attention of psychology which is, after all, one of the sciences of the human being? But within the flood of relevant literature, only one psychological title is forthcoming: "De psychologie der verzuiling" (The Psychology of Pillarization) by Verwey-Jonker (1957), a lady generally known as a sociologist. It should be pointed out, however, that she was part of a generation that had not yet drawn the dividing line between the academic disciplines, as is nowadays done with frequently dire consequences. She was trained in a period when sociology and psychology still related to each other as brothers, albeit with a sometimes fratricidal struggle (as has often been the case in the establishment of these disciplines as separate fields; just compare the highly psychological works of Weber on the one hand with the many cultural reflections of Freud and Wundt on the other). Everything that human beings do can be studied by psychology, although it is not always simple and although psychology will never be the only discipline to study it. Indeed, there are no phenomena that are accessible to psychology alone.

But apart from this somewhat epistemological consideration, pillarization itself demands a psychological approach. Confining the research to sociological and political questions alone certainly does no justice to the multi-faceted aspects of the empirical phenomenon. In an effort to avoid getting caught in the abstract – no minor consideration – let us examine the most frequently quoted description (though far from a definition!) of the phenomenon by the Roman Catholic historian Rogier. He described some facets of the pillarization for his part of the population as follows:

> a community within whose borders one not only cast one's vote in the community's political party, subscribed to a Catholic newspaper, a Catholic women's magazine, a Catholic pictorial and a Catholic youth magazine, and gave one's children the pleasure of a strictly Catholic education from kindergarten to the university, but also held fast to one's Catholic affiliation in listening to the radio, going on a trip, buying life insurance, cultivating the arts, pursuing the sciences and engaging in sports. (1956, p. 613)

This impressionistic description touchingly recalls a few of the features of pillarization that I have in mind: those who belonged to a particular pillar could live and die without having had much contact at all with members of the other pillars. Each of the pillars was self-sufficient to a very high degree, each had its own social climate, style, language, etc. A religious remark made in 1930 would have been a reasonably reliable basis for predicting the person's entire linguistic style, choice of clothing and family life. One would have known the party she voted for, the radio programs she listened to and the ones that were off-limits for her children, her ethics and her morality, etc. And the same reasoning works the other way round: if one knew that a certain person had voted for the Catholic People's Party, one would stand a fairly good chance of knowing how she prayed, how she dressed, how she spent her leisure time, what her opinion was concerning sexuality and marriage,

---

[1] Although remnants of the system are still present, the breakdown of pillarization began in the 1960s (cf. Kruijt and Goddijn 1961; Duffhues and Vugt 1980).

which trade union he belonged to, what Christian names he would never give his children, etc.[2] These are aspects, which constituted a special, separate social environment, that must be taken into account when one speaks of pillars and pillarization.[3]

Hellemans (1985) points out that two dimensions can be distinguished in the picture painted by Rogier: (1) those participating in a pillar form a community, a subculture; and (2) within that community is a network of organizations from several domains which are coordinated ideologically.[4] In taking a broad look at pillarization research we notice that most of the attention is focused on the second dimension of the phenomenon. Studies have been done to determine how the various population groups were organized, how their organizations were connected, what roles were played by certain members of the elite (networking) and to what extent the pillarization was complete: how many Calvinists actually voted for the Anti-Revolutionaire Partij or were members of the Nederlandse Christelijke Radio Vereniging (Dutch Christian Radio Association), etc. Sociologists have studied pillarization mainly as the way in which ideological groups succeeded in exercising social control over their supporters by means of organizational networks. Political scientists have often treated pillarization as a way of regulating political conflicts in a society characterized by "segmented pluralism" (Ellemers 1984). As far as the first dimension is concerned a great deal of research remains to be done on the specific characteristics of the social environments, the subculture, style, and mentality.[5]

---

[2] Irwin et al. (1987) speak of "gaps between the various population groups", and focus their attention on behavior at the polls as an example of the influence and importance of pillarization. In 1958 this was still a "virtually impeccable product of the pillarization mentality. (...) One could use this method to declare the party preference of 72% of the voting population" (Andeweg 1981, p. 86).

[3] Laarse provides us with a more detached description than Rogier, but he refers just as much to organizational dimensions as to aspects of mentality. He describes pillarization as "the phenomenon in which people increasingly carry out their social activities within complexes of organizations on the basis of religious-ideological loyalties (this as distinct from kinship, rank, or social class), which encompass several areas of community life and which mutually compete for a share of governmental power and financial resources. It therefore involves not only the emergence of organizational and political ties, but equally the formation of social-cultural ideas concerning the identity of the pillars" (1989, p. 29).

[4] In fact, everything that is featured in the often more popular literature as a pejorative description of the social environment of the pillars should be added to dimension 1: narrow-mindedness, submissiveness, aggression towards other groups, self-importance, authoritarianism, etc. – things that continue to create bitter memories of the pillarized past for many people today. Certainly these negative experiences do not apply to everyone, always and in every domain, yet the fact that they existed is undeniable. Indeed, it is thought that even the terms "pillar" and "pillarization" are palliative and legitimizing designations for what many (especially during the 1930s, cf. Ellemers 1984, p. 141) experienced as an effort to keep the people of the Netherlands divided. They often spoke disapprovingly of "parochialism."

[5] Hellemans (1985) confines "pillar" and "pillarization" to only those situations in which both dimensions are present. This reluctance to make broad use of the terms makes it possible for him to distinguish pillarization from other phenomena that are only partially related. Thus the existence of a subculture alone (such as that of the blacks in the United States) cannot be called a pillar if it lacks an integrated network of organizations. On the other hand, a neo-corporative conglomerate, a network distinct from a random network, cannot be called a pillar if it lacks the support of a distinctive social climate. Thus pillarization is indeed a way of segregating or segmenting a pluralistic society but conversely not every form of segregation or segmentation is a form of pillarization.

Introduction: "Pillarization"

When examining the recent literature concerning pillarization, we can detect a new trend: the flood of studies on the macro level has been followed by more and more studies on the meso level and various authors are urging that the agenda of future research focus on the people and the life within the pillars themselves (Bosscher 1987, pp. 91–92). Besides handling large-scale theories and concepts such as "social movements" and "networks" sociologists should be more receptive to personal motives, perceptions, and ideological contents (Bornewasser 1988, p. 206). The history of pillarization should be studied more in terms of latent functions and less in terms of manifest functions (Dierickx 1986, p. 538). This sort of research already exists to a certain extent, but it is being carried out more by historians than by sociologists (cf. Bruin 1985; Blom 1981; Koppenjan 1986, 1987; Laarse 1989; Maassen 1987; Reinalda 1992). Research that is more closely tied to the course of events on the micro level, and which pays more attention to the motives and feelings of the "ordinary people" who ultimately formed the pillar, is something to which psychologists could also contribute, were it not for the fact that they generally seem to regard history as a "forbidden garden".[6] Perhaps psychologists could also be of help in turning attention to the "religious factor" once again. Remarkable in this regard is the criticism leveled at a number of dissertations defended at the University of Amsterdam as formulated by J. de Bruijn, professor of history and director of the Historical Documentation Center for Dutch Protestantism at the Free University. Although completely in line with the desideratum by Bosscher cited above (1987) – i.e. historical research should pay attention to details and not be directed at sociological portrayals executed with a broad brush – DeBruijn is not satisfied with the work of such authors as Laarse (1989), Groot (1992), Leenders (1992), Wolffram (1993), and Miert (1994). His objection is that these authors are too preoccupied with the phenomenology and the sociology of pillarization and are just standing on the sidelines. According to DeBruijn, these historians, through their sociologically informed view, have the tendency to reduce spiritual movements to economic and social factors. And what really gets his goat – as a professor at a confessional university – is that they fail to recognize the authentic and autonomous character of religion and world view as a factor *sui generis* in the historic process (DeBruijn 1998, p. 65). Evidently, DeBruijn expects that such recognition would be forthcoming if only historians would acknowledge the motives, background, and inspiration of those participating in pillarization. But whether he is correct or not remains to be seen. There is, after all, a whole flood of literature – precisely from the sociological side – that treats the motives of pillarization organizers.

---

[6] In his introduction to historical psychology, Peeters (1994) correctly points out that within the ranks of psychology there has traditionally been much resistance to accepting the impact of "mentality" or – to use Duijker's more formal phrasing (1981) – cognitive behavioral determinants (1994, p. 30).

The Motives Behind Pillarization

In searching for the motives behind pillarization, we can take an overview of the entire body of social-scientific research (cf. Dekker and Ester 1996; Duffhues 1987; Ellemers 1996; cf. also Winkeler 1996a, b). J.P. Kruijt, one of the founding fathers of sociology in the Netherlands, regarded pillarization as a structural phenomenon. He described it as a way in which religion or denominations organized themselves, even within those institutional spheres which are not primarily connected to religion (Kruijt 1957; Kruijt et al. 1959). The most important motives mentioned in the research initiated by Kruijt are: emancipation, protection, social control, conflict regulation, and a response to modernization. Let us take a brief look at each one.[7]

According to the emancipation hypothesis, pillarization was a reaction against the social deprivation suffered by certain segments of the population (cf., e.g. Hendriks 1971). This hypothesis was first formulated by Verwey-Jonker (1962) who dealt with four movements from this perspective: Calvinists, Roman Catholics, socialists, and women. This view has been advanced mainly by denominational historians and sociologists (Ellemers 1984, p. 129). In recent years, however, the emancipation hypothesis has lost its support. Although emancipation does explain the merging of certain social groups (workers, for instance) it does not explain the division into different confessional alliances. If an ideologically defined group had wanted to attain social mobility via the school system, wouldn't it have made more sense to send the children to the (subsidized) public schools than to the denominational schools, which in the nineteenth and part of the twentieth century were much more poorly equipped? (Righart 1986, pp. 29–30) "Emancipation," in retrospect, has all the trappings of a typical reconstruction and legitimization formulated by an elite, since it is not likely that a rational concept of pillarization as an instrument of emancipation existed in the nineteenth century, nor that "ordinary" people allied themselves with pillarized organizations in order to consciously emancipate themselves (cf. also Stuurman 1983). Moreover, once the "emancipation" had succeeded and social equality had been reached, when the pillars were proportionally represented in Parliament and even *dominated* in the government, the pillarization process kept right on going.

The protection hypothesis, developed in particular by Thurlings (1971) for the Catholic segment of the population, seems more plausible. It asserts that pillarization was based on the wish of confessional minorities to protect the integrity of their faith and the autonomy of their church against surrounding threats. The churches wanted to protect their members from secularization, loss of faith, class struggles, materialism, and the whole complex of factors that threatened the influence and the power of the church (cf. for descriptions: Dierickx 1986; Duffhues 1980).

---

[7] Naturally what we are considering here is limited to the situation in the Netherlands. For hypotheses on the situation in Belgium, cf. among others Huyse (1984), Aelst and Walgrave (1998), for international-comparative studies, cf. Righart (1986), Lijphart (1992).

In this context, however, we must ask whether such "protection" was only pastorally motivated, or whether the churches may also have had a political objective: the elimination of socialism, their greatest opponent at the end of the nineteenth century (Righart 1986, p. 30). For Dierickx, this hypothesis is an excessively simple explanation: "the fact that Catholic bishops and socialist trade leaders were very sympathetic towards the fortunes of their particular subcultures does not prove that protecting those subcultures was their only objective and pillarization their only strategy" (1986, p. 538).

The motive of social control is mainly raised in objection to the emancipation hypothesis (cf. Doorn 1956). According to this line of reasoning, pillarization was principally a deliberate top-down attempt by elites to acquire and safeguard their power positions. As pillarization was rooted in an institutional exchange of social rewards and punishments, and as it was reinforced by in-group socialization, it created a basis for elites to exert social control (cf. Bax 1988). Equally adamant in emphasizing the role of elites are the hypotheses that have to do with a moral and civilizing offensive. These terms were originally used in reference to nineteenth century attempts by the bourgeois to discipline the working class (cf. Stuurman 1983; Verrips-Rouken 1987).

The politicological study by Lijphart (1975), one of the first from a foreign perspective, presents pillarization as a way in which political conflicts were regulated in a society characterized by an extraordinary degree of political cleavage or "segmented pluralism". Lijphart's monograph stimulated other political scientists to apply his model of "consociational democracy" or "Proporzdemokratie" to societies other than the Dutch (e.g. Northern Ireland, Belgium, Switzerland, Austria, Cyprus, Lebanon, Malaysia, Canada, and others, cf. Lijphart 1992).

Pillarization can also be regarded as a particular way in which a relatively small society, characterized by "segmented pluralism" and a relatively high degree of particularism, tries to cope with processes of modernization (cf. Ellemers 1984, 1996). Pillarization is then regarded as a specific process during a specific period of time in a specific kind of society.

Of course, other points of view have also been voiced. Goudsblom (1979), for instance, emphasizes aspects of national integration and state formation. But it is unnecessary to provide a full overview here of the motives and objectives that have been put forward in connection with pillarization in the Netherlands. The brief survey just presented will suffice to demonstrate the nature of the various social-scientific views and also to expand the view of the phenomenon. Valuable and necessary as these studies are (and have been), each and every one of them tends to lose sight of the first aspect of "Lebenswelt," of "mentality," mentioned by Rogier and differentiated by Hellemans. Indeed, each of these hypotheses leaves us with the problem that they fail to provide a picture of what was happening at grassroots level: there is no mention of the perspectives and motives of "ordinary" people. The postulated hypotheses (insofar as they were at all a product of motivating reasoning), originate in the minds of the elite. But why did "the ordinary people" go along with pillarization? What was it that made people associate themselves and support organizations in such a way that in the end they lived within a pillar entirely? We might put it even more critically: why did people allow themselves to be shut up within a pillar?[8] Other proposals to study pillarization under the guise of "modernization" (Ellemers 1984; Hellemans 1985) also fail to provide an answer. Pillarization was certainly a path to modernization, but the question remains: why modernization by means of a pillar? What is needed on this point is additional research, and especially research that is of a *different nature* (Bornewasser 1988, p. 206; Dierickx 1986, p. 583); such research could do more justice to the factor of (religious) identity in this process. (Questioning the conscious or at least publicly articulated inspiration and motives does not prove to be successful in this regard, despite what DeBruijn appears to believe.) Furthermore, and this is completely contrary to what DeBruijn (1998) is postulating, the background and inspiration for pillarization is by no means exclusively religious. Indeed, one of the first corrections made to Kruijt's seminal research was to recognize that pillarization was not a phenomenon evident amongst religious groups alone. The various hypotheses that have been put forward all possess a certain plausibility, but they do not hold true at all times and in all places, and certainly do not suffice to explain the entire history of pillarization in the Netherlands. Instead of struggling to find a single all-embracing hypothesis, a common denominator that would serve to "explain" all of pillarization, we should try taking a different route. We might try working with one pillar at a time, or even with a local constellation of pillars, and attempt to reach an overview of the factors that played a role in pillarization. In line with the various desiderata that historians have proposed, I would also like to argue for more detailed studies at the micro level, for a closer look at what actually took place at a pillar's base. In this way, we can grasp and try to understand what the people themselves have mentioned as their reasons for doing what they did. Mentality and other psychological factors could also then be taken into account. This may in turn throw new light on questions concerning the motives of those who participated in the pillarization.

The Beginnings of Pillarization: Case Study – Calvinist Mental Health Care

In the following section I will use a case study to attempt to understand a few aspects of the Calvinist pillarized mentality around the year 1900. We shall deal with origins of pillarization within the Calvinist community in the area of mental health care, and more specifically with the establishment of the Association of Christian Care for the Mentally Ill on November 9, 1884. This association quickly

---

[8] Because that, according to the opinion of many participants afterwards, is exactly what happened. Just compare the common terms that were used at the time and on behalf of the "doorbraak" (the breakthrough of the pillarized system) that took place after the Second World War.

expanded to become one of the most powerful organizations in the area of Dutch mental health care. It rapidly founded a series of asylums, one of them being "Veldwijk" where Doetje Reinsberg-Ypes, whom we encountered in the last chapter, had been hospitalized. The association also set up a number of related sister organizations, was later responsible for the emergence of an umbrella organization, and attempted to promote the growth of a specifically Calvinist psychiatry and psychology, etc. We shall not examine here the way in which the Calvinist pillar organized itself in this area, but the way in which it involved its grassroots supporters and induced them to support its initiatives, thus helping to get pillarization off the ground.

What we are confronted with is a phenomenon well-known in the Netherlands precisely because of pillarization but still essentially remarkable: that the Association sought a *religious* basis for its *psychiatric* work. Its goal was "the advancement of Christian care according to the Word of God for the insane and the mentally ill" based on "the Holy Scriptures according to the declaration of the Calvinist churches" (formulations in the Annual Reports of the Association). In language saturated with religious expressions, Calvinist-minded people were called on to support the Association's initiative, to admit their patients to its care, and to work as health care professionals in its institutions. To avoid burdening the reader with endless quotes, I will summarize. The Association's appeal reveals two distinct aspects: (1) this work (care of the mentally ill) must be carried out according to Jesus' will and in Jesus' name; it is a Christian duty, and (2) this work should be done in a Calvinist context.

The second point is of special significance in relation to pillarization. Working in psychiatry from a basis of Christian inspiration and motivation (aspect one) but in an existing, "neutral" (i.e. non-confessional) hospital was deemed inadequate. The work had to be carried out in Calvinist hospitals, directed by Calvinist professionals according to Calvinist principles, etc. When adapted to scores of other social sectors, it is this second point that results in the formation of a "pillar." Therefore, let us examine it more closely. When speaking of existing psychiatric institutions the Association referred to "institutions where the blood of Christ is unknown." Without denying the quality of existing institutions, the founders of the Association all agreed "that these institutions, in which the only Savior, the merciful and almighty Physician of troubled souls and bodies, is not honored and worshiped as the Lord, are insufficient; that, on the contrary, they, in many respects, are deemed to inflict harm on these sufferers" (AR*1*, p. 4).[9] In its second Annual Report, the Association reports that at the opening of its first institution, Veldwijk (1 January 1886), R. Klinkert (1857–1886), the first physician-director, gave a speech in which he demonstrated the importance of the connection between faith and science, including the practice of psychiatry (AR2, p. 15). In the speech given by D.K. Wielenga (1845–1902) at this opening, the then vice-chairman of the Association stated that he

---

[9] "AR" stands for the Annual Report of the Association of Christian Care for the Mentally Ill.

expected more from Christian[10] care for psychiatric patients than from any other: "... by the grace of God, we here can resort to the help of factors that cannot be brought to bear there"[11] (Wielenga 1885–1886, p. 48).[12] Such factors are, according to Wielenga, the power of the Lord's Word, the Christian speech, and praying in the Lord's name. At the third annual meeting of the Association, president Lindeboom (1845–1933) gave a programmed address: *De beteekenis van het Christelijk Geloof voor de Geneeskundige Wetenschap, in 't bizonder voor de Psychiatrie* (The Significance of Christian Faith for the Healing Sciences, especially Psychiatry, 1887). For the time being, this became the pattern: not only were the annual reports and lectures stamped with the sanctimonious language that characterized the Calvinists of that period,[13] but it was repeatedly declared that because of the Calvinist religion the Association would be completely different to other organizations, and that a new psychiatry – a *Calvinist* psychiatry – would be developed, or had already been developed, based on the Calvinist religion.

Thus at the sixth annual meeting, Lindeboom stated that the basis for both psychiatric theory and practice within the Association should be the Bible (AR*6*, p. 53). Again and again, the Association pointed out its objections to neutral institutions: "The greatest drawback (...) is that Christ, the almighty Physician, the merciful High Priest, is banned from those places. The Bible is suppressed, and it is contended that reading this book promotes insanity rather than healing it" (AR*12*, p. 12). Thus the thinking in neutral institutions is completely incorrect, for "true religion, revealed in the Holy Scriptures, is medicinal. (...) Health care provided according to God's Word has a salutary influence on the mentally ill." In his opening speech at the thirteenth general annual meeting, Lindeboom stated, "Our goal is to convert the medical sciences, to capture the lectern of physicians and psychiatrists and to proclaim to all the world: Christ the Consoler!" (AR*14*, p. 15). And in 1899 he declares that the Christian attendant is better and can do more than his "humanist" counterpart, for "he has the fullness of Christ, in Whom all treasures and gifts are hidden" (AR*17*, p. 18).

Nevertheless, as I demonstrated in an earlier study (Belzen 1989a), the Association never succeeded in developing its own Calvinist psychiatry. What it did was to take on and adopt existing psychiatry and to express it in Calvinist language.

---

[10] Read: Calvinist. During this period, the Calvinists were strongly inclined to claim the designation "Christian" exclusively for themselves. Although the Christian identity was not explicitly denied to others, the conviction was repeatedly expressed that the Calvinist religion was the most pure, the most in conformity with the Holy Scriptures, and that Calvinism was "Christianity par excellence." So Calvinists did not hesitate to call their activities and organizations "Christian" (instead of, and more correctly, "Calvinist"). Roman Catholics, by the way, often participated in this usage and generally referred to Calvinists as the "Christians."

[11] That is, in non-Calvinist, especially "neutral" (i.e. non-confessional), institutions.

[12] The text was issued once again during the high point of pillarization in the *Gedenkboek uitgegeven bij het vijftig jarig bestaan der Vereeniging* (Commemorative Book Issued on the Occasion of the Association's Fiftieth Anniversary) (pp. 9–26), privately published in 1935.

[13] Mainly a linguistic style borrowed from the Authorized Dutch translation of the Bible and from eighteenth century spiritual authors.

Its hospitals were organized just like all the others in the Netherlands and functioned in the same way, except that everything was done in Calvinist style and involved the use of the practices and customs then current in the Calvinist world. Despite the high aspirations and the attempts that were made – a professorial chair was even established at the Free University, and various specific organizations were formed in order to implement the program of Calvinist psychiatry (Belzen 1989c, 1998b) – ordinary psychiatric practice in Calvinist, Catholic, and neutral hospitals in the Netherlands was identical. It must be pointed out, however, that psychiatry does not just consist of professional activities, principles and theory, and corresponding (or non-corresponding), treatment and care. At least up until the Second World War, all this took place in an asylum which in many respects resembled a "total institution" (Goffman 1961) in which the patient and the personnel were entirely absorbed in a clearly recognizable organizational relationship cut off from the outside world, with a specific way of life and an atmosphere all its own. And in this respect there were indeed significant differences between the psychiatry of the Association and other forms of psychiatry. The Association's psychiatry was different because its people – the patients but especially the personnel – were different: they were Calvinists. The people working in these institutions had been socialized in a Calvinist climate and performed religious practices and ceremonies in a Calvinist way; they lived, thought, and spoke in a Calvinist manner; thus they were the ones who gave the entire setting its "Calvinist" atmosphere.

The Association was an integral part of the Calvinist community. Its leaders came from that part of the population, as did its health care workers and other personnel. It preferred to admit Calvinist patients to its institutions. There, the language was Calvinist, the songs and prayers were Calvinist, Calvinist religious services were held, job applicants were all tested on their Calvinist identity, and employees were monitored during their entire period of service to make sure they preserved the Calvinist heritage. These people were Calvinists, and their Calvinist customs permeated every aspect of their lives. If you were to meet someone who had been raised in a good Calvinist home, you would know (at least in principle), his thoughts on family life and sexuality, the place of women, games and leisure, reading material and radio, State and society, and many other things. All of this meant that Calvinists differed from other population groups in a number of ways. And since the increasing pillarization was keeping people from having almost any contact with other population groups and was allowing them to glory in the sun of their own identity, each pillarized part of the nation (with perhaps the Calvinists and the Catholics at the top) firmly believed that it was fundamentally different from the others. In this case, the notion even extended to the theory and practice of psychiatry. The pillars still had so little knowledge of each other that even incorrect preconceptions of other people were maintained and even reinforced.

These differences in atmosphere and mentality should not be underestimated (cf., e.g., Kruijt 1943). Before the Second World War, the division between the pillars, especially between the various religious groups of Calvinists and Catholics, was very deep, and the number of related differences is almost endless to today's observer. However, there are hardly any lists containing such differences, and those who do dare to take on such a task realize that their enumerations are only a beginning. The psychologist A. Chorus (1909–1998), in an article of 1943, mentions just a few examples in a series of variables. These include differences in names given to children, clothing, hair style, language, facial expressions, body language, manners, habits, character traits. Here are a few examples. Christian names such as Aard, Barend, Dievertje, Bram, and Menno were particularly popular amongst Protestants. Latin names, or names with some Latinate connection, were rare with Protestants but common amongst Catholics: Clemens, Aloysius, Clara, Odilia, Constant, Monica. According to Chorus, Protestants were "generally simpler in their style of clothing, more sober. They avoid decoration, dress as unostentatiously as possible, choose more subdued and sober colors. The Catholic has more of a preference for decoration, embellishments and ornaments" (Chorus 1943, p. 39). So the Catholic is more fashion-conscious than the dyed-in-the-wool Protestant. There were also countless linguistic differences in the Dutch spoken by the various groups that could be traced back to different formulations and phrases in their own particular religious literature. These were noticeable even in the smallest details: "from his first uttered words, the Catholic says "*op de eerste plaats*" ["first of all"], influenced by the Mechel Catechism; the Protestant says "*in de eerste plaats, tweede plaats*" because it is the preferred phrase used in the Authorized Version of the Bible" (Chorus 1964, p. 122). The way Catholics furnished their homes was influenced by a church full of images and a liturgy full of symbols. Catholic houses could be recognized by the saints that were displayed in the form of statues or prints, with everything preferably as colorful as possible. "Protestantism renounced images and held fast to the invisible God and the Word of the Bible. In place of statues, the Protestant has texts and proverbs in the living room and bedroom: sober, abstract, and somewhat cold, with a tendency towards moralization" (p. 122). Whether the differences were always as pronounced as was supposed by Chorus (who was himself a Catholic) and those from whom he derived his examples can no longer be easily determined. For instance, Chorus writes about things like facial expressions: "Among Protestants these are generally more severe, somber, more closed, and sometimes more dour. Their glance in particular seems more confident, sometimes haughty, and often aggressive (the typical "*geuzenkop*"!).[14] Take a look at people as they leave church: the Catholics are lighthearted and go (or went) to the village for a nip or a glass of beer. The Protestants seem much stiffer when they leave church, as though stooped under a curse" (Chorus 1943, p. 41).

But these differences still do not explain the one feature which later so often gave rise to critical questions (ideological) discussions, and surprised incomprehension: the solid conviction that the organizations within the pillars differed fundamentally from each other, not only in atmosphere and mentality, but in virtually every aspect, even

---

[14] In translation something like: *geuzen*-head. *Geuzen*: reference to a kind of guerrilla fighter from the period 1568–1648, when the former Netherlands was wresting itself from Spanish (Roman Catholic) domination.

including their psychiatric theory and practice. They do not explain the repeated insistent claim that a unique, Calvinist psychiatry had been developed which differed fundamentally in principle and practice from the psychiatry being practiced elsewhere. Our case study is limited to psychiatry, but it would be very easy to expand it to include numerous other domains such as some – in fact all! – scientific disciplines (the reason for founding and maintaining the Free University as a Christian institution), upbringing and education, press and media, etc.[15] Various studies have now given us adequate evidence that the nature of the activities that developed in this pillarized context did not usually differ from what was going on in other pillars (cf., e.g., Sturm 1988; Os and Wieringa 1980). In addition (and especially relevant for our case study), assertions such as those made when the Association was founded, claiming that existing psychiatry was anti-religious, proved to be simply not true. The other, non-Calvinist hospitals also provided church services, allowed patients to receive visits from clergymen, and respected religious feelings and customs (cf. Belzen 1989a). The State Inspectors who monitored conditions and institutions for the mentally ill always argued in favor of an adequate religious treatment of patients (cf., e.g., the *Verslagen van (de Inspectie van) het Staatstoezicht op Krankzinnigen en Krankzinnigengestichten* (Reports of State Supervision (and Inspectors) for the Mentally Ill and for Institutions for Mental Illness)).

This is an important point, providing us with a paradox and a further perspective for analysis. For if it is true that the existing psychiatry was not anti-religious, then the argument behind the previously mentioned second aspect of the Association's appeal is seriously impaired – the very argument that served to legitimize the pillarization of psychiatry. Had it not been stated that psychiatric work based on Christian motives should be segregated in Calvinist hospitals (and later, hospitals belonging to the Calvinist pillar), because everywhere else "the Bible was being suppressed" etc.? And now it turns out that the Bible and religion were not being suppressed. How is this to be understood? Did the Calvinist spokesmen mislead their followers? And were the followers so naive as to believe something that obviously was not true? It probably had nothing to do with either being misled or being naive, and we will have to search for a more fundamental explanation.

Brief History of the Calvinist Mind

First of all, however, it should be remembered that what we are dealing with here is a variation of the phenomenon of the *struggle of establishment* (cf. Elias and Scotson 1965). There are a variety of familiar mechanisms involved in legitimizing the existence of particular organizations: presenting them as exclusive, pretending to own something that is a necessary supplement or corrective to what already

---

[15] In a later period, critics of pillarization would often poke fun at something that does seem to sum up the passion of pillarized existence: a Roman Catholic Goat Breeders' Association.

exists, denying that such a supplement or corrective exists elsewhere, polarization, portraying others as opponents, etc. As Bruin (1985) demonstrated in a related field (the denominational school struggle in the Netherlands), and Ellenberger described for psychoanalysis, these mechanisms form legends and myths that take on a life of their own (Ellenberger 1970, p. 547).[16]

Second, and even more important for us as a point of psycho-historic interest: when the Calvinists described the outside world, including existing psychiatric hospitals, as nonreligious, this was not an intentional distortion of the outside world, but their perception of it. As is known from psychology, a perception is not a (photographic), registration of the outside world, but an interpretation of sensory impressions, an interpretive process whereby cognitive processes, frames of reference and patterns of expectation interact with invariable data. To understand a perception, it is therefore necessary to study both that which is being perceived and the person who is doing the perceiving. In applying this simple principle to our paradox (i.e. that existing psychiatry was not anti-religious, but that the Calvinists experienced it as such), we should study the Calvinists themselves, the Calvinist mind, if we want to gain any understanding at all of the Calvinist perception of the outside world as being non-religious and even anti-religious. A brief look at their history can be helpful in understanding the Calvinist mentality.

The Dutch Calvinists who founded the Association and organized their lives in pillarized form belonged to groups that emerged as ecclesiastical bodies after breaking away from the Netherlands Reformed Church. The largest group, numerically speaking – the A-Calvinists[17] – is particularly important in the history of the

---

[16] Also see Sulloway (1979) and Brinkgreve (1984). The main point of focus here is the "myth of the great resistance" (Brinkgreve 1984, p. 71): portraying the outside world as hostile. Yet we also encounter another great myth: that of the "lonely and original hero." The Association very much prided itself in "its" family health care program (placing patients within guest families instead of in an institution) and "its" pavilion system (housing patients in units of a limited size that were initially under the direction of a married couple). It gladly presented these initiatives as their own and particular practice, and some even went so far as to claim that they were based on the Bible and theology. The fact was, however, that such "treatment" existed before the establishment of the Association and had even been suggested to the Association by others. But indeed, once they had taken over these methods and furnished them with a Calvinist religious setting and legitimation, the Association, with its great energy, generally did work harder on them than others had done before.

[17] A-Calvinists are the ecclesiastical communities that trace their origins back to the so-called "Afscheiding" (Separation) of 1834 (and shortly thereafter). The genealogy of the B-Calvinists goes back to 1886 (the Doleantie (Secession), under the leadership of A. Kuyper). Most of the A-Calvinists joined forces in 1869 to become the *Christelijk Gereformeerde kerk* (the Christian Reformed Church). The communities descending from the Doleantie formed the *Nederduitsch Gereformeerde kerken* (the Lower German Reformed churches). Both of these merged in 1892, not without difficulty, to form what is today known as the *Gereformeerde* (strict Reformed, or Calvinist) churches in the Netherlands. Not without difficulty, because the groups were quite divided in their experience of faith and in their relation to the "outside world." The differences in mentality still exist to a certain extent. In many places today, people are able to say whether the local Calvinist church was originally an A or a B congregation.

Association: most of its founders and leaders were among this group. An important factor behind the schism of 1834 was dissatisfaction with the course being followed by the then Netherlands Reformed Church, having to do with the spread of liberalism and with theology that had disintegrated into "rationalistic supra-naturalism." This church was orienting itself more towards human reason than towards revelation. The influence of the Enlightenment was dominant, the old Calvinist confession, as laid down at the famous Synod of Dordt (1618–1619), no longer functioned. This, at any rate, was the opinion of a rather large group of orthodox believers. Quite a number of them felt that the church should return to its roots and to the true doctrine, and if the national church passed up this opportunity, then believers at the local level should take matters into their own hands. In 1834, the congregation in Ulrum was the first to separate, with the firm intention to return to the earlier ecclesiastical confession and to a religious life.[18] This step had serious consequences. The government of the Netherlands was closely tied to the Netherlands Reformed Church[19] and did not want trouble within the ranks. The separated congregations "were unlawful and would not be tolerated" (compare Holtrop 1984, p. 95). The reprisals were severe, as reported by even non-Calvinist historians: "There was much suffering among the Separatists, mostly by civil prosecution, which came very hard because in general it affected and humiliated the weakest members of society; it also involved the quartering of soldiers in the houses of the Separatists" (Mönnich 1962, p. 225), the imprisonment of their leaders, and the confiscation of church goods from the separated congregations. After agreeing to apply for official recognition (as a new church, and therefore not as the rightful continuation of the "older" Dutch church, as they had originally declared), most of them withdrew in social isolation.

From the writings of the Separatists we now know that they regarded themselves (and this is of psychological significance), and *continued* to regard themselves as an aggrieved group, unjustly treated, humiliated, debased, and mocked. The insults that were applied to them were words that they themselves continued to repeat into the next century to illustrate their debased position, as it were: they were obscurantists (Bilderdijk's *"dompers"*), holier-than-thous (Da Costa's *"fijnen"*), the missing army of Groen (*"den veldheer-zonder-leger"* general without an army), and Kuyper's night school (*"nachtschool"*) (Rullman, quoted in Hendriks 1971, p. 97). They were evidently a group with an extremely wounded self-image. According to Hendriks, this self-image reflected the opinion of them held by the outside world and was proof of their social inferiority. They saw and described themselves as an unimportant folk, as "simple little people, caps on their heads, greasy jackets – a very common folk indeed" (quoted in Hendriks 1971, p. 206). It is this feeling of

---

[18] Its minister, H. de Cock, formulated a manifesto for the occasion bearing the title *Akte van Afscheiding of Wederkeering* (Act of Separation, or a Return to our Roots).

[19] Consider, for example, the fact that the "General Regulations for the Board of the Reformed Church" was drawn up by a Royal Decree dated 7 January 1816, and that members of the various executive organs were appointed by the King himself (Vree 1984, p. 38).

having been unfairly treated, discriminated against, despised, that we also find in their depictions of how non-religious psychiatry regarded them, their faith, and their initiative to establish Calvinist care for the mentally ill.

Injured and misunderstood, they retreated not only from the Netherlands Reformed Church but also from many areas of life that they regarded as dangerous. They went on to form a religious minority with its own largely autarkic subculture. Since the 1850s a series of new developments began to take place in Dutch society, and there was evidence of increasing cultural and social differentiation in many sectors (cf. Hendriks 1971) from which the Separatists were not able to completely distance themselves. Neither were people like Lindeboom, the founder of the Association, interested in doing so. But he did not want to "hand himself over" to an outside world that had shown such hostility to the Calvinists. His solution was this: let us embark on these various new and necessary activities taking place in so many sectors of life, but on our own terms. He firmly believed that, armed with a Calvinist exegesis of the Bible, one could engage in these activities as capably, and even more capably, than anyone else. Given this mentality, it is also understandable that Calvinists were no longer willing to entrust their psychiatric patients to the existing institutions. Religion was not suppressed in these institutions, to be sure – but for separated Calvinists that was not enough. Even in the area of mental health, they insisted on maintaining their own religiously colored culture. If in such institutions meals did not begin and end with prayer and Bible reading, if the Psalms were not sung there, if church attendance was left to everyone's own initiative, if services might even be led by Roman Catholic and free-thinking Protestant clergy – then such institutions were places "where Christ did not reside." It is in this light that we must understand the Calvinists' conviction that "institutions, in which the only Savior, the merciful and almighty Physician of troubled souls and bodies, is not honored and worshiped as the Lord, are insufficient; that, on the contrary, they, in many respect, are deemed to inflict harm on these sufferers." Given this Separatist mentality, together with the holy conviction that their own theologically legitimized subculture contained the only truth, one can understand why Calvinists distrusted any institution whose annual report did not begin with thanks to God for the blessings received in the last year, and why they insisted that such places "had broken with Christ." Examples like these abound. Dutch psychiatry was not anti-religious; it was, however, usually a-religious, without religious obligations and/or identity, and therefore non-Calvinist in any case (Belzen 1989a). The Calvinist could not recognize himself in this kind of psychiatric practice, nor could he feel at home there.

The solution, they thought, could only be found in the establishment of a distinctive psychiatry under a Calvinist "canopy" (cf. Berger 1967). This process of establishment and then of expansion went hand in hand with passionate speeches and bold claims: "We want to convert the sciences; in our psychiatry, theory and practice are grounded in Scripture; Calvinist religion is a medicine." These notions, however, should be regarded as expressions of enthusiasm with the rapid establishment and growth of the Association. They serve to legitimize the initiative and to inspire the grassroots. The same is true for the claim that existing psychiatry was hostile to religion. Most of these aspects, these rallying-cries, did not surface until the establishment of the Association and the opening of a separate hospital had in fact taken place; they cannot in themselves have been motivating factors.

Far more than the anti-Calvinist character of medical science, the motivating factor behind the founding of the Association may have been the desire to maintain a separate identity and culture, even in a psychiatric hospital. Once the hospital was established, the Calvinists in fact seemed satisfied: Calvinist psychiatry had been realized. In this way they did not abandon their isolation, but, indeed, continued it even within the realm of psychiatry. Many other sectors would follow, until "the modern world had been carefully copied within a separate culture, in which religious ideology was linked with rational and differentiated organizational forms" (Righart 1986, p. 35) – in other words, until the Calvinist pillar had become a reality. The fact that, e.g., the treatment offered in their own institution in no way differed from that being offered in any other, and that the content of a textbook written by a Calvinist neurologist was barely distinguishable from any other Dutch textbook in that field,[20] was not very problematic. It was a Calvinist climate that prevailed in the institution, a Calvinist spirit that filled the pages of the book, written from a Calvinist position and with a Calvinist interpretation. The Calvinist could recognize himself there; he could feel at home and be himself.

At annual meetings, in memorial speeches and in the classroom, the Calvinists continued to emphasize that this psychiatry was based on Calvinist principles and was therefore different. In doing so they overestimated the "being different" and extended it to areas where there were actually no differences at all: in psychiatric theory and treatment.[21] But the very fact of being separate, the absence of contacts with the other pillars, made it impossible to introduce a corrective to this assumption. It is true that those at the top of the organization were concerned. Should not the Calvinist identity affect more than climate alone? Should we not develop and practice a psychiatry that is also Calvinist in content? But for an "ordinary" Calvinist, born in a Calvinist family, raised in a Calvinist environment, trained and employed in a Calvinist institution and married to a Calvinist partner, these questions would rarely arise.[22]

---

[20] For an elaboration of these and other examples, see Belzen 1989a.

[21] In my *Psychopathologie en religie* (1989a), I draw a comparison with the York Retreat, a home for psychiatric patients founded by English Quakers in 1796. Amidst all the similarities between the York Retreat and the asylums of the Association, one of the most important differences was that the Quakers did not pretend to be practicing (or want to practice) a fundamentally new psychiatry based on religion. The result of both initiatives was approximately the same, however: a psychiatry that followed the general trends, but within the confines of a specific religious subculture. For the York Retreat see, among others: Scull (1982) and Digby (1985).

[22] Compare Hendriks (1971), who responded to the fact that at that time there was mention of "specific Christian constitutional laws, science, art, marriage, family, and much more" by wondering what this meant in concrete terms. He concluded that "the term 'Christian culture' does not imply a cultural pattern that is radically different from the Western cultural pattern as such, but is a specific variant of that Western cultural pattern in which certain norms and values are rejected and replaced by others" (p. 179). I am inclined to alter this conclusion somewhat and to regard Calvinist language, customs, and climate, even more than other norms and values, as the attributes of the "specific Christian" (Calvinist) culture.

Religion and Identity

We need to look at some aspects of the history of the mentality of the Dutch Calvinists described above with a somewhat finer lens. The advantage of opting for a psychological perspective (rather than additional arguments concerning the motives, conscious or otherwise, behind pillarization, as DeBruijn (1998) proposed), is that it provides a better insight into the role of religion in general. Indeed, what the above retrospective fails to explain is the rigid character of the pillarization mentality. In connection with pillarization, we are often told (naturally by critics), how those living within the pillars ended up slowly but surely cutting themselves off completely from fellow citizens belonging to different pillars, how mutual stereotypes and prejudices settled in, and even how people began fostering animosity towards each other.[23] The cultural differences briefly described above – linguistic habits, Christian names, clothing styles, decoration, etc. – were manifold, and they functioned as distinguishing characteristics, but from a factual point of view they are no more than shibboleths. In fact, the Dutch people we are discussing here still shared far more similarities than they did differences. After all, the difference between "in *de eerste plaats*" and "op *de eerste plaats*", for example, is a minor linguistic variation. Like so many others, Sigmund Freud insisted that it is precisely the minor differences between people who are otherwise alike that form the basis of feelings of strangeness and hostility between them. He suggested "to derive from this 'narcissism of minor differences' the hostility which in every human relation we see fighting successfully against feelings of fellowship and overpowering the commandment that all men should love one another" (Freud 1918/1963, p. 199). He admitted that the formula "narcissism of minor differences" did not explain very much, and in later years he tried, although not explicitly, to create a link with his concept of the death instinct,[24] an attempt whose success we may very well question. Perhaps we had better take the formula as an indication of the direction in which we must turn for a deeper understanding of the phenomenon itself. Even so, first let us try thematizing a few aspects of the more or less unconscious "driving force" behind pillarization suggested above: striving to preserve one's identity as a group.

---

[23] In his well-known monograph *Das unbekannte Holland* (1984), Zahn contradicts the very widespread image (and self-image) of the Dutch and states that tolerance is not a national virtue, but a behavioral norm born of practical realism and necessity. In his opinion, pillarization was not the result of forbearance. Rather, in the segregation of the various population groups, pillarization embodied just the opposite: merely putting up with outsiders. The sociologist Van Doorn also wrote that people within the pillars were free "to denounce everyone else to their hearts' content – and no one need concern himself with anyone on the outside" (Doorn 1985, p. 31).

[24] "I gave this phenomenon the name of 'narcissism of minor differences,' a name which does not do much to explain it. We can now see that it is a convenient and relatively harmless satisfaction of the inclination to aggression, by means of which cohesion between the members of the community is made easier" (Freud 1930/1961, p. 114).

In this last context, "narcissism of minor differences" can indeed be very functional. It may prove more useful to draw clear lines between oneself and quite similar individuals or groups than between oneself and very different ones, such as foreigners (Elms 1994, p. 168).

The notion of "identity" is a term familiar to both sociology and psychology, yet with two different meanings. For sociologists and social-psychologists, "identity" refers to membership in a social group and to the integration of the individual in that group (cf. Lewin 1948). When the psychoanalyst Erikson (1956) uses the term "ego-identity" he means the integration and stability of the individual personality. On the empirical level, however, the contents of these two concepts may be related to a greater or lesser degree. In order to conceptualize this relationship and the extent to which it occurs, Sherif and Cantril's concept of "ego-involvement" may be used: "the ego is a genetic formation made up of a host as a frame of reference by means of which he makes those judgments that affect *him*; that define for *him* success and failure; that determine *his* loyalties and allegiances; that spell out what he conceives to be *his* role, *his* status, *his* class. Judgments and behavior resulting from this identification of oneself with a certain constellation of values we can properly term "ego-involved'" (1947, pp. 152–153). So a high level of ego-involvement means that the social identity of the individual in question is also part of his ego-identity and his self-definition. Examples of the way that this functions are legion. We may think, for example, of someone who cannot bear to hear his family criticized. Being a member of the "xyz" family in this case means more than bearing a social label so one's name can be found in the telephone book, it is also a matter of self-definition. Or, regarding religious convictions, they are adhered to in the case of high "ego-involvement" not only because of their intrinsic plausibility but also because they are a part of "me" (Beit-Hallahmi 1989, p. 100). As has been satisfactorily shown in psychological and social-scientific literature, religion can fulfill numerous psychic and social functions, both beneficial and harmful. It can fulfill a function by raising one's self-esteem, for instance, because it offers a social identity. In this way, religion can compensate for objective suffering or a feeling of inferiority by creating a group identity of the "elect" people who really are superior despite their worldly misery (because these particular believers are presumed – or better still, presume themselves – to possess the truth and the promise about future salvation).

Might this not have been the case with the Calvinists – an "ego-identity" in line with the social identity, in which the following sorts of components played a role: "we may be a small group, socially despised and restricted, but we possess the true exegesis of the Holy Scriptures. We have to watch out for the outside world, because their attitude towards us is hostile. That's why we can't work together with them, for if we do, it would eventually lead to the loss or debasement of our most precious possession: our faith." (This is apart from whether that "outside world" was really as hostile as the Calvinists perceived it to be. A psychological reality is different from any other kind of reality, historical, social, or otherwise.) In any case, these are the aspects (and sensitivities) that were alluded to when the Association was founded, even in the context of the establishment of something that did not belong to the essence of religion and to which the outside world had not demonstrated any hostility: Calvinist psychiatry.

But let's go a step further and introduce a psychodynamic point of view in the interpretation of the psychological factors that may have played a role among the Calvinists during the period of pillarization. Freud's formula "narcissism of minor differences" makes one think of the work of a later psychoanalyst, Heinz Kohut (1971, 1977, 1985), some of whose ideas we encounter in the last chapter and who did indeed provide an important stimulus to psychohistorical research by postulating a "group self" analogous to the individual self, in order to define the underlying psychological basis of group cohesion and fragmentation (cf. Strozier and Offer 1985). Like that of the individual, the "group self" consists of three constituents, each of which can manifest itself as a self-object transference. (Kohut discovered and postulated three such transferences – mirror, idealizing, and alter ego transference – to exist next to the drive transference already known within classical psychoanalysis. Each of these self-object transferences is a reactivation of a frustrated developmental need.) Groups not only share an ego ideal (Freud 1921/1955), but also a kind of "subject-bound grandiosity" or a grandiose self, providing cohesive glue. Groups also share ideals – be they religious, cultural, or political – as bases for the cohesion of the "group self". Kohut used these ideas to illuminate some characteristics of the psychoanalytic community and, more important, of Nazi Germany. He believed that the assumption of power and the resulting terror by the Nazis in Germany could not be explained by "events" only, but that they showed something of a chronic weakness in Germany's group self-structures in the pre-Hitler period. Because of its importance, I will quote a somewhat longer passage:

> It does not seem to me that the blow of having lost World War I and of having to pay reparations should be considered as the psychological basis for Germany's readiness to espouse the Hitlerian remedy for its self-pathology. The Nazis clearly exploited German sensibilities in order to harness the ensuing narcissistic rage in the service of their vengeful atrocities and of a vengeful war. Nevertheless, we are not dealing here with the primary manifestations of a diseased group self but with the secondary symptoms of an underlying self disorder. The disease itself, as would be the case with an individual patient, was silent. What the skilled psychohistorian must look for now, in retrospect, is evidence for a sense of group depression, a lack of vitality, and a sense of discontinuity in time and of fragmentation in space. Behind the noisy rage was a despair that the demands for respect and the legitimate needs for a merger with powerful ego ideals were not only responded to in action but before Hitler received no effectively communicative recognition through words or by other symbolic means. Basing myself openly and unashamedly on the profound insights about man's self and its experiences and reactions that are obtained in individual psychoanalytic treatment of patients with self pathology, I suggest that the psychological illness of pre-Hitler Germany was not caused by the external adversities to which Germany was exposed at that time. Of course they mattered, especially since these adversities occurred not only in the realm of power and greatness via defeat and poverty but also in the realm of ideals. But the real issue was the absence of an empathic matrix that would have recognized and acknowledged the emotional needs of the German group self exposed to such external adversities. (Kohut 1985, pp. 85–86)

Kohut's hypothesis concerning pre-Hitler Germany might also be of use in trying to understand something of the mentality of the Calvinists during the pillarization period.[25] If we follow the Kohut hypothesis (which can only be done briefly and tentatively here), and depict the Calvinists at the beginning of pillarization as having a deficient "group self", we then obtain insight into several other aspects of their behavior. The triumphalism and the self-satisfaction that would, at a later stage, radiate from the group during the process of pillarization would then indicate arrested narcissistic needs (not necessarily to be identified with pathological aberrations).[26] The changes that took place in the Calvinists' overt self-image (i.e. from a marginal and inferior group before pillarization to the one group that called itself "the root of the national character" and in the 1930s regarded itself as the "true church"), then represent a revival of that normal phase in the grandiose self in which the gleam in the mother's eye that mirrors the child's exhibitionistic displays, and other forms of maternal participation made in response to the child's narcissistic-exhibitionistic enjoyment, confirm the child's self-esteem and, by gradually increasing selectivity of those responses, begin to channel it into realistic directions (cf. Lee and Martin 1991, p. 129). For the Calvinists of the nineteenth century, the absence of an empathic matrix may have led to disturbances in the process of transformation towards a stable self, towards mature forms of narcissism, resulting in the continued existence of a primitive, unrealistic grandiosity that manifested itself once again during pillarization. Likewise, the idealization that Calvinists exhibited towards their own leaders, particularly towards Abraham Kuyper (1837–1920), may be understood from this perspective. Kuyper, who has been called "the bell-ringer of the common people" was a driving force behind the Calvinist mobilization. He founded a separate political party, published a separate newspaper and weekly magazine, established a separate university (the Free University in Amsterdam), and became the Prime Minister with the first (1901–1905) of a series of "confessional" cabinets. Although he had his share of criticism, his photograph hung in people's living rooms, his theology directed their spirituality, and his newspapers provided their political orientation. In a word (the Calvinists own!) he was the "God-given leader." Kohut's perspective allows us to understand such an excessive idealization as a narcissistic transference that was needed to overcome arrested,

---

[25] Please note: I have intentionally said "*something* of the mentality" because (of course) this hypothesis only provides us with partial insight. In this essay we have formed a picture of some aspects of the history and mentality of the Calvinists. These background facts and psychological hypotheses presented are by no means expected to simply hold true for other pillarized population groups in the Netherlands who were nevertheless characterized to the same degree by animosity and "narcissism of minor differences." And conversely, if the reasoning presented here could not be applied to the non-Calvinist population groups who exhibited the same kind of characteristics, this does not constitute an argument against the validity of the reasoning in the case of the Calvinists. Indeed, the same behavior can have a very different psychological structure with different persons (or groups).

[26] Thurlings (1971) described an analogous development within the "dominant upper current" of Dutch Catholics: defensiveness (1860–1900), regained self-confidence (1900–1925), extroverted triumphalism (1925–1940), and reserved confidence (1945–1960). For a biographical overview of Catholic life in the Netherlands in the 19th and 20th centuries, see also Winkeler (1996a, b).

unmet developmental needs. Just as an individual self cannot exist without self-objects, so a "group self" requires a self-object to maintain a sense of well-being. Through a nation's or institution's idealizing self-object relationship to, e.g., a leader, the group's self well-being is restored. Indeed, religion itself may function as such a (healthy) self-object, for both a person or a group.[27]

These reflections cannot be elaborated on here; they are presented only by way of hypotheses which may, however, result in the posing of new and additional questions. For example, new research could be done on the person and position of Kuyper from the point of view of his function as a self-object. The greater the need to idealize, the greater the risk that the "group self" will choose someone needing to be idealized, and the greater the risk that the group and the leader will collude to fulfill one another's needs (Schlauch 1993, p. 38). To what extent was this the case in the relationship between Kuyper and the Calvinists? Speaking more generally, further research is needed to demonstrate whether this "understandable connection" (in the sense of Weber, Simmel and Jaspers), concerning identity, formulated with reference to the development of Calvinist mental health care, can help us understand the aspects of pillarization discussed here when applied to other areas. Literature that presents life within the pillar in a descriptive way, or even that criticizes it (often from the inside) seems to confirm the hypothesis in any case.[28] At least the motive of "preserving our identity" in connection with the Calvinist mentality and expressed in theological-ideological language,[29] helps us to understand why the elite (who may have been similarly inspired themselves), were able to win over the grassroots, why "ordinary" people thought that the only way to give shape to their (modern) Christian lives was within the seclusion of what would later become a pillar. It was to this (deficient), sense of self and identity, with the related notions concerning "others" (the outside world), that the organizers of the Calvinist pillar appealed. And it was this appeal, thus formulated, that stirred people. In future research on pillarization, de-pillarization, and re-pillarization, it might prove useful

---

[27] Among other things, in order to do justice to this observation, Grotstein introduced a further differentiation in the conceptualizing of prenarcissistic self-objects: "There is a considerable difference phenomenologically between background objects and interpersonal objects which are impressed into service as self-objects. The concept of self-object, I strongly maintain, transcends far more than just simply the mother or father. It includes tradition, heredity, the mother country, the neighborhood, etc." (Grotstein 1983, p. 85). Evidently, religion and the church can also be added here.

[28] Cf. for instance the description of "Calvinist life when we were young" by Booy (1956); cf. also Gooyer (1964), Kaam (1964).

[29] Many years later, Calvinist authors would start to point out that faith and theology had been too closely identified with certain lifestyles, and that failing to comply with certain practices (e.g., not sending children to Calvinist schools or not voting for the Calvinist ARP party) had been too readily connected with "abandoning the faith." In the period we are discussing here, the emergence and peaking of pillarization, this differentiation was not the general pattern, however. Seen from another angle, it cannot be expected that present-day churchgoers would respond to the sort of appeal that was made in those days by constructing a pillar, since religion for them is more differentiated from other areas of life. On the other hand, it is striking that the very groups that reject any division between religion and state/education/etc., have today become receptive to re-pillarization tendencies.

to attempt to gain more insight into what these aspects had to do with people's actual experience. Analyses could be made of the exact contents of the orations made by leaders in support of pillarized organizations: What did they appeal to? What were their arguments? From what source did their arguments derive their strength? Why did "ordinary" people join in, and what was done with those who refused to comply? (Since we cannot assume that the relationship described here worked automatically, or that all had a high ego involvement with regard to the Calvinist identity.) Was there pressure involved, and if so, how? And how was it made legitimate? Those who prefer working from a non-psychoanalytical framework may find potentially fruitful schemata for description and classification in social-psychological theories on group observation and prejudice, for instance.

In short, there still seem to be quite a number of possibilities for further interdisciplinary study involving history, sociology and psychology. In any case, a psychological approach, or a partial approach that is influenced by psychology, could contribute to a somewhat clearer picture of the "ordinary people", the majority of those who participated in the historical-sociological process known as pillarization. When we want to understand the role of religion, in whatever respect and in whatever context, we need psychology. In particular, we shall need the various forms of cultural psychology, as the multitude of ways in which human psychic functioning and cultural structures are inter-weaved and mutually constitutive are the challenging, interesting and pressing theme of any cultural psychology.

Bibliography

Aalders, C. (1980). *Spiritualiteit: Over geestelijk leven vroeger en nu.* [Spirituality: Yesterday and today] 's Gravenhage: Boekencentrum.
Abma, R. (1983). *"Methodisch zonder confessie." Uit de geschiedenis van de Nijmeegse psychologie.* [Methodical without confession: From the history of the Nijmegen psychology] Nijmegen: Katholieke Universiteit Nijmegen, Psychologisch Laboratorium (internal report).
Aelst, P. van & Walgrave, S. (1998). Voorbij de verzuiling? [Beyond pillarization?] *Tijdschrift voor Sociologie, 19*, 55–87.
Agger, E.M. (1988). Psychoanalytic perspectives on sibling relationships. *Psychoanalytic Inquiry, 8*, 3–30.
Åkerberg, H. (1975). *Omvändsele och kamp: En empirisk religionspsykologisk undersökning av den unge Nathan Söderbloms religiösa utveckling 1866–1894.* [Conversion and struggle: an empirical psychological study of the religious development of the young Nathan Söderblom 1866–1894] Doctoral dissertation, University of Lund, Sweden (*Studia Psychologiae Religionum Lundensia, 1*).
Åkerberg, H. (1978). Attempts to escape: A psychological study on the autobiographical notes of Herbert Tingsten 1971–1972. In T. Källstad (Ed.), *Psychological studies on religious man* (pp. 71–92). Stockholm: Almqvist & Wiksell.
Åkerberg, H. (1985). *Tillvaron och religionen: Psykologiska studier kring personlighet och mystik.* [Existence and religion: psychological studies in personality and mysticism] Lund: Studentlitteratur.
Akthar, S. & Parens H. (Eds.) (2001). *Does God help? Developmental and clinical aspects of religious belief.* New York: Aronson.
Allport, G.W. (1937). *Personality: A psychological interpretation.* New York: Holt.
Allport, G.W. (1950). *The individual and his religion: A psychological interpretation.* New York: Macmillan.
Allport, G.W. (1960). Religion and prejudice. In *Personality and social encounter* (pp. 257–267). Boston: Beacon Press.
Allport, G.W. (1962). Prejudice: Is it societal or personal? *Journal of Social Issues, 18*, 120–174.
Anders, G. (1956). *Die Antiquiertheit des Menschen: Über die Seele im Zeitalter der zweiten industriellen Revolution.* [The antiquity of mankind: the soul during the second industrial revolution] München: Beck.
Andeweg, R.B. (1981). De burger in de Nederlandse politiek [The citizen in Dutch politics]. In R.B. Andeweg, A. Hoogerwerf & J. J. A. Thomassen (Eds.), *Politiek in Nederland* [Politics in the Netherlands] (pp. 79–102). Alphen aan de Rijn: Samson.
Andrae, T. (1926). *Mystikens psykologi.* [The psychology of mysticism] Stockholm: Diakonistyrelsen.
Andrae, T. (1932). *Die Frage der religiösen Anlage religionsgeschichtlich beleuchtet.* [On the problem of the genuine religious disposition: A perspective from the history of religion] Uppsala: Universitets Årsskrift.

Andresen, J. (Ed.) (2001). *Religion in mind: Cognitive perspectives on religious belief, ritual, and experience*. Cambridge: Cambridge University Press.

Angel, H. -F. (2006). *Religiosität: Anthropologische, theologische und sozialwissenschaftliche Klärungen*. Stuttgart: Kohlhammer.

Appelsmeyer, H., Kochinka, A. & Straub, J. (1997). Qualitative Methoden. [Qualitative methods] In J. Straub, W. Kempf & H. Werbik (Eds.), *Psychologie: Eine Einführung* [Psychology: An introduction] (pp. 709–742). München: Deutscher Taschenbuch Verlag.

Ariès, Ph. & Béjin, A. (Eds.) (1984/1986). *Western sexuality: Practice and precept in past and present times*. Oxford: Blackwell.

Argyle, M. (2000). *Psychology and religion: An introduction*. London/New York: Routledge.

Argyle, M., & Beit-Hallahmi, B. (1975). *The social psychology of religion*. London: Routledge & Kegan Paul.

Armon-Jones, C. (1986). The thesis of constructionism. In R. Harré (Ed.), *The social construction of emotions* (pp. 32–56). Oxford: Blackwell.

Aronson, H. B. (2004). *Buddhist practices on Western ground: Reconciling Eastern ideals and Western psychology*. Boston/London: Shambala.

Atran, S. (2002). *In gods we trust: The evolutionary landscape of religion*. Oxford/New York: Oxford University Press.

Atran, S. (2007). Religion's cognitive and social landscape: An evolutionary perspective. In: J. Valsiner & A. Rosa (Eds.), *Cambridge Handbook of Sociocultural Psychology* (pp. 454–476). New York: Cambridge University Press.

Austin, J.L. (1962). *How to do things with words*. New York: Oxford University Press.

Averill, J.R. (1982). *Anger and aggression: an essay on emotion*. New York: Springer.

Averill, J.R. (1985). The social construction of emotion: with special reference to love. In K. J. Gergen & K.E. Davis (Eds.), *The social construction of the person* (pp. 89–109). New York: Springer.

Ayele, H., Mulligan, T., Gheorghiu, S., & Reyes Ortiz, C. (1999). Religious activity improves life satisfaction for some physicians and older patients. *Journal of the American Geriatrics Society*, 47, 453–455.

Baerveldt, C. & Voestermans, P. (1996). The body as a selfing device: The case of anorexia nervosa. *Theory and Psychology*, 6, 693–714.

Bairoch, P. (1993). *Economics and world history: Myth and paradoxes*. New York: Harvester Wheatsheaf.

Bakhtin, M. (1929/1973). *Problems of Dostoevsky's poetics*. (2nd ed.) Ann Arbor, MI: Ardis.

Batson, C.D., Schoenrade, P. & Ventis, W. L. (1993). *Religion and the individual: A social-psychological perspective*. New York: Oxford University Press.

Batson, C.D. & Ventis, W. L. (1982). *The religious experience: A social-psychological perspective*. New York: Oxford University Press.

Bax, E.H. (1988). *Modernization and cleavage in Dutch society: A study of long term economic and social change*. (Doctoral dissertation, University of Groningen, the Netherlands.)

Becker, U. (Ed.) (1993). *Nederlandse politiek in historisch en vergelijkend perspectief* [Dutch politics in historical and comparative perspective]. Amsterdam: Spinhuis.

Beile, H. (1998). *Religiöse Emotionen und religiöses Urteil*. [Religious emotions and religious judgment] Ostfildern: Schwabenverlag.

Beit-Hallahmi, B. (1989). *Prolegomena to the psychological study of religion*. London/ Toronto: Associated University Press.

Beit-Hallahmi, B. (1992). Between religious psychology and the psychology of religion. In M. Finn & J. Gardner (Eds.), *Object relations theory and religion: Clinical applications* (pp. 119–128). Westport, CT/London: Praeger.

Beit-Hallahmi, B. (1993). Three ideological traditions and the psychology of religion. *The International Journal for the Psychology of Religion*, 3 (2), 95–96.

Beit-Hallahmi, B. & Argyle, M. (1997). *The psychology of religious behaviour, belief and experience*. London/New York: Routledge.

Belzen, J.A. (1989a). *Psychopathologie en religie: Ideeën, behandeling en verzorging in de gereformeerde psychiatrie, 1880–1940* [Psychopathology and religion: Ideas, treatment and care in Calvinist psychiatry, 1880–1940]. Kampen: Kok.

Belzen, J.A. (1989b). Godsdienst, psychopathologie en moord: Historische en cultuurpsychologische notities. [Religion, psychopathology, and murder: Historical and cultural-psychological observations] *Amsterdams Sociologisch Tijdschrift, 16*, 115–128.
Belzen, J.A. (1989c). Theological influences and aspirations in psychology. *Storia della Psicologia, 1*, 26–38.
Belzen, J.A. (1990). Psychopathologie und Religion. [Psychology and religion] *Archiv für Religionspsychologie* [Archive for the Psychology of Religion], *19*, 167–188.
Belzen, J.A. (1991a). *Rümke, religie en godsdienstpsychologie: Achtergronden en vooronderstellingen.* [Rümke, religion, and psychology of religion: Background and presuppositions] Kampen: Kok.
Belzen, J.A. (1991b). Religie in de rapportage pro justitia : Enkele cultuur- en godsdienstpsychologisch relevante casus. [Religion in reportage on issues of justice: A number of cases with relevance to cultural psychology and psychology of religion] In F. Koenraadt (Ed.), *Ziek of schuldig?* [Ill or guilty?] (pp. 175–190). Amsterdam: Rodopi.
Belzen, J.A. (1991c). Verzuiling en mentaliteit: Pleidooi voor een interdisciplinaire benadering. [Pillarization and mentality: A plea for an interdisciplinary approach] *Amsterdams Sociologisch Tijdschrift,* [Amsterdam Journal of Sociology] *17* (4), 46–67.
Belzen, J.A. (1995–1996). Sketches for a family portrait of psychology of religion at the end of modernity. *Journal of Psychology of Religion, 4/5*, 89–122.
Belzen, J.A. (1996a). Spiritualiteit als zinvol leven: Profiel van een cultuurpsychologische benadering. [Spirituality as meaningful living: A profile of a cultural psychological approach] *Nederlands Theologisch Tijdschrift,* [Dutch Journal of Theology] *50,* 1–21.
Belzen, J.A. (1996b). Beyond a classic? Hjalmar Sundén's Role Theory and contemporary narrative psychology. *International Journal for the Psychology of religion, 6,* 181–199.
Belzen, J.A. (1996c). Die blühende deutsche Religionspsychologie in der Zeit vor dem Zweiten Weltkrieg und eine niederländische Quelle zur Geschichte der deutschen Psychologie. [The prosporing German psychology of religion before World War II and a Dutch source of the history of German psychology] In H. Gundlach (Ed.), *Untersuchungen zur Geschichte der Psychologie und der Psychotechnik* [Investigations on the history of psychology and psychotechnology] (pp. 75–94). München/Wien: Profil.
Belzen, J. A. (1997a). *Hermeneutical approaches in psychology of religion.* Amsterdam/Atlanta: Rodopi.
Belzen, J.A. (1997b). The historico-cultural approach in the psychology of religion: perspectives for interdisciplinary research. *Journal for the Scientific Study of Religion,* 1997, *36* (3), 358–371.
Belzen, J.A. (1997c). The inclusion of the excluded? A paradox in the historiography of psychology of religion. *Teori & Modelli: Rivista di Storia e Metodologia della Psicologia, 2* (2), 41–64.
Belzen, J.A. (1998a). Religious mania and criminal non-culpability: Religious and psychiatric reactions to a case of manslaughter in The Netherlands (1900). *Law and Psychiatry, 21* (4), 433–445.
Belzen, J.A. (1998b). "Searching for the soul": Religious factors in Leendert Bouman's development of a "psychological psychiatry." *History of Psychiatry, 9,* 303–333.
Belzen, J.A. (1999a). The cultural-psychological approach to religion: Contemporary debates on the object of the discipline. *Theory and Psychology, 9,* 229–256.
Belzen, J.A. (1999b). Religion as embodiment: Cultural-psychological concepts and methods in the study of conversion among "bevindelijken." *Journal for the Scientific Study of Religion, 38* (2), 236–253.
Belzen, J.A. (2000a). *Aspects in contexts: Studies in the history of psychology of religion.* Amsterdam/Atlanta: Rodopi.
Belzen, J.A. (2000). Psychology is history: On the necessity for psychology of religion to reflect its own history. In J. A. Belzen (Ed.), *Aspects in contexts: Studies in the history of psychology of religion* (pp. 11–23). Amsterdam/Atlanta: Rodopi.
Belzen, J.A. (2001a). *Psychohistory in psychology of religion: Interdisciplinary studies.* Amsterdam/Atlanta: Rodopi.
Belzen, J.A. (2001b). Religion as an object of empirical research: Psychohistory as exemplary interdisciplinary approach. In J. A. Belzen (Ed.), *Psychohistory in psychology of religion: Interdisciplinary studies* (pp. 7–20). Amsterdam/Atlanta: Rodopi.

Belzen, J.A. (2001c). The introduction of psychology of religion to the Netherlands: Ambivalent reception, epistemological concerns, and persistent patterns. *Journal for the History of the Behavioral Sciences*, *37*, 45–62.

Belzen, J.A. (2001–2002). Der deutsche Herold der Religionspsychologie. [The German herald of the psychology of religion] *Temenos*, 37/38, 39–69.

Belzen, J.A. (2002a). Developing scientific infrastructure: The International Association for the Psychology of Religion after its reconstitution. *Newsletter of Division 36 (Psychology of Religion) of the American Psychological Association*, *27* (2), 1–12.

Belzen, J.A. (2002b). Die Gleichzeitigkeit des Ungleichen: Anmerkungen zur Entwicklung der Religionspsychologie im niederländischen Sprachraum. [The simultaneity of the unequal: Comments on the development of the psychology of religion in the Dutch speaking world] In Chr. Henning & E. Nestler (Eds), *Konversion: Zur Aktualität eines Jahrhundertthemas* [Conversion: Topicality of a centenarian theme] (pp. 117–144). Frankfurt: Lang.

Belzen, J.A. (2003). God's mysterious companionship: Cultural psychological reflections on mystical conversion among Dutch "Bevindelijken." In J. A. Belzen & A. Geels (Eds.), *Mysticism: A variety of psychological approaches* (pp. 263–292). Amsterdam/New York: Rodopi.

Belzen, J.A. (2004a). *Religie, melancholie en zelf: Een historische en psychologische studie* [Religion, melancholy and self: A historical and psychological study]. Kok: Kampen.

Belzen, J.A. (2004b). Spirituality, culture and mental health: Prospects and risks for contemporary psychology of religion. *Journal of Religion and Health*, *43*, 291–316.

Belzen, J.A. (2005a). In defense of the object: Spirituality, culture and the psychology of religion. *International Journal for the Psychology of Religion*, *15*, 1–16.

Belzen, J.A. (2005b). The varieties, the principles and psychology of religion: Unremitting inspiration from a different source. In J. Carrette (Ed.), *William James and "The Varieties of Religious Experience": A centenary celebration* (pp. 58–78). London/New York: Routledge.

Belzen, J.A. (2006). The varieties of functions of religious experience: James' *Varieties* reconsidered. *Archives de Psychologie*, *72*, 49–65.

Belzen, J.A. (2007). *Psychologie en het raadsel van de religie: Beschouwingen bij een eeuw godsdienstpsychologie in Nederland*. [Psychology and the mystery of religion: Reflections on a century of psychology of religion in the Netherlands] Amsterdam: Boom.

Belzen, J.A. (Ed.) (2009a). *Changing the scientific study of religion: Beyond Freud?* Dordrecht: Springer.

Belzen, J.A. (2009b). Ideology, politics and personality: Shaping forces in Dutch psychology of religion, 1907–1957. *History of Psychology*, *12*, 157–182.

Belzen, J.A. & Geels, A. (Eds.) (2008). *Autobiography and the psychological study of religious lives*. Amsterdam-New York: Rodopi.

Belzen, J.A. & Lans, J. M. van der (Eds.) (1986). *Current issues in the psychology of religion*. Amsterdam: Rodopi.

Berelson, B. R. & Steiner, G. A. (1964). *Human behaviour: An inventory of scientific findings*. New York: Harcourt.

Berg, J.H. van den (1958). *Psychologie en geloof: Een kroniek en een standpunt*. [Psychology and religion: A chronicle and a point of view] Nijkerk: Callenbach.

Berge, H. van den (1997). Uit pestepidemie blijkt onmacht van de mens. [The epidemic of plague reveals the impotence of man] *Reformatorisch Dagblad* [Reformed Newspaper] June 3, 1997.

Berger, P. (1967). *The sacred canopy*. New York: Doubleday.

Berger, P.L. (1974). Some second thoughts on substantive versus functional definitions of religion. *Journal for the Scientific Study of Religion*, *13*, 125–133.

Bernard, L. L. (1924). *Instinct*. New York: Holt.

Berndt, T.J., Cheung, P. C., Lau, S. & Hau, K. (1993). Perceptions of parenting in mainland China, Taiwan, and Hong Kong: Sex differences and societal differences. *Developmental Psychology*, *29*, 156–164.

Bernstein, R.J. (1983). *Beyond objectivism and relativism*. Oxford: Blackwell.

Berry, J.W. (1992). *Cross-cultural psychology: Research and applications*. Cambridge: Cambridge University Press.

Bibliography

Beth, K. (1927). *Religion und Magie: Ein religionsgeschichtlicher Beitrag zur psychologischen Grundlegung der religiösen Prinzipienlehre.* [Religion and magic: A religion-historical contribution to the psychological foundation of the theory of religious principles] Leipzig/Berlin: Teubner.

Beth, K. (1931a). Religion als Metabiontik. I. Der Fall R. Sch. *Zeitschrift für Religionspsychologie* (Beiträge zur religiösen Seelenforschung und Seelenführung), *4*, 25–37.

Beth, K. (1931b). Religion als Metabiontik. II. Madeleine Sémer. *Zeitschrift für Religionspsychologie* (Beiträge zur religiösen Seelenforschung und Seelenführung), *4*, 145–156.

Beumer, J.J. (1993). *Intimiteit en solidariteit: Over het evenwicht tussen dogmatiek, mystiek en ethiek.* [Intimacy and solidarity: On the balance between dogmatics, mysticism, and ethics] Baarn: Ten Have.

Bhugra, D. (Ed.) (1996). *Psychiatry and religion: Context, consensus and controversies.* London/New York: Routledge.

Billig, M. (1987). *Arguing and thinking: A rhetorical approach to social psychology.* Cambridge: Cambridge University Press.

Billig, M. (1991). *Ideology and opinions: Studies in rhetorical psychology.* London: Sage.

Billmann-Mahecha, E. (2001). Kulturpsychologie. [Cultural psychology] In G. Wenninger (Ed.), *Lexikon der Psychologie.* [Dictionary of psychology] Vol. 2 (pp. 405–408). Heidelberg: Spektrum.

Black, D.M. (2006). *Psychoanalysis and religion in the 21st century: Competitors or collaborators?* New York: Routledge.

Blattner, J., Gareis, B. & Plewa, A. (Eds.) (1992). *Handbuch der Psychologie für die Seelsorge.* Band 1: *Psychologische Grundlagen.* [Handbook of psychology for pastoral care. Volume 1: Foundations of psychology] Düsseldorf: Patmos.

Blattner, J., Gareis, B. & Plewa, A. (Eds.) (1993). *Handbuch der Psychologie für die Seelsorge.* Band 2: *Angewandte Psychologie.* [Handbook of psychology for pastoral care. Volume 2: Applied psychology] Düsseldorf: Patmos.

Blom, J.C.H. (1981). *Verzuiling in Nederland, in het bijzonder op lokaal niveau, 1850–1925* [Pillarization in the Netherlands, with a focus on the local level, 1850–1925]. Amsterdam: Historisch Seminarium van de Universiteit van Amsterdam.

Blom, J.C.H. (2006). The Netherlands since 1830. In J. C. H. Blom & E. Lamberts (Eds.), *History of the Low Countries* (New Edition) (pp. 393–470). New York/Oxford: Berghahn Books.

Blom, J.C.H. & Talsma, J. (2000). *De verzuiling voorbij: Godsdienst, stand en natie in de lange negentiende eeuw* [Beyond pillarization: religion, class and nation in the long 19th century]. Amsterdam: Spinhuis.

Boehnlein, J.K. (2000). *Psychiatry and religion: The convergence of mind and spirit.* Washington, DC: American Psychiatric Press.

Boer, Th. de (1980/1983). *Foundations of a critical psychology.* Pittsburgh: Duquesne University Press.

Boesch, E.E. (1983). *Das Magische und das Schöne: Zur Symbolik von Objekten und Handlungen.* [Magic and beauty: On symbolism of objects and acts] Stuttgart/Bad Cannstatt: Frommann-Holzboog.

Boesch, E.E. (1991). *Symbolic action theory and cultural psychology.* Berlin/Heidelberg: Springer.

Boesch, E.E. (2000). *Das lauernde Chaos: Mythen und Fiktionen im Alltag.* [Chaos lies on the lurk: Myths and fictions in daily life] Bern: Huber.

Boesch, E.E. (2005). *Von Kunst bis Terror: Über den Zwiespalt in der Kultur.* [From art to terror: On the discord in culture] Göttingen: Vandenhoeck & Ruprecht.

Boesch, E. & Straub, J. (2006). Kulturpsychologie. Prinzipien, Orientierungen, Konzeptionen [Psychology of culture: Principles, orientations, conceptions]. In H.-J. Kornadt & G. Trommsdorff (Eds.), *Kulturvergleichende Psychologie* [Psychology of comparative culture] (*Enzyklopädie der Psychologie.* Serie VII. Themenbereich C *"Theorie und Forschung"*) (pp. 25–95). Göttingen: Hogrefe.

Booy, T. (1956). *Een stille omwenteling: Het gereformeerde leven in onze jeugd* [A silent revolution: The Calvinist life in our youth]. Amsterdam: Ten Have.

Bornewasser, J.A. (1988). De katholieke zuil in wording als object van columnologie [The genesis of the Catholic pillar as object of columnology]. *Archief voor de Geschiedenis van de Katholieke kerk in Nederland* [Archives for the History of the Catholic Church in the Netherlands], 168–212.

Bosscher, D.F.J. (1987). Het protestantisme [Protestantism]. In P. Luykx & N. Bootsma (Eds.), *De laatste tijd: Geschiedschrijving over Nederland in de 20e eeuw* [Recent times: Historiography of the Netherlands in the 20th century]. Utrecht: Spectrum.

Bouman, L. (1901). Un cas important d'infection psychique. [A significant case of psychic infection] *Psychiatrische en Neurologische Bladen*, [Journal of Psychiatry and Neurology] 5, 106–117.

Bourdieu, P. (1977). *Outline of a theory of practice*. New York: Cambridge University Press.

Bourdieu, P. (1980/1990). *The logic of practice*. Cambridge: Polity Press.

Bourdieu, P. (1993). *The field of cultural production*. Cambridge/New York: Polity Press/ Columbia University Press.

Bourdieu, P. & Wacquant, L. J. D. (1992). *An introduction to reflexive sociology*. Chicago, Ill.: University of Chicago Press.

Bouvy, A.-M (Ed.) (1994). *Journeys into cross-cultural psychology*. Lisse: Swets & Zeitlinger.

Boyer, P. (2001). *Religion explained: The evolutionary origins of religious thought*. New York: Basic Books.

Braam, A.W., Sonnenberg, C. M., Beekman, A. T. F., Deeg, D. J. H. & Tilburg, W. van (2000). Religious denomination as a symptom-formation factor of depression in older Dutch citizens. *International Journal of Geriatric Psychiatry, 15*, 458–466.

Brienen, T. (1978). *Bevinding: Aard en functie van de geloofsbeleving*. [Bevinding: The nature and function of the experience of faith] Kampen: Kok.

Brienen, T. (Ed.) (1986). *De Nadere Reformatie*. [The Further Reformation] Den Haag: Boekencentrum.

Brienen, T. (Ed.) (1989). *De Nadere Reformatie en het Gereformeerd Piëtisme*. [The Further Reformation and Reformed Pietism] Den Haag: Boekencentrum.

Brienen, T. (2003). Mystiek van de Nadere Reformatie. [Mysticism of the Further Reformation] In J. Baers, G. Brinkman, A. Jelsma & O. Steggink (Eds.), *Encyclopedie van de mystiek: Fundamenten, tradities, perspectieven* [Encyclopedia of mysticism: Foundations, traditions, perspectives] (pp. 753–759). Kampen/Tielt: Kok/Lannoo.

Brinkgreve, C. (1984). *Psychoanalyse in Nederland* [Psychoanalysis in the Netherlands]. Amsterdam: Arbeiderspers.

Brown, L.B. (1987). *The psychology of religious belief*. London: Academic Press.

Browning, D.S. (1987). *Religious thought and the modern psychologies: A critical conversation in the theology of culture*. Philadelphia: Fortress.

Bruin, A. A. de (1985). *Het ontstaan van de schoolstrijd: Onderzoek naar de wortels van de schoolstrijd in de Noordelijke Nederlanden gedurende de eerste helft van de 19e eeuw; een cultuurhistorische studie* [The emergence of the school funding controversy: Research on the roots of the school funding controversy in the northern Netherlands during the first half of the 19th century; a cultural-historical study]. (Doctoral dissertation, University of Leiden, The Netherlands).

Brümmer, V. (Ed.) (1991). *Interpreting the universe as creation*. Kampen: Kok.

Bruner, J. (1990). *Acts of meaning*. Cambridge, MA: Harvard University Press.

Bruner, J. (1992). The narrative construction of reality. In H. Beilin & P. B. Putall (Eds.), *Piaget's theory: Prospects and possibilities* (pp. 229–248). Hillsdale: Erlbaum.

Bruner, J. (1997). *The culture of education*. Cambridge, MA: Harvard University Press.

Bucher, A.A. (2004). *Psychobiographien religiöser Entwicklung: Glaubensprofile zwischen Individualität und Universalität*. [Psychobiographies of religious development: Religious profiles between individuality and universality] Stuttgart: Kohlhammer.

Bucher, A.A. (2007). *Psychologie der Spiritualität. Handbuch*. [Psychology of spirituality. A handbook.] Weinheim: Beltz.

Bühler, K. (1908). Nachtrag: Antwort auf die von W. Wundt erhobenen Einwände gegen die Methode der Selbstbeobachtung an experimentell erzeugten Erlebnissen. [Afterword: Response

to Wundt's objections to the method of self-observation in experimentally produced experiences] *Archiv für die Gesamte Psychologie*, [Archive for all Psychologies] *12*, 93–123.
Bühler, K. (1909). Zur Kritik der Denkexperimente. [Critics of thought experiments] *Zeitschrift für Psychologie*, [Journal of Psychology] *51*, 108–118.
Bühler, K. (1927). *Die Krise der Psychologie*. [The crisis of psychology] Jena: Fischer.
Bulkeley, K. (2005). *Soul, psyche, brain. New Directions in the study of religion and brain-mind science*. New York. Palgrave.
Burke, P. (1980). *Sociology and history*. London: Allen & Unwin.
Cahan, E.D. & White, S. H. (1992). Proposals for a second psychology. *American Psychologist*, *47*, 224–235.
Capps, D. (1997). *Men, religion and melancholia: James, Otto, Jung and Erikson*. New Haven/London: Yale University Press.
Capps, D. (2000). *Jesus: A psychological biography*. St. Louis: Chalice.
Capps, D. (Ed.) (2001). *Freud and Freudians on religion: A reader*. New Haven/London: Yale University Press.
Capps, D. & Dittes, J. E. (Eds.) (1990). *The hunger of the heart: Reflections on the Confessions of Augustine*. West Lafayette, IN: Society for the Scientific Study of Religion.
Carrette, J. (Ed.) (2005). *William James and "The Varieties of Religious Experience": A centenary celebration*. London/New York: Routledge.
Carrette, J. & King, R. (2005). *Selling spirituality: The silent takeover of religion*. Abingdon/New York: Routledge.
Carroll, M.P. (1986). *The cult of the Virgin Mary: Psychological origins*. Princeton: Princeton University Press.
Carroll, M.P. (2002). *The penitente brotherhood: Patriarchy and Hispano-Catholicism in New Mexico*. Baltimore: John Hopkins University Press.
Carruthers, M.J. (1990). *The book of memory: A study of memory in medieval culture*. Cambridge: Cambridge University Press.
Cashwell, C.S. & Young, J.S. (Eds.) (2005). *Integrating spirituality and religion into counselling: A guide to competent practice*. Alexandria, VA: American Counseling Association.
Cermak, L.S. (1989). Synergistic ecphory and the amnestic patient. In H. L. Roediger & I. M. Craik (Eds.), *Varieties of memory and consciousness* (pp. 121–131). Hillsdale: Erlbaum.
Chorus, A. (1943). Psychologische verschillen tussen protestanten en katholieken in Nederland [Psychological differences between Protestants and Catholics in the Netherlands]. *Het Gemenebest* [The Commonwealth], 34–57, 65–89.
Chorus, A. (1964). *De Nederlander innerlijk en uiterlijk: Een karakteristiek* [The Dutchman, inside and out: A portrait]. Leiden: Sijthoff.
Christensen, S.M. & Turner, D.R. (1993). *Folk psychology and the philosophy of mind*. Hillsdale, NJ: Lawrence Erlbaum Associates.
Clarke, I. (Ed.) (2001). *Psychosis and spirituality: Exploring the new frontier*. London: Whurr.
Clément, C. & Kakar, S. (1993). *La folle et le saint*. [The lunatic and the saint] Paris: Éditions du Seuil.
Cohen, C.L. (1986). *God's caress: the psychology of puritan religious experience*. New York: Oxford University Press.
Cohen, E. (2007). *The mind possessed: The cognition of spirit possession in an Afro-Brazilian religious tradition*. Oxford/New York: Oxford University Press.
Cole, M. (1995). Culture and cognitive development: From cross-cultural research to creating systems of cultural mediation. *Culture & Psychology*, *1*, 25–54.
Cole, M. (1996). *Cultural psychology: A once and future discipline*. Cambridge, MA: Belknap Press/Harvard University Press.
Coon, D.J. (1992). Testing the limits of sense and science. American experimental psychologists combat spiritualism, 1880–1920. *American Psychologist*, *47*, 143–151.
Corbett, L. (1996). *The religious function of the psyche*. London/New York: Routledge.
Corbin, A. (1982/1986). *The foul and the fragrant: Odor and the French social imagination*. Leamington: Berg.

Crawford, V.M & Valsiner, J. (1999). Varieties of discursive experience in psychology: Culture understood through the language used. *Culture & Psychology, 5,* 259–269.

Crocket, C. (2007). *Interstices of the Sublime: Theology and psychoanalytic theory.* New York: Fordham University Press.

Csordas, Th.J. (1990). Embodiment as a paradigm for anthropology. *Ethos, 18,* 5–47.

Cushmann, Ph. (1990). Why the self is empty: Toward a historically situated psychology. *American Psychologist, 45,* 599–611.

Danziger, K. (1990). *Constructing the subject: Historical origins of psychological research.* Cambridge: Cambridge University Press.

Danziger, K. (1997). *Naming the mind: How psychology found its language.* London: Sage.

Danziger, K. (2001a). Wundt and the temptations of psychology. In R.W. Rieber & D.K. Robinson (Eds.), *Wilhelm Wundt in history: The making of a scientific psychology* (pp. 69–94). New York: Kluwer/ Plenum.

Danziger, K. (2001b). The unknown Wundt: Drive, apperception and volition. In R. W. Rieber & D.K. Robinson (Eds.), *Wilhelm Wundt in history: The making of a scientific psychology* (pp. 95–120). New York: Kluwer/ Plenum.

Danziger, K. (2008). *Marking the mind: A history of memory.* Cambridge: Cambridge University Press.

Darley, J. & Batson, C. D. (1973). From Jerusalem to Jericho: A study of situational and dispositional variables in helping behavior. *Journal of Personality and Social Psychology, 27,* 100–108.

Day, J.M. (1993). Speaking of belief: Language, performance, and narrative in the psychology of religion. *International Journal for the Psychology of Religion, 3,* 213–230.

Day, J. (2002). Religious development as discursive construction. In C. A. M. Hermans, G. Immink, A. de Jong & J. van der Lans (Eds.), *Social constructionism and theology* (pp. 63–89). Leiden: Brill.

DeBruijn, J. (1998). De betekenis van documentatiecentra voor het kerkelijk erfgoed [The significance of documentation centers for the church's legacy]. In J. de Bruijn, P. N. Holtrop & B. Woelderink (Eds.), *"Een lastige erfenis": Kerkelijke archieven van de twintigste eeuw* ["A troublesome legacy": Church archives of the twentieth century] (pp. 51–70). Zoetermeer: Meinema.

Deconchy, J.-P. (1987). [Review of J.A. Belzen & J.M. van der Lans (1986), *Current issues in the psychology of religion*]. *Archives de Sciences Sociales des Religions, 63,* 305–306.

Dekker, G. & Peters, J. (1989). *Gereformeerden in meervoud: Een onderzoek naar levensbeschouwing en waarden van de verschillende gereformeerde stromingen.* [Being Reformed in the plural: An inquiry into the philosophy of life and values of the different currents] Kampen: Kok.

Dekker, P. & Ester, P. (1996). Depillarization, deconfessionalization and de-ideologization: Empirical trends in Dutch society, 1958–1992. *Review of Religious Research, 37*(4), 325–341.

Delany, P. (1969). *British autobiography in the seventeenth century.* London: Routledge & Kegan Paul.

Delumeau, J. (1982/1990). *Sin and fear: The emergence of a western guilt culture, 13th-18th centuries.* New York: Saint Martin's Press.

Demos, J. (1988). Shame and guilt in early New England. In C. Z. Stearns & P. N. Stearns (Eds.), *Emotion and social change: Toward a new psychohistory* (pp. 69–86). New York: Holmes & Meier.

Denzin, N.K. & Lincoln, Y.S. (Eds.) (2000). *Handbook of qualitative research.* (2nd. ed.) Thousand Oaks, CA: Sage.

Derks, F.C.H. (1990). *Religieuze attitudetheorieën.* [Religious atittude theories] (Doctoral dissertation, University of Nijmegen, The Netherlands).

Dewey, J. (1938/1963). *Experience and education.* New York: Macmillan.

Diener, E. & Diener, M. (1995). Cross-cultural correlates of life satisfaction and self-esteem. *Journal of Personality and Social Psychology, 68,* 653–663.

Dierickx, G. (1986). De sociologen en de verzuiling: Over het nut van deterministische en strategische paradigmata [Sociologists and pillarization: On the usefulness of deterministic and strategic paradigms]. *Tijdschrift voor Sociologie* [Journal for Sociology], *7,* 509–549.

Digby, A. (1985). *Madness, morality and medicine: A study of the York Retreat, 1796–1914*. Cambridge: Cambridge University Press.
Dijksterhuis, E.J. (1986). *The mechanization of the world picture: Pythagoras to Newton*. Princeton: Princeton University Press.
Dilthey, W. (1894/1964). Ideen über eine beschreibende und zergliedernde Psychologie. [Ideas on a descriptive and an analysing psychology] In *Gesammelte Schriften*. [Complete works] Band 5 (pp. 139–241). Stuttgart: Teubner.
Dilthey, W. (1910). Der Aufbau der geschichtlichen Welt in den Geisteswissenschaften. [The construction of the historical world in the humanities] In *Gesammelte Schriften*. [Complete works] Bd. 7 (pp. 79–188). Stuttgart: Teubner.
Diriwächter, R. (2004). Völkerpsychologie: The synthesis that never was. *Culture & Psychology, 10*, 85–109.
Dittes, J.E. (1973). Beyond William James. In C. Y. Glock & P. H. Hammond (Eds.), *Beyond the classics? Essays in the scientific study of religion* (pp. 291–354), New York: Harper and Row.
Dixon, S.L. (1999). *Augustine: The scattered and gathered self*. St. Louis, Mo: Chalice Press.
Dockett, K.H., Dudley-Grant, G.R. & Bankart, C.P. (Eds.) (2003). *Psychology and Buddhism: From individual to global community*. New York/Dordrecht: Kluwer Academic/Plenum Publishers.
Doorn, J.A.A. van (1956). Verzuiling: Een eigentijds systeem van sociale controle [Pillarization: A contemporary system of social control]. *Sociologische Gids* [Sociological Guide], *5*, 41–49.
Doorn, J.A.A. van (1985). Tolerantie als tactiek [Tolerance as tactic]. *Intermediair* [Intermediary], *21* (51), 31.
Driesch, H. (1925). *The crisis in psychology*. Princeton, NJ: Princeton University Press.
Duffhues, T. (1980). Het georganiseerd katholicisme in Nederland. [Organized Catholicism in the Netherlands] *Jaarboek van het Katholiek Documentatie Centrum* [Yearbook of the Catholic Documentation Center], *10*, 135–159.
Duffhues, T. (1987). Staat "de wankele zuil" nog overeind? Een verkenning van de recente literatuur over verzuiling en ontzuiling [Is "the shaky pillar" still standing? An exploration of the recent literature on pillarization and depillarization]. *Jaarboek van het Katholiek Documentatie Centrum* [Yearbook of the Catholic Documentation Center], *17*, 134–162.
Duffhues, T. & Vugt, J. van (1980). Literatuur over verzuiling en ontzuiling [Literature on pillarization and depillarization]. *Jaarboek van het Katholiek Documentatie Centrum* [Yearbook of the Catholic Documentation Center], *10*, 161–170.
Duijker, H.C.J. (1981). Mentaliteit: Een gedragsdeterminant? [Mentality: A determinant of behaviour?] *Symposium, 3*, 129–138.
Dunde, S.R. (Ed.) (1993). *Wörterbuch der Religionspsychologie*. [Dictionary of psychology of religion] Gütersloh: Mohn.
Durkheim, E. (1912). *Les formes élémentaires de la vie religieuse: Le système totémique en Australie*. [The elementary forms of religious life] Paris: Alcan.
Eckardt, G. (Ed.) (1997). *Völkerpsychologie: Versuch einer Neuentdeckung. Texte von Lazarus, Steinthal und Wundt*. [Folk psychology: Attempt to a rediscovery. Texts by Lazarus, Steinthal and Wundt] Weinheim: Psychology VerlagsUnion.
Eckensberger, L. H. (1995). Activity of action: Two different roads towards an integration of culture into psychology? *Culture & Psychology, 1*, 67–80.
Edie, J.M. (1987). *William James and phenomenology*. Bloomington: Indiana University Press.
Edwards, D. & Potter, J. (1992). *Discursive psychology*. London: Sage.
Eigen, M. (1981). The area of faith in Winnicott, Lacan and Bion. *International Journal of Psychoanalysis, 62*, 413–433.
Eigen, M. (1998). *The psychoanalytic mystic*. London: Free Association Books.
Elias, N. (1939/1978–82). *The civilizing process* (2 vols.). Oxford: Blackwell.
Elias, N. & Scotson, J.L. (1965). *The established and the outsiders: A sociological inquiry into community problems*. London: Cass.
Ellemers, J.E. (1984). Pillarization as a process of modernization. *Acta Politica, 19*, 129–144.
Ellemers, J.E. (1996). Pillarization as a process of modernization. *Acta Politica, 31*, 524–538.

Ellenberger, H.F. (1970). *The discovery of the unconsciousness*. New York: Basic Books.
Ellens, J. H. (Ed.) (2004). *The destructive power of religion: Violence in Judaism, Christianity, and Islam*. Volume 2: *Religion, psychology, and violence*. Westport, CT/London: Praeger.
Ellens, J.H. & Rollins, W.G. (Eds.) (2004). *Psychology and the Bible*. (four volumes) Westport, CT/London: Praeger.
Elms, A.C. (1994). *Uncovering lives: The uneasy alliance of biography and psychology*. New York: Oxford University Press.
Emmons, R.A. & Paloutzian, R.F. (2003). The psychology of religion. *Annual Review of Psychology*, 54, 377–402.
Erikson, E.H. (1956). The problem of ego identity. *Journal of the American Psychoanalytic Association*, 4, 56–118.
Erikson, E.H. (1958). *Young man Luther: A study in psychoanalysis and history*. New York: Norton.
Eugen, M. (1981). The area of faith in Winnicott, Lacan and Bion. *International Journal of Psychoanalysis*, 62, 413–433.
Evans, D. (1996). *An introductory dictionary of Lacanian psychoanalysis*. London/New York: Routledge.
Faber, M.D. (2004). *The psychological roots of religious belief: Searching for angels and the parent-god*. Amherst, NY: Prometheus.
Faiver, C, Ingersoll, R. E., O'Brien, E. & McNally, C. (2001). *Explorations in counselling and spirituality: Philosophical, practical and personal reflections*. Belmont, CA: Wadsworth/Thomson Learning.
Farberow, N. L. (Ed.) (1963). *Taboo topics*. New York: Prentice Hall.
Fèbvre, L. (1942/1982). *The problem of unbelief in the sixteenth century: The religion of Rabelais*. Cambridge, MA: Harvard University Press.
Feil, E. (1986). *Religio: Die Geschichte eines neuzeitlichen Grundbegriffs vom Frühchristentum bis zur Reformation*. [Religio: The history of a modern basic concept from Early Christianity to Reformation] Göttingen: Vandenhoeck & Ruprecht.
Feil, E. (1997). *Religio*. Band II: *Die Geschichte eines neuzeitlichen Grundbegriffs vom Frühchristentum bis zur Reformation* (ca. 1540–1620). [Religio: The history of a modern basic concept from Early Christianity to Reformation] Göttingen: Vandenhoeck & Ruprecht.
Festinger, L., Riecken, H. W. & Schachter, S. (1956). *When prophecy fails*. Minneapolis: University of Minnesota Press.
Fitzgerald, T. (2000). *The ideology of religious studies*. New York: Oxford University Press.
Fitzgerald, T. (2007). *Discourse on civility and barbarity*. New York: Oxford University Press.
Flick, U., Kardorff, E. von & Steinke, I. (Eds.) (2000). *Qualitative Forschung: Ein Handbuch*. [Qualitative research: A handbook] Hamburg: Rowohlt.
Florijn, H. (1991). *De Ledeboerianen: Een onderzoek naar de plaats, invloed en denkbeelden van hun voorgangers tot 1907*. [The Ledeboerians: A study of the place, influence, and ideas of their ministers up until 1907] Houten: Den Hertog.
Fogel, A. (1993). *Developing through relationships*. New York: Harvester Wheatsheaf.
Fortmann, H.M.M. (1964–1968). *Als ziende de Onzienlijke: Een cultuurpsychologische studie over de religieuze waarneming en de zogenaamde religieuze projectie*. [Seeing the Unseeable: A cultural-psychological study on religious perception and the so-called religious projection] (4 vols.) Hilversum: Brand.
Fortmann, H.M.M. (1968). *Hindoes en boeddhisten: Dagboekaantekeningen en reisbrieven*. [Hindus and Buddhists: Diary notes and journey letters] Baarn: Ambo.
Fortmann, H.M.M. (1971). *Inleiding tot de cultuurpsychologie*. [Introduction to the psychology of culture] Baarn: Ambo.
Foucault, M. (1975/1977). *Discipline and punish: The birth of the prison*. London: Lane.
Fox, D. & Prilleltensky, I. (Ed.) (1997). *Critical psychology: An introduction*. London: Sage.
Frame, M.W. (2003). *Integrating religion and spirituality into counselling*. Pacific Grove, CA: Thomson/Brooks/Cole.
Freud, S. (1907/1959). Obsessive actions and religious practices. In *The standard edition of the complete psychological works of Sigmund Freud*, vol. 9 (transl. & ed. J. Strachey; pp. 115–127). London: Hogarth.

Freud, S. (1910/1964²). Leonardo da Vinci and a memory of his childhood. In *The standard edition of the complete psychological works of Sigmund Freud*, vol. 11 (transl. & ed. J. Strachey; pp. 63–137). London: Hogarth.

Freud, S. (1913/1964⁴). Totem and taboo. In *The standard edition of the complete psychological works of Sigmund Freud*, vol. 13 (transl. & ed. J. Strachey; pp. 1–161). London: Hogarth.

Freud, S. (1914/1975). Zur Einführung des Narzißmus. [Introduction to narcism] In *Freud: Studienausgabe*. Vol. 3 (Eds. A. Mitscherlich, A. Richards & J. Strachey; pp. 37–68). Frankfurt: Fischer.

Freud, S. (1917/1971⁵). *Introductory lectures on psycho-analysis.* (*The standard edition of the complete psychological works of Sigmund Freud*, vol. 15; transl. & ed. J. Strachey). London: Hogarth.

Freud, S. (1918/1963). The taboo of virginity. In *The standard edition of the complete psychological works of Sigmund Freud*, vol. 16 (transl. & ed. J. Strachey; pp. 7–122). London: Hogarth.

Freud, S. (1921/1955). Group psychology and the analysis of the ego. In *The standard edition of the complete psychological works of Sigmund Freud*, vol. 18 (transl. & ed. J. Strachey; pp. 69–143). London: Hogarth.

Freud, S. (1927/1961). The future of an illusion. In *The standard edition of the complete psychological works of Sigmund Freud*, vol. 21 (transl. & ed. J. Strachey; pp. 1–56). London: Hogarth.

Freud, S. (1928/1961). A religious experience. In *The standard edition of the complete psychological works of Sigmund Freud*, vol. 21 (transl. & ed. J. Strachey; pp. 167–172). London: Hogarth.

Freud, S. (1930/1961). Civilization and its discontents. In *The standard edition of the complete psychological works of Sigmund Freud*, vol. 21 (transl. & ed. J. Strachey; pp. 64–145). London: Hogarth.

Freud, S. (1933/1964²). New introductory lectures on psycho-analysis. In *The standard edition of the complete psychological works of Sigmund Freud*, vol. 22 (transl. & ed. J. Strachey; pp. 5–182). London: Hogarth.

Freud, S. (1960). *Briefe 1873–1939* (Ed. E. L. Freud). Frankfurt a.M.: Fischer.

Fromm, E. (1950). *Psychoanalysis and religion*. New Haven: Yale University Press.

Fukuyama, M. A. & Sevig, T. D. (1999). *Integrating spirituality into multicultural counselling*. London: Sage.

Funder, D. (2002). Why study religion? *Psychological Inquiry*, *13*, 213–214.

Gadamer, H. G. (1960/1986). *Truth and method*. New York: Crossroad.

Gadlin, H. (1992). Lacan explicated [review of J. Scott Lee (1990), *Jacques Lacan*]. *Contemporary Psychology*, *37* (9), 888.

Gauld, A. & Shotter, J. (1977). *Human action and its psychological investigation*. London: Routledge and Kegan Paul.

Gay, V.P. (1989). *Understanding the Occult: Fragmentation and repair of the Self*. Minneapolis: Fortress Press.

Geels, A. (1980). *Mystikerna Hjalmar Ekström 1885–1962*. [Mystic Hjalmar Ekström 1885–1962] Malmö: Doxa.

Geels, A. (1989). *Skapande mystik: En psykologisk studie av Violet Tengbergs religiösa visioner och konstnärliga skapande*. [Creative mysticism: a psychological study of Violet Tengberg's religious visions and artistic creations] Löberöd: Plus Ultra.

Geels, A. (1991). *Att möta Gud i kaos: Religiösa visioner i dagens Sverige*. [Encounter with God in chaos: Religious visions in contemporary Sweden] Stockholm: Norstedts Förlag.

Geels, A. (1997). *Subud and the Javanese mystical tradition*. Richmond (GB): Curzon.

Geertz, C. (1973). *The interpretation of cultures*. New York: Basic Books.

Geertz, C. (1983). *Local knowledge: Further essays in interpretive anthropology*. New York: Basic Books.

Geertz, C. (1997). Learning with Bruner. *The New York Review*, April 10, 22–24.

Gehlen, A. (1961). *Anthropologische Forschung zur Selbstbegegnung und Selbstentdeckung des Menschen*. [Anthropological research for selfencountering and selfdiscovering of mankind] Hamburg: Rowohlt.

Gergen, K.J. (1973). Social psychology as history. *Journal of Personality and Social Psychology*, *26* (2), 309–320.

Gergen, K.J. (1985). The social constructionist movement in modern psychology. *The American Psychologist, 40,* 266–275.

Gergen, K.J. (1993). Belief as relational resource. *The International Journal for the Psychology of Religion, 3* (4), 231–235.

Gergen, K.J. (1994). *Realities and relationships: Soundings in social construction.* Cambridge, MA: Harvard University Press.

Gergen, K.J. (1999). *Invitation to social construction.* London: Sage.

Gerth, H. & Mills, C. W. (1953). *Character and social structure: The psychology of social institutions.* New York: Harcourt/Brace.

Ginzburg, C. (1986/1989). *Clues, myths, and the historical method.* Baltimore: John Hopkins University.

Girgensohn, K. (1921/1930). *Der Seelische Aufbau des Religiösen Erlebens: Eine religionspsychologische Untersuchung auf Experimenteller Grundlage.* [The psychological structure of religious experiences: A religious-psychological investigation based on experimental research] Gütersloh: Bertelsmann.

Giorgi, A. (1976). Phenomenology and the foundations of psychology. In W. J. Arnold (Ed.), *Conceptual foundations of psychology* (pp. 281–408). Lincoln/London: University of Nebraska Press.

Glaser, B.G. & Strauss, A. L. (1967). *The discovery of grounded theory: Strategies for qualitative research.* Chicago: Aldine.

Glock, C.Y. & Stark, R. (1965). *Religion and society in tension.* Chicago: Harper & Row.

Godin, A. (1987). [Review of J.A. Belzen & J.M. van der Lans (1986), *Current issues in the psychology of religion*]. *Lumen Vitae, 47,* 455.

Goffman, E. (1951). Symbols of class status. *British Journal of Sociology, 2,* 294–304.

Goffman, E. (1961). *Asylums: Essays on the social situation of mental patients and other inmates.* Chicago: Aldine.

Goldberger, N.R. & Veroff, J.B. (Eds.) (1995). *The culture and psychology reader.* New York/London: New York University Press.

Gomperts, W.J. (1992). *De opkomst van de sociale fobie: Een sociologische en psychologische studie naar de maatschappelijke verandering van psychische verschijnselen.* [The rise of social phobia: a sociological and psychological study into the societal change of psychic phenomena] Amsterdam: Bert Bakker.

Gone, J.P., Miller, P.J. & Rappaport, J. (1999). Conceptual narrative as normatively oriented: The suitability of past personal narrative for the study of cultural identity. *Culture & Psychology, 5,* 371–398.

Gooyer, A.C. de (1964). *Het beeld der vad'ren: Een documentaire over het leven van het protestants-christelijk volksdeel in de twintiger en dertiger jaren* [The image of the fathers: A documentary on the life of the Protestant community during the twenties and thirties]. Baarn: Bosch & Keuning.

Gorsuch, R.L. (1984). Measurement: The boon and bane of investigating the psychology of religion. *American Psychologist, 39,* 201–221.

Goudsblom, J. (1979). De Nederlandse samenleving in ontwikkelingsperspectief. [Dutch society from developmental perspective] *Symposium, 1,* 8–27.

Graafland, C. (1991). Bevinding. In W. Aantjes (Ed.), *Gereformeerden en het gesprek met de cultuur.* [The Reformed and the dialogue with culture] Zoetermeer: Boekencentrum.

Grad, H., Blanco, A., & Georgas, J. (Eds.) (1996). *Key issues in cross-cultural psychology.* Lisse: Swets & Zeitlinger.

Greil, A.L. & Bromley, D.G. (Eds) (2003). *Defining religion: Investigating the boundaries between the sacred and the secular.* Oxford: Elsevier Science.

Groenendijk, L.F. (1993). De spirituele autobiografie als bron voor onze kennis van de religieuze opvoeding en ontwikkeling van Nederlandse piëtisten [The spiritual autobiography as source for our knowledge of the religious upbringing and development of Dutch pietists]. In L. F. Groenendijk & J. C. Sturm (Eds.), *Leren geloven in de lage landen: Facetten van de geschiedenis van de religieuze opvoeding* [Learning to believe in the low countries: Facets of the

history of religious education] (pp. 57–90). Amsterdam: Vrije Universiteit (Department of Historical Pedagogy).
Groot, A.D. de (1961/1969). *Methodology: Foundations of inferences and research in the behavioral sciences.* (transl. J.A.A. Spiekerman) The Hague: Mouton.
Groot, F. (1992). *Roomsen, rechtzinnigen en nieuwlichters: Verzuiling in een Hollandse plattelandsgemeente, Naaldwijk 1850–1930* [Catholics, Reformed and modernists: Pillarization in the Dutch country town of Naaldwijk, 1850–1930]. Hilversum: Verloren.
Grotstein, J. (1983). Some perspectives in self psychology. In A. Goldberg (Ed.), *The future of psychoanalysis* (pp. 165–201). New York: International Universities Press.
Grünbaum, A.A. (1928). *Het ik-bewustzijn en de psychische ontwikkeling.* [Self-consciousness and psychological development] Utrecht: s.n.
Guignon, C. (1998). Narrative explanation in psychotherapy. *American Behavioral Scientist, 41*, 558–577.
Gundry, M.R. (2006). *Beyond psyche: The symbol and transcendence in C.G. Jung.* New York. Lang.
Guntrip, H. (1969). Religion in relation to personal integration. *British Journal of Medical Psychology, 42*, 323–333.
Guthrie, S.E. (1993). *Faces in the clouds: A new theory of religion.* New York: Oxford University Press.
Haartman, K. (2004). *Watching and praying: Personality transformation in eighteen century British Methodism.* Amsterdam: Rodopi.
Hall, G.S. (1904). *Adolescence: Its psychology and its relations to physiology, anthropology, sociology, sex, crime, religion, and education,* (2 vols.) New York: Appleton.
Hall, G.S. (1917). *Jesus, the Christ, in the light of psychology.* New York: Doubleday.
Hansen-Löve, A. (1986). Der Diskurs der Konfessionen. [The discussion among the confessions] In F. Dostojewski, *Der Jüngling* [The young man] (pp. 874–910). Munich: Piper.
Harinck, C. (1980). *De bekering.* [Conversion] Utrecht: Den Hertog.
Harré, R. (Ed.) (1986). *The social construction of emotions.* Oxford: Blackwell.
Harré, R. (1992). The second cognitive revolution. *American Behavioral Scientist,* 36, 3–7.
Harré, R. & Gillett, G. (1994). *The discursive mind.* London: Sage.
Harré, R. & Stearns, P. (1995). *Discursive psychology in practice.* London: Sage.
Haußig, H.-M. (1999). *Der Religionsbegriff in den Religionen: Studien zum Selbst-und Religionsverständnis in Hinduismus, Buddhismus, Judentum, Islam.* Berlin/Bodenheim: Philo.
Haute, P. van (1993). Zijn en zelf. [Being and self] In J. M. Broekman, H. Feldmann & P. van Haute, *Ziektebeelden* [Images of illness] (pp. 151–179). Leuven: Peeters.
Heelas, P. & Woodhead, L. (2005). *The spiritual revolution: Why religion is giving way to spirituality.* Oxford: Blackwell.
Heidegger, M. (1927). *Sein und Zeit.* Tübingen: Niemeyer.
Hellemans, S. (1985). Elementen van een algemene theorie van verzuiling [Elements of a general theory of pillarization]. *Tijdschrift voor Sociologie* [Journal for Sociology], *6*, 235–258.
Helminiak, D.A. (1996). *The human core of spirituality: Mind as psyche and spirit.* Albany, NY: State University of New York Press.
Hemminger, H. (2003). *Grundwissen Religionspsychologie: Ein Handbuch für Studium und Praxis.* [Basic knowledge of the psychology of religion: A handbook for study and practice] Freiburg: Herder.
Hendriks, J. (1971). *De emancipatie der gereformeerden: Sociologische bijdrage tot de verklaring van enige kenmerken van het huidige gereformeerde volksdeel* [The emancipation of the Calvinists: Sociological contribution to the explanation of several features of today's Calvinist population]. Alphen aan de Rijn: Samson.
Henning, C., Murken, S. & Nestler, E. (Eds.) (2003). *Einführung in die Religionspsychologie.* [Introduction to the psychology of religion] Paderborn etc.: Schöningh.
Heppe, H. (1879/1979). *Geschichte des Pietismus und der Mystik in der Reformirten Kirche, namentlich der Niederlande.* [History of pietism and mysticism in the Reformed Church, notably in The Netherlands] Kampen: Goudriaan.

Herdt, G. & Stephen, M. (Eds.) (1989). *The religious imagination in New Guinea*. New Brunswick/ London: Rutgers University Press.

Hermans, H.J.M. (1967). *Motivatie en prestatie*. [Motivation and performance] Amsterdam: Swets & Zeitlinger.

Hermans, H.J.M. (1970). A questionnaire measure of achievement motivation. *Journal of Applied Psychology*, 54, 353–363.

Hermans, H.J.M. (1971). *Prestatiemotief en faalangst in gezin en onderwijs, tevens handleiding bij de Prestatie Motivatie Test voor Kinderen (PMT-K)*. [Motivation of performance and fear of failure: Manual to the Performance Motivation Test for Children] Amsterdam: Swets & Zeitlinger.

Hermans, H.J.M. (1974). *Waardegebieden en hun ontwikkeling*. [Fields of positioning and their development] Amsterdam: Swets & Zeitlinger.

Hermans, H.J.M. (1981). *Persoonlijkheid en waardering*. Deel 1: *Organisatie en opbouw der waarderingen*. [Personality and positioning. Part 1: Organization and construction of positions] Lisse: Swets en Zeitlinger.

Hermans, H.J.M. (1999a). Dialogical thinking and self-innovation. *Culture & Psychology*, 5, 67–87.

Hermans, H.J.M. (1999b). The innovative potentials of agreement and disagreement in dialogical history. *Culture & Psychology*, 5, 491–498.

Hermans, H.J.M. (2001a). The dialogical self: Toward a theory of personal and cultural positioning. *Culture & Psychology*, 7, 243–281.

Hermans, H.J.M. (2001b). The construction of a personal position reportoire: Method and practice. *Culture & Psychology*, 7, 323–365.

Hermans, H.J.M. (2002). Special issue on the Dialogical Self. *Theory & Psychology*, 12 (2).

Hermans, H.J.M. (2003). Special issue on the Dialogical Self. *Journal of Constructivist Psychology*, 16 (2).

Hermans, H.J.M. & Dimaggio, G. (2007). Self, identity, and globalization in times of uncertainty: A dialogical analysis. *Review of General Psychology*, 11, 31–61.

Hermans, H.J.M. & Hermans-Jansen, E. (1995). *Self-narratives: The construction of meaning in psychotherapy*. New York: Guilford Press.

Hermans, H.J.M. & Hermans-Jansen, E. (2003). Dialogical processes and the development of the self. In J. Valsiner & K.L. Connolly (Eds.), *Handbook of developmental psychology* (pp. 534–559). London: Sage.

Hermans, H.J.M. & Kempen, H.J.G. (1993). *The dialogical self: Meaning as movement*. San Diego, CA: Academic Press.

Hermans, H.J.M. & Kempen, H.J.G. (1998). Moving cultures: The perilous problem of cultural dichotomies in a globalizing society. *American Psychologist*, 53, 1111–1120.

Hermans, H.J.M., Kempen, H.J.G. & Loon, R.J.P. van (1992). The dialogical self: Beyond individualism and rationalism. *American Psychologist*, 47, 23–33.

Hermans, H.J.M., Rijks, T.I. & Kempen, H.J.G. (1993). Imaginal dialogues of the self: Theory and method. *Journal of Personality*, 61 (2), 207–236.

Hermsen, E. (2006). *Faktor Religion: Geschichte der Kindheit vom Mittelalter bis zur Gegenwart*. [Factor religion: History of childhood from the Middle Ages to the present] Köln: Böhlau.

High, D.M. (1967). *Language, persons and beliefs: Studies in Wittgenstein's "Philosophical Investigations" and religious uses of language*. New York: Oxford University Press.

Hijweege, N.H. (2004). *Bekering in bevindelijk gereformeerde kring: Een psychologische studie*. [Conversion among bevindelijken: A psychological study] Kampen: Kok.

Hill, P.C. et al. (2000). Conceptualizing religion and spirituality: Points of commonality, points of departure. *Journal for the Theory of Social Behaviour*, 30, 51–77.

Hill, P.C. & Hood, R.W. (Eds.) (1999). *Measures of religiosity*. Birmingham: Religious Education Press.

Hill, P.C. & Pargament, K.I. (2003). Advances in the conceptualization and measurement of religion and spirituality: Implications for physical and mental health research. *American Psychologist*, 58, 64–74.

Hill, P.C., Pargament, K.I., Hood, R.W. Jr., McCullough, M.E., Sawyers, J.P., Larson, D.B. & Zinnbauer, B. (2000). Conceptualizing religiosity and spirituality: Points of commonality. *Journal for the Theory of Social Behavior*, *30*, 50–77.
Hof, W.J. op 't (1987). *Engelse piëtistische geschriften in het Nederlands, 1598–1622*. [English Pietist writings in Dutch] Rotterdam: Lindenberg.
Hoffman, D. (1982). *Der Wege zur Reife: Eine religionspsychologische Untersuchung der religiösen Entwicklung Gerhard Tersteegens*. [The way to maturity: A psychological investigation of Gerhard Tersteegen's religious development] Ph.D. dissertation, University of Lund, Sweden (*Studia Psychologiae Religionum Lundensia, 3*).
Holm, N.G. (1987). *Joels Gud: En religionspsykologisk studie*. [Joel's God: A study in psychology of religion] Åbo: Åbo Akademi.
Holm, N.G. (1990). *Einführung in die Religionspsychologie*. [Introduction to the psychology of religion] München/Basel: Reinhardt.
Holtrop, P.N. (1984). De Afscheiding: Breekpunt en kristallisatiepunt [The Schism: Breaking point and crystallization point]. In W. Bakker et al. (Eds.), *De Afscheiding van 1834 en haar geschiedenis* [The Schism of 1834 and its history] (pp. 62–99). Kampen: Kok.
Holzkamp, K. (1980). Zu Wundts Kritik an der experimentellen Erforschung des Denkens. [On Wundt's criticism on the experimental study of thought] In W. Meischner & A. Metge (Eds.), *Wilhelm Wundt: Progressives Erbe, Wissenschaftsentwicklung und Gegenwart* [Wilhelm Wundt: Progressive legacy, scientific development and modernity] (pp. 141–153). Leipzig: Karl-Marx-Universität.
Homans, P. (Ed.) (1968). *The dialogue between theology and psychology*. Chicago/London: University of Chicago Press.
Homans, P. (1970). *Theology after Freud: An interpretative inquiry*. New York.
Homans, P. (1979). *Jung in context: Modernity and the making of a psychology*. Chicago: University of Chicago Press.
Homans, P. (1989). *The ability to mourn: Disillusionment and the social origins of psychoanalysis*. Chicago: University of Chicago Press.
Hood, R.W. Jr. (1975). The construction and preliminary validation of a measure of reported mystical experience. *Journal for the Scientific Study of Religion*, *14*, 29–41.
Hood, R.W. (Ed.) (1995). *Handbook of religious experience*. Birmingham, AL.: Religious Education Press.
Hood, R.W. (1998). When the spirit maims and kills: Social psychological considerations of the history of serpent handling sects and the narrative of handlers. *International Journal for the Psychology of Religion*, *8*, 71–96.
Hood, R.W. Jr. (2000). American psychology of religion and The Journal for the Scientific Study of Religion. *Journal for the Scientific Study of Religion*, *39*, 531–543.
Hood, R.W. (2001). *Dimensions of mystical experiences: Empirical studies and psychological links*. Amsterdam/New York: Rodopi.
Hood, R.W. Jr. (2003a). The relationship between religion and spirituality. In A. L. Griel & D.G. Bromley (Eds.), *Defining religion: Investigating the boundaries between the sacred and the secular* (pp. 241–264). Oxford: JAI, Elsevier Science. (*Religion and the Social Order*, Vol. 10).
Hood, R.W. Jr. (2003b). Conceptual and empirical consequences of the unity thesis. In J.A. Belzen & A. Geels (Eds.), *Mysticism: A variety of psychological perspectives* (pp. 17–54). Amsterdam/New York: Rodopi.
Hood, R.W. & Belzen, J.A. (2005). Methods in the psychology of religion. In R. Paloutzian & C. Park (Eds.), *Handbook of the psychology of religion and spirituality* (pp. 62–79). Guilford, New York and London.
Hood, R.W., Spilka, B., Hunsberger, B., & Gorsuch, R. (1996). *The psychology of religion: An empirical approach*. (second edition) New York: Guilford.
Hood, R.W. Jr., Hill, P.C. & Spilka, B. (2009). *The psychology of religion: An empirical approach*. (4th ed.) New York: Guilford.
Hood, R.W. & Morris, R.J. (1985). Conceptualization of quest: A critical rejoinder to Batson. *Review of Religious Research*, *26*, 391–397.

Hood, R.W. Jr. & Williamson, W.P. (2008). *Them that believe: The power and meaning of the Christian serpent handling tradition*. Berkely, CA: University of California Press.

Hoorn, W. van & Verhage, T. (1980). Wilhelm Wundt's conception of the multiple foundations of scientific psychology. In W. Meischner & A. Metge (Eds.), *Wilhelm Wundt: Progressives Erbe, Wissenschaftsentwicklung und Gegenwart* [Wilhelm Wundt: Progressive legacy, scientific development and modernity] (pp. 107–120). Leipzig: Karl-Marx-Universität.

Howard, G.S. (1991). Culture tales: A narrative approach to thinking, cross-cultural psychology and psychotherapy. *American Psychologist, 46*, 187–197.

Hudson, W.D. (1968). *Ludwig Wittgenstein: The bearing of this philosophy upon religious belief*. London: Lutterworth.

Huls, B. (1986). Historische veranderingen in geheugenprocessen bij kinderen. [Historical changes in childrens' memory processes] In H. F. M. Peeters & F. J. Mönks (Eds.), *De menselijke levensloop in historisch perspectief* [The human course of life in historical perspective] (pp. 139–153). Assen/Maastricht: Van Gorcum.

Hume, H. (1997). Psychological concepts, their products and consumers. *Culture & Psychology, 3*, 115–136.

Hunt, R.A. (1972). Mythological-symbolic religious commitment: The LAM-scale. *Journal for the Scientific Study of Religion, 11*, 42–52.

Hutch, R.A. (1991). Mortal body, studying lives: Restoring Eros to the psychology of religion. *International Journal for the Psychology of Religion, 1*, 193–210.

Hutschemaekers, G.J.M. (1990). *Neurosen in Nederland: Vijfentachtig jaar psychische en maatschappelijk onbehagen*. [Neuroses in The Netherlands: 85 years of psychic and societal discomfort] Nijmegen: SUN.

Hutsebaut, D. (1986). [Review of J.A. Belzen & J.M. van der Lans (1986), *Current issues in the psychology of religion*]. *Psychologica Belgica, 26*, 268–269.

Huyse, L. (1984). Pillarization reconsidered. *Acta Politica, 19*, 145–158.

Ingleby, D. & Nossent, S. (1986). Cognitieve ontwikkeling en historische psychologie. [Cognitive development and historical psychology] In H. F. M. Peeters & F. J. Mönks (Eds.), *De menselijke levensloop in historisch perspectief* [The human course of life in historical perspective] (pp. 122–138). Assen/Maastricht: Van Gorcum.

Irwin, G.A., Eijk, C. van der, Hosteyn, J. M. van & Niemöller, B. (1987). Verzuiling, issues, kandidaten en ideologie in de verkiezingen van 1986 [Pillarization, issues, candidates and ideologies in the elections of 1986]. *Acta Politica, 22*, 129–179.

Iyengar, S.S & Lepper, M.R. (1999). Rethinking the value of choice: A cultural perspective on intrinsic motivation. *Journal of Personality & Social Psychology, 76* (3), 349–366.

Jacobs, J.L. & Capps, D. (Eds.) (1997). *Religion, society and psychoanalysis: Readings in contemporary theory*. Boulder: Westview Press.

Jahoda, G. (1993). *Crossroads between culture and mind: Continuities and change in theories of human nature*. Cambridge, MA: Harvard University Press.

Jahoda, G. (2007). *A history of social psychology: From the eighteenth century Enlightenment to the Second World War*. Cambridge/New York: Cambridge University Press.

James, W. (1890). *The principles of psychology*. London: MacMillan.

James, W. (1902/1907). *Die religiöse Erfahrung in ihrer Mannigfaltigkeit: Materialien und Studien zu einer Psychologie und Pathologie des religiösen Lebens*. [The varieties of religious experience] Leipzig: Hinrich.

James, W. (1902/1958). *The varieties of religious experience: A study in human nature*. New York: Mentor Books.

James, W. (1902/1982). *The varieties of religious experience: A study in human nature*. Hammondsworth: Penguin.

James, W. (1902/2002). *The varieties of religious experience: A study in human nature*. London/New York: Routledge.

Janse, C.S.L. (1985). *Bewaar het pand: De spanning tussen assimilatie en persistentie bij de emancipatie van de bevindelijk gereformeerden*. [Guard what has been entrusted to you: The tension between assimilation and persistence in the case of the emancipation of the 'bevindelijke' Reformed] Houten: Den Hertog.

Jaspers, K. (1917/1997). *General psychopathology.* (transl. J. Hoenig) Baltimore: John Hopkins University Press.
Jaspers, K. (1922). *Psychologie der Weltanschauungen.* Berlin: Springer.
Johnson, E.L. & Jones, S.L. (Eds.) (2000). *Psychology & Christianity.* Downers Grove, IL: InterVarsity Press.
Johnson, M. (1987). *The body in the mind: The bodily basis of meaning, imagination and reason.* Chicago, Ill.: University of Chicago Press.
Jones, J.W. (1991). *Contemporary psychoanalysis and religion: Transference and transcendence.* New Haven: Yale University Press.
Jones, J.W. (1996). *Religion and psychology in transition: Psychoanalysis, feminism and theology.* New Haven/London: Yale University Press.
Jones, J.W. (2008). *Blood that cries out from the earth: The psychology of religious terrorism.* Oxford/New York: Oxford University Press.
Jong, O.J. de, Spijker, W. van 't & Florijn, H. (1992). *Het eigene van de Nadere Reformatie.* [The characteristic features of the Further Reformation] Houten: Den Hertog.
Jonte-Pace, D. (2001). *Speaking the unspeakable: Religion, misogyny and the uncanny mother in Freud's cultural texts.* Berkeley: University of California Press.
Jonte-Pace, D. (2003). *Teaching Freud.* New York: Oxford University Press/American Academy of Religion.
Jonte-Pace, D. & Parsons, W.B. (Eds.) (2001). *Religion and psychology: Mapping the terrain. Contemporary dialogues, future prospects.* London/New York: Routledge.
Josselson, R. & Lieblich A. (Eds.) (1993). *The narrative study of lives.* Vol. 1. London: Sage.
Judd, C. (1926). *The psychology of social institutions.* New York: Macmillan.
Jung, C.G. (1938/1969²). Psychology and religion. In *The collected works of C.G. Jung,* vol. 11 (eds. H. Read, M. Fordham & G. Adler; pp. 3–105). Princeton, NJ: Princeton University Press.
Jung, C.G. (1967/2003). *The Spirit in man, art and literature.* London/New York: Routledge.
Jüttemann, G. & Thomae, H. (1987). *Biographie und Psychologie.* [Biography and psychology] Berlin: Springer.
Kaam, B. van. (1964). *Parade der mannenbroeders* [Parade of the brothers]. Wageningen: Zomer & Keuning.
Kääriäinen, K. (1989). *Discussion on scientific atheism as a soviet science, 1960–1985.* Helsinki: Suomalainen Tiedeakatemia.
Kaiser, P. (2007). *Religion in der Psychiatrie: Eine (un)bewußte Verdrängung?* Göttingen: Vandenhoeck & Ruprecht.
Kakar, S. (1982). *Shamans, mystics and doctors: A psychological inquiry into India and its healing traditions.* Boston: Boston Press.
Kakar, S. (1991). *The analyst and the mystic: Psychoanalytic reflections on religion and mysticism.* Chicago: University of Chicago Press.
Källstad, T. (1974). *John Wesley and the bible: A psychological study.* Uppsala: Acta Universitatis Upsaliensis.
Källstad, T. (1978). *Psychological studies on religious man.* Stockholm: Almqvist & Wiksell.
Källstad, T. (1987). *Levande mystik: En psykologisk undersökning av Ruth Dahlens religiösa upplevelser.* [Living mysticism: a psychological investigation of Ruth Dahlen's religious development] Delsbo: Åsak.
Kalweit, P. (1908). Das religiöse apriori. [The religious a priori] *Theologische Studien und Kritiken,* [Theological Studies and Reviews] *81,* 139–156.
Kamper, D. (Ed.) (1977). *Über die Wünsche: Ein Versuch zur Archäologie der Subjektivität.* [On the desires: An essay in the archeology of subjectivity] München/Wien: Hanser.
Kant, I. (1787/1956). *Kritik der reinen Vernunft.* [Critique of pure reason] (2nd edition) Wiesbaden: Casel.
Kehoe, N.C. & Gutheil, Th.G. (1993). Ministry or therapy: The role of transference and countertransference in a religious therapist. In M. L. Randour (Ed.), *Exploring sacred landscapes: Religious and spiritual experiences in psychotherapy.* New York: Columbia University Press.

Kernberg, P.F. & Richards, A.K. (1988). Siblings of preadolescents: Their role in the development. *Psychoanalytic Inquiry*, *8*, 51–65.
Kerr, F. (1986). *Theology after Wittgenstein*. Oxford: Blackwell.
Ketterij, C. van de (1972). *De weg in woorden: Een systematische beschrijving van piëtistisch woordgebruik na 1900*. [The way in words: A systematic account of pietistic word usage after 1900] Assen: Van Gorcum.
King, J.O. (1983). *The iron of melancholy: Structures of spiritual conversion in America from the Puritan conscience to Victorian neurosis*. Middletown, CN: Wesleyan University Press.
Kippenberg, H. (2001). Was sucht die Religionswissenschaft unter den Kulturwissenschaften? [The place of the study of religion in the study of culture] In H. Appelsmeyer & E. Billman-Mahecha (Eds.), *Kulturwissenschaft: Felder einer prozeßorientierten wissenschaftlichen Praxis* (pp. 240–275). [The study of culture: Fields of a process orientated academic practice] Weilerswist: Velbrück.
Kirkpatrick, L.A. (2005). *Attachment, evolution and the psychology of religion*. New York: Guilford.
Kitayama, S. & Cohen, D. (Eds.) (2007). *Handbook of cultural psychology*. New York: Guilford.
Kitayama, S., Duffy, S. & Uchida, Y. (2007). Self as cultural mode of being. In S. Kitayama & D. Cohen (Eds.), *Handbook of cultural psychology* (pp. 136–174). New York: Guilford.
Klessmann, M. (2004). *Pastoralpsychologie: Ein Lehrbuch*. [Pastoral psychology: A textbook] Neukirchen: Neukirchener Verlag.
Klünker, W.U. (1985). *Psychologische Analyse und Theologische Wahrheit: Die Religionspsychologische Methode Georg Wobbermins*. [Psychological analysis and theological truth: Georg Wobbermin's psychological-religious method] Göttingen: Vandenhoeck & Ruprecht.
Knorr Cetina, K. (1999). *Epistemic cultures: How the sciences make knowledge*. Cambridge, MA: Harvard University Press.
Knorr Cetina, K. & Grathoff, R. (1988). Was ist und was soll kultursoziologische Forschung? [Socio-cultural investigation: What it is and what it should be] *Soziale Welt*, *Sonderband* [Social World, Special edition] *6*, 21–36.
Koch, S. & Leary, D.E. (Eds.) (1985). *A century of psychology as science*. New York: McGraw Hill.
Koenig, H.G. (Ed.) (1998). *Handbook of religion and mental health*. San Diego: Academic Press.
Kohut, H. (1966/1985). Forms and transformations of narcissism. In *Self psychology and the humanities: Reflections on a new psychoanalytic approach* (pp. 97–123). New York: Norton.
Kohut, H. (1971). *The analysis of the self: A systematic approach to the psychoanalytic treatment of narcissistic personality disorders*. New York: International Universities Press.
Kohut, H. (1977). *The restoration of the self*. New York: International Universities Press.
Kohut, H. (1979). The two analyses of Mr. Z. *International Journal of Psycho-Analysis*, *60*, 3–27.
Kohut, H. (1985). *Self psychology and the humanities*. New York: Norton.
Kohut, H. & Wolf, E. (1978). The disorders of the self and their treatment: An outline. *International Journal of Psycho-Analysis*, *59*, 413–425.
Kojève, A. (1947). *Introduction à la lecture de Hegel: Leçons sur la phénoménologie de l'esprit*. Paris: Gallimard.
Koppenjan, J. (1986). Verzuiling en interconfessionaliteit in Nederlands-Limburg 1900–1920 [Pillarization and interconfessionality in Dutch Limburg 1900–1920]. *Tijdschrift voor Sociale Geschiedenis* [Journal for Social History], *12*, 109–134.
Koppenjan, J. (1987). De Limburgse School: Interconfessionalisme en stadsorganisatie [The Limburg School: Interconfessionalism and urban organisation]. *Tijdschrift voor Sociale Geschiedenis* [Journal for Social History], *13*, 87–93.
Kotre, J. (1995). *White gloves: How we create ourselves through memory*. New York: Free Press.
Kripall, J.J. (1995). *Kali's child: The mystical and the erotic in the life and teaching of Ramakrishna*. Chicago: University of Chicago Press.
Kripall, J. (2008). From paradise to paradox: The psychospiritual journey of John Heider. In J. A. Belzen & A. Geels (Eds.), *Autobiography and the psychological study of religious lives*. Amsterdam/New York: Rodopi (in press).

Kruijt, J.P. (1943). Mentaliteitsverschillen in ons land in verband met godsdienstige verschillen [Differences in mentality in our country and their relationship to religious differences]. *Mensch en Maatschappij* [Man and Society], *19*, 1–28; 65–83.
Kruijt, J.P. (1957). Levensbeschouwing en groepssolidariteit in Nederland [Philosophy of life and group solidarity in the Netherlands]. *Sociologisch Jaarboek* [Sociological Yearbook], *2*, 29–65.
Kruijt, J.P. et al. (1959). *Verzuiling* [Pillarization]. Zaandijk: Heijnis.
Kruijt, J.P. & Goddijn, W. (1961). Verzuiling en ontzuiling als sociologisch proces [Pillarization and depillarization as a sociological process]. In A. N. J. den Hollander et al. (Eds.), *Drift en koers: Een halve eeuw sociale verandering in Nederland* [Current and course: A half century of social change in the Netherlands] (pp. 227–263). Assen: Van Gorcum.
Kuhn, T.S. (1962). *The structure of scientific revolutions*. Chicago: University of Chicago Press.
Kusch, M. (1999). *Psychological knowledge: A social history and philosophy*. London/New York: Routledge.
Laan, M.C. van der (1994). Kohuts zelfpsychologie en de problematiek van tweede-generatie-oorlogsgetroffenen [Kohut's self psychology and the problem of second generation war victims]. *Tijdschrift voor Psychotherapie* [Journal for Psychotherapy], *20* (5), 279–292.
Laarse, R. van der (1989). *Bevoogding en bevinding: Heren en kerkvolk in een Hollandse provinciestad, Woerden 1780–1930* [Paternalism and the experience of God: Gentlemen and common churchgoers in the Dutch provincial town of Woerden, 1780–1930]. (Doctoral dissertation, University of Amsterdam, The Netherlands.)
Lacan, J. (1949/1977). The mirror stage as formative of the function of the I. In *Écrits: A selection* (pp. 1–7). London: Tavistock.
Lacan, J. (1953). Some reflections on the ego. *International Journal for Psycho-Analysis*, *34*, 11–17.
Lacan, J. (1966). *Écrits*. [Writings] Paris: Seuil.
Lakatos, I. (1978). *The methodology of scientific research programmes*. Cambridge: Cambridge University Press.
Lakoff, G. & Johnson, M. (1980). *Metaphors we live by*. Chicago: University of Chicago Press.
Lamiell, J.T. (2003). Rethinking the role of quantitative methods in psychology. In J. A. Smith, R. Harré & L. van Langenhove (Eds.), *Rethinking methods in psychology* (pp. 143–161). London: Sage.
Lans, J.M van der (1986). Introduction to the plenary debate: Two opposed viewpoints concerning the object of the psychology of religion. In J.A. Belzen & J.M. van der Lans, (Eds.), *Current issues in the psychology of religion* (pp. 76–81). Amsterdam: Rodopi.
Lans, J.M. van der (1991a). Interpretation of religious language and cognitive style: A pilot study with the LAM-scale. In H.N. Malony (Ed.), *Psychology of religion: Personalities, problems, possibilities* (pp. 295–312). Grand Rapids, MI: Baker.
Lans, J.M. van der (1991b). What is psychology of religion about? Some considerations concerning its subject matter. In H.N. Malony (Ed.), *Psychology of religion: Personalities, problems, possibilities* (pp. 313–323). Grand Rapids, MI: Baker.
Laucken, U. (1998). *Sozialpsychologie: Geschichte, Hauptströmungen, Tendenzen*. [Social psychology: History, principal trends, tendencies] Oldenburg: BIS.
Lave, J., Murtaugh, M. & De la Rocha, O. (1984). The dialectic of arithmetic in grocery shopping. In B. Rogoff & J. Lave (Eds.), *Everyday cognition: Its development in social context* (pp. 67–94). Cambridge: Harvard University Press.
Leary, D.E. (1990). *Metaphors in the history of psychology*. New York: Cambridge University Press.
Le Bon, G. (1903). *The crowd*. London: Fisher Unwin.
Lee, F., Hallanhan, M. & Herzog, T. (1996). Explaining real life events: How culture and domain shape attributions. *Personality and Social Psychology Bulletin*, *22*, 732–741.
Lee, R.R. & Martin, W. (1991). *Psychotherapy after Kohut: A textbook of self psychology*. Hillsdale, NJ: The Analytic Press.
Leenders, J.M.M. (1992). *Benauwde verdraagzaamheid, hachelijk fatsoen: Families, standen en kerken te Hoorn in het midden van de negentiende eeuw* [Anxious tolerance, precarious respectability: Families, social position and churches in Hoorn in the mid-nineteenth century]. The Hague: Stichting Hollandse Historische Reeks.

Leezenberg, M. & Vries, G. de (2001). *Wetenschapsfilosofie voor geesteswetenschappen.* [Philosophy of science for the humanities] Amsterdam: Amsterdam University Press.

Leontiev, A. (1978). *Activity, consciousness and personality.* Englewoods Cliffs, NJ: Prentice-Hall.

Leontiev, A. (1981). *Problems of the development of the mind.* Moscow: Progress.

Leuba, J. (1896). *Studies in psychology of religious phenomena: The religious motive, conversion, facts and doctrines.* Worcester, MA: Orpha.

Leupin, A. (2004). *Lacan today: Psychoanalysis, science, religion.* New York: Other.

Levin, H. (1970). The quixotic principle: Cervantes and other novelists. In M.W. Bloomfield (Ed.), *The interpretation of narrative: Theory and practice* (pp. 45–66). Cambridge, MA: Harvard University Press.

Levine, M. (2000). *The positive psychology of Buddhism and yoga: Paths to a mature happiness with a special application to handling anger.* Mahwah, NJ/London: Erlbaum.

Lewin, K. (1948). *Resolving social conflicts.* New York: Harper.

Lieburg, F.A. van (1991). *Levens van vromen: Gereformeerd piëtisme in de achttiende eeuw.* [The lives of the devout: Calvinist pietism in the eighteenth century] Kampen: De Groot Goudriaan.

Lijphart, A. (1975). *The politics of accommodation: Pluralism and democracy in the Netherlands.* Berkeley: University of California Press.

Lijphart, A. (1976). Verzuiling [Pillarization]. In A. Hoogerwerf (Ed.), *Verkenningen in de politiek, Deel 2* [Exploring politics, Part 2]. Alphen aan den Rijn: Samson.

Lijphart, A. (1992). Verzuiling en pacificatie als empirische en normatieve modellen in vergelijkend perspectief [Pillarization and pacification as empirical and normative models in comparative perspective]. *Acta Politica, 27*, 323–332.

Lillard, A. (1998). Ethnopsychologies: Cultural variations in theories of mind. *Psychological Bulletin, 123*, 1–32.

Lindeboom, L. (1887). *De beteekenis van het christelijk geloof voor de geneeskundige wetenschap, in het bijzonder voor de psychiatrie* [The significance of Christian faith for the healing sciences, especially psychiatry]. Heusden: Gezelle Meerburg.

Loewenthal, K.M. (1995). *Mental health and religion.* London: Chapman & Hall.

Loewenthal, K.M. (2000). *The psychology of religion: A short introduction.* Oxford: Oneworld.

Loewenthal, K. (2007). *Religion, culture and mental health.* Cambridge/New York: Cambridge University Press.

Lonner, W.J. & Hayes, S. A. (2007). *Discovering cultural psychology: A profile and selective readings of Ernest E. Boesch.* Charlotte, NC: Information Age Publishing.

Lorenzer, A. (1977). *Sprachspiel und Interaktionsformen: Vorträge und Aufsätze zu Psychoanalyse, Sprache und Praxis.* [Language game and forms of interaction: lectures and papers on psychoanalysis, language and praxis] Frankfurt am Main: Suhrkamp.

Lowe, D.M. (1982). *History of bourgeois perception.* Chicago: University of Chicago Press.

Luria, A.R. (1971). Towards the problem of the historical nature of psychological processes. *International Journal of Psychology, 6*, 259–272.

Luria, A.R. (1976). *Cognitive development: Its cultural and social foundations.* Cambridge, MA: Harvard University Press.

Luria, A.R. (1979). *The making of a mind.* Cambridge, MA: Harvard University Press.

Luria, A.R. (1981). *Language and cognition.* Washington/New York: Winston/Wiley.

Maassen, J. (1987). Interconfessionalisme [Interconfessionalism]. *Tijdschrift voor Sociale Geschiedenis* [Journal for Social History], *13*, 74–86.

Malony, H.N. (1997). A proposal for a psychology of religious expression. In J.A. Belzen & O. Wikström (Eds.), *Taking a step back: Assessments of the psychology of religion.* Stockholm/Uppsala: Almqvist & Wiksell Intern./Acta Universitatis Upsaliensis.

Malony, H.N. & Lovekin, A. (1985), *Glossolalia: Social and psychological perspectives.* New York: Oxford University Press.

Mancuso, J.C. & Sarbin, T.R. (1983). The self-narrative in the enactment of roles. In T.R. Sarbin & K.E. Scheibe (Eds.), *Studies in social identity* (pp. 233–253). New York: Praeger.

Marcus, P. (2003). *Ancient religious wisdom, spirituality, and psychoanalysis*. Westport, CT/London: Praeger.
Markus, H. R., Kitayama, S. & Heiman, R. J. (1996). Culture and "basic" psychological principles. In E.T. Higgins & A.W. Kruglanski (Eds.), *Social psychology* (pp. 857–913). New York/London: Guilford Press.
Marler, P.L. & Hadaway, C.K. (2002). "Being Religious" or "Being Spiritual" in America: A Zero-Sum Proposition? *Journal for the Scientific Study of Religion*, 41, 289–300.
Matsumoto, D. (1994a). *Cultural influences on research methods and statistics*. Pacific Grove, CA: Brooks/Cole.
Matsumoto, D. (1994b). *People: Psychology from a cultural perspective*. Pacific Grove, CA: Brooks/Cole.
Matsumoto, D. (1996). *Culture and psychology*. Pacific Grove, CA: Brooks/Cole.
Mauss, M. (1938/1985). A category of the human mind: The notion of person; the notion of self (trans. W.D. Halls). In M. Carrithers, S. Collins & S. Lukes (Eds.), *The category of the person: Anthropology, philosophy, history* (pp. 1–25). Cambridge: Cambridge University Press.
McAdams, D.P. (1993). *The stories we live by: Personal myths and the making of the self*. New York: Morrow.
McAdams, D.P. (1994a). Can personality change? Levels of stability and growth in personality across the lifespan. In T.F. Heatherton & J.L. Weinberger (Eds.), *Can personality change?* (pp. 299–313). Washington, DC: American Psychological Association.
McAdams, D.P. (1994b). *The person: An introduction to personality psychology*. (2nd ed.) Fort Worth, TX: Harcourt Brace.
McAdams, D.P. (1999). Personal narratives and the life story. In L.A. Pervin & O. John (Eds.), *Handbook of personality: Theory and research* (2nd ed.; pp. 478–500). New York: Guilford Press.
McAdams, D.P. (2005). What psychobiographers might learn from personality psychology. In: William Todd Schultz (Ed.), *Handbook of psychobiography* (pp. 64–73). New York: Oxford University Press.
McAdams, D.P. (2006). *The redemptive self: Stories Americans live by*. New York: Oxford University Press.
McCutcheon, R.T. (Ed.) (1999). *The insider/outsider problem in the study of religion*. London/New York: Cassell.
McCutcheon, R.T. (2003). *Manufacturing religion: The discourse on sui generis religion and the politics of nostalgia*. New York: Oxford University Press.
McDargh, J. (1983). *Psychoanalytic object relations theory and the study of religion: On faith and the imaging of God*. Lanham, Md.: University Press of America.
McDargh, J. (1993). Rebuilding fences and opening gates: Vergote on the psychology of religion. *The International Journal for the Psychology of Religion*, 3 (2), 87–93.
McDougall, W. (1909). *An introduction to social psychology*. (2nd edition) Boston: Luce.
McGuire, M.B. (1990). Religion and the body: Rematerializing the human body in the social sciences of religion. *Journal for the Scientific Study of Religion*, 29, 283–296.
McKim, D.K. (1992). The mainline Protestant understanding of conversion. In H. N. Malony & S. Southard (Eds.), *Handbook of religious conversion* (pp. 123–136). Birmingham, Al.: Religious Education Press.
Mead, G.H. (1934). *Mind, self, and society*. Chicago: University of Chicago Press.
Meissner, W.W. (1984). *Psychoanalysis and religious experience*. New Haven: Yale University Press.
Meissner, W.W. (1992). *Ignatius of Loyola: The psychology of a saint*. New Haven: Yale University Press.
Meissner, W.W. (1995). *Thy kingdom come: Psychoanalytic perspectives on the Messiah and the millennium*. Kansas City: Sheed & Ward.
Meissner, W.W. (1996). The pathology of beliefs and the beliefs of pathology. In E. Shanfransky (Ed.), *Religion and the clinical practice of psychology* (pp. 241–268). Washington, DC: American Psychological Association.
Meissner, W.W. (1997). *Vincent's religion: The search for meaning*. New York: Lang.

Merleau-Ponty, M. (1945/1962). *Phenomenology of perception.* London: Routledge.
Merwe, W.L. & Voestermans, P. P. (1995). Wittgenstein's legacy and the challenge to psychology. *Theory & Psychology, 5* (1), 27–48.
Messer, S.B., Sass L.A. & Woolfolk, R.L. (Eds.) (1988). *Hermeneutics and psychological theory.* Brunswick, NJ: Rutgers University Press.
Miert, J. van (1994). *Wars van clubgeest en partijzucht: Liberalen, natie en verzuiling, Tiel en Winschoten 1850–1920* [Aversion to the club mentality and party-mindedness: Liberals, nation and pillarization in Tiel and Winschoten, 1850–1920]. Amsterdam: Amsterdam University Press.
Miller, J.G. (1999). Cultural psychology: Implications for basic psychological theory. *Psychological Science, 10*, 85–91.
Miller, J.G. (2001). The cultural grounding of social psychological theory. In A. Tesser & N. Schwarz (Eds.), *Blackwell handbook of social psychology.* Vol. 1: *Intrapersonal processes* (pp. 22–43). Oxford: Blackwell.
Miller, J.G. (2002). Culture and the self: Implications for psychological theory. In N.J. Smelser & P.B. Baltes (Eds.), *International encyclopedia of the social and behavioral sciences.* England: Elsevier Science.
Miller, J.G. & Bersoff, D.M. (1994). Cultural influences on the moral status of reciprocity and the discounting of endogenous motivation. *Personality and Social Psychology Bulletin, 20*, 592–602.
Miller, W.R. (Ed.) (2002). *Integrating spirituality into treatment: resources for practitioners.* Washington: American Psychological Association.
Miller, W.R. & Delaney, H.D. (Eds.) (2005). *Judeo-Christian perspectives on psychology: Human nature, motivation and change.* Washington: American Psychological Association.
Miller, W.R. & Thoresen, C.E. (2003). Spirituality, religion, and health: An emerging research field. *American Psychologist, 58*, 24–35.
Misiak, H. & Sexton, V. S. (1973). *Phenomenological, existential and humanistic psychologies: A historical essay,* New York/London: Grune & Stratton.
Misra, G. & Gergen, K.J. (1993). On the place of culture in psychological science. *International Journal of Psychology, 28* (2), 225–243.
Moghaddam, F.M., Taylor, D.M. & Wright, S.C. (1993). *Social psychology in cross-cultural perspective.* New York: Freeman.
Mönnich, C.W. (1962). De kerken der Hervorming sinds 1813 [The churches of the Reformation since 1813]. In A.G. Weiler et al. (Eds.), *Geschiedenis van de Kerk in Nederland* [History of the church in the Netherlands]. Utrecht/Antwerpen: Spectrum.
Mooij, A.W.M. & Widdershoven, G.A.M. (1992). *Hermeneutiek en psychologie: Interpretatie in theorievorming, onderzoek en psychotherapie.* [Hermeneutics and psychology: Interpretation in theorizing, research and psychotherapy] Meppel: Boom.
Morris, M.W., Nisbett, R.E. & Peng, K. (1995). Causal understanding across domains and cultures. In D. Sperber, D. Premack & A.J. Premack (Eds.), *Causal cognition: A multidisciplinary debate* (pp. 577–612). Oxford: Oxford University Press.
Moscovici, S. (1998). Social consciousness and its history. *Culture & Psychology, 4*, 411–429.
Moss, D.M. (1977). Narzißmus, Empathie und die Fragmentierung des Selbst: Ein Gespräch mit Heinz Kohut. [Narcism, empathy and the fragmentation of the self: An interview with Heinz Kohut] *Wege zum Menschen,* [Roads to man] *29*, 49–68.
Much, N. (1995). Cultural psychology. In J.A. Smith, R. Harré & L. van Langenhove (Eds.), *Rethinking psychology* (pp. 97–121). London: Sage.
Much, N.C. & Mahapatra (1995). Constructing divinity. In R. Harré & P. Stearns (Eds.), *Discursive psychology in practice* (pp. 55–86). London: Sage.
Murisier, E. (1892). *Maine de Biran: Esquisse d'une psychologie religieuse.* [Maine of Biran: Sketch of a psychology of religion] Paris: Jouve.
Murisier, E. (1901). *Les maladies du sentiment religieux.* [The diseases of the religious sentiment] Paris: Alcan.
Nase, E. & Scharfenberg, J. (Eds.) (1977). *Psychoanalyse und Religion.* [Psychoanalysis and religion] Darmstadt: Wissenschaftliche Buchgesellschaft.

Neeleman, J. & Persand, R. (1995). Why do psychiatrists neglect religion? *British Journal of Medical Psychology*, 68, 169–178.
Neisser, U. (1976). *Cognition and reality*. San Francisco: Freeman.
Newberg, N., d'Aquili, E.G. & Rause, V. (2001). *Why God won't go away: Brain science and the biology of belief*. New York : Ballantine Books.
Nielsen, K. (1982). *Introduction to the philosophy of religion*. London: Macmillan.
Nørager, T. (1996). Metapsychology and discourse: A note on some neglected issues in the psychology of religion. *International Journal for the Psychology of Religion*, 6, 139–149.
Obeyesekere, G. (1981). *Medusa's hair*. Chicago: University of Chicago Press.
Obeyesekere, G. (1985). Depression, Buddhism, and the work of culture in Sri Lanka. In A. Kleinman & B. Good (Eds.), *Culture and depression: Studies in the anthropology and cross-cultural psychiatry of affect and disorder* (pp. 134–152). Berkeley: University of California Press.
O'Connor, K.V. (1997). Reconsidering the psychology of religion: Hermeneutical approaches in the contexts of research and debate. In J.A. Belzen (Ed.), *Hermeneutical approaches in psychology of religion* (pp. 85–108). Amsterdam: Rodopi.
O'Connor, K.V. (1998). Religion and mental health: A review of Antoine Vergote's approach in "Guilt and desire." *International Journal for the Psychology of Religion*, 8, 125–148.
Oelze, B. (1991). *Wilhelm Wundt: Die Konzeption der Völkerpsychologie*. [Wilhelm Wundt: Conception of a folk psychology] Münster: Waxmann.
Olbrich, E. (1986). De levensloop in de moderne tijd: historische perspectieven en levensloopsychologie. [The course of life in modern time: historical perspectives and psychology of the course of life] In H. F. M. Peeters & F. J. Mönks (Eds.), *De menselijke levensloop in historisch perspectief* [The human course of life in historical perspective] (pp. 84–100). Assen/Maastricht: Van Gorcum.
Olson, R.P. (Ed.) (2002). *Religious theories of personality and psychotherapy: East meets west*. New York/London/Oxford: Haworth.
Os, M. van, & Wieringa, W.J. (Eds.) (1980). *Wetenschap en rekenschap, 1880–1980: Een eeuw wetenschapsbeoefening aan de Vrije Universiteit* [Science and accountability, 1880–1980: A century of scientific inquiry at the Free University]. Kampen: Kok.
Otto, R. (1917/1976). *The idea of the Holy: An inquiry into the non-rational factor in the idea of the divine and its relation to the rational*. Oxford: Oxford University Press.
Ouwerkerk, C. van (1986). *In afwezigheid van God: Voorstudies tot een psychologie van het geloof*. [In absence of God: Preliminary studies to a psychology of belief] Den Haag: Boekencentrum.
Palmer, M. (1997). *Freud and Jung on religion*. New York/London: Routledge.
Paloutzian, R.F. (1996). *Invitation to the psychology of religion*. (2nd ed.) Boston/London: Allyn & Bacon.
Paloutzian, R.F. & Kirkpatrick, L. E. (Eds.) (1995). Religious influences on personal and societal well-being. *Journal of Social Issues*, 51, no.2 (special issue).
Paloutzian, R.F. & Park, C.L. (Eds.) (2005). *The handbook of the psychology of religion and spirituality*. New York/London: Guilford.
Paranjpe, A. C. (1998). *Self and identity in modern psychology and Indian thought*. New York/London: Plenum Press.
Pargament, K.I. (1990). God help me: Toward a theoretical framework of coping for the psychology of religion. *Research in the Social Scientific Study of Religion*, 2, 195–224.
Pargament, K.I. (1997). *The psychology of religion and coping: Theory, research, practice*. New York/London: Guilford Press.
Pargament, K.J. (1999). The psychology of religion *and* spirituality? Yes and no. *International Journal for the Psychology of Religion*, 9, 3–16.
Pargament, K.I. (2007). *Spiritually integrated psychotherapy: Understanding and addressing the sacred*. New York/London: Guilford Press.
Pargament, K.I., Maton, K.I. & Hess, R.E. (Eds.) (1992). *Religion and prevention in mental health: Research, vision, and action*. New York: Haworth Press.
Parsons, W.B. (1999). *The enigma of the oceanic feeling: Revisioning the psychoanalytic theory of mysticism*. New York/Oxford: Oxford University Press.

Parsons, W.B., D. Jonte-Pace & S.E. Henking (Eds.) (2008). *Mourning religion*. Charlottesville: University of Virginia Press.

Patton, M.Q. (2002). *Qualitative research and evaluation methods*. (3rd ed.) Thousand Oaks, CA: Sage.

Paul, H. (1910). Über Völkerpsychologie. [On folk psychology] *Süddeutsche Monatshefte*, [South-German Monthly] 7 (2), 363–373.

Peeters, H.F.M. (1974). *Mensen veranderen: Een historisch-psychologische verhandeling*. [People change: A historical-psychological essay] Meppel: Boom.

Peeters, H.F.M. (1993). Mentaliteitsgeschiedenis en psychologie. [History of mentalities and psychology] *Nederlands Tijdschrift voor de Psychologie*, [Dutch Journal for Psychology] 48 (5), 195–204.

Peeters, H.F.M. (1994). *Hoe veranderlijk is de mens? Een inleiding in de historische psychologie* [How changeable is the human being? An introduction to historical psychology]. Nijmegen: SUN.

Pepper, S. (1942). *World hypotheses*. Berkeley, CA: University of California Press.

Pfister, O. (1910). *Die Frömmigkeit des Grafen Ludwig von Zinzendorf: Ein psychoanalytischer Beitrag zur Kenntnis der religiösen Sublimierungsprozesse und zur Erklärung des Pietismus*. [Count Ludwig von Zinzendorf's piety: A psychoanalytic contribution to the knowledge of the religious sublimation and to the explanation of pietism] Leipzig: Deuticke.

Pfister, O. (1926). *Die Legende Sundar Singhs: Eine auf Enthüllungen protestantischer Augenzeugen in Indien gegründete religionspsychologische Untersuchung*. [The legend of Sundar Singh: An investigation in psychology of religion based on disclosures by protestant witnesses] Bern: Haupt.

Pfister, O. (1944/1948). *Christianity and fear: A study in history and in the psychology and hygiene of religion*. London: Allen & Unwin.

Phillips, D.Z. (1991). *From fantasy to faith: The philosophy of religion and twentieth-century literature*. London: Macmillan.

Phillips, D.Z. (1993). *Wittgenstein and Religion*. New York: St. Martin's Press.

Piedmont, R.L. (1999). Does spirituality represent the sixth factor of personality? Spiritual transcendence and the five-factor model. *Journal of Spirituality*, 67, 985–1013.

Pietzcker, C. (1983). *Einführung in die Psychoanalyse des literarischen Kunstwerks*. [Introduction to the psychoanalysis of the literary artwork] Würzburg: Köninghausen & Neumann.

Plante, T.G. & Sherman, A.C. (Eds.) (2001). *Faith and health: Psychological perspectives*. New York: Guilford.

Platvoet, J.G. & Molendijk, A.L. (Eds.) (1999). *The pragmatics of defining religion: Contexts, concepts, and contests*. Leiden: Brill.

Pollack, D. (1995). Was ist Religion? Probleme der Definition. [What is religion? Problems of definition] *Zeitschrift für Religionswissenschaft*, [Journal for the Study of Religion] 3, 163–190.

Pollmann, T. (1999). *De letteren als wetenschappen*. [Liberal arts as a science] Amsterdam: Amsterdam University Press.

Pomerleau, C.S. (1980). The emergence of women's autobiography in England. In E. C. Jelinek (Ed.), *Women's autobiography: Essays in criticism* (pp. 21–38). Bloomington: Indiana University Press.

Popp-Baier, U. (1998). *Das Heilige im Profanen: Religiöse Orientierungen im Alltag. Eine qualitative Studie zu religiösen Orientierungen von Frauen aus der charismatisch-evangelischen Bewegung*. [The sacred in the profane: Religious orientations in everyday life. A qualitative studie of religious orientations of women in the charismatic-evangelical movement] Amsterdam/Atlanta: Rodopi.

Popp-Baier, U. (2003). Qualitative Methoden in der Religionspsychologie. [Qualitative methods in psychology of religion] In R.-Ch. Henning, S. Murken & E. Nestler (Eds.), *Einführung in die Religionspsychologie* [Introduction to the psychology of religion] (pp. 184–229). Paderborn etc.: Schöningh.

Popp-Baier, U. (2010). From religion to spirituality - Megatrend in contemporary society or methodological artefact? A contribution to the secularization debate from psychology of religion. /Journal of Religion in Europe, 3/, 1–34.

Popper, K.R. (1934/1959). *The logic of scientific discovery*. London: Hutchinson.

Portmann, A. (1951). *Zoologie und das neue Bild vom Menschen: Biologische Fragmente zu einer Lehre vom Menschen.* [Zoology and the new image of man; biological fragments for a new doctrine of mankind] Basel: Schwabe.
Post, H. (1989). *Pillarization: An analysis of Dutch and Belgian society.* Aldershot [etc.]: Avebury.
Pruyser, P.W. (1983). *The play of imagination: Toward a psychoanalysis of culture.* New York: International Universities Press.
Pultz, W. (2007). *Nüchternes Kalkül: Nahrungsabstinenz im 16. Jahrhundert.* [Calculations of fasting: Food abstinence in the 16th century] Köln: Böhlau.
Putman, W. (1998). *Godsbeelden en levensverhaal: Een onderzoek met behulp van de Waarderingstheorie en de Zelfkonfrontatiemethode naar de betekenis van persoonlijke godsbeelden.* [Images of God and lifestory: A study to the meaning of personal images of God, with the help of the Valuation Theory and the Self Confrontation Method] Tilburg: Tilburg University Press.
QSR International. (n.d.). NVIVO [Computer software]. Retrieved February 7, 2006, from http://www.qsr.com/au/products/productoverwiew/product_overview.htm
Quispel, G. (Ed.) (1976). *Mystiek en bevinding.* [Mysticism and "Bevinding"] Kampen: Kok.
Radley, A. (1996). Displays and fragments: Embodiment and the configuration of social worlds. *Theory and Psychology, 6,* 559–576.
Ragan, C.P., Malony, H.N. & Beit-Hallahmi, B. (1980). Psychologists and religion: Professional factors and personal belief. *Review of Religious Research, 21,* 208–217.
Ramachandran, V.S. & Blakeslee, S. (1998). *Phantoms in the brain: Probing the mysteries of the human mind.* New York: Morrow.
Rambo, L.R. (1992). The psychology of conversion. In H.N. Malony & S. Southard (Eds.), *Handbook of religious conversion* (pp. 159–177). Birmingham: Religious Education Press.
Rambo, L.R. (1993). *Understanding religious conversion.* New Haven, CT: Yale University Press.
Randour, M. L. (Ed.) (1993). *Exploring sacred landscapes: Religious and spiritual experiences in psychotherapy.* New York: Columbia University Press.
Rappard, J. F. H. van & Sanders, C. (1990). Theorie in de psychologie. [Theory in psychology] In P.J. van Strien & J. F. H. van Rappard (Eds.), *Grondvragen van de psychologie: Een handboek theorie en grondslagen* [Foundational issues in psychology: A manual for theory and foundations] (pp. 33–44). Assen: Van Gorcum.
Ratner, C. (1991). *Vygotsky's sociohistorical psychology and its contemporary applications.* New York: Plenum.
Ratner, C. (1993). A sociohistorical psychological approach. In S.C. Hayes, L.J. Hayes, H.W. Reese & Th. R. Sarbin (Eds.) (1993). *Varieties of scientific contextualism* (pp. 169–186). Reno, NV: Context Press.
Ratner, C. (1996). Activity as a key concept for cultural psychology. *Culture & Psychology, 2,* 407–434.
Ratner, C. (2002). *Cultural psychology: Theory and method.* New York: Kluwer/Plenum.
Ratner, C. (2008). *Cultural psychology, cross-cultural psychology and indigenous psychology.* Hauppage, NY: NOVA.
Reich, K.H. (1990). Rituals and social structure: The moral dimension. In H.-G. Heimbrock & H. B. Boudewijnse (Eds.), *Current studies on rituals: Perspectives for the psychology of religion* (pp. 121–134). Amsterdam/Atlanta: Rodopi.
Reich, K.H. (2004). Psychology of religion and neurobiology: Which relationship? *Archiv für Religionspsychologie* [Archive for the Psychology of Religion], *26,* 117–134.
Reinalda, B. (1992). The weak implantation of the early Catholic and Socialist workers' movement in Nijmegen. *Tijdschrift voor Sociale Geschiedenis* [Journal for Social History], *18,* 404–424.
Reinsberg, A.R. (1898). *De bekeeringsgeschiedenis van eene vijftigjarige wereldlinge, daarna eene twee in een halfjarige bezetene des duivels op Veldwijk en nu eene verloste en wedergeborene in Jezus Christus, haar Verlosser en Zaligmaker, Die het voor haar zal voleinden nu en tot in der eeuwigheid* [The conversion story of a fifty-year-old mortal, afterwards possessed by the devil at Veldwijk for two and a half years and now redeemed and reborn in Jesus Christ, her Redeemer and Saviour, Who will accomplish all things for her, now and forever]. The Hague: s.n.

Ribot, T. (1884/1894). *The diseases of the will.* Chicago: Open Court.
Ribot, T. (1896/1903). *The psychology of the emotions.* New York: Scribner.
Richards, P.S. & Bergin, A.E. (Eds.) (1997). *A spiritual strategy for counseling and psychotherapy.* Washington: American Psychological Association.
Richards, P.S. & Bergin, A.E. (Eds.) (2000). *Handbook of psychotherapy and religious diversity.* Washington: American Psychological Association.
Richards, P.S. & Bergin, A.E. (Eds.) (2004). *Religion and psychotherapy: A case book.* Washington: American Psychological Association.
Ricoeur, P. (1965/1970). *Freud and philosophy: An essay on interpretation.* New Haven, Conn.: Yale University Press.
Ricoeur, P. (1977/1992). The question of proof in Freud's psychoanalytic writings. In J.B. Thompson (Ed. & transl.), *Hermeneutics and the social sciences* (pp. 247–273). New York: Cambridge University Press.
Ricoeur, P. (1981). *Hermeneutics and the human sciences.* Cambridge: Cambridge University Press.
Righart, J.A. (1986). *De katholieke zuil in Europa: Het ontstaan van verzuiling onder katholieken in Oostenrijk, Zwitserland, België en Nederland* [The Catholic pillar in Europe: The emergence of pillarization among Catholics in Austria, Switzerland, Belgium and the Netherlands]. Meppel: Boom.
Rizzuto, A.M. (1979). *The birth of the living God: A psychoanalytic study.* Chicago: University of Chicago Press.
Rizzuto, A.M. (1996). Psychoanalytic treatment and the religious patient. In E.P. Shafranske (Ed.), *Religion and the clinical practice of psychology.* Washington: American Psychological Association.
Rizzuto, A.-M. (1998). *Why did Freud reject God? A psychodynamic interpretation.* New Haven/London: Yale University Press.
Roberts, R.C. & Talbot, M.R. (Eds.) (1997). *Limning the psyche: Explorations in Christian psychology.* Grand Rapids/Cambridge: Eerdmans.
Robinson, D.N. (1995). *An intellectual history of psychology.* (3rd ed.) Madison, WI: University of Wisconsin Press.
Röckelein, H. (Ed.) (1993). *Biographie als Geschichte.* [Biography as history] Tübingen: Diskord.
Roels, F.J.M.A. (1918). *De toekomst der psychologie.* [The future of psychology] Den Bosch: Teulings.
Roels, F.J.M.A. (1919–1920). Godsdienstpsychologie en apologetiek. [Psychology of religion and apologetics] *De Beiaard*, [The Carillon] *4* (2), 337–359.
Roels, F.J.M.A. (1928). Cultuurpsychologie en psychotechniek. [Psychology of culture and psychotechnics] *Mededeelingen van het psychologisch laboratorium R.U.Utrecht*, [Announcements of the Psychological Laboratory University of Utrecht] 77–95.
Rogier, L.J. (1956). *Katholieke herbeleving: Geschiedenis van katholiek Nederland, 1853–1953* [Reliving the Catholic experience: History of the Catholic Netherlands, 1853–1953]. The Hague: Pax.
Rollins, W.G. (1999). *Soul and psyche: The bible in psychological perspective.* Minneapolis, MN: Fortress.
Rooy, P.de (2005). *Republiek van rivaliteiten: Nederland sinds 1813* [Republic of rivalries: The Netherlands since 1813]. Amsterdam: Mets en Schilt.
Rosenau, P.M. (1992). *Post-modernism ands the social sciences.* New Jersey: Princeton University Press.
Rosenberg, S.D., Rosenberg, H.J. & Farrell, M.P. (1992). In the name of the Father. In G.C. Rosenwald & R.L. Ochberg (Eds.), *Storied lives: The cultural politics of self-understanding* (pp. 41–59). New Haven: Yale University Press.
Roth, P.A. (1987). *Meaning and method in the social sciences: A case for methodological pluralism.* Ithaca: Cornell University Press.
Rubin, J.H. (1994). *Religious melancholy and protestant experience in America.* New York: Oxford University Press.

Ruler, A.A. van (1971). Ultra-gereformeerd en vrijzinnig. [Ultra-reformed and liberal] *Wapenveld*, [Field of Arms] *21*, 13–52.
Rümke, H.C. (1939/1952). *The psychology of unbelief*. London: Rockliff.
Rümke, H.C. (1956/1981). De neurotische doublures van het menselijk lijden [The neurotic duplicates of human suffering]. In *Vorm en inhoud: Een keuze uit de essays van H.C. Rümke* [Form and content: A selection from the essays by H.C. Rümke] (pp. 209–217). Utrecht: Bohn, Scheltema & Holkema.
Runyan, W. (1982). *Life histories and psychobiography: explorations in theory and method*. New York: Oxford University Press.
Runyan, W. (1988). *Psychology and historical interpretation*. New York: Oxford University Press.
Rutten, F.J.Th. (1937). *Het domein der godsdienstpsychologie*. [The field of the psychology of religion] Nijmegen: Centrale Drukkerij.
Rutten, F.J.Th. (1947). *De overgang van het agrarische volkstype in het industriële*. [The transition of the agricultural to the industrial type] Amsterdam: Koninklijke Nederlandse Academie van Wetenschappen.
Rutten, F.J.Th. (1954). Verschil tussen de Amerikaanse en Europese benadering der psychologische problemen. [Difference between the American and European approach to psychological problems] *De Tijd*, [The Times] June 17, 3.
Rutten, F.J.Th. (1975). Een lijstje titels uit de wereldliteratuur. [A list of titles from world literature] *Gedrag*, [Behavior] *6*, 391–392.
Ruysch, W.P. (1900). Godsdienstwaanzin. [Religious mania] *Psychiatrische en Neurologische Bladen*, [Journal of Psychiatry and Neurology] *4*, 87–99.
Sacks, O. (1990). Neurology and the soul. *The New York Review of books*, November 22.
Sampson, E.E. (1996). Establishing embodiment in psychology. *Theory and Psychology*, *6*, 601–620.
Sanders, C. & Rappard, J.F.H. van (1982). *Tussen ontwerp en werkelijkheid: Een visie op de psychologie*. [Between design and reality: a perspective on psychology] Meppel: Boom.
Sanders, C., & Rappard, J.F.H. van (1987). *Filosofie van de psychologische wetenschappen*. [Philisophy of the psychological sciences] Leiden: Nijhoff.
Santner, E.L. (2001). *On the psychotheology of everyday life: Reflections on Freud and Rosenzweig*. Chicago/London: University of Chicago Press.
Sarbin, T.R. (Ed.) (1986a). *Narrative psychology: The storied nature of human conduct*. New York: Praeger.
Sarbin, T.R. (1986b). The narrative as a root metaphor for psychology. In T.R. Sarbin (Ed.), *Narrative psychology: The storied nature of human conduct* (pp. 3–21). New York: Praeger.
Sarbin, T.R. (1986c). Emotion and act: Roles and rhetoric. In R. Harré (Ed.), *The social construction of emotions* (pp. 83–97). Oxford: Blackwell.
Sarbin, T.R. (1992). Metaphors of unwanted conduct: A historical sketch. In D.E. Leary (Ed.), *Metaphors in the history of psychology* (pp. 300–330). New York: Cambridge University Press.
Sarbin, T.R. (1993). The narrative as the root metaphor for contextualism. In S.C. Hayes, L. J. Hayes, H.W. Reese & T.R. Sarbin (Eds.), *Varieties of scientific contextualism* (pp. 51–65). Reno, NV: Context Press.
Sarbin, T.R. & Kitsuse, J. I. (Eds.) (1994). *Constructing the social*. London: Sage.
Sarbin, T.R. & Scheibe, K. E. (Eds.) (1983). *Studies in social identity*. New York: Praeger.
Schafer, R. (1983). *The analytic attitude*. New York: Basic Books.
Scheibe, K.E. (1998). *Self studies: The psychology of self and identity*. Westport, CT: Praeger.
Schlauch, C. (1993). The intersecting-overlapping self: Contemporary psychoanalysis reconsiders religion again. *Pastoral Psychology*, *42*, 21–43.
Schleiermacher, F.D.E. (1799/1958). *On religion: Speeches to its cultured despisers* (transl. J. Oman; introd. R. Otto). New York: Harper & Row.
Schneider, C.M. (1990). *Wilhelm Wundts Völkerpsychologie: Entstehung und Entwicklung eines in Vergessenheit geratenen, Wissenschaftshistorisch Relevanten Fachgebietes*. [Wilhelm

Wundt's folk psychology: Foundation and development of a forgotten and in perspective of the history of science relevant field of study] Bonn: Bouvier.
Schivelbusch, W. (1977/1979). *The railway journey: Trains and travel in the 19th century.* New York: Urizen Books.
Schönau, W. (1991). *Einführung in die psychoanalytische Literaturwissenschaft.* [Introduction to the psychoanalytical literary theory] Stuttgart: Metzger.
Schram, P.L. (1983). Conventikels. [Conventicles] In J. M. Vlijm (Ed.), *Buitensporig geloven: Studies over randkerkelijkheid* [Believing exorbitantly: Studies of church life on the margins] (pp. 50–69). Kampen: Kok.
Schultz, W.T. (2005). *Handbook of psychobiography.* Oxford/New York: Oxford University Press.
Schumaker, J.F. (Ed.) (1992). *Religion and mental health.* New York: Oxford University Press.
Scull, A.T. (1982). *Museums of madness: The social organization of insanity in nineteenth-century England.* Harmondsworth: Penguin.
Segal, R.A. (2006). *The Blackwell companion to the study of religion.* Malden, MA/Oxford: Blackwell.
Shafranske, E.P. (Ed.) (1996a). *Religion and the clinical practice of psychology.* Washington: American Psychological Association.
Shafranske, E.P. (1996b). Religious beliefs, affiliations, and practices of clinical psychologists. In E.P. Shafranske (Ed.), *Religion and the clinical practice of psychology* (pp. 149–161). Washington: American Psychological Association.
Sharpe, E.J. (1986). *Comparative religion: A history.* Illinois: Open Court.
Sherif, M. & Cantril, H. (1947). *The psychology of ego-involvements, social attitudes & identifications.* New York: Wiley.
Shore, B. (1996). *Culture in mind: Cognition, culture and the problem of meaning.* Oxford: Oxford University Press.
Shotter, J. (1989). Social accountability and the social construction of "You." In J. Shotter & K.J. Gergen (Eds.), *Texts of identity* (pp. 133–151). London: Sage.
Shotter, J. (1992). "Getting in touch": The meta-methodology of a postmodern science of mental life. In S. Kvale (Ed.), *Psychology and postmodernism* (pp. 58–73). London: Sage.
Shotter, J. (1993a). *Conversational realities: Constructing life through language.* London: Sage.
Shotter, J. (1993b). *Cultural politics of everyday life: Social construction, rhetoric and knowing of the third kind.* Buffalo: University of Toronto Press.
Shotter, J. & Gergen, K.J. (Eds.) (1989). *Texts of identity.* London: Sage.
Shweder, R.A. (1991). *Thinking through cultures: Expeditions in cultural psychology.* Cambridge, MA: Harvard University Press.
Shweder, R.A. & Bourne, E.J. (1984). Does the concept of the person vary cross-culturally?. In R.A. Shweder & R.A. Levine (Eds.), *Culture theory: Essays on mind, self, and emotion* (pp. 158–199). New York: Cambridge University Press.
Siegel, A.M. (1996). *Heinz Kohut and the psychology of the self.* London/New York: Routledge.
Sierksma, F. (1950). *Phaenomenologie der religie en complexe psychologie: Een methodologische bijdrage.* [Phenomenology of religion and complex psychology. A methodological contribution] Assen: Van Gorcum.
Sierksma, F. (1956/1980). *De religieuze projectie: Een anthropologische en psychologische studie over de projectie-verschijnselen in de godsdiensten.* [The religious projection: an anthropological and psychological study of projection phenomena in the religions] Groningen: Konstapel.
Sims, A. (1994). "Psyche": Spirit as well as mind? *British Journal of Psychiatry, 165,* 441–446.
Simao, L.M. (2008). Ernst Boesch' holistic cultural psychology. In R. Diriwächter & J. Valsiner (Eds.), *Striving for the whole: Creating theoretical syntheses* (pp. 131–150). New Brunswick, NJ: Transaction.
Skinner, B. F. (1953). *Science and human behavior.* New York: Macmillan.
Slik, F. W. P. van der (1992). *Overtuigingen, attituden, gedrag en ervaringen: Een onderzoek naar de godsdienstigheid van ouders en van hun kinderen.* [Beliefs, attitudes, behaviour and experi-

ences: A study on the religiousness of parents and their children] (doctoral dissertation, University of Tilburg, The Netherlands) Helmond: Wibro Dissertatiedrukkerij.
Slone, D.J. (2004). *Theological incorrectness: Why religious people believe what they shouldn't*. New York: Oxford University Press.
Smith, H. (2001). *Why religion matters: The fate of the human spirit in an age of disbelief*. San Francisco: HarperCollins.
Smith, J.A., Harré, R. & Langenhove, L. van (Eds.) (1995). *Rethinking psychology*. London: Sage.
Smith, J.A., Harré, R. & Langenhove, L. van (Eds.) (1995/2003). *Rethinking methods in psychology*. London: Sage.
Smith, J.A., Harré, R. & Langenhove, L. van (2003). Introduction. In J.A. Smith, R. Harré & L. van Langenhove (Eds.), *Rethinking methods in psychology* (pp. 1–8). London: Sage.
Söderblom, N. (1908). *Studier av religionen*. [The study of religion] Stockholm: Diakonistyrelsen.
Söderblom, N. (1916). *Das Werden des Gottesglaubens: Untersuchungen über die Anfänge der Religion* (Ed. R. Stuebe) [The development of belief in God. On the origins of religion]. Leipzig: Hinrichs.
Söderblom, N. (1939). *The living God: Basal forms of personnel religions*. London: s.l.
Sonntag, M. (Ed.) (1990). *Von der Machbarkeit des Psychischen*. [The manipulability of the psychic] Pfaffenweiler: Centaurus.
Sperry, L. (2001). *Spirituality in clinical practice: New dimensions in psychotherapy and counseling*. London: Brunner-Routledge.
Sperry, L. & Shafranske, E. P. (Eds.) (2005). *Spiritually integrated psychotherapy*. Washington, DC: American Psychological Association.
Spiegelberg, H. (1972). *Phenomenology in psychology and psychiatry*. Evanston: North-Western University Press.
Spiegelberg, H. (1982). *The phenomenological movement: A historical introduction*. (3rd ed.) Den Haag: Mouton.
Spilka, B., Hood, R.W., Hunsberger, B. & Gorsuch, R.L. (2003). *The psychology of religion: An empirical approach*. (3rd ed.) New York: Guilford.
Spranger, E. (1910/1974). *Philosophie und Psychologie der Religion*. [Philosophy and psychology of religion] (In: *Gesammelte Schriften*, [Complete works] Band 9; Ed. H. W. Bähr) Tübingen: Niemeyer. (previously unpublished text of a lecture)
Sprinker, M. (1980). Fictions of the self: The end of autobiography. In J. Olney (Ed.), *Autobiography: Essays theoretical and critical* (pp. 321–342). Princeton: Princeton University Press.
Stace, W.T. (1960). *Mysticism and philosophy*. Philadelphia: Lippincott.
Stählin, W. (1910). [Review of E. D. Starbuck (1909), *Religionspsychologie*]. *Archiv für die gesamte Psychologie*, [Archive for all Psychologies] *18*, 1–9.
Stählin, W. (1911). Religionspsychologie. [Psychology of religion] *Noris, Bayerisches Jahrbuch für Protestantische Kultur*, [Noris, Bavarian Annual for Calvinist Culture] *11*, 46–49.
Stählin, W. (1912). Die Verwendung von Fragebogen in der Religionspsychologie. [The use of questionnaires in the psychology of religion] *Zeitschrift für Religionspsychologie*, [Journal for the Psychology of Religion] *5*, 394–508.
Stählin, W. (1914a). Zur Psychologie und Statistik der Metaphern: Eine methodologische Untersuchung. [On the psychology and the statistics of metaphors: A methodological investigation] *Archiv für die Gesamte Psychologie*, [Archive for all Psychologies] *31*, 297–425.
Stählin, W. (1914b). Experimentelle Untersuchungen über Sprachpsychologie und Religionspsychologie. [Experimental investigations on the psychology of language and the psychology of religion] *Archiv für Religionspsychologie* [Archive of the Psychology of Religion], *1*, 117–194.
Stam, H.J. (Ed.) (1998). *The body and psychology*. London: Sage.
Starbuck, E.D. (1899). *The psychology of religion: An empirical study of the growth of religious consciousness*. New York: Scribner.
Starbuck, E.D. (1899/1909). *Religionspsychologie: Empirische Entwicklungsstudie Religiösen Bewußtseins*. [The psychology of religion] (transl. Fr. Beta) Leipzig: Klinkhardt (Philosophisch-soziologische Bücherei, Bd. XIV, XV)

Stern, W. (1909). [Review of W. James (1909), *Die religiöse Erfahrung in ihrer Mannigfaltigkeit*]. *Deutsche Literaturzeitung*, [German Journal of Literature] *30* (8), 465–468.
Stern, W. (1917). *Die menschliche Persönlichkeit*. [The human personality] Leipzig: Barth.
Stevenson, D.H., Eck, B.E. & P.C. Hill (2007). *Psychology & Christianity integration. Seminal works that shaped the movement*. Batavia, Ill.: Christian Association for Psychological Studies.
Stifoss-Hanssen, H. (1999). Religion *and* spirituality: What a European ear hears. *The International Journal for the Psychology of Religion, 9*, 25–33.
Stigler, J.W., Shweder, R.A. & Herdt, G. (Eds.) (1990). *Cultural psychology: Essays on comparative human development*. Cambridge: Cambridge University Press.
Stollberg, D. & Wienold, K. (1987). [Review of J.A. Belzen & J.M. van der Lans (1986), *Current issues in the psychology of religion*]. *Theologische Literaturzeitung*, [Journal of Theological Literature] *112*, 551–552.
Straub, J. & Werbik, H. (Hg.) (1999). *Handlungstheorie: Begriff und Erklärung des Handelns im interdisziplinären Diskurs*. [Theory of action: Concept and interpretation of action in a interdisciplinary debate] Frankfurt a. M.: Campus.
Strean, H. (1994). *Psychotherapy with the orthodox Jew*. New York: Jason Aronson.
Strien, P.J. van (1986). *Praktijk als wetenschap: Methodologie van het sociaal-wetenschappelijk handelen*. [Practice as science: Methodology of social-scientific action] Assen: Van Gorcum.
Strien, P. J. van (1990). Definitie en domein van de psychologie. [Definition and field of psychology] In P.J. van Strien & J.F.H. van Rappard (Eds.), *Grondvragen van de psychologie: Een handboek theorie en grondslagen* [Foundational issues in psychology: A manual for theorety and foundations] (pp. 12–32). Assen: Van Gorcum.
Strien, P.J. van (1993). The historical practice of theory construction. *Annuals of Theoretical Psychology, 8*, 149–227.
Strozier, C.B. & Offer, D. (1985). New directions: Heinz Kohut. In C.B. Strozier & D. Offer (Eds.), *The leader: Psychohistorical essays* (pp. 73–78). New York/London: Plenum Press.
Strycker, S. (1977). Development in "two social psychologies": Toward an appreciation of mutual relevance. *Sociometry, 40*, 145–160.
Sturm, J.C. (1988). *Een goede gereformeerde opvoeding: Over neo-calvinistische moraalpedagogiek (1880–1950) met speciale aandacht voor de nieuw-gereformeerde jeugdorganisaties* [A good Calvinist upbringing: On neo-Calvinistic moral pedagogy (1880–1950) with special focus on the neo-Calvinist youth organizations]. Kampen: Kok.
Stuurman, S. (1983). *Verzuiling, kapitalisme en patriarchaat: Aspecten van de ontwikkeling van de moderne staat in Nederland* [Pillarization, capitalism and patriarchy: Aspects of the development of the modern state in the Netherlands]. Nijmegen: SUN.
Suèr, H. (1969). *Niet te geloven: De geschiedenis van een pastorale commissie*. [Don't you believe it: The history of a pastoral committee] Bussum: Paul Brand.
Sulloway, F.J. (1979). *Freud, biologist of the mind: Beyond the psychoanalytic legend*. London: Basic Books.
Sundén, H. (1959/1966). *Die Religion und die Rollen: Eine psychologische Untersuchung*. [Religion and roletheory: A psychological investigation] Berlin: Töpelmann.
Sundén, H. (1987). Saint Augustine and the Psalter in the light of role-psychology. *Journal for the Scientific Study of Religion, 26* (3), 375–382.
Süskind, H. (1914). Zur Theologie Troeltsch [On the theology of Troeltsch]. *Theologische Rundschau*, [Theological Prospect] *17*, 1–13, 53–62.
Tamminen, K. (1991). *Religious development in childhood and youth: An empirical study*. Helsinki: Suomalainen Tiedeakatemia.
Tennekes, J. (1969). De "oud gereformeerden." [The "Old-Reformed"] *Mensch en maatschappij*, [Man and Society] *44*, 365–385.
Terwee, S. (1989). *Hermeneutics in psychology and psychoanalysis*. New York: Springer.
Terwee, S.J.S. (1990). De beide methodologische hoofdstromen. [The two methodological mainstreams] In P. J. van Strien & J. F. H. van Rappard (Eds.), *Grondvragen van de psychologie: Een handboek theorie en grondslagen* [Foundational issues in psychology: A manual for theorety and foundations] (pp. 228–240). Assen: Van Gorcum.

Thomas, K. (1971). *Religion and decline of magic: Studies in popular beliefs in 16th and 17th century England*. London: Weidenfeld & Nicolson.
Thurlings, J.M.G. (1971). *De wankele zuil: Nederlandse katholieken tussen assimilatie en pluralisme* [The shaky pillar: Dutch Catholics between assimilation and pluralism]. Deventer: Van Loghum Slaterus.
Tillich, P. (1952). *The courage to be*. New Haven, CN: Yale University Press.
Toulmin, S. (1960). *The philosophy of science*. New York: Harper & Row.
Toulmin, S. (1990). *Cosmopolis: The hidden agenda of modernity*. Chicago: University of Chicago Press.
Triandis, H.C. (1994). The 20th century as an aberration in the history of psychology. *Contemporary Psychology, 39*, 9–11.
Triandis, H.C. (1995). *Individualism and collectivism*. New York: Basic Books.
Triandis, H.C. (2007). Culture and psychology: A history of the study of their relationship. In S. Kitayama & D. Cohen (Eds.), *Handbook of cultural psychology* (pp. 59–76). New York: Guilford.
Troeltsch, E. (1905). *Psychologie und Erkenntnistheorie in der Religionswissenschaft: Eine Untersuchung über die Bedeutung der kantischen Religionslehre für die heutige Religionswissenschaft*. [Psychology and epistemology in the science of religion: An investigation in the meaning of the Kantian theory on religion for the contemporary science of religion] (Lecture, presented at the International Congress of Arts and Sciences in St. Louis) Tübingen: Mohr.
Turner, L. (2008). *Theology, psychology and the plural self*. Farnham, UK: Ashgate.
Uleyn, A.J.R. (1986). Zingevingsvragen en overdrachtsproblemen in de psychotherapie [Questions of meaning and transference problems in psychotherapy]. In M. Kuilman & A. Uleyn, *Hulpverlener en zingevingsvragen* [Counselor and questions of meaning] (pp. 35–67). Baarn: Ambo.
Utsch, M. (2005). *Religiöse Fragen in der Psychotherapie: Psychologische Zugänge zu Religiosität und Spiritualität*. Stuttgart: Kohlhammer.
Valsiner, J. (2001). The first six years: Culture's adventure in psychology. *Culture & Psychology, 7*, 5–48.
Valsiner, J. & Rosa, A. (Eds.) (2007). *Cambridge handbook of sociocultural psychology*. New York: Cambridge University Press.
Valsiner, J. & VanderVeer, R. (2000). *The social mind*. New York: Cambridge University Press.
VandeKemp, H. (1992). G. Stanley Hall and the Clark School of Religious Psychology. *American Psychologist, 47* (2), 290–298.
VanderLeeuw, G. (1926). Über einige neuere Ergebnisse der psychologischen Forschung und ihre Anwendung auf die Geschichte, insonderheit die Religionsgeschichte. [On some new results of psychological research and its application on history, especially on history of religion] *Studi e Materiali di Storia delle Religione, 2*, 1–43.
VanderLeeuw, G. van der (1928). Strukturpsychologie und Theologie. [Psychology and Theology] *Zeitschrift für Theologie und Kirche, 9*, 321–349.
VanderLeeuw, G. van der (1932). Godsdienstpsychologie. [Psychology of religion] In *Winkler Prins Algemeene Encyclopedie*, 5th ed., Vol. 8, 350.
Vandermeersch, P. (1974/1991). *Unresolved questions in the Freud/Jung debate on psychosis, sexual identity and religion*. Leuven: Leuven University Press. (Louvain Philosophical Studies 4)
VanderMeiden, A. (1981). *Welzalig is het volk: Een bijgewerkt en aangevuld portret van de zwarte-kousen kerken*. [Blessed are the people: An edited and enlarged portrait of the Black Stocking churches] Baarn: Ten Have.
Varela, F.J., Thompson, E. & Rosch, E. (1997). *The embodied mind*. Cambridge, MA: MIT press.
Velde, H. te & Verhage, H. (Eds.) (1996). *De eenheid & de delen: Zuilvorming, onderwijs en natievorming in Nederland, 1850–1900*. [Unity and parts: Pillarization, education and nation in the Netherlands, 1850–1900] Amsterdam: Spinhuis.

Vellenga, S.J. (1994). Bevindelijk gereformeerden en hun geestelijke gezondheidszorg. [Reformed "bevindelijken" and their mental health care] *Maandblad Geestelijke volksgezondheid*, [Monthly for Mental Health Care] *49*, 962–975.

Veresov, N. (1999). *Undiscovered Vygotsky: Etudes on the pre-history of cultural-historical psychology*. Frankfurt: Lang.

Vergote, A. (1978/1988). *Guilt and desire: Religious attitudes and their pathological derivatives*. (transl. M.H. Wood) New Haven, CT/London: Yale University Press.

Vergote, A. (1983/1997). *Religion, belief and unbelief: A psychological study*. Amsterdam: Rodopi/Leuven: Leuven University Press.

Vergote (1986). Introduction to the plenary debate: Two opposed viewpoints concerning the object of the psychology of religion. In J.A. Belzen & J.M. van der Lans (Eds.), *Current issues in the psychology of religion* (pp. 67–75). Amsterdam: Rodopi.

Vergote, A. (1993). What the psychology of religion is and what it is not. *The International Journal for the Psychology of Religion*, *3*, 73–86.

Vergote, A. (1995). Debate concerning the psychology of religion. *The International Journal for the Psychology of Religion*, *5*, 119–123.

Vergote, A. & Tamayo, A. (1980). *The parental figures and the representation of God: A psychological and cross-cultural study*. The Hague: Mouton.

Verrips-Rouken, K. (1987). Lokale elites en beschavingsoffensieven, Langbroek 1870–1920 [Local elites and civilizing offensives, Langbroek 1870–1920]. *Sociologisch Jaarboek* [Sociological Yearbook], 165–181.

Verwey-Jonker, H. (1957). De psychologie van de verzuiling [The psychology of pillarization]. *Socialisme en Democratie* [Socialism and Democracy], *14*, 30–39.

Verwey-Jonker, H. (1962). De emancipatiebewegingen [The emancipation movements]. In A. N. J. den Hollander et al. (Eds.), *Drift en koers: Een halve eeuw sociale verandering in Nederland* [Current and course: A half century of social change in the Netherlands]. Assen: Van Gorcum.

Vijver, F.J.R. van de, Hemert, D.A. van & Poortinga, Y.H. (2008). *Multilevel analysis of individuals and cultures*. New York: Erlbaum.

Visser, J. (1987). [Review of J.A. Belzen & J.M. van der Lans (1986), *Current issues in the psychology of religion*]. *Nederlands Theologisch Tijdschrift*, *41*, 170–171.

Voestermans, P.P.L.A. (1992). Cultuurpsychologie: van cultuur in de psychologie naar psychologie in "cultuur." [Cultural psychology: From culture in psychology to psychology in "culture"] *Nederlands Tijdschrift voor de Psychologie*, [Dutch Journal of Psychology] *47*, 151–162.

Voestermans, P. & Verheggen, T. (2007). *Cultuur en lichaam: Een cultuurpsychologisch perspectief op patronen in gedrag*. [Culture and body: A cultural-psychological perspective on behavioural patterns] Malden, MA/Oxford: Blackwell/Heerlen: Open Universiteit Nederland.

Vorbrodt, G. (1904). *Beiträge zur Religiösen Psychologie: Psychobiologie und Gefühl*, [Contributions to religious psychology: Psychobiology and feelings] Leipzig: Deichert.

Vorbrodt, G. (1909). Übersetzungs-Vorwort. [Preface by the translator] In E. D. Starbuck, *Religionspsychologie: Empirische Entwicklungsstudie Religiösen Bewusstseins* [Psychology of religion] (pp. v-xxv), Leipzig: Klinkhardt.

Vorbrodt, G. (1911). Vorwort des Herausgebers. [Preface by the editor] In Th. Flournoy, *Experimentaluntersuchungen zur Religions-, Unterbewußtseins- und Sprachpsychologie*. [Experimental investigations to the psychology of religion, of the subconscious, and of language] Vol. 1: *Beiträge zur Religionspsychologie* [Contributions to the psychology of religion] (pp. i–lii). Leipzig: Eckardt.

Vorbrodt, G. (1918). [Review of T. K. Oesterreich (1917), *Einführung in die Religionspsychologie als Grundlage für Religionsphilosophie und -geschichte*]. *Zeitschrift für Angewandte Psychologie und Psychologische Sammelforschung*, [Journal for the Applied Psychology] *15*, 439–443.

Vovelle, M. (1982/1990). *Ideologies and mentalities*. Cambridge: Polity Press.

Vree, J. (1984). De Nederlandse Hervormde kerk in de jaren voor de Afscheiding [The Netherlands Reformed Church in the years before the Schism]. In W. Bakker et al. (Eds.), *De Afscheiding van 1834 en haar geschiedenis* [The Schism of 1834 and its history] (pp. 30–61). Kampen: Kok.

Vroom, H.M. (1988). *Religies en de waarheid*. [Religions and the truth] Kampen: Kok.

Vygotsky, L.S. (1930/1971). The development of higher psychological functions. In J. Wertsch (Ed.), *Soviet activity theory*. Cambridge (MA): Blackwell.
Vygotsky, L.S. (1934/1987). *Thinking and speech*. New York: Plenum.
Vygotsky, L.S. (1978). *Mind in society: The development of higher psychological processes*. (Ed. & trans. M. Cole) Cambridge, MA: Harvard University Press.
Vygotski, L.S. (1998). *Collected works*. Vol. 5. New York: Plenum.
Wang, Q. & Brockmeier, J. (2002). Autobiographical memory as cultural practice: Understanding the interplay between memory, self and culture. *Culture & Psychology, 8*, 45–64.
Wang, Q. & Ross, M. (2007). Culture and memory. In S. Kitayama & D. Cohen (Eds.), *Handbook of cultural psychology* (pp. 645–667). New York/London: Guilford.
Watson, J.B. (1913). Psychology as the behaviorist views it. *Psychological Review, 20,* 158–177.
Watts, F. (2002). *Theology and psychology*. Hants, UK: Ashgate.
Watts, F. (Ed.) (2007). *Jesus and psychology*. London: Darton, Longman and Todd.
Watts, F., Nye, R. & Savage, S. (2002). *Psychology for Christian ministry*. London/New York: Routledge.
Weber, M. (1904/1984). *Die protestantische Ethik*. Vol. 1. Gütersloh: Mohn.
Wertsch, J.V. (1991). *Voices of the mind: A sociocultural approach to mediated action*. London: Harvester Wheatsheaf.
West, W. (2000). *Psychotherapy & spirituality: Crossing the line between therapy and religion*. London/Thousand Oaks, CA/New Delhi: Sage.
Westerhof, G.J. (1994). *Statements and stories: Towards a new methodology of attitude research*. Amsterdam: Thesis.
Westhoff, H. (1996). *Geestelijke bevrijders: Nederlandse katholieken en hun beweging voor geestelijke volksgezondheid in de twintigste eeuw*. [Spiritual redemptors: Dutch Catholics and their movement for mental public health in the 20th century] Nijmegen: Valkhof.
Whitehouse, H. & Laidlaw, J. (Eds.) (2004). *Ritual and memory: Toward a comparative anthropology of religion*. Walnut Creek: Altamir.
Whitehouse, H. & Martin, L.H. (Eds.) (2004). *Theorizing religions past: Archeology, history and cognition*. Walnut Creek: Altamir.
Widdershoven, G.A.M. & Boer, Th. de (Eds.) (1990). *Hermeneutiek in discussie*. [Hermeneutics in discussion] Delft: Eburon.
Wielenga, D.K. (1885–1886). Rede gehouden bij de opening van Veldwijk op 28 januari 1886 [Speech given at the opening of Veldwijk on 28 January 1886]. *Jaarverslag van de Vereeniging tot Christelijke Verzorging van Geestes- en Zenuwzieken* [Annual Report of the Association of Christian Care for the Mentally Ill], *2,* 37–53.
Wikström, O. (1980). Kristusbilden i Kristinebergsgruvan: Historiska och religionspsykologiska aspekter. [Figures of Christ in Kristineberggrave: historical and psychological aspects] *Kyrkohistorisk Årsskrift, 80,* 99–112.
Williamson, W.P. (2000). The experience of religious serpent handling: A phenomenological study. *Dissertation Abstracts International, 6* (2B), 1136.
Wilshire, B. (1968). *William James and phenomenology*. Bloomington: Indiana University Press.
Windelband, W. (1894/1904). *Geschichte und Naturwissenschaft*. [History and the science of nature] (3rd ed.) Strasburg: Heitz.
Winer, J.A. & Anderson, J.W. (Eds.) (2007). *Religion and spirituality: Psychoanalytic perspectives*. Catskill, NY: Mental Health Resources.
Winkeler, L. (1996a). Geschiedschrijving sedert 1945 over het katholiek leven in Nederland in de 19e en 20e eeuw [Historiography since 1945 on Catholic life in the Netherlands in the 19th and 20th centuries] (part I). *Trajecta, 5,* 111–133.
Winkeler, L. (1996b). Geschiedschrijving sedert 1945 over het katholiek leven in Nederland in de 19e en 20e eeuw [Historiography since 1945 on Catholic life in the Netherlands in the 19th and 20th centuries] (part II). *Trajecta, 5,* 213–242.
Wittgenstein, L. (1921/1981). *Tractatus Logico-Philosophus*. London/New York: Routledge.
Wittgenstein, L. (1953). *Philosophical investigations*. Oxford: Blackwell.
Wittgenstein, L. (1958). *Philosophical investigations*. (2nd ed.; transl. G.E.M. Anscombe) New York: McMillan.

Wittgenstein, L. (1980). *Remarks on the philosophy of psychology.* Vols. I and II. Oxford: Blackwell.
Wobbermin, G. (1901). *Theologie und Metaphysik: Das Verhältnis der Theologie zur Modernen Erkenntnistheorie und Psychologie.* [Theology and metaphysics: The relationship of modern theory of insight to psychology] Berlin: Duncker.
Wobbermin, G. (1907/1914). "Aus dem Vorwort zur ersten Auflage" and "Vorwort zur zweiten Auflage." ["Preface to the first edition" and "Preface to the second edition"] In W. James, *Die Religiöse Erfahrung in ihrer Mannigfaltigkeit: Materialien und Studien zu einer Psychologie und Pathologie des Religiösen Lebens* [Varieties of religious experience] (pp. iii–xxxi). Leipzig: Hinrich.
Wobbermin, G. (1910). Der gegenwärtige Stand der Religionspsychologie (Aufgabe, Methode und Hauptprobleme). [The contemporary state of the art of the psychology of religion] *Zeitschrift für Angewandte Psychologie und Psychologische Sammelforschung,* [Journal for the Applied Psychology] *3,* 488–540.
Wolfradt, U. & Müller-Plath, G. (2003). Quantitative Methoden in der Religionspsychologie. [Quantitative methods in the psychology of religion] In C. Henning, S. Murken & E. Nestler (Eds.), *Einführung in die Religionspsychologie* [Introduction to the psychology of religion] (pp. 164–183). Paderborn etc.: Schöningh.
Wolffram, D.J. (1993). *Bezwaarden en verlichten: Verzuiling in een Gelderse provinciestad, Harderwijk 1850–1925* [The troubled and the enlightened: Pillarization in the provincial town of Harderwijk, Gelderland, 1850–1925]. Amsterdam: Het Spinhuis.
Wong, P.T.P. & Fry, P.S. (Eds.) (1998). *The human quest for meaning: A handbook of psychological research and clinical applications.* Mahwah/London: Erlbaum.
Wulff, D.M. (1997). *Psychology of religion: Classic and contemporary.* (2nd ed.) New York: Wiley.
Wulff, D. (2003). A field in crisis. Is it time to start over? In H.M.P. Roelofsma, J.M.T. Corveleyn, & J.W. van Saane (Eds.), *One hundred years of psychology of religion* (pp. 11–32). Amsterdam: VU University Press.
Wundt, W. (1883). *Logik: Eine Untersuchung der Principien der Erkenntnis und der Methoden wissenschaftlicher Forschung.* Teil 2: *Methodenlehre.* [Logic: An investigation of the principles of knowledge and the methods of scientific research. Part 2: Methodology] Stuttgart: Enke.
Wundt, W. (1886). *Ethik: Eine Untersuchung der Tatsachen und Gesetze des Sittlichen Lebens.* [Ethics: An investigation of the facts and laws of moral life] Stuttgart: Enke.
Wundt, W. (1888). Über Ziele und Wege der Völkerpsychologie. [On targets and methods of folk psychology] *Philosophische Studien,* [Philosophical Studies] *4,* 1–27.
Wundt, W. (1900–1909). *Völkerpsychologie: Eine Untersuchung der Entwicklungsgesetze von Sprache, Mythos und Sitte.* [Folk psychology: An investigation of the laws of development of language, mythe and mores] Leipzig: Engelmann.
Wundt, W. (1900/1921). *Völkerpsychologie: Eine Untersuchung der Entwicklungsgesetze von Sprache, Mythos und Sitte.* Teil 1: *Die Sprache.* [Folk psychology: An investigation of the developmental laws of language, mythe and mores. Part 1: Language] (4th ed.) Stuttgart: Kröner.
Wundt, W. (1900/1997). Völkerpsychologie: Eine Untersuchung der Entwicklungsgesetze von Sprache, Mythos und Sitte. Einleitung. [Folk psychology: An investigation of the laws of development of language, mythe and mores. Introduction] In G. Eckardt, (Ed.), *Völkerpsychologie: Versuch einer Neuentdeckung. Texte von Lazarus, Steinthal und Wundt* [[Folk psychology: Attempt to a rediscovery. Texts by Lazarus, Steinthal and Wundt] (pp. 239–270). Weinheim: Psychology VerlagsUnion.
Wundt, W. 1905/1920. *Völkerpsychologie: Eine Untersuchung der Entwicklungsgesetze von Sprache, Mythos und Sitte.* Vierter Band: *Mythos und Religion.* [Folk psychology: An investigation of the laws of development of language, mythe and mores. Vol. 4: Myth and religion] (3rd ed.) Stuttgart: Kröner.
Wundt, W. (1907). Über Ausfrageexperimente und über die Methoden zur Psychologie des Denkens. [Experiments in cross-examination and the methods of the psychology of reason] *Psychologische Studien,* [Psychological Studies] *3,* 301–360.

Wundt, W. (1908). Kritische Nachlese zur Ausfragemethode. [Critical check of the method of cross-examination] *Archiv für die Gesamte Psychologie*, [Archive for all Psychologies] *11*, 445–459.
Wundt, W. (1911). *Probleme der Völkerpsychologie*. [Problems of folk psychology] Leipzig: Wiegand.
Wundt, W. (1915). *Völkerpsychologie*. Vol. 6: *Mythos und Religion* [Myth and religion] (3rd part). Leipzig: Kröner.
Wundt, W. (1918). *Völkerpsychologie*. Vol. 9: *Das Recht*. [The law] Leipzig: Kröner.
Wundt, W. (1920). *Erlebtes und Erkanntes*. [Autobiography] Stuttgart: Kröner.
Wuthnow, R. (1998). *After heaven: Spirituality in America since the 1950s*. Berkeley: University of California.
Wuthnow, R. (2001). Spirituality and spiritual practice. In R.K. Fenn (Ed.). *The Blackwell companion to sociology of religion* (pp. 306–320). Oxford: Blackwell.
Wysling, H. (1982). *Narziβmus und illusionäre Existenzform: Zu den Bekenntnissen des Hochstaplers Felix Krull*. [Narcism and illusory forms of existence: On the testimonies of the swindler Felix Krull] Bern: Francke.
Yin, R.K. (1989). *Case study research: Design and methods*. (rev. ed.) London: Sage.
Yinger, J.M. (1970). *The scientific study of religion*. New York: Macmillan.
Young-Eisendraht, P. & Muramoto, S. (Eds.) (2002). *Awakening and insight: Zen Buddhism and psychotherapy*. Hove/New York: Brunner-Routledge/Taylor & Francis.
Young-Eisendrath, P. & Miller, M.E. (2000). *The psychology of mature spirituality: Integrity, wisdom, transcendence*. London/Philadelphia, PA: Routledge/Taylor & Francis.
Zahn, E. (1984). *Das unbekannte Holland: Regenten, Rebellen und Reformatoren*. [The unknown Holland: Regents, rebels and reformers] Berlin: Siedler.
Zeegers, W. (1988). *Andere tijden, andere mensen: De sociale representatie van identiteit*. [Different times, different people: The social representation of identity] Amsterdam: Bakker.
Zinnbauer, B.J. & Pargament, K.J. (2005). Religiousness and spirituality. In R.F. Paloutzian & C.L. Park (Eds). *Handbook of the psychology of religion and spirituality* (pp. 21–42). New York: Guilford.
Zinnbauer, B.J. et al. (1997). Religion and spirituality: Unfuzzying the fuzzy. *Journal for the Scientific Study of Religion*, *36*, 549–564.
Zinnbauer, B.J., Pargament, K. I. & Scott, A. B. (1999). The emerging meanings of religiousness and spirituality: Problems and prospects. *Journal of Personality*, *67*, 889–919.
Zwaal, P. van der (1997). *De achtste vrije kunst: Psychoanalyse als retorica*. [The eighth liberal art: Psychoanalysis as rhetoric] Meppel: Boom.
Zwemer, J. (1992). *In conflict met de cultuur: De bevindelijk gereformeerden en de Nederlandse samenleving in het midden van de twintigste eeuw*. [In conflict with culture: Reformed "bevindelijken" and mid-20th century Dutch society] Kampen: De Groot Goudriaan.

Index

A
Aalders, C., 150
Abma, R., 140
Aelst, P. van, 220
Agger, E.M., 204
Åkerberg, H., 34
Akthar, S., 165
Allah, 15
Allport, G.W., 39, 54, 57, 58, 71, 92, 126
Althusser, L., 139
Amma, Sri, 99
Anders, G., 31
Anderson, J.W., 17
Andeweg, R.B., 218
Andrae, T., 34, 44
Andresen, J., 51
Angel, H.-F., 6
Appelsmeyer, H., 78
Argyle, M., 8, 126
Ariès, Ph., 31
Armon-Jones, C., 26, 42, 61
Aronson, H.B., 5
Atatürk, M.K., 204
Atran, S., 38
Augustine (Saint), 34, 58, 189
Austin, J.L., 158
Averill, J.R., 26, 158
Avila, Teresa of, 34
Ayele, H., 70

B
Baerveldt, C., 160
Bairoch, P., 32
Bakthin, M., 140
Bankart, C.P., 5
Barthes, R., 139
Batson, C.D., 6, 54, 58, 64, 80, 163, 166
Bax, E.H., 221

Becker, U., 216
Beile, H., 92
Beit-Hallahmi, B., 8, 55, 58, 233
Béjin, A., 31
Benedict, R., 138
Berelson, B. R., 101
Berge, H. van den, 155
Berger, P.L., 59, 139, 230
Bergin, A.E., 7, 8, 58, 91
Berg, J.H. van den, 56, 110
Berkeley, G., 57
Bernard, L.L., 57
Berndt, T.J., 43
Bernstein, R.J., 159
Berry, J.W., 13
Bersoff, D.M., 43
Beth, K., 39
Beumer, J.J., 150, 156
Bhugra, D., 58
Bilderdijk, W., 229
Billig, M., 24
Billmann-Mahecha, E., 40
Black, D.M., 17
Blakeslee, S., 51
Blattner, J., 90
Blom, J.C.H., 216, 219
Boas, F., 149
Boehnlein, J.K., 165, 171
Boer, Th. de, 26, 27
Boesch, E.E., 14, 16, 37, 38, 125, 162
Booy, T., 236
Bornewasser, J.A., 219, 222
Bosscher, D.F.J., 219
Bouman, L., 174, 175, 179
Bourdieu, P., 19, 28, 45, 65, 94, 160, 161
Bourne, E.J., 42
Bouvy, A.-M., 13
Boyer, P., 51, 126
Braam, A.W., 70

Brentano, F. von, 132
Brienen, T., 150, 156
Brinkgreve, C., 228
Brockmeier, J., 125
Bromley, D.G., 8
Browning, D.S., 6
Brown, L.B., 25
Bruin, A.A. de, 219, 228
Brümmer, V., 63
Bruner, J., 24, 41, 60, 77, 139, 181
Bucher, A.A., 13, 34
Buddha, Gautama, 94
Bühler, K., 23, 110, 117, 118
Bunyan, J., 150
Burke, P., 32
Bush, G.W., 85
Buytendijk, F.J.J., 136, 139, 141

C
Cahan, E.D., 123
Calvin, J., 188
Cantril, H., 233
Capps, D., 6, 7, 34, 88, 126
Carrette, J., 83, 104
Carroll, M.P., 34, 126
Carruthers, M.J., 31
Cashwell, C.S., 7
Cermak, L.S., 185
Chorus, A., 226
Christensen, S.M., 73
Clarke, I., 165
Clément, C., 61
Cock, H. de, 229
Cohen, C.L., 32
Cohen, D., 13, 40–42, 60
Cohen, E., 13, 14, 40, 41, 51, 60, 97, 126
Cole, M., 10, 60, 123–125, 139
Coombs, C.H., 134
Coon, D.J., 71
Corbett, L., 5, 58
Corbin, A., 31
Costa, I. da, 229
Crawford, V.M., 125
Crocket, C., 6, 59
Csordas, Th. J., 160
Cushmann, Ph., 157

D
Danziger, K., 31, 39, 101, 103, 117, 118, 127, 140
d'Aquili, E.G., 51
Darley, J., 80

Darwin, Ch., 57, 140
Da Vinci, Leonardo, 34
Day, J.M., 64, 81
DeBruijn, J., 219, 222, 232
Deconchy, J.-P., 54
Dekker, G., 149, 156
Dekker, P., 220
Delaney, H.D., 91
Delany, P., 188
Delumeau, J., 31
Demos, J., 32
Denzin, N.K., 80
Derks, F.C.H., 54
Descartes, R., 55
Dewey, J., 45, 123
Diener, E., 42
Diener, M., 42
Diepen, A.F., 140
Dierickx, G., 219–222
Digby, A., 231
Dijksterhuis, E.J., 167
Dilthey, W., 11, 102, 103, 132, 167
Dimaggio, G., 129
Diriwächter, R., 118
Dittes, J.E., 34, 88, 104
Dixon, S.L., 34
Dockett, K.H., 5
Don Quixote, 183
Doorn, J.A.A. van, 221, 232
Driesch, H., 102
Dudley-Grant, G.R., 5
Duffhues, T., 217, 220
Duffy, S., 42
Duijker, H.C.J., 219
Dunde, S.R., 32
Durkheim, E., 43, 138

E
Eckardt, G., 118, 120, 122
Eck, B.E., 7
Eckensberger, L.H., 125
Edie, J.M., 110
Edwards, D., 24
Elias, N., 11, 26, 227
Ellemers, J.E., 218, 220–222
Ellenberger, H.F., 228
Ellens, J.H., 7
Elms, A.C., 233
Emmons, R.A., 69, 73, 75, 81
Engels, F., 45
Erikson, E.H., 33, 34, 39, 178, 233
Ester, P., 220
Eugen, M., 59
Evans, D., 199

F

Faber, M.D., 17
Faiver, C., 17
Farberow, N.L., 83
Farrell, M.P., 194
Fèbvre, L., 31, 32
Feil, E., 8, 64
Festinger, L., 34, 99, 156
Fitzgerald, T., 5, 8
Flick, U., 77
Florijn, H., 156
Flournoy, Th., 111, 112, 114, 115
Fogel, A., 130
Fortmann, H.M.M., 134, 136–143
Foucault, M., 26, 139
Fox, D., 9, 83
Frame, M.W., 7
Freud, S., 6, 29, 34, 39, 54, 62, 65, 71, 72, 98, 105, 120, 126, 137, 138, 169, 186, 189, 190, 195, 199, 201, 208, 217, 232, 234
Fromm, E., 39, 59, 126
Fry, P.S., 91
Fukuyama, M.A., 7
Funder, D., 90

G

Gadamer, H.G., 76
Gadlin, H., 33
Galileo, 140
Gauld, A., 76
Gay, V.P., 198, 200
Geels, A., 33–35, 88, 97, 126
Geertz, Cl., 18, 27, 46, 60, 65, 149, 167
Gehlen, A., 27
Gergen, K.J., 16, 24, 28, 31, 93, 130, 139, 148, 157–159, 162
Gerth, H., 47
Gibson, J.J., 73
Gillett, G., 24
Ginzburg, C., 30
Giorgi, A., 23, 24
Girgensohn, K., 6, 39, 115, 135, 138
Glaser, B.G., 76
Glock, C.Y., 63
Goddijn, W., 217
Godin, A., 54
Goffman, E., 161, 225
Goldberger, N.R., 60
Gomperts, W.J., 39, 148
Gone, J.P., 16
Gooyer, A.C. de, 236
Gorsuch, R.L., 80
Goudsblom, J., 221
Graafland, C., 156

Grad, H., 13
Grathoff, R., 66
Greil, A.L., 8
Groenendijk, L.F., 192
Groen van Prinsterer, G., 229
Groot, A.D. de, 75
Groot, F., 219
Grotstein, J., 236
Grünbaum, A.A., 132
Guignon, C., 183
Gundry, M.R., 6
Guntrip, H., 59
Gutheil, Th.G., 60
Guthrie, S.E., 51, 126

H

Haartman, K., 34, 88
Hallanhan, M., 42
Hall, G.S., 33, 34, 71, 92, 105, 126
Hallowell, A.I., 138
Hansen-Löve, A., 207
Harinck, C., 156
Harré, R., 24, 157, 158
Hauser, Kaspar, 28
Haußig, H.-M., 8
Haute, P. van, 182
Hayes, S.A., 37
Heelas, P., 55
Hegel, G.W.F., 182
Heidegger, M., 63, 129, 133, 160, 168, 182
Heider, J., 89
Heiman, R.J., 60
Hellemans, S., 218, 221, 222
Helminiak, D.A., 93
Hemminger, H., 8
Hendriks, J., 220, 229–231
Henning, C., 103
Heppe, H., 150
Herder, J.G., 60
Herdt, G., 34
Hermans, H.J.M., 125, 129, 130, 133, 139, 140, 142, 143, 184, 191, 212
Hermans-Jansen, E., 139, 142
Hermsen, E., 31
Herzog, T., 42
Hess, R.E., 58, 167
High, D.M., 63
Hijweege, N.H., 97, 125, 149, 156
Hill, P.C., 10, 11, 69, 72
Hitler, A., 234
Höffding, Harald, 115
Hoffman, D., 34
Hof, W.J. op 't,' 150
Holmes, Sherlock, 30

Holm, N.G., 34, 39
Holtrop, P.N., 229
Holzkamp, K., 117
Homans, P., 6, 58, 88
Hood, R.W., 7, 8, 10, 11, 16, 54, 56, 72, 75, 80, 81, 97, 103, 104, 156, 166
Hoogveld, J., 131
Hoorn, W. van, 116
Howard, G.S., 46
Hudson, W.D., 63
Huizinga, J., 31
Huls, B., 31
Hume, D., 57
Hume, H., 140
Hunt, R.A., 64
Husserl, E., 7, 111, 132
Hutch, R.A., 147, 149, 162
Hutschemaekers, G.J.M., 31
Hutsebaut, D., 54
Huyse, L., 220

I
Ingleby, D., 31
Irwin, G.A., 218
Iyengar, S.S., 43

J
Jacobs, J.L., 6
Jahoda, G., 44, 60
James, W., 9, 11, 56, 65, 71, 92, 98, 101, 104–112, 114–116, 118, 119, 121, 123, 126, 127, 130, 140, 184, 186, 212
Janse, C.S.L., 156
Jaspers, K., 86, 98, 126, 135, 236
Jesus (Christ) of Nazareth, 7, 34, 171, 176, 177, 186, 190, 207, 223
Johnson, E.L., 7
Johnson, M., 160
Jones, J.W., 6, 7, 59, 126
Jones, S.L., 7
Jong, O.J. de, 156
Jonte-Pace, D., 6, 126
Josselson, R., 24
Judd, C., 123
Jung, C.G., 5, 6, 34, 39, 59, 65, 87, 138
Jüttemann, G., 29

K
Kaam, B. van, 236
Kääriäinen, K., 85

Kaiser, P., 165
Kakar, S., 39, 61, 64
Kalasi, 49, 50
Källstad, T., 34
Kalweit, P., 58
Kamper, D., 31
Kant, I., 55–57, 92
Kardiner, A., 138
Kardorff, E. von, 77
Kehoe, N.C., 60
Kempen, H.J.G., 125, 129, 130, 133, 138–140, 142, 143, 184, 191, 212
Kempis, Thomas à, 150
Kernberg, P.F., 204
Kerr, F., 63
Ketterij, C. van de, 156
King, J.O., 32
King, R., 83
Kippenberg, H., 8
Kirkpatrick, L.A., 51, 53
Kitayama, S., 13, 40–42, 60
Kitsuse, J.I., 157, 183
Klessmann, M., 6, 90
Klinkert, R., 223
Kluckhohn, C., 138
Kluckhohn, F.R., 138
Klünker, W.U., 106
Knorr Cetina, K., 66, 140
Kochinka, A., 78
Koch, S., 70, 71
Koenig, H.G., 165, 171
Koffka, K., 115
Kohut, H., 195–201, 203–205, 212, 234, 235
Kojève, A., 182
Koppenjan, J., 219
Kotre, J., 14, 185
Kripall, J., 89
Kripall, J.J., 39, 88, 126
Krishnamurti, 89
Kruijt, J.P., 217, 220, 222, 225
Kuhn, T.S., 18, 34, 75, 178
Külpe, O., 112, 114, 115, 117, 132
Kusch, M., 122
Kuyper, A, 228, 229, 235, 236
Kuyper, H.H., 209

L
Laan, M.C. van der, 198
Laarse, R. van der, 218, 219
Lacan, J., 27, 48, 62, 65, 138, 160, 168, 182, 194, 199, 200
Laidlaw, J., 14

Index

Lakatos, I., 75
Lakoff, G., 160
Lamiell, J.T., 78
Lampe, 56
Langenhove, L. van, 76, 102
Lans, J.M. van der, 54, 55, 58, 64
Laucken, U., 40
Lave, J., 42, 61
Lazarus, M., 122
Leary, D.E., 70–72
Le Bon, G., 57
Lee, F., 42
Leenders, J.M.M., 219
Lee, R.R., 235
Leezenberg, M., 102
Le Goff, J., 31
Leibniz, G.W., 55
Lenin (Vladimir Iljitsj Oeljanov), 92
Leontiev, A., 46, 47, 123
Lepper, M.R., 43
Le Roy Ladurie, E., 31
Leuba, J.H., 92, 105, 109
Leupin, A., 6
Levine, M., 5
Levin, H., 169
Lévi-Strauss, C., 137
Levy-Bruhl, L., 137
Lewin, K., 233
Lieblich, A., 24
Lieburg, F.A. van, 156, 188
Lijphart, A., 216, 220, 221
Lillard, A., 42
Lincoln, Y.S., 80
Lindeboom, L., 224, 230
Linton, R., 138
Lodenstein, J. van, 150
Loewenthal, K.M., 8, 163
Lonner, W.J., 37
Loon, R.J.P. van, 130
Lorenzer, A., 29
Lovekin, A., 6
Lowe, D.M., 31
Loyola, Ignatius of, 34
Luckmann, Th., 139
Luria, A.R., 46, 123, 139
Luther, M., 178, 188

M
Maassen, J., 219
Mahapatra, M., 162
Malony, H.N., 6, 55
Mancuso, J.C., 46, 170
Marbe, K., 118

Marcus, P., 5
Markus, H.R., 60
Martin, L.H., 14, 168
Martin, W., 235
Marx, K., 45, 137
Mary (Mother of Jesus), 15
Maslow, A.H., 39, 126
Maton, K.I., 58, 167
Matsumoto, D., 40, 60
Mauss, M., 47
McAdams, D.P., 130, 183, 191, 212
McCutcheon, R.T., 5, 9
McDargh, J., 55, 59
McDougall, W., 57
McGuire, M.B., 147–149, 162
McKim, D.K., 153
Mead, G.H., 11, 123, 139, 184
Mead, M., 138, 149
Meissner, W.W., 7, 17, 34, 35, 39, 126, 204
Mel, K., 177
Merleau-Ponty, M., 27, 110, 129, 139, 160
Merwe, W.L., 27, 160
Messer, A., 115
Messer, S.B., 26
Michotte, A., 132, 136
Miert, J. van, 219
Miller, J.G., 14, 41–43
Miller, M.E., 5
Miller, W.R., 7, 42, 86, 91
Mills, C.W., 47
Misiak, H., 110
Misra, G., 28
Moghaddam, F.M., 13
Molendijk, A.L., 8, 86
Mönnich, C.W., 229
Mooij, A.W.M., 26
Morris, M.W., 42
Morris, R.J., 54
Moscovici, S., 138, 140
Moses, 104
Moss, D.M., 196
Much, N.C., 16, 49, 50, 64, 162
Müller-Plath, G., 103
Muramoto, S., 5
Murisier, E., 114
Murphy, N., 25

N
Nase, E., 54
Neeleman, J., 171
Neisser, U., 76
Newberg, N., 51
Nielsen, K., 63

Nietzsche, F.W., 160
Nisbett, R.E., 42
Nørager, T., 35, 125
Nossent, S., 31
Notten, J.W.A., 202, 205, 207, 209, 213
Nye, R., 6, 90

O
Obeyesekere, G., 45, 64, 162
O'Connor, K.V., 160, 168
Oelze, B., 118, 120, 122
Offer, D., 234
Olbrich, E., 31
Olson, R.P., 7
Os, M. van, 227
Otto, R., 56, 57, 92
Ouwerkerk, C. van, 53
Ovid, 199

P
Palmer, M., 6
Paloutzian, R.F., 13, 25, 53, 69, 73, 75, 81, 83, 103
Pannenberg, W., 6
Paranjpe, A.C., 40, 94
Parens H., 165
Pargament, K.I., 11, 55, 58, 65, 70, 72, 91, 167
Park, C.L., 13, 25, 83, 103
Parsons, W.P., 6, 39, 126
Patton, M.Q., 80
Paul, H., 122
Peeters, H.F.M., 31, 38, 219
Peng, K., 42, 54
Pepper, S., 168
Persand, R., 171
Peters, J., 149, 156
Pfister, O., 34, 39
Phillips, D.Z., 63
Piaget, Jean, 73
Piedmont, R.L., 93
Pietzcker, C., 197, 209
Plante, T.G., 165
Platvoet, J.G., 8, 86
Poincaré, J.H., 101
Pollack, D., 64
Pollmann, T., 102
Pomerleau, C.S., 188
Popp-Baier, U.L., 56, 81, 84, 97, 103, 125
Popper, Karl, 74, 75
Portmann, A., 27
Post, H., 216
Potter, J., 24
Prilleltensky, I., 9, 83

Pruyser, P.W., 39
Pultz, W., 32
Putman, W., 143

Q
Quispel, G., 150

R
Radley, A., 161
Ragan, C.P., 103
Ramachandran, V.S., 51
Rambo, L.R., 70, 157, 192
Randour, M.L., 58
Rappard, J.F.H. van, 25
Ratner, C., 13, 24, 40, 41, 46, 47, 60, 125
Rause, V., 51
Reich, K.H., 51, 59
Reinalda, B., 219
Reinsberg-Ypes, D., 187, 206, 223
Ribot, Th., 114
Richards, A.K., 204
Richards, P.S., 7, 8, 58, 91
Rickert, H.J., 11, 102
Ricoeur, P., 26, 62, 167, 168, 182, 194
Riecken, H.W., 34, 99, 156
Righart, J.A., 220, 221, 231
Rijks, T.I., 125, 129, 130, 142, 184, 191, 212
Ritschl, A., 106
Rizzuto, A.M., 7, 34, 39, 60, 72
Roberts, R.C., 7, 91
Robinson, D.N., 71, 72, 77
Röckelein, H., 33
Roels, F.J.M.A., 131–136, 141, 142
Rogers, C., 110
Rogier, L.J., 217, 218, 221
Rollins, W.G., 7, 88
Rooy, P. de, 216
Rosa, A., 13, 40, 60
Rosch, E., 73
Rosenau, P.M., 70, 73
Rosenberg, H.J., 194
Rosenberg, S.D., 194
Ross, M., 14
Roth, P.A., 70
Rubin, J.H., 32
Ruler, A.A. van, 173
Rullman, J.C., 229
Rümke, H.C., 32, 211
Runyan, W.Mac, 31
Rutten, F.J.Th., 131, 134–136
Ruysch, W.P., 174

S

Sacks, O., 160
Sampson, E.E., 16, 157, 160, 162
Sanders, C., 25
Santner, E.L., 6, 59
Sarbin, Th.R., 26, 46, 130, 157, 158, 170, 177, 183
Satan, 175, 177, 206
Savage, S., 6, 90
Savornin Lohman, A.F. de, 207
Schachter, S., 34, 99
Schafer, R., 27
Scharfenberg, J., 54
Scheibe, K.E., 162, 183, 185
Schillebeeckx, E., 6
Schivelbusch, W., 31
Schlauch, C., 236
Schleiermacher, F.D.E., 56, 76, 106
Schliemann, H., 204
Schneider, C.M., 118, 120
Schoenrade, P., 6, 54, 64, 80, 163, 166
Schönau, W., 207
Schram, P.L., 153
Schultz, W.T., 33
Schumaker, J.F., 166
Schweitzer, Albert, 196
Scotson, J.L., 227
Scott, A.B., 86
Scribner, S., 139
Scull, A.T., 231
Segal, R.A., 5
Sevig, T.D., 7
Sexton, V.S., 110
Shafranske, E.P., 8, 58, 103, 171
Shankar, Sri Ravi, 97
Sharpe, E.J., 44
Sheets-Johnstone, M., 160
Sherif, M., 233
Sherman, A.C., 165
Shore, B., 60
Shotter, J., 24, 49, 60, 76, 93, 156, 158, 159
Shweder, R.A., 42, 60, 124, 158
Siegel, A.M., 199
Sierksma, F., 44
Simao, L.M., 37
Simmel, G., 236
Sims, A., 171
Singh, Sadhu Sundar, 34
Skinner, B.F., 65
Slik, F.W.P. van der, 54
Slone, D.J., 51
Smith, H., 75
Smith, J.A., 76, 102
Söderblom, N., 34, 44
Sonntag, M., 31
Sperry, L., 7, 8, 58
Spiegelberg, H., 110
Spijker, W. van 't, 156
Spilka, B., 16, 81, 126, 186, 214
Spranger, E., 57
Sprinker, M., 184
Spurgeon, Ch.H., 150
Stace, W.T., 97
Stählin, W., 39, 112–116, 118, 119, 123, 128
Stam, H.J., 27, 160
Starbuck, E.D., 105, 108–113, 115, 119, 123
Stark, R., 63
Stearns, P., 24, 158
Steiner, G. A., 101
Steinke, I., 77
Steinthal, H., 122
Stendhal (Marie-Henri Beyle), 204
Stephen, M., 34
Stern, W., 109, 132
Stevenson, D.H., 7
Stifoss-Hanssen, H., 55
Stollberg, D., 54
Strasser, S., 141
Straub, J., 14
Strauss, A.L., 76, 137
Strean, H., 60
Strien, P.J. van, 25, 29, 53
Strozier, C.B., 234
Strycker, S., 123
Sturm, J.C., 227
Stuurman, S., 220, 221
Suèr, H., 137
Sulloway, F.J., 228
Sundén, Hj., 34, 39, 48
Süskind, H., 57, 58

T

Talbot, M.R., 7, 91
Talsma, J., 216
Tamayo, A., 65
Tamminen, K., 70
Teelinck, W., 150
Tennekes, J., 151
Terwee, S.J.S., 26, 73
Thomae, H., 29
Thomas, K., 32
Thompson, E., 73
Thoresen, C.E., 86
Thurlings, J.M.G., 220, 235
Tillich, P., 6, 58
Tolmin, E.C., 134
Toulmin, S., 75
Triandis, H.C., 44
Troeltsch, E., 57, 58, 92, 106, 107, 110

Turner, D.R., 73
Turner, L., 6

U
Uchida, Y., 42
Uleyn, A.J.R., 202
Utsch, M., 165

V
Valsiner, J., 13, 40, 60, 125, 129
VandeKemp, H., 105
VanderLeeuw, G., 34
Vandermeersch, P., 6
VanderMeiden, A., 151, 152, 188
VanderVeer, R., 140
Varela, F.J., 73
Velde, H., 216
Vellenga, S.J., 156
Ventis, W.L., 54, 64
Veresov, N., 46
Vergote, A., 6, 17, 23, 34, 39, 48, 49, 53–56, 61, 65, 69, 72, 160, 209, 210
Verhage, H., 216
Verhage, T., 116
Verheggen, T., 27, 160, 163
Veroff, J.B., 60
Verrips-Rouken, K., 221
Verwey-Jonker, H., 217, 220
Vico, 60
Vijver, F.J.R. van de, 40
Visser, J., 54
Voestermans, P.P.L.A., 27, 149, 157
Voetius, G., 150
Vorbrodt, G., 107–112, 116, 128
Vovelle, M., 31
Vree, J., 229
Vries, G. de, 102
Vroom, H.M., 63
Vugt, J. van, 217
Vygotsky, L.S., 25, 46, 47, 123, 139

W
Wacquant, L.J.D., 160, 161
Walgrave, S., 220
Wang, Q., 14, 125
Watson, J.B., 132
Watts, F., 6, 7, 90
Weber, M., 43, 124, 217, 236
Werbik, H., 14

Wertsch, J.V., 139, 191
Westerhof, G.J., 113
Westhoff, H., 136
West, W., 7
Whitefield, G., 150
Whitehouse, H., 14
White, S.H., 123
Whiting, B.B., 138
Whiting, J.W.M., 138
Widdershoven, G.A.M., 26
Wielenga, D.K., 223, 224
Wienold, K., 54
Wieringa, W.J., 227
Wikström, O., 34
Williamson, W.P., 81, 97
Wilshire, B., 110
Windelband, W., 78, 102
Winer, J.A., 17
Winkeler, L., 220, 235
Winkler, C., 131
Wittgenstein, L., 44, 49, 50, 63, 71, 74, 128, 158, 161
Wobbermin, G., 106–112, 116
Wolf, E., 198
Wolffram, D.J., 219
Wolfradt, U., 103
Wong, P.T.P., 91
Woodhead, L., 55
Wulff, D.M., 7, 39, 69, 72, 75, 81, 103, 110, 118, 127
Wundt, W., 10, 11, 13, 25, 35, 101, 103, 104, 115–126, 128, 129, 132, 136, 139, 217
Wuthnow, R., 55
Wysling, H., 207

Y
Yinger, J.M., 59
Yin, R.K., 78
Young-Eisendraht, P., 5
Young, J.S., 7

Z
Zahn, E., 232
Zeegers, W., 39
Zinnbauer, B.J., 11, 55, 86
Zinzendorf, Nicolaus Ludwig, Graf von, 34
Zwaal, P. van der, 182
Zweig, Arnold, 189
Zwemer, J., 156